Antique Trader ®
JEWELRY
PRICE GUIDE

EDITED BY KYLE HUSFLOEN
CONTRIBUTING EDITOR MARION COHEN

Published by
Antique Trader Books, A Division of

**krause
publications**

**700 E. State Street • Iola, WI 54990-0001
Telephone: 715/445-2214
Web: www.krause.com**

Please, call or write us for our free catalog of antiques and collectibles publications.
Our toll-free number to place an order or obtain a free catalog
is 800-258-0929 or please use our regular business telephone, 715-445-2215.

Library of Congress Catalog Number: 2001086548
ISBN: 0-87349-222-6

Printed in the United States of America

Table of Contents

Introduction

Jewelry has held a special place for humankind since prehistoric times, both as an emblem of personal status and as a decorative adornment worn for its sheer beauty. This tradition continues today. We should keep in mind, however, that it was only with the growth of the industrial revolution that jewelry first became cheap enough so that even the person of modest means could own a piece or two.

Only since around the mid-19th century did certain forms of jewelry, especially pins and brooches, begin to appear on the general market as a mass-produced commodity and the Victorians took to it immediately. Major production centers for the finest pieces of jewelry remained in Europe, especially Italy and England, but less expensive pieces were also exported to the booming American market and soon some American manufacturers also joined in the trade. Especially after the Civil War era, when silver and gold supplies grew tremendously in the U.S., jewelry in silver or with silver, brass or gold-filled (i.e. gold-plated) mounts began flooding the market here. By the turn of the 20th century all the major mail-order companies and small town jewelry shops could offer a huge variety of inexpensive jewelry pieces aimed at not only the feminine buyer but also her male counterpart.

As with all types of collectibles, yesterday's trinket can become today's treasure and so it is with jewelry. Today jewelry collecting ranks as one of the most popular areas of collecting and with millions of pieces on the market any collector, no matter what their budget, can find fascinating and attractive jewelry to collect. Of course the finest and rarest examples of antique or "preowned" estate jewelry can run into the many thousands of dollars, but thanks to the mass-production of jewelry over the last century and a half, there is lots for the less well-heeled to enjoy.

Inexpensive jewelry of the late 19th and early 20th century is still widely available and often at modest prices. Even more in demand today is what is called "costume jewelry," that is, well-designed jewelry produced of inexpensive materials and meant to carefully accent a lady's ensemble. The idea was launched in the 1920s by the famous French clothing designer Coco Chanel and her inspiration immediately took root. From that time forward any lady of taste could afford well-designed and attractive pieces which mirrored the glitziest bijoux but were available at a fraction of the cost. Today costume jewelry of the 20th century has become one of the most active areas in the field of collecting and some of the finest pieces, signed by noted designers and manufacturers, can reach price levels nearly equal to much earlier and scarcer pieces.

Whether you prefer the glittering and gaudy or the subtle and elegant, jewelry offers the collector a vast realm to choose from. In addition to being an investment the owner also has the opportunity to wear and share the beauty or whimsey of a piece of our past.

I hope you will enjoy the selection of jewelry pieces we have brought together in this guide. We have basically divided our listings into several major sections: Antique and Vintage Jewelry (1800-1920), including a special section on American Painted Porcelain Jewelry, Modern (1920-1960s), Estate (1960-present) and Watches. Also, there is a major section on Costume Jewelry and for work on this latter section I owe a great debt to our Contributing Editor Marion Cohen. Marion has collected and dealt in fine Costume Jewelry for many years and shares her expertise with readers of *The Antique Trader Weekly* in her question and answer column, "Inside the Costume Jewelry Box." In addition Marion has written feature articles on her favorite field and has been a regular contributor to our *Antique Trader Antiques & Collectibles Price Guide*. My sincere thanks to Marion for her major contribution to this new reference. I greatly appreciate it as I know our readers will.

In addition to Marion Cohen's contributions, I'd like to thank Dorothy Kamm, collector, author and authority on American Hand-painted Porcelain, who shares a lovely selection of antique painted porcelain pieces with us here. Thanks are also due to a number of major auction houses around the country who were generous enough to share information and photographs recorded in their recent jewelry sales. They are listed in our Special Contributors section.

In preparing our listing my editors and I have done our best to provide detailed and accurate descriptions of the pieces included but as always, the reader should use the prices listed only as a guide. Jewelry prices, as in every other major collecting field, are influenced by a number of factors including local demand, quality, condition and rarity. As market prices have risen in recent years it has become ever more important for the collector to shop and buy with care. Learn as much as you can about your favorite area of jewelry and keep abreast of market trends and stay alert to warning about alterations, repairs or reproductions that can be found on the market. Use this book as reference and general guide to broaden your understanding and appreciation of the wonderful world of jewelry collecting and it can serve you well.

Good luck and happy collecting!

Kyle Husfloen, Editor

Special Note from Marion Cohen

My thankful appreciation to those who so generously allowed their costume jewelry collections to be catalogued and photographed for this book: Davida Baron, Paula Beck, Robert Cirillo, Roselyn Gerson and Joan Orlen.

A special thank you to my photographer Robert Cohen for his beautiful costume jewelry photographs, my editor Kyle Husfloen for his excellent suggestions, and also to my husband Julius Cohen for his help and moral support.

Please note: Though listings have been double checked and every effort has been made to ensure the accuracy, neither the compilers, editors nor publisher can assume responsibility for any losses that might be incurred as a result of consulting this guide, or of errors, typographical or otherwise.

Special Feature
Collecting Costume Jewelry

Costume jewelry...what is it? To say that it's jewelry made of inexpensive materials is only part of the story. It's a personal adornment old as mankind. In early historic times shells, animal bones teeth and feathers were used as personal ornaments. Ancient civilizations produced jewelry made of glass, ceramics, iron, copper and bronze.

During the mid to late 19th century, mass production made it possible for the average woman to purchase inexpensive jewelry. Daytime jewelry of the 19th century was the forerunner of 20th century costume jewelry. Hair jewelry, jet, gutta percha, bog oak, black glass jewelry, pinchbeck as well as gold-filled and sterling silver jewelry were popular. Shell cameos were available in gold-filled and silver mountings as well as in precious 14k and 18k gold. Garnet jewelry set in gold-plated brass, copper, gunmetal, silverplate on copper, celluloid and enamel on sterling were some of the materials used in daytime jewelry.

Sears Roebuck catalogs enabled almost every woman to afford at least one piece of finely made inexpensive jewelry. Amber and coral beads, gold-filled and sterling lockets and gold-filled festoon necklaces set with "fine imitation diamonds" could be purchased for less than $3. Gold-filled and rolled gold-plated bangle bracelets, expansion bracelets and chain link bracelets were also available at these low prices. Daytime jewelry imitated the designs of precious jewelry and the more "real" it looked, the better.

During this time it became stylish for some women to show off their wealth with precious jewelry. The more precious jewelry someone wore, the richer she was and rich women, and those who aspired to be, looked down at inexpensive jewelry as "sham jewelry" or "imitation jewelry."

Two art movements of the late 19th and early 20th century helped make non-precious jewelry more acceptable to fashionable women. The Arts and Crafts and Art Nouveau artisans felt that their art was an expression of the design and the materials used weren't as important as the design itself. Their work showed that beauty and craftsmanship were not limited to expensive metals and precious stones. Jewelry was made of glass, ivory, enamels tortoiseshell and freshwater pearls.

Rene Lalique, a jewelry craftsman of the time, used glass and a variety of semi-precious gemstones in his designs. These art designs made jewelry of inexpensive materials more acceptable to the public, but it wasn't until after World War I that costume jewelry was created and became widely accepted.

After the grim reality of a world war, to show off one's wealth became socially inappropriate. Dress designer Coco Chanel saw costume jewelry as the mark of the post-war liberated woman who dressed to please herself and not to display her wealth. She designed original and conspicuously fake costume jewelry to complement her clothing collection. She did not try to disguise the fact that these art forms were made of inexpensive materials and that they did not imitate precious jewelry. She also went against the conventions of the time by mixing precious and costume jewelry as accessories for her clothing collections.

Art Deco became the major art and design movement of the 1920s. Geometric forms and bright colors replaced the snake-like gale-swept curves and pastel colors of Art Nouveau. Art Deco motifs emphasized speed and movement and were influenced by Native American, African, Egyptian, Chinese, Japanese art.

Elsa Schiaparelli and other dress designers also began designing their own jewelry for their costume designs and, by 1933, the term "Costume Jewelry" came into use. During the 1930s costume jewelry, originally a fun fashion accessory, became a fashion necessity for the Depression-poor public. An inexpensive clip or pin could extend the wardrobe for a woman who couldn't afford new clothing and many makers of costume jewelry helped to meet this need. Coro, founded in the first decade of the 20th century, produced thousands of different designs each month. Its production ranged from higher end fashion jewelry to very inexpensive jewelry marketed in 5 and 10 cents stores. The United States division of Coro discontinued production in the 1970s and the Canadian division in 1996.

Trifari was founded in 1918 as a maker of hair ornaments. In the 1920s women bobbed their hair and when combs became passé, Trifari turned to making costume jewelry. By 1930 designer Alfred Philippe joined the company. His designs made costume jewelry become totally acceptable to fashion conscious women when First Lady Mamie Eisenhower, wife of president Dwight D. Eisenhower, commissioned him to design sets of costume jewelry for both of her inaugural balls in 1953 and 1957. In doing so, she became the first wife of a president to wear costume jewelry to her inaugural ball. Trifari continues making lovely costume jewelry designs today.

Eisenberg originally started as a women's clothing firm in 1880. An attractive piece of jewelry made with Swarovski crystals was attached to each dress to appeal to customers and increase sales. By the 1930s theft of the pins from the dresses became so great that Eisenberg made a separate line of costume jewelry to sell to the public. Eisenberg is still in business today and continues making fine rhinestone jewelry.

Miriam Haskell founded her own jewelry company in 1924 in New York City. Her designs were not mass produced but each one was made by hand. Many designs featured beads, seed pearls and rhinestones put together with tiny wires on an openwork metal background. Her very pretty, detailed style was continued by her assistant Frank Hess in 1953 when she fell ill. Miriam Haskell jewelry is still being made today.

Wartime restrictions of metals affected the costume jewelry industry during the 1940s. Metals such as brass, copper, chrome and nickel were commandeered by the government for the war effort. Sterling silver, which was not needed for the war, became a base metal for costume jewelry and was also plated with gold. Other materials including plastic, glass, leather, fabric and straw were used to meet the increased public demand for costume jewelry.

The 1950s and 1960s were prosperous decades for the nation and for the costume jewelry industry as well. People were very fashion conscious and had money to spend and women looked for designer names as indicative of good quality costume jewelry.

By the 1970s, women no longer followed the fashion trends and many costume jewelry makers went out of business, but some survived and are still in business today.

During the 1980s. celebrities such as Princess Diana of England, Madonna and Michael Jackson helped revive an interest in costume jewelry. Collecting vintage costume jewelry became the hot new hobby and continues into the 21st century.

Originally not meant to last any longer than the clothing it accessorized, costume jewelry did survive as many women saved it for its beauty and continued to wear it. More than merely jewelry made of inexpensive materials it is art, design and fine craftsmanship. It is a reflection of its time and representative of art and design movements of those times. It's a wonderful 20th century accessory which continues to be made in the 21st. But best of all, costume jewelry is not only meant to be collected, but to be worn and enjoyed!

Marion Cohen

Special Contributors

The editors wish to thank the following sources for sharing their information and photographs for this volume:

Marion Cohen
P.O. Box 39
Albertson, NY 11507

Dorothy Kamm
P.O. Box 7460
Port St. Lucia, FL 34985-7460
(561) 465-4008
e-mail: dorothy.kamm@usa.net
Author: "Painted Porcelian Jewelry and Buttons, Identification & Value Guide"

Cooksey Shugart
P.O. Box 3147
Cleveland, TN 37320
Author: "Complete Price Guide to Watches"

For other photographs and data, we sincerely express appreciation to the following auctioneers, galleries and individuals: Antiquorum Auctioneers, 609 Fifth Avenue, Suite 503, New York, New York 10017; Butterfield and Dunning Auctioneers, 220 San Bruno Avenue, San Francisco, California 94103; Susan Eberman, Bedford, Indiana; William Doyle Galleries, 175 East 87th Street, New York, New York 10128; DuMouchelles, 409 East Jefferson, Detroit, Michigan 48226; Robert G. Jason-Ickes, Olympia, Washington; Sloan Auctioneers and Appraisers, 8861 NW 18th Terrace, Suite 100, Miami, Florida 33172; Skinner, Inc., 357 Main Street, Bolton, Massachusetts 01740 and Weschler's Auctioneers and Appraisers, 909 "E" Street, NW, Washington, D.C. 20004

Note: For further listings on auctioneers, appraisers, dealers and experts on all types of jewelry refer to *Maloney's Antiques & Collectibles Resource Directory 5th Edition* by David J. Maloney,

Jr., published by Antique Trader Books, a Division of Krause Publications, Iola, Wisconsin 54990. To order or receive our free catalog, call 800-258-0929.

Auction Houses with Special Jewelry Sales

Antiquorum Auctioneers
609 Fifth Avenue, Suite 503
New York, NY 10017

Butterfield & Dunning Auctioneers
220 San Bruno Avenue
San Francisco, CA 94103

William Doyle Galleries
175 East 87th Street
New York, NY 10128

DuMouchelles
409 East Jefferson
Detroit, MI 48226

Sloan Auctioneers & Appraisers
8861 NW 18th Terrace, Suite 100
Miami, FL 33172

Skinner, Inc.
357 Main Street
Bolton, MA 01740

Weschler's Auctioneers & Appraisers
909 "E" Street NW
Washington, DC 20004

On the Cover...

Front cover: Left to right: American Painted Porcelain watch chatelaine, $115, courtesy of Dorothy Kamm, Port St. Lucia, Florida; an amber rhinestone duette clip, $100-125, courtesy of Marion Cohen, photo by Robert Cohen, Albertson, New York; hooded cobra rhinestone pin, $85-115, courtesy of Marion Cohen, photo by Robert Cohen, Albertson, New York; antique gold-plated and faux gemstone bracelet, $80-100, courtesy of Marion Cohen, photo by Robert Cohen, Albertson, New York.

ANTIQUE

American Painted Porcelain

American painted porcelain jewelry comprises a unique category. While the metallic settings and porcelain medallions were inexpensive, the painted decoration was a work of fine art. The finished piece possessed greater intrinsic value than costume jewelry of the same period because it was a one-of-a-kind creation, but one that was not as expensive as real gold and sterling silver settings and precious and semi-precious jewels. Note that signatures are rare, backstamps lacking.

Dorothy Kamm

Bar pin, decorated w/pink roses & greenery, brass-plated bezel, ca. 1880s, 7/16 x 1 1/2" $30

Bar pin, decorated w/pink roses on a pale green ground, burnished gold tips & brass-plated bezel, ca. 1900-1915, 2 5/8" w. 50

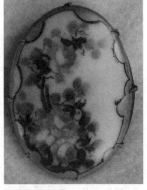

Belt Buckle Brooch with Roses

Belt buckle brooch, oval, decorated w/roses & greenery on a polychrome ground, burnished gold scalloped border outlined in black, gold-plated bezel, ca. 1900-1917, 1 15/16 x 2 11/16' (ILLUS.) 110

Belt Buckle Brooch with Violets

Belt buckle brooch, oval, decorated w/deep purple violets on a graduating yellow to dark green background, brass-plated bezel, ca. 1900-17, 1 3/4 x 2 1/8" (ILLUS.) 100

Belt buckle brooch, oval, decorated w/yellow roses, burnished gold rim & brass-plated bezel, 1 7/8 x 2 3/8" 115

Belt Buckle Brooch with Pink Roses

Belt buckle brooch, oval, decorated w/pink roses, burnished gold scrolls at top & burnished gold edge, brass-plated bezel, ca. 1900-17, 1 7/8 x 2 5/8" (ILLUS.) 90

Brooch with Water Lily

Brooch, diamond-shaped, decorated w/a water lily & waterscape w/white enamel highlights, sky & clouds in background, burnished gold rim, gold-plated bezel, ca. 1930s-1940s, 7/8" sq. (ILLUS.).. **35**

Brooch with Iris & Enamel Decoration

Brooch, oval, decorated w/a conventional-style lavender iris & green leaves outlined in black on a yellow lustre ground w/white enamel highlights on petal edges & yellow enamel highlights on flower centers, burnished gold rim, gold-plated bezel, ca. 1900-20, 1 5/8 x 2 1/8" (ILLUS.).................... **75**

Brooch with Pansy Decoration

Brooch, oval, decorated w/a large red & purple pansy on a burnished gold ground, gold-plated bezel, 1 1/2 x 1 7/8" (ILLUS.).................... **75**

Scenic Landscape Brooch

Brooch, oval, decorated w/a sunset landscape scene w/house by stream, trees in background, burnished gold rim, gold-plated bezel, 1 1/2 x 1 15/16" (ILLUS.).......... **115**

Water Lily Decorated Brooch

Brooch, oval, decorated w/a water lily on a watery blue green background, gold-plated bezel, ca. 1900-20, 1 5/8 x 2 1/16" (ILLUS.)................. **50**

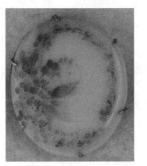

Brooch w/Forget-me-knots Decoration

Brooch, oval, decorated w/forget-me-nots on a pale yellow center w/pale blue border, gold-plated bezel, signed "A. Jibbing," ca. 1900-20, 1 3/8 x 1 1/2" (ILLUS.)............... **75**

Blue Brooch with Roses

Brooch, oval, decorated w/pink & white & ruby roses & green leaves on a rich blue ground w/white enamel highlights, burnished gold border & rim, gold-plated bezel, ca. 1940s, 1 1/2 x 2" (ILLUS.) **65**

Brooch with Wild Roses Decoration

Brooch, oval, decorated w/pink wild roses & buds w/green leaves on an ivory ground, gold-plated bezel, ca. 1900-20, 1 5/8 x 2 1/16" (ILLUS.)................................... **65**

Brooch with Tropical Scene

Brooch, rectangular, decorated w/a tropical scene of palm tree in white on a platinum ground, painted by Olive Commons, Miami, Florida, sterling silver bezel, ca. 1920s-1940s, 3/4 x 1" (ILLUS.)................................... **80**

Brooch with Pansy Decoration

Brooch, round, decorated w/a white pansy on a matte black ground, gold-plated bezel, ca. 1890-1910, 1 1/8" d. (ILLUS.)............................ **30**

Brooch, decorated w/a conventional-style trillium w/raised paste & burnished gold pistols & burnished gold background, brass-plated bezel, ca. 1910-15, 1 9/16" d.................................... **35**

Brooch, decorated w/violets on a light yellow brown ground w/raised paste scrolled border covered w/burnished gold & burnished gold rims, gold-plated bezel, ca. 1890-1920, 1 1/2" d. **45**

Brooch, horseshoe shape, decorated w/pink & ruby roses on a green & yellow ground, white enamel highlights & burnished gold tips, ca. 1880s - 1915, 1 1/4 x 1 1/2" **65**

Brooch with Forget-me-nots

Brooch, lozenge shape, decorated w/forget-me-nots on a pink & pale yellow ground w/white enamel highlights & burnished gold rim, brass-plated bezel, ca. 1890-1920, 7/8 x 1 5/8" (ILLUS.) **35**

Brooch, oval, decorated w/a tropical Florida scene, burnished gold border & brass-plated bezel, ca. 1920s, 1 1/2 x 2" **60**

Brooch with Pansy Decoration

Brooch, oval, decorated w/purple pansies on a pale yellow & violet background w/white enamel highlights & raised paste scrolled border covered w/burnished gold, brass-plated bezel, ca. 1880-1915, 1 1/2 x 2" (ILLUS.) **75**

Brooch, oval, decorated w/a conventional-style Colonial dame in light blue & yellow w/opal lustre background & burnished gold rim, brass-plated bezel, ca. 1915-25, 1 5/8 x 2 1/8" **55**

Brooch/pendant, heart shape, decorated w/daisies on a light shading to dark blue ground, gold-plated bezel, ca. 1900-20, 1 13/16 x 2" **50**

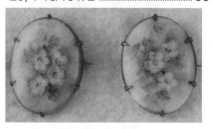
Brooches with Forget-me-nots

Brooches, oval, decorated w/forget-me-nots on a pale pink & blue ground w/white enamel highlights on petal edges, burnished gold rims, gold-plated bezels, gold wear, ca. 1900-20, 13/16 x 1", pr. (ILLUS.) **70**

Cuff Pin with Forget-me-not

Cuff pin, rectangular, decorated w/a forget-me-not on a burnished gold ground, gold-plated bezel, ca. 1900-15, 1/4 x 1" (ILLUS.) **12**

Cuff pin, rectangular, decorated w/a purple iris outlined & bordered in burnished gold, brass-plated bezel, ca. 1900-15, 1/4 x 1 1/6".................. 15

Flapper Pin

Flapper pin, oval, decorated w/a stylized, elegant red-haired woman wearing blue dress & fur stole, pink flower & large comb in her hair, white ground w/burnished gold border, gold-plated bezel, ca. 1922-30, 1 11/16 x 2 1/8" (ILLUS.) 85

Flapper pin, oval, decorated w/bust of stylized red-haired flapper on a pastel polychrome ground, burnished gold rim & brass-plated bezel, ca. 1924-28, 1 5/8 x 2 1/8" 75

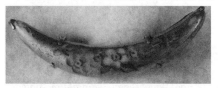

Crescent-shaped Handy Pin

Handy pin, crescent shape, decorated w/forget-me-nots & leaves on a burnished gold ground, gold-plated bezel, ca. 1890-1915, gold wear, 1 13/16" w. (ILLUS.)......... 30

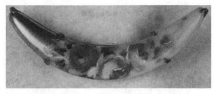

Handy Pin with Roses

Handy pin, crescent shape, decorated w/pink & ruby roses & green leaves on an ivory ground, w/white enamel highlights & one burnished gold tip, gold-plated bezel, ca. 1890-1915, 2 3/16" w. (ILLUS.)............................45

Handy pin, decorated w/forget-me-nots w/white enamel highlights & rounded burnished gold tips, ca. 1890-1915, 1 1/2" w...............................35

Handy pin, crescent shape, asymmetrically decorated w/a purple pansy on an ivory ground, burnished gold tip & brass-plated bezel, ca. 1880-1915, 2" w. 35

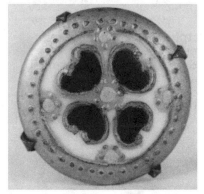

Hat Pin with Enamel Decoration

Hatpin, circular head, decorated w/a conventional geometric design in raised paste dots & scrolls, covered w/burnished gold, turquoise enamel jewels, cobalt blue flat enamel, gold-plated bezel, ca. 1905-20, 1" d., 6 3/8" shaft (ILLUS.).................... 105

Hat Pin with Roses

Hatpin, circular head, decorated w/pink roses & greenery on a pale blue & yellow ground, burnished gold border, gold-plated bezel, ca. 1890-1920, some gold wear, 1" d., 7 3/4" shaft (ILLUS.) **110**

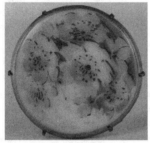

Hat Pin Decorated w/Wild Roses

Hatpin, circular head, decorated w/wild pink & white roses & greenery w/yellow enamel accents in flower centers, burnished gold border, gold-plated bezel, ca. 1890-1915, 1 1/4" d., 9" shaft (ILLUS.) **185**

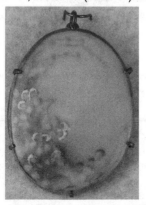

Pendant w/Forget-me-not Decoration

Pendant, oval, decorated w/forget-me-nots on a pastel polychrome ground w/white enamel highlights & burnished gold rim, gold-plated bezel, ca. 1900-25, 1 1/4 x 1 3/4" (ILLUS.) **50**

Pendant, decorated w/a purple pansy w/white enamel center accents & burnished gold border, gold-plated bezel, ca. 1880s-1914, 1" d. **50**

Scarf pin, decorated w/violets, brass-plated bezel & shank, ca. 1880-1920, medallion 1 1/4" d., shank 3" l. **45**

Portrait Shirt Waist Button

Shirtwaist button, round w/shank, decorated w/a girl's profile on multicolored ground, burnished gold rim, 1 7/16" d. (ILLUS.) **75**

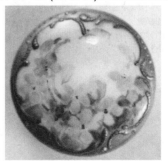

Shirt Waist Button w/Forget-me-nots

Shirtwaist button, round w/shank, decorated w/forget-me-nots, raised paste scrolled border covered w/burnished gold, signed "GHL," 1 1/26" d. (ILLUS.) **30**

Shirtwaist button, decorated w/a central design of pink roses w/outer pale blue band, inner & outer raised paste scrolled borders covered w/burnished gold, ca. 1890s, 1" d. **35**

Heart-shaped Shirt Waist Buttons

Shirtwaist buttons, heart-shaped, decorated w/pink roses, raised paste scrolled border covered w/burnished gold, ca. 1890-1910, 1 1/8 x 1 3/16", pr. (ILLUS.) **70**

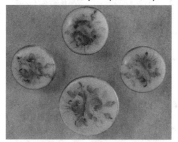

Shirt Waist Set w/Roses

Shirtwaist buttons, round w/shanks, decorated w/pink roses & greenery on a pastel polychrome ground, burnished gold rims, ca. 1900-20, gold wear, 5/8" d., one 7/8" d., the set (ILLUS.) **50**

Shirt Waist Buttons with Three Color Roses

Shirtwaist buttons, decorated w/white, pink & ruby roses on a polychrome background w/raised paste scrolled border covered w/burnished gold, ca. 1890-1910, 3/4" d., pr. (ILLUS.) **70**

Shirtwaist buttons, decorated w/violets on an ivory ground w/white enamel highlights & burnished gold rims, signed "E," ca. 1890-1920, 1 1/16" d. **60**

Shirtwaist set: oval brooch & pr. of oval cuff links; decorated w/blue forget-me-nots on an ivory background w/white enamel highlights, brass-plated mounts, ca. 1900-10, brooch w/burnished gold free-form border & rim, 1 3/8 x 1 3/4", cuff links w/burnished gold rims, 13/16 x 1 1/16", the set **250**

Shirt Waist Set w/Violets

Shirtwaist set, oval cuff links & three round buttons w/shanks, decorated w/clusters of violets on pale yellow ground, burnished gold rim, gold-plated bezel on cuff links, ca. 1900-15, cuff links 3/4 x 1 1/4", buttons 1 1/4" d., the set (ILLUS.) **175**

Watch Chatelaine

Watch chatelaine, oval, decorated w/a woman wearing a rose-colored bodice, light shading to dark warm green ground, set in gold-plated rim w/twisted gold edge, ca. 1880s, 1 1/8 x 1 3/8" (ILLUS.) **115**

General (1800-1920)

Archer's ring, stone, yellowish green stone suffused w/emerald green, approx. 30.5 mm. in diameter, 5.2 mm. in thickness, Qing Dynasty, China **10,000-15,000**

Bar pin, citrine, garnet & peridot, Victorian Renaissance Revival style, five collet-set pear-shaped drops of citrine, garnet & peridot, each suspended from a box-set rose-cut diamond w/a pearl accent on either end, 18k yellow gold mount, signed "Giuliano," w/original box (repair to back) **2,185**

Bar pin, diamond & platinum, set w/19 old European-cut diamonds, engraved gallery **1,725**

Bar pin, diamond, set w/a row of ten old mine-cut diamonds, the center suspending a knife-edge bar w/old mine-cut diamond terminal, French assay mark, Edwardian **1,150**

Bar pin, diamond, the knife-edge design curved in a whiplash line, centered by a spray of prong-set round diamonds, platinum-topped 18k yellow gold mount, Swedish hallmark, Edwardian **578**

Bar pin, enamel & diamond, platinum & rose gold bar w/diamond highlights surmounted by a black enamel flower & an old European-cut diamond, ca. 1915 .... **345**

Bar pin, garnet, centered by a row of collet-set demantoid garnets w/beaded accents

within an openwork scalloped frame, platinum-topped 15k yellow gold mount, ca. 1910 .... **518**

Bar pin, gold (14k yellow) w/lobed terminals & wiretwist accents (discoloration to one side) **230**

Victorian Gold Bar Pin

Bar pin, gold (15k yellow), navette-shaped, centered w/an octagonal-cut peridot, flanked on either side by foliate devices set w/half-pearls & two rubies, hallmarked "G," Victorian, w/fitted box (ILLUS.) **1,035**

Bar pin, gold, Art Nouveau style, centered by a disk depicting a female bust in relief, 18k yellow gold, marked "RL" (minor dents to back) **288**

Bar pin, gold & quartz, centering a tri-color gold pictorial scene w/rose-cut diamond highlight within a bar set w/gold quartz, scallop & gold bead edge, Victorian **748**

Bar pin, komai, scenic design in silver & gold, ca. 1905, Japan **350-650**

Antique Natural Pearl Bee Pin

Bar pin, pearl, a row of natural pearls w/model of a bee at the center w/a natural pearl & faceted ruby body, ruby eyes & rose-cut diamond-set wings, the bee in silver-topped 18k yellow gold on an 18k yellow gold pin w/safety mechanism, ca. 1890 (ILLUS.) **1,725**

Victorian Bar Pin

Bar pin, pearl & citrine, 14k yellow gold mount centered by a marquise citrine w/oval citrine terminals outlined by freshwater pearls, two missing, Victorian (ILLUS.) **316**

Bar pin, platinum & diamond, openwork design w/an alternating pattern of old European-cut diamonds & square-cut synthetic sapphires, platinum-topped 14k yellow gold mount **345**

Bar pin, sapphire, pearl & 14k gold, designed w/five collet-set sapphires spaced by freshwater pearls, Edwardian **230**

Bar pin, sapphire & pearl, designed w/five collet-set sapphires spaced by freshwater pearls, 14k gold, Edwardian ... **230**

Barrette, diamond, designed w/119 rose-cut diamonds, silver topped gold, French hallmark & assay marks, Edwardian **1,150**

Barrette, diamond & pearl, rectangular open design set w/ten collet-set old European-cut diamonds approx. total wt. 0.60 cts. & spaced by ten cultured pearls, 14k yellow gold mount, solder evident, Victorian **431**

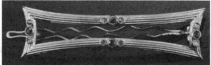

Antique Gold Barrette

Barrette, gold (18k), diamond & ruby, a shaped & reeded design, surmounted by clusters of collet-set rose-cut diamonds & rubies (ILLUS.) **690**

Belt, silver & pottery, Satsuma medallions set in silver w/silver links, designs of flowers in colors & gilt, ca. 1910, Japan, 24" w. **475-775**

Belt buckle, enamel & 14k gold, Egyptian Revival style, each half features a winged goddess, possibly Isis, in profile, between her arms is a large carved turquoise scarab, a symbol of rebirth & rejuvenation, fan-shaped lotus w/multicolor enamels surrounds the face of the Goddess w/two smaller blossoms emerging from the stylized phoenix, which supports both Goddess & beetle, two diamonds, symbolizing sun disks, are set alternatively in the Goddess' hand & on top of the toe..... **12,650**

Belt buckle, komai, oval scenic views of Japan, signed, ca. 1910, 2 1/4" l **1,000-1,500**

Belt buckle, sterling silver, Art Nouveau style, two repoussé plaques of female faces w/flowing hair & flower blossoms, hallmark for William B. Kerr & Co. **288**

Belt hook, bronze, inlaid w/gold & turquoise, rounded on one side, the other side tapering toward the dragon's head hook, malachite encrustation overall, Eastern Zhou period, China, 7 1/4" l. (losses, repaired)........ **2,500-3,500**

Belt hook, jadeite, white, spade form, carved in relief w/a pair of chilong, the hook formed by the head of a dragon, the stone an even pale greenish white, 18th-19th c., China, 4" l..... **1,000-1,500**

Bracelet, bangle-type, 14k gold, hinged, w/lion's head & bead terminals, cabochon ruby eye, bead & wiretwist decoration, engraved "Grace," Victorian..................... **1,265**

Bracelet, bangle-type, 14k yellow gold, hinged design, top w/applied gold geometric design centered by an oval foliate motif, beaded & wiretwist accents (minor damage) **489**

Etruscan Gold Bangle Bracelet

Bracelet, bangle-type, 18k gold, Victorian Etruscan Revival style, hinged knot design w/ball terminals, overall bead & wiretwist decoration (ILLUS.) **2,415**

Art Nouveau Style Bangle Bracelet

Bracelet, bangle-type, Art Nouveau style pierced & chased foliate design in 14k yellow gold, 7 1/2" (ILLUS.) **1,035**

Citrine, Diamond & Enamel Bracelet

Bracelet, bangle-type, citrine, diamond & enamel, hinged design centering a large, faceted, heart-shaped citrine surrounded by old mine- & rose-cut diamonds w/two triangular-shaped citrines on the sides, each decorated w/rose-cut diamonds set in trefoil designs, mounted in 14k yellow gold w/royal blue enameled background, 6 1/2" (ILLUS.) **3,450**

Bracelet, bangle-type, diamond & amethyst, hinged bangle w/openwork foliate top set w/pear-shaped & oval amethysts & rose-cut diamonds set in silver, 18k yellow gold mount, European hallmarks **920**

Edwardian Bangle Bracelet

Bracelet, bangle-type, diamond, enamel, platinum & gold, the tested 14k yellow gold mount set on the top portion w/a filigree platinum chase-work floral design set w/93 round old European- and rose-cut diamonds weighing about 1.l75 carats within a cobalt blue guilloché enamel field, ca. 1910, Edwardian (ILLUS.) **2,760**

Bracelet, bangle-type, diamond & gold, the tested 14k yellow gold mount fitted on the top portion w/an S-form design set w/11 old mine-cut diamonds weighing about 1 carat, together w/original leather & felt-lined fitted presentation box, last quarter 19th c. **489**

Bracelet, bangle-type, garnet, hinged & set throughout w/faceted garnets, the top designed as a bypass & centered by a garnet horseshoe, ca. 1860, Victorian **863**

Edwardian Bangle Bracelet

Bracelet, bangle-type, gold (14k yellow) & amethyst, hinged design centered by a prong-set rectangular-cut amethyst within an openwork foliate frame, dated 1908, Edwardian (ILLUS.) **690**

Bracelet, bangle-type, gold (15k), the top designed as a three dimensional salamander, the body embellished w/an engraved scroll & floral motif, red stone cabochon eyes, double hinged tail wraps around to form the bangle, registry marks "class I, parcel 5, May 16, 1850," England **2,300**

Bracelet, bangle-type, gold (18k), Archaeological Revival style, hinged design w/three curved sections decorated w/Greek letters, alternating w/carved carnelian scarabs, w/wiretwist accents, monogram for Castellani, ca. 1875 .... **8,625**

Bracelet, bangle-type, gold (18k) & diamond, narrow hinged band set w/12 old mine-cut diamonds **978**

Bracelet, bangle-type, gold (18k yellow) & amethyst, the hinged band set w/six oval amethyst cabochons w/wiretwist accents, hallmark, Victorian (minor overall wear) **1,495**

Bracelet, bangle-type, gold & diamond, centered by a rose-cut diamond flanked by oval yellow stones, framed by 14 rose-cut diamonds, bead & scroll motif rose gold hinged mount, Victorian **1,150**

Bracelet, bangle-type, gold, opal, ruby & enamel, black enamel medallions centered w/an opal & ruby floral design surrounded by raised gold designs & engraving, France, ca. 1840 .... **1,288**

Victorian Pietra Dura Bracelet

Bracelet, bangle-type, gold & pietra dura, the hinged 10k rose gold mount surmounted by an oval hardstone plaque inlaid w/a bouquet of flowers flanked by gold leaves, Victorian (ILLUS.) **575**

Bracelet, bangle-type, gold, turquoise & diamond, a center decoration of diamonds & six cabochon turquoise on either side of the center surrounded by small diamonds, ca. 1890 .... **1,232**

Bracelet, bangle-type, lapis, pearl & 14k yellow gold, Etruscan Revival, hinged design, the top centered by a line of pyramid-shaped lapis flanked by rows of seed pearls & granulation, European hallmarks (missing one pearl, some dents, repair) **1,265**

Bracelet, bangle-type, sapphire & diamond, Etruscan Revival style, bead-set w/three sapphires & two round diamonds, accented w/rosettes & beads on edge, 18k yellow gold, interior engraved "Lung-Tsing, 1889," Victorian, in original box **3,680**

Bracelet, diamond, centered by rose-cut & collet-set old European-cut diamond openwork links, millegrain accents, completed by open bar links, platinum-topped 18k yellow gold mount, French hallmarks & assay marks, Edwardian **805**

Bracelet, diamond, early Art Deco style, gradually tapering & articulated design set w/14 old mine-cut diamonds, each within a rose-cut diamond-set frame & bordered w/smaller round diamonds, mounted in platinum, ca. 1915, 7 1/4" l. **16,100**

Bracelet, diamond, flexible, segmented, strap w/a central row of eight old European-cut diamonds framed by a plaque decorated w/pavé-set old European-cut diamonds, mounted in platinum, ca. 1905, 6 3/4" l. **23,575**

Diamond & Gold Toggle Bracelet

Bracelet, diamond & gold, a horseshoe & toggle design bead-set w/old European-cut diamonds, silver-topped gold mount w/open curved link chain, 15k gold, English hallmarks, Victorian (ILLUS.)............................. **1,725**

Gold Bracelet w/Emeralds & Diamonds

Bracelet, emerald, diamond & gold, articulated barrel-shaped links w/the 16 center link section set w/an emerald flanked by rose-cut diamonds, ca. 1880, Victorian, w/original box (ILLUS.) .. **2,875**

Gold & Enamel Hand Bracelet

Bracelet, enamel & 18k yellow gold, flexible gold & white enamel links w/foliate repoussé spacers completed by a hand clasping a basket of blue enamel flowers, surmounted by pink stones, French assay mark, chips & repair to enamel, Victorian (ILLUS.)............................... **2,300**

Bracelet, enamel & gold, hinged panels inlaid w/cobalt blue enamel decorated w/an overall pattern of gold flecks, 18k yellow gold mount, 6 3/4" l. (minor enamel loss to one panel) **1,495**

Bracelet, enamel & pearl, centered by a baroque pearl surrounded by engraved bi-color 18k gold leaves & hinged curved sections w/green enamel stripes, French import mark, adjustable from 6 1/2 to 7 1/4" l. (repair to tongue of clasp) **1,840**

Bracelet, gold (10k yellow), designed as a lion's head w/diamond in the mouth, red stone eyes, oval & baton links, Edwardian, 7 1/4" l. **403**

Victorian Multicolored Gold Bracelet

Bracelet, gold (14k multicolored), designed w/13 mottled "patchwork" plaques, each joincd by small straight pins & highlighted w/two small sapphires & a diamond, hallmark for A.J. Hedges & Co., Victorian, ca. 1880s (ILLUS.)................... **1,725**

Bracelet, gold (14k yellow), adjustable mesh "belt" w/central knot surmounted by a cultured pearl & rose-cut starburst motif................... **1,150**

Art Nouveau Slide Bracelet

Bracelet, gold (14k yellow), Art Nouveau style, slide-type composed of 11 individual diamond-set female silhouettes (ILLUS.)................. **2,070**

Antique Gold Snake Bracelet

Bracelet, gold (14k yellow), designed as a coiled snake of flexible braided gold wire w/ruby eyes (ILLUS.).............. **1,725**

Bracelet, gold (14k yellow) & diamond, tubular bangle-type w/center openwork lion mask design w/scrolled mane, round old European-cut diamond in mouth, eyes set w/single-cut diamonds (added later), inscription on verso, ca. 1900, Edwardian..... **978**

Bracelet, gold (14k yellow), enamel & pearl, slide-type, woven mesh band set w/a circular slide decorated w/shades of blue & black enamel & centered by a cultured pearl, culminating w/a tassel, Victorian, approx. 38.2 dwt............................. **1,265**

Bracelet, gold (14k yellow), flexible mesh design, the rectangular slide w/applied shield form plaque & black enamel & seed pearl accents, foxtail fringe terminal, Victorian (minor damage to mesh)............................. **690**

Gold Bracelet

Bracelet, gold (14k yellow), flexible plaque design alternating round floret links w/concave barrel-shaped stations, ca. 1900 (ILLUS.).. **1,380**

Bracelet, gold (14k yellow), slide-type, mesh, the quatrefoil slide w/seed pearl accents, black enamel tracery & foxtail tassels, Victorian........ **748**

Bracelet, gold (14k yellow), the gold mesh chain accented by a slide w/a pearl center, beaded & tracery accents, Victorian....................... **978**

Bracelet, gold (14k yellow) & turquoise, Arts & Crafts style, designed w/alternating oval turquoise-set links & foliate links w/seed pearl accents, hallmark for Bippart, Griscom & Osborn (minor repair evident to back) **748**

Diamond & Emerald Bracelet

Bracelet, gold (18k), diamond & emerald, four openwork plaques centered by bezel-set old mine-cut diamond & emerald clusters flanked by diamond & emerald peacocks, each plaque joined by cabochon emerald links, French assay & hallmarks (ILLUS. of part) **1,495**

Bracelet, gold (18k) & diamond, textured fancy links centered by a foliate cluster w/enamel flowers & a prongset old European-cut diamond **2,185**

Gold Snake Bracelet

Bracelet, gold (18k), snake form, flexible woven design w/sapphire & rose-cut diamond-set head & eyes, minor dent near tail, European hallmark (ILLUS.) **6,325**

Bracelet, gold (18k yellow), braided foxtail chain, the clasp decorated w/beaded accents, Victorian **690**

Gold & Enamel Snake Bracelet

Bracelet, gold (18k yellow), enamel & diamond, designed as a hinged flexible coiled snake, the body w/guilloché pink enamel & adorned w/six old mine-cut & rose-cut diamonds set in silver, enamel damaged, Victorian (ILLUS.) **4,750**

Bracelet, gold & diamond, pink gold filigree links w/a center medallion containing three diamonds set in white gold, ca. 1900, center medallion 1/2" w., overall 7" l. **672**

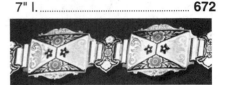

Victorian Gold & Enamel Bracelet

Bracelet, gold & enamel, the hinged rectangular plaques inlaid w/champleve enamel in white, navy & rust, 18k yellow gold mount, Victorian, 7 3/4" l. (ILLUS.) **805**

Bracelet, gold & mixed metal, Damascene-style, hinged design cuff centered by a circular plaque depicting a horse & rider in relief flanked by six-pointed stars w/foliate & beaded accents **1,150**

Bracelet, hardstone intaglio, the six oval plaques depicting classical figures & scenes, 18k yellow gold mountings, separated by trace links, French import marks, 7" l. (chip to back of one, surface scratches) **920**

Etruscan Revival Style Lapis Bracelet

Bracelet, lapis & 18k yellow gold, Etruscan Revival style, center bezel-set round lapis flanked by two oval lapis-set links within gold wiretwist frames, gold bead & floral filigree detail, French import mark, 7" l. (ILLUS. of part) **1,035**

Lapis Lazuli & Diamond Bracelet

Bracelet, lapis lazuli & diamond, an open, flexible design w/six ornate sections, each centering a round cabochon-cut lapis lazuli capped w/a rose-cut diamond w/gold fleur-de-lis designs & rose-cut diamonds on each side, attached to round snake chain borders, mounted in 18k yellow gold, two diamond points missing, 7 1/4" l. (ILLUS. of part) **2,300**

Bracelet, moonstone, double row of 50 prong-set cabochon moonstones, silver mount, 7" l. **920**

Bracelet, moonstone, seven bezel-set moonstones set in a diamond shaped cartouche alternating w/seven freshwater pearls, 14k yellow gold, 7 3/4" l. **1,380**

Bracelet, pearl, Arts & Crafts style, five prong-set multicolored blister pearls joined by gold grape & leaf design links, completed by a baroque pearl drop accented w/a double-sided gold leaf finding, 14k yellow gold, 7 3/8" l. **403**

Bracelet, pearl & diamond, hinged design, top centered by a cultured pearl framed in old mine-cut diamonds, flanked by six collet-set diamonds w/foliate accents, all set in silver-topped 14k yellow gold **633**

Bracelet, pearl & gold (18k yellow), Art Nouveau style, the lozenge-shaped links chased & engraved in a poppy motif, alternating w/semi-baroque pearl links, French gold marks, 7" l. **1,495**

Edwardian Seed Pearl Bracelet

Bracelet, pearl, mesh design of seed pearl & platinum links, bezel-set diamond spacers w/millegrain accents, Edwardian, 7 3/4" l. (ILLUS. of part) **8,625**

Pearl, Sapphire & Diamond Bracelet

Bracelet, pearl, sapphire & diamond, flexible, strap type, designed w/seven rows of natural seed pearls centering a cushion-shaped, faceted sapphire, surrounded by a square frame of 14 old mine- & old European-cut diamonds, decorated w/three small rectangular-shaped plaques each w/a centerline of square French-cut sapphires flanked by two rows of small round diamonds, mounted in platinum w/18k white gold catch, ca. 1900, approx. 6 1/2" l. (ILLUS.) ... **12,075**

Bracelet, pearl, set at intervals w/grey, ivory & yellow pearls, probably natural, platinum chain, Edwardian, 7 1/2" l. **863**

Bracelet, portrait-type, oval bust portraits of three children within platinum-topped 14k gold & old European-cut diamond frames joined by later platinum nautical links, Edwardian, 8" l. **2,300**

Ruby, Diamond & Pearl Bracelet

Bracelet, ruby, diamond & pearl, each section set w/rubies in an "X" motif & centered by a row of old mine-cut diamonds, enhanced by a border of old mine-cut diamonds & pearls, one ruby missing, one section detached, lead solder, silver mount (ILLUS.) **13,800**

Bracelet, sapphire & diamond, a flexible design set w/seven oval-shaped, cabochon-cut sapphires, gradually tapering in size, each separated by a row of five old mine-cut diamonds, mounted in platinum & 18k yellow gold, 7 1/4" l. **10,925**

Bracelet, sterling silver, large curb links w/a center circular gilt clasp surmounted by a spider, No. 162X, hallmark for Schiebler **546**

Bracelet, turquoise & pearl, three rows of seed pearls & irregular-shaped American turquoise spacers, gilt metal mount, ca. 1890 .... **259**

Antique Gold Bracelet/Brooch

Bracelet/brooch, gold, ruby & diamond, wide mesh bracelet w/diamond accents w/detachable brooch of old mine-cut diamonds & cushion-cut rubies, pinched collet settings, ropetwist accents (ILLUS.) **5,750**

Bracelets, bangle-type, 14k gold, designed as identical hinged bangles, the tops surmounted by rose & textured gold ornaments, ca. 1870, Victorian, pr. **3,105**

Gold & Enamel Cuff Bracelet

Bracelets, bangle-type, enamel & 14k gold, hinged cuff-style, engraved w/black tracery enamel foliate motifs, Victorian, pr. (ILLUS. of one) **1,265**

Bracelets, bangle-type, gold (14k), hinged design decorated w/applied multicolor 14k gold butterfly & floral motif, coiled gold wire border, 14k yellow gold mount, dated 1883, signed "E.W. Schurmann, Philadelphia," pr. (minor dents to back) **2,990**

Bracelets, gold (14k bicolor), hinged design, twisted gold accents, rose & yellow gold, boxed, pr. **288**

Victorian Slide Bracelet

Bracelets, gold (14k yellow), slide-type, flexible mesh design, the shield shape slide w/black enamel tracery & applied bicolor gold clover leaf plaque w/seed pearl accent, foxtail fringe terminal, Victorian, pr. (ILLUS. of one) **1,265**

Bracelets, hairwork, friendship-type, woven tubes of hair forming a twist, chase decorated clasps containing braided hair, 6 1/2" l., matching pr. (damage) **121**

Brooch, amethyst, Arts & Crafts style, bar pin top w/a tapering collet-set cultured pearl & 14k yellow gold oak leaf design centered by an emerald-cut amethyst, Edward Oakes **6,210**

Brooch, amethyst & pearl, Arts & Crafts style, prong-set w/faceted amethysts & split pearls, gold bead accents, gilt mount, by Dorrie Nossiter, England **1,093**

Brooch, amethyst, pearl & diamond, Arts & Crafts style, five bezel-set amethysts, enhanced by baroque pearls & an old mine-cut diamond, surrounded by platinum leaves in a 14k yellow gold mount w/scroll & bead accents, attributed to Edward Oakes **4,025**

Brooch, amethyst, pearl & enamel, centered by a bezel-set square-cut amethyst, suspending a festoon of basse taille enamel leaves interrupted by five seed pearls, 14k yellow gold mount, hallmark for Whiteside & Blank, Edwardian **748**

Aquamarine & Diamond Brooch

Brooch, aquamarine & diamond, centered by an emerald-cut aquamarine within an open wirework, millegrain & rose-cut diamond frame w/four green gold florets & collet-set aquamarine terminals, 14k yellow gold mount, Russian hallmarks, Edwardian, one diamond missing (ILLUS.) **2,990**

Brooch, beryl & diamond, the oval shape centered by a prong-set cabochon beryl framed by prong-set old European-cut diamonds, 18k yellow gold mount **575**

Brooch, bow-form, plaited hair within a platinum-topped yellow gold frame w/rose-cut diamond accents, Edwardian **460**

Brooch, carved moonstone, depicting the profile of a classical figure, cushion-cut ruby & diamond highlights, 18k yellow gold wiretwist & beaded frame, Edwardian (some minor surface scratches) **1,955**

Brooch, coral & pearl & 14k gold, modeled as a daisy, accented w/seed pearls & drops, Victorian (solder, chip to drop) **230**

Brooch, diamond & 14k gold, designed as a bow w/rose-cut diamonds, green glass grape cluster & seed pearl accents, possibly Russian .. **1,035**

Brooch, diamond & 14k white gold, a starburst design set of old mine-cut diamonds **1,380**

Brooch, diamond & 18k gold, center bust portrait of lady w/flowers in hair, framed within a circle of 39 rose-cut diamonds, signed "C & Co.," Victorian **978**

Art Nouveau Griffin Brooch

Brooch, diamond & 18k yellow gold, Art Nouveau style, designed as a griffin accented w/a prong-set rose-cut diamond in mouth, on a scrolled branch terminating in a diamond & pearl drop (ILLUS.) **978**

Diamond Corsage Brooch

Brooch, diamond, a floral & leaf design, decorated w/old mine- & rose-cut diamonds, the five flowerheads en tremblant, mounted in silver-topped 18k yellow gold, several detachable sections, ca. 1830 (ILLUS.) **6,900**

Art Nouveau Diamond Brooch

Brooch, diamond, Art Nouveau style, graceful open-work w/lozenge-shaped design centering a large old mine-cut diamond w/old mine- & rose-cut diamond accents, one small rose-cut diamond missing, mounted in platinum-topped 18k yellow gold (ILLUS.) **5,060**

Diamond Bow Brooch

Brooch, diamond, bow design set w/173 rose-cut diamonds set in a platinum & 18k yellow gold mount, some diamonds missing to under-gallery, French hallmarks, No. 6113 (ILLUS.) **6,900**

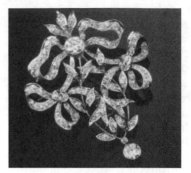

Edwardian Diamond Bow Brooch

Brooch, diamond, bow & swag design set throughout w/bead & collet-set diamonds, platinum-topped 14k gold, Edwardian (ILLUS.) **4,255**

Brooch, diamond, buckle form, set w/old European-cut diamonds, platinum-topped 18k yellow gold mount, signed "Tiffany & Co." (one diamond missing) **3,910**

Brooch, diamond, Caduceus design w/snake's body composed of rose-cut diamonds set in silver, coiled around a 14k yellow gold staff surmounted by a semi-baroque pearl, head & eyes set w/foil backed garnets, 14k yellow gold pin stem, Victorian (one rose-cut diamond missing) **575**

Brooch, diamond, centered by a rose-cut diamond-set buckle, millegrain accents, within a black silk ribbon & gold wire bow, platinum-topped 18k yellow gold mount **230**

Brooch, diamond, circular design centered by a cushion-shaped glass plaque surrounded by 30 collet-set cushion-cut diamonds, silver-topped 14k yellow gold mount, ca. 1820, Georgian . **5,405**

Brooch, diamond, crescent design w/21 bead-set old mine-cut diamonds, approx. total wt. 1.15 cts., silver-topped gold mount **1,610**

Brooch, diamond, crescent shape w/five prong-set old European-cut diamonds, platinum-topped 18k yellow gold mount, signed "Pickslay & Co." **22,713**

Brooch, diamond, depicting a swallow in flight, decorated w/rose-cut fiamonds, mounted in silver-topped 14k yellow gold, ca. 1880 .... **2,875**

Brooch, diamond, diamond-set starburst design centered by an old European-cut diamond **2,875**

Emerald & Diamond Butterfly Brooch

Brooch, diamond & emerald, modeled as a butterfly w/en tremblant wings set w/old mine & Swiss-cut diamonds & calibré-cut emeralds, the body also set w/emeralds & diamonds, ruby eyes & diamond-studded antennae, mounted in 18k yellow gold & platinum (ILLUS.) **3,220**

Brooch, diamond & enamel, blue guilloché enamel plaque w/central applied, rose-cut diamond accents, silver-topped 18k gold mount, Edwardian **7,705**

Diamond & Enamel Eagle Brooch

Brooch, diamond & enamel, modeled as an eagle, the body designed w/pavé-set rose-cut diamonds, feathers & head decorated w/shaded guilloché enamel, talon suspending a pearl drop, silver-topped gold mount, French import mark (ILLUS.) **4,370**

Brooch, diamond, floral spray design collet- & bead-set w/old European & rose-cut diamonds, freshwater pearl & ruby accents, silver top, 18k yellow gold mount **748**

Brooch, diamond, floral spray design set w/rose-cut diamonds w/cabochon red stone accents, 18k yellow gold-backed sterling silver mount, ca. 1800, Georgian (lead solder evident to back) **1,035**

Diamond Flower Brooch

Brooch, diamond, flower design centered by a collet-set old European-cut diamond, surrounded by numerous collet & bead-set diamonds, platinum-topped 18k gold, signed "Marcus & Co.," Edwardian (ILLUS.) **19,550**

Diamond Brooch

Brooch, diamond, garland style decorated w/24 old mine-cut diamonds & rose-cut diamonds, mounted in platinum, ca. 1890, numbered w/French hallmarks & maker's mark (ILLUS.) **2,990**

Brooch, diamond, modeled as a basket w/overhead handle, filled w/flowers, 100 bead-set diamonds, platinum-topped gold mount, Edwardian (minor lead solder) **4,025**

Brooch, diamond, openwork design of a footed basket holding flowers, set w/round- & rose-cut diamonds, ruby, sapphire & green stone accents, platinum-topped 18k yellow gold, French hallmarks, ca. 1900 (abrasions to colored stones)......... **2,300**

Brooch, diamond & pearl, bow design set w/75 old mine-cut diamonds terminating in an old mine-cut diamond & rose-cut diamond capped baroque pearl, silver-topped gold mount.............................. **10,925**

Diamond & Pearl Bow Brooch

Brooch, diamond & pearl, four-loop bow design set w/approximately 153 old mine-cut diamonds, suspending a natural pearl drop, diamond-set cap, silver-topped 18k yellow gold mount, European hallmarks (ILLUS.)................................... **17,250**

Brooch, diamond, pearl & garnet, designed as a flowerhead, centered w/a demantoid garnet surrounded by eight old-European-cut dia-

monds, the five open looped petals set w/diamonds, garnets & split pearls, 15k gold mount, Edwardian...................... **3,335**

Edwardian Flowerhead Brooch

Brooch, diamond, pearl & garnet, designed as a flowerhead, set w/a demantoid garnet surrounded by eight old European-cut diamonds, petals set w/diamonds, garnets & split pearls, 15k gold mount, Edwardian (ILLUS.). **3,335**

Brooch, diamond & pearl, modeled as a bird on a branch, bead-set w/old European-cut diamonds, ruby eye, baroque pearl body, 14k gold mount (solder to back).. **2,875**

Edwardian Flower Basket Brooch

Brooch, diamond, pearl & platinum, flower basket design, openwork platinum grill surmounted by pearl & diamond flowers, set throughout w/41 round brilliant- & single-cut diamonds & 21 pearls in shades of pink, grey & cream, millegrain accents, minor gold solder, Edwardian (ILLUS.)......................... **6,325**

Diamond Pinwheel Brooch

Brooch, diamond, pinwheel design set w/old European-cut diamonds, openwork 14k yellow gold mount (ILLUS.) **2,990**

Brooch, diamond & platinum, centered by an old mine-cut diamond in a lacy filigree mount set throughout w/rose- & single-cut diamonds, millegrain accents, French assay mark, Edwardian **7,475**

Brooch, diamond & platinum, set w/round & old European-cut diamonds, centered by an old European-cut diamond flanked by two collet-set diamonds, millegrain accents, 18k white gold findings, Edwardian **4,888**

Late Edwardian Diamond Brooch

Brooch, diamond & platinum, the circular openwork floral filigree design centering a round diamond, approx. .50 ct., additionally adorned w/204 round diamonds, total approx. 4.50 cts., signed "T.B. Starr," Edwardian, approx. 17.3 dwt. (ILLUS.) **12,650**

Brooch, diamond & ruby, designed as a swallow, 14k gold & silver enhanced by rose-cut diamonds, ruby eye, Victorian **3,163**

Delicate Early Butterfly Brooch

Brooch, diamond, ruby, garnet, moonstone, gold & platinum, butterfly-shaped, the 14k yellow gold & platinum top openwork mount set w/two oval & one round cabochon moonstone weighing about 9 carats surrounded by 42 old mine- and European-cut diamonds weighing about 1.15 carats, the eyes set w/two round faceted rubies weighing about .10 carats, the back of the head set w/one round faceted demantoid garnet weighing about .20 carats, early 20th c., 2" w. (ILLUS.) **6,325**

Brooch, diamond & silver, feather design set w/48 rose- & old mine-cut diamond melée (minor solder) **805**

Brooch, diamond, starburst design centered by a cushion-cut sapphire, measuring approx. 6.42 x 6.50 x 2.50 mm. within a diamond-set 14k yellow gold mount, approx. total diamond wt. 1.92 cts. **1,553**

Brooch, diamond, stylized heart w/central flower motif in an openwork design flanked by scrolls w/bead-set rose-cut diamonds & collet-set old European-cut diamonds, platinum-topped gold mount, approx. 75 diamonds **1,150**

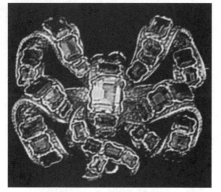

Emerald Bow Brooch

Brooch, emerald & 18k yellow gold, a ribbon bow design set throughout w/square-cut emeralds, the gold frame enhanced w/floral engraving, ca. 1860 (ILLUS.) **3,450**

Art Nouveau Dragonfly Brooch

Brooch, enamel, 14k yellow gold, garnet, ruby & diamond, Art Nouveau style dragonfly design w/green & white guilloché enamel wings edged w/seed pearls, demantoid garnet eyes, ruby & diamond accents, minor chips to enamel, hallmark for Riker Bros. (ILLUS.) **2,645**

Art Nouveau Style Portrait Brooch

Brooch, enamel & 18k yellow gold, Art Nouveau style portrait brooch, scalloped shell shape w/pink iridescent champlevé enamel, rose-cut diamond accent, French assay mark (ILLUS.) **1,610**

Brooch, enamel, Art Nouveau style, lily designed w/white petals set w/a circular-cut diamond on a green translucent lily pad, hallmark for Krementz & Co. (enamel loss) **1,380**

Brooch, enamel, Art Nouveau style orchid design in shades of pale pink & green iridescent enamel, highlighted by a seed pearl, 14k gold, hallmark for Whiteside & Blank **690**

Art Nouveau Floral Design Pieces

Brooch, enamel, Art Nouveau style, orchid design, purple, pink & green enamel petals accented w/an old mine-cut diamond, minor chip to enamel (ILLUS. bottom right)....................................... **1,610**

Brooch, enamel & diamond, depicting a bird in flight, grey & burgundy enamel w/gold beak & legs, beak suspending a small old mine-cut diamond, mounted in 18k yellow gold, ca. 1890, w/hallmarks.................................... **1,610**

Arts & Crafts Moonstone Brooch

Brooch, enamel, moonstone & 18k yellow gold, Arts & Crafts style, the circular shape decorated w/an overall vine motif against a shaded blue enamel ground, centered by a bezel-set moonstone, some enamel loss near edges, signed "Tiffany & Co." on applied plaque (ILLUS.)............................ **5,750**

Brooch, enamel, opal, diamond & pearl, navette-shaped w/an opal center surrounded by rose-cut diamonds & seed pearls, within a green guilloché & white enamel frame, 18k yellow gold mount............................... **748**

Brooch, enamel, openwork design of a lily w/burgundy enameling, green enameled leaves, an old mine-cut diamond at the top of stem, a free-hanging pearl drop at the base, mounted in 18k yellow gold................................. **1,265**

Brooch, enamel & pearl, oval portrait design w/female profile within a red shell guilloché enamel background, framed within a pearl & old European-cut diamond frame w/gold ribbon accents, 18k yellow gold mount, ca. 1900 (some nicks to enamel) .. **978**

Brooch, garnet, a round mounting set w/47 round faceted garnets, ca. 1890 .... **504**

Brooch, garnet & enamel, Victorian Revival style, a bezel-set garnet carbuncle within a circular & quatrefoil frame accented by white enamel & beaded accents, 14k yellow gold mount, rear locket compartment (tiny dents) **518**

Brooch, gemstone & pearl, Arts & Crafts style, floral spray design prong-set w/various colored gems in shades of lilac, yellow, pink & green, including colored sapphires, kunzite, emerald & amethyst w/seed pearl accents, gilt silver mount, by Dorrie Nossiter **2,760**

Brooch, gold (14k) & pearl, reticulated date "1892," three pearl accents, boxed **173**

Brooch, gold (14k yellow), Arts & Crafts style, set to one side w/an opal doublet, in an openwork design of leaves, tendrils & beaded accents, attributed to Edward Oakes (crazing to opal) **1,150**

Brooch, gold (14k yellow), circular design w/ram's head centered by a spherical pendant, Victorian Revival (minor dents) **575**

Brooch, gold (14k yellow), diamond & enamel, designed as an eight-point star set w/old mine-cut & round diamonds, black enamel detail, engraved heart & foliate yellow gold mount set w/round diamonds, Victorian **2,070**

Brooch, gold (14k yellow), Egyptian Revival style, carved steatite scarab surrounded by a coiled gold snake w/diamond accent **920**

Brooch, gold (14k yellow) & gems, Arts & Crafts style, centered by a large cabochon stone flanked by graduating cabochon gemstones, beaded accents **978**

Gold & Gem-set Brooch

Brooch, gold (14k yellow) & gems, rectangular form set w/a clipped corner modified rectangular-cut tourmaline w/overall applied foliate & bead motifs, collet-set diamond & demantoid garnet accents, Edward Oakes, accompanied by copy of original drawing (ILLUS.) **7,015**

Brooch, gold (18k), Art Nouveau style, an eagle w/textured gold body, depicted in flight, holding a pearl, ruby & diamond accents, French hallmarks **2,645**

Brooch, gold (18k yellow), Art Nouveau style, circular form w/center depicting relief-molded woman's profile w/border of leaf accents bead-set w/six oval sapphires & rose-cut diamond accents **1,380**

Brooch, gold (18k yellow), designed as a bridled horse's head w/textured mane & ears, rose gold reins, ca. 1910 (pin stem not gold) **575**

Gold & Enamel Ribbon Brooch

Brooch, gold (22k yellow), enamel & diamond, a floral engraved ribbon design w/blue enamel knot set w/old mine-cut diamonds, suspending a blue enamel locket, the scalloped edge accented w/gold & center-set w/diamonds set in a star shape, ca. 1860 (ILLUS.) **4,025**

Brooch, gold & crystal, reverse intaglio circular form depicting a bird in flight within an 18k yellow gold frame accented by four gold cubes, Victorian (minor solder evident) **690**

Antique Bullfight Brooch

Brooch, gold & enamel, a three-dimensional scene depicting a bullfighter & a bull in polychrome enamel, rose-cut diamond accents, 18k yellow gold mount, signed "Duval," minor wear to enamel, French hallmarks (ILLUS.) **978**

Brooch, gold, enamel & diamond, 10k pink gold setting w/an oval blue enamel medallion framed by bold pink border engraved in the form of a serpent & centered by a mine-cut diamond, glass panel on reverse, ca. 1850, 1 x 1 1/4" **616**

Brooch, gold, enamel & diamond, a blue enamel shield-shaped medallion w/18k gold & diamonds applied in a floral form topped w/a crown of gold & seed pearls & inlaid w/gemstones, ending in a ribbon design w/a center diamond, 19th c., 1 1/2 x 2" **1,288**

Brooch, gold, enamel, opal & ruby, a 14k gold floral filigree setting centered by a star-shaped enameled medallion w/a circle of opals surrounding a cabochon ruby, ca. 1920 .... **224**

Brooch, gold, enamel & pearl, 10k yellow gold oval setting w/a blue enameled medallion surrounded by small pearls, centered by gold inlay in floral designs set w/diamonds, glass panel on reverse, ca. 1850, 1 x 1 1/4"... **728**

Miniature Portrait Brooch

Brooch, gold, miniature portrait-type, the circular plaque depicting Marie Antoinette, surrounded by 18k yellow gold feather motif frame accented by pearl & rose diamond flowers, French hallmark (ILLUS.) **690**

Brooch, gold, modeled as a violin w/bi-color 18k gold body & white gold strings, verso engraved in French (some scratches) **1,380**

Brooch, gold & pearl, 18k yellow gold orchid-form setting centered by a pearl, ca. 1900, 1 1/4 x 2" **532**

Brooch, gold & pearl, 18k yellow gold orchid-form setting set w/pearls, signed "LC," ca. 1900, 2 1/4 x 3 1/2" **952**

Brooch, gold, pietra dura, two birds nesting on a floral branch, 10k yellow gold frame w/gold bead & floret decoration, Victorian **748**

Floral Micromosaic Brooch

Brooch, micromosaic, an oval floral design mosaic w/some flowers in relief, 18k yellow gold frame decorated w/vine tendrils & scrollwork, verso locket compartment, Victorian (ILLUS.) **1,725**

Victorian Micromosaic Brooch

English Georgian Silver & Gold Brooch

Brooch, gold & sterling silver, large curved cut-out blossom & leaf sprig design, England, Georgian era, late 18th - early 19th c. (ILLUS.) **1,200**

Brooch, gold-plate, gold, enamel & diamond, an oval blue enamel medallion centered by white gold scrolling floral work set w/diamonds in a floral-form design, ca. 1850, 1 x 1 1/8" **448**

Brooch, hairwork, elaborate gold-filled frame w/grape cluster & vine motif, beveled edge glass over braided brown hair, reverse inscribed "Maggie Bewington" (old repairs) **132**

Brooch, micromosaic, center malachite ground w/micromosiac of the Vatican within a gold wiretwist & scalloped frame, 18k yellow gold mount, Vatican hallmarks, Victorian (ILLUS.) **2,300**

Brooch, micromosaic, depicting the Pantheon, set within an oval malachite plaque & a textured 18k gold frame, Victorian (cracks to malachite) **259**

Brooch, micromosaic, oval, depicting a group of polychrome bathing birds perched on a gold-colored tureen set in a cobalt blue hardstone plaque, surrounded by a later 18k gold frame, Victorian (chips to stone & loss to mosaic) **1,093**

Brooch, micromosaic, polished black onyx oval stone set w/a polychromatic mosaic of St. Peter's Square, 14k yellow gold mount, ca. 1850 .. **518**

Art Nouveau Moonstone & Enamel Brooch

Brooch, moonstone & enamel, Art Nouveau style centered by an oval moonstone within a foliate blue green enamel & 18k yellow gold mount w/sapphire accents, signed "Tiffany & Co.," boxed (ILLUS.)......................... **17,250**

Moonstone & Sapphire Brooch

Brooch, moonstone & sapphire, Arts & Crafts style, four bezel-set moonstones joined by a foliate design of collet-set sapphires & seed pearls, 14k yellow gold, attributed to Edward Oakes (ILLUS.)............................... **2,645**

Victorian Pearl & Diamond Brooch

Brooch, natural pearl & diamond, composed of three rosettes, each centering a natural round pearl surrounded by old mine-cut diamonds separated by diamond-set trefoil designs, the center rosette suspending three large old mine-cut diamonds in a free-hanging frame of small pearls & diamonds w/a free-hanging old mine- and rose-cut diamond accented bow design drop on either side, each terminating w/a pear-shaped pearl drop decorated at the top w/rose-cut diamonds, center portion detachable to be worn as a pendant, mounted in silver & silver-topped 18k yellow gold, three small rose-cut diamonds missing, ca. 1865 (ILLUS.)................................. **14,950**

Brooch, opal & diamond, centered by an oval opal surrounded by a diamond-set scroll motif frame, 14k yellow gold mount................................**1,725**

Brooch, opal & diamond, crescent-shaped design w/graduated round opals bordered by old European-cut diamonds, 18k yellow gold mount, signed "T.B. Starr" (crazing to two opals) **1,725**

Arts & Crafts Jeweled Brooch

Brooch, pearl, amethyst, aquamarine, ruby & gold, Arts & Crafts style, wreath design centered by a prong-set oval amethyst cabochon surrounded by clusters of wire-set seed pearls & prong-set carved emerald leaves, faceted amethysts, lavender star rubies & aquamarines, silver mount wire gold bead accents, by Dorrie Nossiter, England (ILLUS.). **3,680**

Brooch, pearl, coral & enamel, the domed oval center pavé-set w/seed pearls & coral, framed w/light blue opaque enamel inset w/coral & pearls, 18k yellow gold mount, locket compartment on reverse, in original fitted box, signed "James Muirhead & Sons, Glasgow," Victorian (minor chips to enamel) **690**

Arts & Crafts Pearl Brooch

Brooch, pearl & diamond, Arts & Crafts style, 14k white gold scrolled openwork rectangular mount w/diamond accents, set w/four freshwater petal-shaped pearls, two w/lavender hue, radiating from a center pearl (ILLUS.) ... **633**

Brooch, pearl & diamond, pinwheel design centered by an old European-cut diamond surrounded by seed pearls, 14k yellow gold mount (pin stem replaced) **431**

Seed Pearl Wing Form Brooch

Brooch, pearl & diamond, wing design center set w/a round old European-cut diamond surrounded by six seed pearls, the wings pavé-set w/split pearls, 14k yellow gold mount, ca. 1900, Victorian (ILLUS.) **1,093**

Serpent & Starburst Brooch

Brooch, pearl, emerald & ruby, designed as a coiled emerald & pearl-set serpent w/pearl in fangs, surmounting a starburst set w/rubies & pearls w/large center prong-set pearl, 18k yellow gold mount, English gold mark, solder to back, 19th c. (ILLUS.).................................. **1,725**

Brooch, pearl & gemstone, a cruciform design set w/five split pearls & four round emeralds within a square frame of 36 old mine-cut diamonds, the corners in a fleur-de-lis motif w/red stone accents, silver-topped 18k yellow gold mount, French hallmarks **1,610**

Brooch, pearl, set throughout w/seed pearls, gold bead & wire rosette accents, suspending three pearl drops, ca. 1900 .... **316**

Brooch, pietra dura, 14k yellow gold floral chase-work decorated mount set w/pietra dura panel depicting a floral still life, Victorian **201**

Brooch, pietra dura, designed as a circular hardstone plaque w/pansies, vermeil wiretwist frame (solder evident to back) **288**

Brooch, pietra dura, oval hardstone centered by a white rose, white & green floral buds within a 14k gold triple wiretwist frame (later clasp) **460**

Brooch, pietra dura, the oval hardstone centered by a red & white flower within an 18k yellow gold wirework frame **374**

Onyx & Diamond Brooch

Brooch, platinum, diamond & onyx, stylized bow design w/a geometric onyx frame flanked by diamond-set terminals, set w/270 rose-cut diamonds, in a platinum-topped 18k yellow gold mount, French hallmark, Edwardian (ILLUS.) **6,325**

Plique-a-jour Brooch

Brooch, plique-a-jour enamel, Art Nouveau style, square openwork naturalistic design centered by three graduated fluted emerald beads within an 18k yellow gold green plique-a-jour frame w/diamond accents, probably originally a buckle, minor enamel loss, signed "Marcus & Co." (ILLUS.) **18,400**

Brooch, portrait-type, miniature, depicting Mary Queen of Scots, oil paint on ivory within a rectangular white paste frame, silver gilt mount, ca. 1800, in original fitted box (loose crystal) **374**

Art Nouveau Ruby & Diamond Brooch

Brooch, ruby & diamond, Art Nouveau style, an open frame w/a stylized wreath design centering a free-hanging oval faceted ruby flanked by two curved rows of old mine-cut diamonds topped w/an old mine-cut diamond, suspended from a pair of pearl-shaped faceted rubies & diamonds, the lower portion decorated w/six rectangular cushion-cut rubies slightly tapering in size, w/old mine- and rose-cut diamonds between the rubies & in the borders, mounted in platinum & 18k yellow gold, signed by Vever, Paris, ca. 1900 (ILLUS.) **10,925**

Fine Victorian Floral Brooch

Brooch, ruby, emerald, sapphire & silver, flower-form, the vermeil silver openwork mount set w/about 115 round faceted rubies weighing about 12 carats, the leafage set w/50 round, square & rectangular-cut emeralds weighing about 5 carats & six ciruclar & cushion-cut blue sapphires weighing about .50 carats, second half 19th c., underside w/some solder repair, 3 3/4" l. (ILLUS.)... **1,725**

Sapphire & Diamond Brooch

Brooch, sapphire, diamond & 18k yellow gold, crescent-shaped design alternating round sapphires & diamonds, ca. 1900 (ILLUS.)... **2,070**

Sapphire & Diamond Slide/Brooch

Brooch, sapphire & diamond, center prong-set cushion-shaped Kashmir sapphire surrounded by ten prong-set old mine-cut diamonds, platinum prongs w/18k yellow gold mount, brooch frame detaches to be worn as a slide, chip to girdle & surface scratches, Edwardian, accompanied by AGL Colored Stone Origin Report No. CS 32685, stating natural sapphire, Kashmir (ILLUS.)...... **88,300**

Brooch, sapphire & diamond, centered by a cushion-shaped sapphire within a diamond-set bezel, surrounded by round diamonds in an openwork foliate design & geometric frame, platinum mount, Edwardian..................... **7,475**

Double Crescent Brooch

Brooch, sapphire & diamond, double crescent design w/one crescent set w/ten cushion shape sapphires w/collet-set diamond accents, the other set w/17 old mine-cut diamonds, platinum mount, 14k white gold pin stem, signed "Yard" (ILLUS.)... **4,715**

Brooch, sapphire & diamond, five cushion-shaped sapphires in yellow gold prong settings surrounded by prong- & bead-set old mine-cut diamonds, mounted in silver & yellow gold, detachable clasp & retractable bail **13,800**

Brooch, sapphire & diamond, rose-cut diamond-set loop design w/oval cabochon sapphire terminals, silver-topped 14k yellow gold mount, Edwardian......................... **575**

Arts & Crafts Jeweled Wreath Brooch

Brooch, sapphire, emerald, ruby & moonstone, Arts & Crafts style wreath design w/prong-set faceted & cabochon sapphires, emeralds & moonstones & clusters of wire-set pearls, highlighted by a sapphire & ruby insect set in 14k yellow gold, gilded silver leaves & mount, by Dorrie Nossiter, England (ILLUS.)............................ **8,625**

Renaissance Revival-style Brooch

Brooch, silver & enamel, Renaissance Revival-style, design of a nesting bird w/three chicks suspended from a garnet-set bar pin top, overall polychrome enamel decoration, Hungarian hallmarks, enamel loss, assayer's mark for 800 silver (ILLUS..)........... **3,220**

Georg Jensen Brooch

Brooch, silver & malachite, Arts & Crafts style, openwork design w/a bird highlighted by bezel-set round malachites, ca.   1915-27, stamped 830 & signed "Georg Jensen, Denmark, No. 165" (ILLUS.)........................ **460**

Brooch, silver metal, Art Nouveau style, raised lady's head w/flowing hair, 2 x 2 1/4"................................ **65**

Brooch, silver-gilt, plique-a-jour enamel, peridot & pearl, Art Nouveau style, the foliate motif centered by a collet-set faceted oval peridot, peridot accents, baroque pearl drop, silver-gilt mount (crazing to one plique panel)......................... **230**

Art Nouveau Sterling Silver Brooch

Brooch, sterling silver, Art Nouveau style, designed as the head of a woman wearing a bonnet, gilt hair & bow, wear to nose & edges of bow, hallmark for Unger Bros. (ILLUS.)............................ **1,035**

Brooch, sterling silver, Arts & Crafts style, scrolled open-work design of a calla lily blossom & leaves, stamped sterling mark, early 20th c., 1 1/2 x 2 3/4" **288**

Arts & Crafts Brooch

Brooch, tourmaline & pearl, Arts & Crafts style, set w/buff-top green tourmalines within millegrained bezels, highlighted by freshwater pearls, (two small pearls missing) rose-cut diamond corners, silver mount, gold pin stem, retractable bail (ILLUS.)................................. **2,070**

Brooch/locket, diamond, memento mori design, centered by an oblong locket containing locks of hair, surrounded by 14 rose-cut diamonds, silver-topped 14k gold mount...... **949**

Brooch/pendant diamond, Art Nouveau style, swag & floral motif set w/old mine- & rose-cut diamonds suspending a pearl drop, silver-topped 18k gold, French assay mark **1,725**

Brooch/pendant, diamond, flowerhead design, set throughout w/49 old mine-cut diamonds, diamond-set bail, silver-topped gold mount (one diamond missing) **2,300**

Brooch/pendant, diamond, gold & seed pearl, round w/fleur-de-lis medallions w/seed pearls between floral mountings w/diamonds, ca. 1900 .... **896**

Gold & Diamond Brooch/Pendant

Brooch/pendant, diamond & gold, shield shape centered w/an old European-cut diamond & six smaller old European-cut diamonds, 18k yellow gold top, 14k gold mount, reverse locket compartment, Victorian (ILLUS.)... **748**

Starburst Design Brooch/Pendant

Brooch/pendant, diamond & gold, starburst design w/scrollwork detail, featuring seven old European-cut diamonds in buttercup settings, further enhanced by 33 smaller round diamonds, 14k yellow gold, retractable bail, signed "Birks" (ILLUS.) **1,725**

Brooch/pendant, diamond & pearl, a circular frame enclosing a pierced & millegrained design of a flower basket set w/rose-cut diamonds & accented w/seed pearls, retractable bail, platinum mount, gold pin stem signed "Tiffany & Co." **1,495**

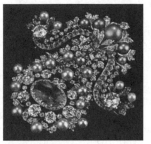

Tiffany Jeweled Brooch/Pendant

Brooch/pendant, diamond, pearl, garnet & sapphire, set throughout w/multicolored natural pearls, fancy color diamonds, pink stones, demantoid garnets & centering an oval pink sapphire, platinum-topped 18k yellow gold, late 19th c., signed "Tiffany & Co." (ILLUS.).......................... **63,000**

Diamond & Pearl Brooch/Pendant

Brooch/pendant, diamond & pearl, ivy leaf design w/old mine- & rose-cut diamonds terminating in a baroque pearl, mounted in silver-topped 18k yellow gold, the end portions of the pendant are detachable to be worn as a brooch, the original chain replaced w/14k white gold chain, one diamond missing (ILLUS.)............................... **5,750**

Diamond Star Brooch/Pendant

Brooch/pendant, diamond, star form centered by old mine-cut light yellow diamond, six old mine-cut diamonds in buttercup settings between star points w/30 old mine-cut diamonds set in star points, silver topped gold mount (ILLUS.)................ **2,530**

Emerald & Diamond Brooch/Pendant

Brooch/pendant, emerald & diamond, a hexagon-cut emerald weighing approx. 6.44 cts. supported by an arch-shaped frame suspending a diamond garland centered by another hexagon-cut emerald weighing approx. 1.60 cts., set throughout w/57 old mine- & rose-cut diamonds, approx. total weight 4.91 cts., silver-topped 14k gold (ILLUS.)... **3,450**

Emerald, Diamond & Pearl Brooch

Brooch/pendant, emerald, diamond & pearl, the garland style decorated w/a laurel motif, centering a large emerald-cut Columbian emerald, framed by small old mine single-cut diamonds w/old mine single- and Swiss-cut diamonds in the floral & leaf designs, accented w/five natural pearls, diamond-set hinged pendant attachment at the top, removable brooch pin, mounted in silver-topped 18k yellow gold, ca. 1900, w/original fitted leather box (ILLUS.) **10,350**

Brooch/pendant, enamel & 14k gold, Art Nouveau style, designed as a lotus blossom flanked by swans w/a shaded green & ivory enamel background, diamond accents, hallmark for Krementz & Co. **1,840**

Brooch/pendant, enamel & 14k yellow gold, Art Nouveau design of an orchid w/light pink, lavender & green enamel petals, maker's mark for Whiteside & Blank **518**

Brooch/pendant, enamel, Art Nouveau pansy design, leaves decorated w/shaded purple & white enamel & edged w/split pearls, circular-cut diamond accent, hallmark for Krementz & Co. **1,380**

Memorial Brooch/Pendant

Brooch/pendant, enamel & gold, memorial-type, designed as a locket w/a central compartment containing blue fabric, surrounded by seed pearls in an 18k yellow gold fleur-de-lis, enameled & engraved oval settings, repair to clasp, reverse hair compartment (ILLUS.) **374**

Brooch/pendant, enamel & pearl, a four-leaf clover design, the leaves outlined w/seed pearls, retractable bail, 14k yellow gold, hallmark for Krementz & Co., Edwardian **1,265**

Brooch/pendant, lapis & pearl, oval lapis framed w/pearls within an 18k yellow gold mount w/applied foliate design, the verso w/hinged compartment, Victorian **690**

Heart-shaped Opal Brooch/Pendant

Brooch/pendant, opal & diamond, the prong-set heart-shaped opal framed by a bead- & prong-set diamond accented silver-topped 14k yellow gold pendant, detachable pin back (ILLUS.) **1,840**

Brooch/pendant, pavé-set old mine-cut diamonds set in a heart-shaped pendant, removable pin stem frame & retractable pendant bail, rear crystal locket compartment, platinum-topped 18k gold, Edwardian **4,313**

Edwardian Pearl Brooch/Pendant

Brooch/pendant, pearl, designed as a cluster of pearls surmounted by an old European-cut diamond-set grapevine motif, platinum-topped 14k gold mount, Edwardian (ILLUS.) **2,530**

Art Nouveau Silver Buckle

Buckle, silver, Art Nouveau style pierced abstract design w/cabochon green stone accents, hallmark for T. Fahrner, signed "K. Poe" (ILLUS.) **3,738**

Cameo bracelet, jasperware, designed w/eight graduated blue & white jasperware plaques depicting classical figures in 14k gold octagonal & oval frames, completed by a hand-engraved box clasp (one jump ring missing) **805**

Cameo bracelet, shell, 14k yellow gold flexible design w/five square links, each set w/a cameo depicting classical profile bust of a woman, each facing to the left, 7 1/2" l. **633**

Garnet Cameo Brooch

Cameo brooch, carved garnet, profile of a woman within a gold & silver mount, surrounded by 30 old mine-cut diamonds spaced by six pearls, French gold marks, removable back, signed at neck "LEBAS" (ILLUS.) **7,475**

Cameo brooch, carved ivory, depicting a lady's head, platinum-topped gold frame w/collet- and bead-set old mine- & rose-cut diamond accents **374**

Cameo brooch, carved sardonyx, the profile of a woman in high relief, within a 14k yellow gold oval frame set w/split pearls, Victorian (repair to back, clasp replaced) **1,093**

Cameo Brooch

Cameo brooch, carved shell depicting the profile of a right facing woman w/high relief-molded roses in her upswept hair & across her shoulder, hairline, gold frame (ILLUS.) **1,150**

Cameo brooch, carved shell depicting the profiles of three classical males & one classical female centered by a ram's head within a 14k gold foliate frame w/bead & wiretwist accents (minor lead solder) **575**

Three Muses Cameo Brooch

Cameo brooch, carved shell, depicting the Three Muses, the center muse within a floral canopy, 14k yellow gold mount, Edwardian (ILLUS.)..... **460**

Cameo brooch, depicting a woman in profile within a pearl, rose-cut diamond & foliate frame, 18k gold mount, ca. 1875........................ **3,795**

Cameo brooch, hardstone, depicting a cherub playing a lyre, framed by pearls, 14k yellow gold foliate mount, Victorian (cameo nicked)..... **1,610**

Fine Hardstone Cameo Brooch

Cameo brooch, hardstone & gold, a tested 14k yellow gold oval framed composed of delicated chased C-scrolls enclosing a hardstone cameo carved in high-relief w/a profile bust of a classical woman, her hair dressed w/leaves & berries, a sleeping ram mounted on her shoulder, early 20th c., 1 3/4 x 2 1/4" (ILLUS.)............ **1,725**

Victorian Cameo Brooch

Cameo brooch, hardstone, oval, depicting a woman & cherub, surrounded by rose-cut diamonds within an ornate pierced 18k yellow mount, Victorian (ILLUS.)..... **2,645**

Fine Victorian Lava Cameo Brooch

Cameo brooch, lava, the tested 10k yellow gold mount set w/a large pea green lava cameo carved in high-relief w/a profile cut of a classical woman, late 19th c., 1 1/2 x 1 3/4" (ILLUS.) **748**

Cameo brooch, shell, 14k yellow gold lattice & beadwork decorated mount set w/a large oval cameo depicting two classical women within a floral landscape, one feeding a duck, the other attending a cherub, 3 x 4"...................... **575**

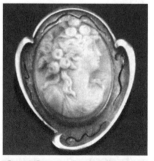

Coral Cameo Brooch/Pendant

Cameo brooch/pendant, carved coral, Art Nouveau style, depicting a woman in profile within a 14k yellow gold whiplash frame, hallmark (ILLUS.) **748**

Edwardian Cameo Brooch/Pendant

Cameo brooch/pendant, carved shell, depicting "Three Graces" within narrow gold frame, Edwardian, 2 1/4" l. (ILLUS.) **325**

Cameo Brooch/Pendant

Cameo brooch/pendant, hardstone, oval onyx cameo depicting the bust of a classical female within a 14k gold foliate frame accented w/26 old mine-cut diamonds, the reverse w/beveled glass compartment, suspended from a bow further set w/11 diamonds (ILLUS.) **3,565**

Cameo brooch/pendant, rectangular gold filigree mounting holding a shell cameo of a young woman w/flowers in her hair, ca. 1880 .... **504**

Victorian Agate Cameo Earrings

Cameo earrings, carved agate, pearl & gold, depicting a female bust within an oval frame in engraved 18k yellow gold w/seed pearl accents, suspended from an engraved gold bow, one pearl missing, lead solder to backs, later findings, Victorian, pr. (ILLUS.)............................... **690**

Cameo earrings, carved lava, putti tops suspending pear-shaped floral & cherub pendants, Victorian, pr....................... **546**

Cameo locket/pendant, agate, depicting the profile of classical woman within an etched green gold laurel leaf frame, fleur-de-lis bail, Victorian **288**

Cameo necklace, carved jasper, the festoon design featuring four oval cameos w/14k yellow gold frames, completed by an 18k yellow gold trace link chain, the clasp labeled "Amitie," boxed **1,380**

Cameo necklace, carved lava, 11 plaques depicting the busts of classical women within oval gilt metal frames, 10k gold trace link chain, Victorian................................. **690**

Tortoiseshell Cameo Pendant

Cameo pendant, carved tortoiseshell facing cameos depicting the heads of classical females set within an 18k gold filigree frame, suspended by shaped wiretwist links, 10" l (ILLUS.)..................................... **863**

Chalcedony Cameo Pendant

Cameo pendant, chalcedony, depicting the bust of a classical male within an oval blue & white enamel frame w/applied gold bead & wiretwist detail, 18k yellow gold mount, engraved "9th Decr. 1873" on reverse, minor chip to cameo, hallmark for Phillips Co. (ILLUS.)........................ **2,185**

Cameo Pendant/Brooch

Cameo pendant/brooch, carnelian & tri-color 18k gold, a three-dimensional turbaned head accented by diamonds & framed by an arch w/columns, scroll & floral motifs, retractable bail, French hallmarks (ILLUS.)............................ **1,955**

Cameo pendant/brooch, hardstone & diamond, oval design depicting the bust of a woman in profile, surrounded by prong-set old European-cut diamonds, 14k yellow gold mount (cracks to hardstone)............... **1,610**

Cameo & Garnet Pendant/Brooch

Cameo pendant/brooch, shell & garnet, 14k yellow gold lattice & beadwork decorated mount set w/a large oval cameo depicting a gladiator & a woman riding a horse-drawn chariot, cherub holding a cornucopia within a clouded field, the frame set w/seven oval buff top garnets, 3 1/2 x 4" (ILLUS.)............ **805**

Cameo & Garnet Pendant/Brooch

Cameo pendant/brooch, shell & garnet, a carved shell cameo depicting a profile bust of a young classical woman & flowers, 14k yellow gold mount set w/33 round cabochon garnets, solder repair to clasp, Edwardian (ILLUS.) **1,093**

Cameo ring, diamond, pearl, moonstone & gold, the tested 14k yellow gold mount set w/a circular carved moonstone cameo depicting a face of a young girl surrounded by six old mine-cut diamonds weighing about .60 carats alternating w/six seed pearls measuring 2.5 mm, last quarter 19th c., size 7 .... **1,725**

Chain, enamel & 14k gold, short & oval gold links separated at intervals w/grey guilloché baton links, swivel clasp, hallmark for Carter, Howe, Gough & Co., together w/silver chain, Edwardian... **575**

Chain, enamel, short & oval 14k gold links separated at intervals w/grey gulloché baton links, swivel clasp, hallmark for Carter, Howe, Gough & Co., together w/a silver chain, Edwardian **575**

Chain, gold (14k), designed w/three fancy link chains in graduating lengths, completed by two 10k engraved square terminals, 21 1/2" l. .. **1,035**

Chain, gold (14k), trace links spaced at intervals by openwork floral repoussé links completed by a later spring ring clasp, Victorian, 31" l. **863**

Chain, gold (14k yellow), fancy trace & curb reeded links completed by a barrel clasp w/applied wiretwist design, Victorian, 17 1/8" l. **431**

Chain, gold (14k yellow) & pearl, a shield-form slide w/pearl accents on a double round link & bead chain, Victorian, 72" l. **920**

Chain, gold (14k yellow), reeded fancy links, each surmounted by a stylized flower, Victorian **748**

Chain, gold (18k), fancy circle links, barrel-shaped clasp dated "1828," 50" l. **3,450**

Chain, gold (18k yellow), box links, engraved foliate motif slide w/red stone accents, 58" l. **403**

Chain, gold (18k yellow), open links w/a figural & rosette accented clasp w/collet-set foil backed pink stones, Victorian, 46 1/2" l. **2,990**

Chain, gold & pearl, Art Nouveau style, 14k yellow gold trace links interrupted at intervals by graduated baroque pearls, swivel hook, hallmark, 56" l. **1,150**

Chain, gold & pearl, ropetwist chain w/oval slide decorated w/seed pearls & applied wiretwist detail, 14k yellow gold, Victorian, 34 1/8" l. **546**

Chain, opal, sapphire & 18k yellow gold, Art Nouveau style, designed w/alternating links of bezel-set opals & round sapphires w/fancy link spacers, completed by a yellow gold curb link chain, 58" l. **2,875**

Chain, pearl & 14k yellow gold, Art Nouveau style, designed w/gold trace links alternating w/freshwater pearls, swivel hook, 50" l. **920**

Chain, silver & enamel, Arts & Crafts style, the double-sided flowerhead links inlaid w/enamel in green & white alternating w/black & white, w/elongated pear-shaped terminals in black, sky blue & yellowish green enamel, hallmark for Bernard Cuzner, for Liberty & Co., 57" l. (overall pitting to enamel, probably from original firing) **1,840**

Gold Chain with Slide

Chain & slide, 14k yellow gold quadruple-link chain w/bicolor gold & diamond slide suspending a tassel, Russian hallmarks, solder evident at clasp, 28" l. (ILLUS. of part) **633**

Chain & slide, pearl, turquoise, enamel & 14k yellow gold, ball slide w/pearl, turquoise & black enamel tracery, rope chain w/black enamel tracery & foxtail fringe terminal, Victorian **748**

Charm bracelet, enamel & 14k gold, trace links decorated w/cobalt blue enamel, 9k engraved padlock charm, 7 1/2" l. **633**

Charm bracelet, gold, a hallmarked 18k yellow gold oval interlocking link design, seven links set w/polished yellow gold beads (three missing), suspending three yellow gold intaglio semiprecious stone watch fobs, France, last quarter 19th c., 7 1/2" l. **1,495**

Chatelaine, gold & gemstones, hand-chased & engraved in a foliate design w/a pair of lions, enameled shields & a crown w/gemstone accents, tri-color 18k gold, European hallmark, "No. 356," (pendant attachments missing) **1,150**

Chatelaine, sterling silver, Art Nouveau style, centered by a round pin w/wheat & geometric design, accented by a shell pincushion, an oval locket w/hallmarks, signed "T & S.," engraved on reverse & a boxing glove-shaped match safe **460**

Chatelaine, sterling silver, Art Nouveau style, the Rococo-inspired top suspending an etui designed as a walnut in repoussé w/gilt interior, a watch key w/braided decorations (minor dents), & a hand-hammered whistle depicting two faces in profile, signed "Tiffany & Co.," hallmark for Schiebler, New York **575**

Chatelaine, sterling silver & hardstone, a hammered silver foliate form centered by a round stone & set w/three bar-linked chains ending w/a pencil, penknife & a miniature valise, impressed mark of the Guild of Handicraft, Birmingham, England, ca. 1900, 2 3/8" w., 10 3/4" l. (nicks to stone) **863**

Sterling Silver Chatelaine

Chatelaine, sterling silver, multi-hook design w/tiered filigree waist plaque incorporating cherubs w/a glass perfume bottle, pencil holder, needle case & egg-shaped thimble holder, English hallmarks, missing one appendage, ca. 1891 (ILLUS.) **863**

Gold & Garnet Chatelaine/Watch

Chatelaine/watch, garnet & gold, white porcelain dial, gilt bar movement, demi-hunter 18k yellow gold case, verso cabochon garnet, suspended from tapering bar links, three-leaf clover garnet & rose-cut diamond top, French gold marks (ILLUS.) **2,875**

Choker, diamond & gold, Edwardian style, three plaques of floral motif, collet & bead-set w/round diamonds on a black velvet band, 18k white gold mount w/yellow gold back.................................. **4,025**

Edwardian Style Choker

Choker, diamond & gold, three plaques of floral motif, collet- & bead-set w/round diamonds, 18k white gold mount, yellow gold back, black velvet band, Edwardian (ILLUS.) **4,025**

Clip, diamond & platinum, designed as a tied floral spray set w/seven round old mine-cut diamonds, approx. 6 cts., additionally set w/86 round-cut diamonds, total approx. 2 cts. & six baguette-cut diamonds, total approx. 2 cts... **9,200**

Clip, gold (18k yellow), diamond, sapphire & ruby, serpent design, the back of the head set w/a cushion-cut blue sapphire, the eyes set w/round faceted rubies, the coiled body platinum-topped & set w/24 rose-cut diamonds, w/added French hallmarked 18k yellow gold ring on underside, 2" l.............. **805**

Clip, gold & enamel, Art Nouveau style, rectangular-shaped cartouche, chased & etched bloomed gold work designed as curving vines, flowerheads & leaves, grey/mauve plique-a-jour enamel, French hallmark & assay marks.............**2,875**

Clip/pendant, diamond, the circular buckle design set w/23 mine-cut diamonds, mounted in silver-topped 18k yellow gold, platinum bail.............................. **460**

Arts & Crafts Sterling Clip

Clips, sterling silver, Arts & Crafts style, oval green agate within a naturalistic openwork mount, signed "Georg Jensen, No. 232," pr. (ILLUS. of one).............**1,840**

Cloak fasteners, gold & sapphire, Art Nouvea style, coiled snakes set w/two bezel-set oval sapphires, connected by a removable curb link chain, 14k yellow gold.... **1,725**

Cloak pin, ruby & diamond, modeled as a sword, the hilt set w/old mine-cut diamonds, ruby accents, pearl terminals, 14k yellow gold mount, 6" l. **748**

Corsage pin, sapphire, adjustable bar pin design w/nine collet-set sapphires & foliate diamond spacers, platinum mount, Edwardian, in original Shreve, Crump & Low box.............................. **575**

Cross pendant, chrysoberyl, 11 crimped collet-set faceted round chrysoberyls mounted in 15k yellow gold, together w/box................................... **518**

Ornate Victorian Cross Pendant

Cross pendant, diamond, silver & gold, the ornate flattened cross in tested 14k yellow gold, the mount w/gold bead & rosette decoration & w/five relief silver floral designs each set w/a rose-cut diamond, suspended from a black silk ribbon, second half 19th c., 2 x 2 1/2" (ILLUS.) **748**

Cross pendant, gold (14k yellow) & garnet, openwork scroll & foliate design w/gold bead at each end & set throughout w/almandine garnets, ca. 1910.................. **345**

Cross pendant, gold, floral chased & engraved 10k yellow gold cross w/seed pearl & black enamel accent, suspended from a shield-shaped clasp w/black enamel tracery, 14k woven gold chain, 20" l. **575**

Cross pendant, gold, silver & rose-cut diamonds, 18k yellow gold w/diamonds set in silver floral shapes in the cross, England, ca. 1800, 1 1/2 x 2 1/2"............................... **1,232**

Cross pendant/brooch, pearl & gold, 21 pearls, 18k yellow gold mount, retractable bail & removable clasp, w/box........ **863**

Cuff buttons, gold (14k bicolor gold), depicting a bird & nest in a circle frame on a square plaque with beaded accents, Victorian, pr.................. **633**

Cuff buttons, pietra dura, rectangular, 14k gold frame w/bead & wiretwist decoration surmounted by an oval floral stone mosaic, pr. **805**

Cuff links, coin, Classical Revival style, each bezel-set coin depicting the profile of a classical Roman warrior within an 18k gold wiretwist frame, pr. **1,093**

Late Victorian Cuff Links

Cuff links, demantoid garnet & diamond, double-sided, each side w/a looped petal form centering a round faceted demantoid garnet w/small rose-cut diamonds set in the petals & borders, mounted in silver-topped 18k yellow gold, ca. 1895, pr. (ILLUS.) . **2,185**

Art Nouveau Gold Cuff Link

Cuff links, gold (14k), Art Nouveau style, oval rose gold bar in a repoussé swirl design, pr. (ILLUS. of one) **345**
Cuff links, gold, 14k, hexagonal w/engraved decoration, ca. 1850, pr. **157**

Gold & Pearl Cuff Link

Cuff links, gold (18k) & pearl, prong-set freshwater pearls connected by figure eight links, signed "Tiffany & Co.," ca. 1910 (ILLUS. of one) **920**
Cuff links, gold (18k yellow) & agate, double sided, centered by collet-set round agate w/gold snake frames, pr... **920**

Gold Bacchus Cuff Links

Cuff links, gold (18k yellow), chased & engraved Bacchus design, collet-set old mine-cut diamond accent, pr. (ILLUS.) **1,725**
Cuff links, gold (18k yellow), double-sided, Art Nouveau style, one side depicting a high relief female profile within a floral design, accented w/small rubies & sapphires, reverse designed from a navette-shaped bar w/high relief floral design, pr. **1,955**
Cuff links, gold (18k yellow) & lapis, Arts & Crafts style double-sided oval plaques within gold frame, beaded accents, signed "F.G. Hale," pr. (minor repair to one) **1,955**

Cuff links, gold, Art Nouveau-style, each depicting a different female bust representing the four seasons, accented by different color gemstones, in a box marked "J. E. Caldwell, Philadelphia," pr. **748**
Cuff links, gold, round w/applied anchors, gold ropetwist accents, Russian hallmark for St. Petersburg, partially obliterated maker's mark, pr... **460**

Art Nouveau Jade Cuff Links

Cuff links, jade, Art Nouveau style, oval jade set within a beaded & grooved 14k yellow gold frame, inscribed "September 2, 1896" & "1909," pr. (ILLUS. of one)... **1,093**

Victorian Pietra Dura Cuff Links

Cuff links, pietra dura, circular form depicting blue swallows & florets against a turquoise background within a 14k yellow gold bead frame, Victorian, pr. (ILLUS.) **690**
Cuff links, quartz, rectangular frame w/bezel-set inlaid golden quartz, 14k rose gold mount, Victorian, pr. **489**

Art Nouveau Style Star Ruby Cuff Link

Cuff links, star ruby & 14k yellow gold, Art Nouveau style, two bezel-set cabochon star rubies attached to a gold twist link, links possibly later, signed "Marcus & Co.," pr. (ILLUS. of one) **518**

Earrings, agate, bezel-set pictorial moss agate edged w/rose-cut diamonds, 18k gold, French import marks, lever back findings, pr. **1,495**

Earrings, agate & gold, round banded agate tops suspending elongated agate teardrops, 18k yellow gold frames w/beaded accents, 2 1/2" l., pr. (minor damage to back of frames) **575**

Earrings, amethyst & zircon, Arts & Crafts style, cluster design of prong-set amethyst & blue zircons, each suspending five cultured pearl drops, gilt silver mount, by Dorrie Nossiter, clip-on, pr. **1,265**

Earrings, bloodstone, Etruscan Revival style, day/night-type, the top w/square bezel-set bloodstone w/applied bead decoration suspending a detachable capped drop, 18k yellow gold mount, pr. **489**

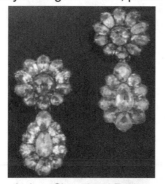

Antique Chrysoberyl Earrings

Earrings, chrysoberyl, golden yellow stones designed as flowerheads suspending similar drops, sterling silver mount, pr. (ILLUS.) **2,530**

Arts & Crafts Jeweled Earrings

Earrings, coral, topaz, zircon, garnet & tourmaline, Arts & Crafts style, designed as a cluster of prong-set faceted gemstones, including topaz, zircon, garnet & tourmaline, w/pearl & gold bead accents, surrounding a coral cabochon & suspending a carved coral pear-shape framing a gem-set drop, by Dorrie Nossiter, England, crack to one bottom stone, pr. (ILLUS. of one) **2,070**

Earrings, cut steel, three navette shaped drops suspended from a triangular section & a round top, Victorian, 2" l., pr. (solder evident on back) **431**

Earrings, diamond, a cascade of flexible old European-cut diamond-set crescents suspending a pear-shaped diamond surrounded by a frame of diamonds, millegraining, mounted in platinum w/later yellow gold plating, 1 1/4" l., pr. **3,910**

Earrings, diamond & emerald, topped by a square-cut emerald, suspending a round old mine-cut diamond, mounted in yellow gold, pr. **18,400**

Earrings, diamond floret tops suspending three tapered pendant drops set throughout w/single, old mine- & old European-cut diamonds, silver-top gold mount, ca. 1900, pr. (later earwires) **1,093**

Victorian Diamond Earrings

Edwardian Basket Earrings

Earrings, diamond, gold & silver, 14k white gold & silver screw-back mount set w/two old mine-cut diamonds weighing about .20 carats suspending a yellow gold & silver top tassel set w/12 graduated old mine-cut diamonds weighing about .50 carats, last quarter 19th c., screw-back added later, pr. (ILLUS.) **1,610**

Earrings, diamond, hinged hoop design w/box-set old European-cut diamonds, 18k yellow gold-topped silver mount, French hallmarks, pr. **2,070**

Earrings, diamond, hoop style, bead-set old mine-cut diamonds set both inside & outside the hoop, platinum-topped 14k yellow gold, pr.. **2,990**

Earrings, diamond, pearl, silver & 14k yellow gold, cushion-shaped old European-cut diamonds suspending a baroque cultured pearl w/diamond-set caps, pr. **3,680**

Earrings, diamond, pendant floral-form, each decorated w/a solitaire old mine-cut diamond suspending a detachable drop w/a floral design w/an attached smaller detachable drop of an acorn, all set w/old mine-cut diamonds, mounted in silver-topped 14k yellow gold, w/fitted leather box, ca. 1890, pr. **9,200**

Earrings, diamond, seed pearl, gold & platinum, a 14k yellow gold & platinum top mount w/an arched design & set w/11 rose-cut diamonds weighing about .15 carats & one seed pearl, suspending a basket of flowers tassel set w/four seed pearls & 25 rose-cut diamonds weighing about .30 carats, Edwardian, ca. 1910, 1" l., pr. (ILLUS.) **2,300**

Earrings, diamond & turquoise, each stamped 14k yellow gold screw-back mount w/a polished yellow gold bead suspending a yellow gold floral pendant, one set w/a greenish blue half turquoise bead surrounded by 11 old mine-cut diamonds, the other set w/a pastel robin's egg blue half turquoise bead surrounded by eleven old mine-cut diamonds, 1" l, pr. (screw back posts added at later date) **575**

Victorian Emerald & Diamond Earrings

Earrings, emerald, diamond, pearl & gold, 18k yellow gold & silver top floral-design openwork mount set w/an oval faceted emerald weighing about .25 carats surrounded by 15 rose-cut diamonds suspending a bluish green cultured pearl tassel measuring 6.8 mm, tassel of later date, second half 19th c., 1 1/2" l., pr. (ILLUS.) **316**

Earrings, enamel & 14k yellow gold, shaped champlevé enamel cartouche w/polychrome floral motif outlined in white enamel, gold ball terminal, Victorian, pr. (enamel loss)..................................... **230**

Antique Persian Bell Drop Earrings

Earrings, enamel & gold, Persian design, gold ring hoop w/yellow metal bell-shaped drop w/three articulated tiers, enhanced by enamel & accented by white bead fringe, pr. (ILLUS.).................... **1,150**

Earrings, gold (14k) & diamond, the ear wire suspending a claw-set old European-cut diamond, pr. **2,070**

Victorian Gold & Diamond Earrings

Earrings, gold (14k yellow), enamel & diamond, an old European-cut diamond set in the center of a round enamel gold-trimmed disk suspending an oval pendant enamel & gold foliate design, further suspending a small diamond-set drop, Victorian, pr. (ILLUS.)............................... **575**

Earrings, gold (15k), anthemion tops suspending an elongated teardrop-shaped reticulated drop w/applied floral decoration at base, pr................ **690**

Earrings, gold (18k yellow) & enamel, Rococo Revival design of repoussé tendrils & scrollwork w/blue & white enamel accents, pr........................ **805**

Earrings, gold (18k yellow), engraved day/night style, pyramid-shaped terminals suspending detachable kite-shaped drops, pr. **3,795**

Earrings, gold (18k yellow), tiered design of shell & scroll motifs in repoussé, Victorian, in fitted box, pr. (repairs, minor dents)............................... **1,265**

Earrings, gold, engraved flowerhead & leaf top suspending gold ball, Victorian, pr. **920**

Earrings, gold & turquoise, Etruscan Revival style, the round tops set w/buff-top turquoise, accented w/black enamel, suspending tapering gold pendants, 18k yellow gold, 2 3/4" l., pr................ **2,300**

Earrings, pearl & diamond, a baroque freshwater pearl suspended from alternating baroque freshwater pearls & platinum collet-set round diamonds, gold findings, later post, Edwardian, pr.................. **1,725**

Earrings, ruby, diamond, gold & silver, tested 14k yellow gold & silver oval button-form top mount set w/one oval faceted ruby weighing about .50 carats surrounded by 16 rose-cut diamonds & 16 round faceted rubies weighing about 1 carat, late 19th c., 3/4 x 1", pr............... **518**

Engagement ring, diamond & platinum, centered by an old mine-cut diamond, flanked by four small round diamonds & two baguette-cut diamonds....................... **4,025**

Engagement ring, diamond & platinum, the engraved mounting set w/a round old mine-cut diamond.................. **2,300**

Engagement ring, diamond & platinum, the filigree mounting set w/a round old mine-cut diamond, four small round diamonds in the mounting.............................. **3,105**

Hair comb, gold, hand-chased in a design of wild roses centered by collet-set round sapphires, 14k yellow gold frame w/tortoiseshell comb, hallmark for Day & Clark (two teeth missing)............... **288**

Hair comb, gold & tortoiseshell, Art Nouveau style, chased gold leaves & C-scrolls in an asymmetrical design, 6 1/8" l............................. **259**

Sterling Silver Comb

Hair comb, sterling silver, engraved scalloped top centered by an openwork thistle design, ca. 1870, signed "Tiffany & Co., No. 4658," in Tiffany & Co. box (ILLUS.).. **1,495**

Hair comb & hairpin, tortoiseshell, roiro ground w/shibayama inlay forming flowers, signed "Matsuyama," ca. 1902-1910, Japan, 4" l. ... **1,000-1,500**

Enamel Violet Hatpin

Hatpin, enamel, designed as a violet w/shaded pale pink enamel petals centered by a prong-set old mine-cut diamond, 18k yellow gold mount, gold-filled pin (ILLUS.)........................... **518**

Headband, gold (14k yellow), engraved foliate motif, hairpin attachments, hallmarked.. **575**

Headband, gold (14k yellow), engraved foliate motif, hairpin attachments, hallmarked.. **575**

Jabot pin, diamond, modeled as a sword bead-set w/round diamonds in silver, ruby accent, 14k gold mount, Edwardian.................................. **633**

Elegant Diamond & Pearl Jabot Pin

Jabot pin, diamond & pearl, the top w/a natural pearl encircled w/rose-cut diamonds which extend & open up into a large circle of rose-cut diamonds (one old mine-cut), the base decorated w/a natural pearl & rose-cut diamonds, mounted in platinum, ca. 1908, numbered & signed "Cartier," Paris (ILLUS.) **2,990**

Diamond Hunting Theme Jabot Pin

Jabot pin, diamond & silver, hunting theme w/rider accented w/enamel, the horse w/bead-set round diamonds set in silver & similar running silver fox terminal (ILLUS.).. **1,035**

Jabot pin, enamel, diamond & pearl, blue & white striped enamel handle, prong-set diamond & seed pearl highlights, ca. 1900, 3 3/4" l. .. **259**

Jabot pin, sterling silver, diamond & enamel, hunting theme, the rider accented w/enamel, the horse w/bead-set round diamonds set in silver w/similar silver fox terminal **1,035**

Lapel pin/locket, silver, Art Nouveau style, a scroll motif suspending a hinged pendant, the central rectangular locket containing a hairwork scene w/a bull on one side & a horse on the other, engraved frame, the lower section a watch key (cracks to crystal on one side of pendant)... **805**

Lavaliere, diamond, centered by a prong-set fancy yellowish brown old European-cut diamond surrounded by a scroll design of prong- & bead-set European-cut white diamonds interspersed w/fancy yellows,

suspending diamond-set drops mounted on a knife-edge bar, completed by a double trace link platinum chain, 16" l. **8,625**

Lavaliere, diamond, openwork foliate mount w/collet- & bead-set diamonds, silver-topped yellow gold mount w/beaded accents, suspended from a silver box link chain w/diamond accent, Edwardian, 11 1/2" l. (break to mount).. **2,760**

Lavaliere, diamond & pearl, centered by an old European-cut diamond within a foliate design set w/seed pearls & freshwater pearls, 14k yellow gold mount, Edwardian **288**

Lavaliere, diamond & pearl, scrolled wire frame set w/eight old mine-cut diamonds, highlighted by six cultured pearls, suspended from a fine trace chain, 16" l · **2,990**

Edwardian Lavaliere

Lavaliere, diamond & platinum, a bow design surmounted by a foliate spray, suspending fringed flexible tails, set throughout w/round diamonds, platinum mount, minor gold solder to back, Edwardian (ILLUS.)................... **1,265**

Lavaliere, diamond & platinum, floral reticulated design set w/20 round old European-cut diamonds, together w/Italian sterling box-link chain of later date, Edwardian, 17 1/2" l. **748**

Lavaliere, diamond, the openwork oval set w/six old mine-cut diamonds & smaller round diamonds & knife-edge bars terminating in two diamond-set drops, one a fancy yellow, completed by a fine trace link chain, Edwardian, 17" l. **3,795**

Lavaliere, diamond, the top designed w/rose-cut diamonds in a C-scroll motif w/calibré blue stone terminals suspending two lines of flexibly-set diamonds ending in diamond-set open circles, silver-topped gold mount, ca. 1915 (needs repair) **1,150**

Lavaliere, gold (14k) & amethyst, centered by an oval amethyst within an openwork scrolled frame surmounted by a seed pearl trefoil, suspending a similar drop, joined by trace link chain, Edwardian, 15" l. **431**

Lavaliere, Jugenstil style, sterling silver & plique-a-jour enamel, openwork sterling mount flower form w/leaves, decorated w/shaded blue enamel & blue stones, freshwater pearl terminal, suspended from a sterling trace link chain, German hallmark **1,093**

Morganite & Diamond Lavaliere

Lavaliere, morganite & diamond, rectangular morganite terminal, diamond-set bow motif shoulders, suspending a faceted pear-shaped morganite, collet-set diamond accents, completed by a fancy link platinum chain, Edwardian, 15 1/2" l. (ILLUS.) **2,645**

Lavaliere, peridot, openwork mount centered by a collet-set peridot, framed by textured gold trefoils w/pink stone highlights, flexibly-set pear-shaped peridot drop, joined by a trace link chain, Edwardian, 15" l. **575**

Lavaliere, platinum, diamond, enamel & pearl, floral & shield design w/a raised floral filigree platinum motif set w/25 round old European-cut & rose-cut diamonds, suspending a pearl tassel, all mounted on a decorated lavender guilloché panel, together w/platinum oval link chain w/white gold-filled jump ring added at a later date, ca. 1910, Edwardian, 18" l. **1,725**

Diamond Lavaliere Pendant

Lavaliere, platinum & diamond, rounded crescent shape w/filigree & foliate diamond accents, centered by a collet-set old European-cut diamond & suspending a row of collet-set old European-cut diamond drops, platinum paperclip link chain, 15 1/2" l. (ILLUS.) **1,840**

Lavaliere, plique-a-jour enamel, depicting a 14k gold bust of a nymph emerging from a background of water lilies flanked by plique-a-jour wings, freshwater pearl terminal, diamond accent, suspended from a trace link chain **431**

Lavaliere/pin, platinum & diamond, floret top suspending a bellflower w/collet-set old European-cut diamond terminal, openwork platinum diamond mount, Edwardian .. **1,840**

Lingerie pins, diamond, each designed in pavé bead-set old mine-cut diamonds, mounted in 14k yellow gold-backed silver, pr. **1,380**

Locket, gold (14k) & enamel, the top w/white guilloché enamel surmounted by a sapphire & rose-cut diamond sautoir motif set in silver, completed by a 14k gold trace link chain, Russian hallmarks, Edwardian (minor enamel loss to edges) **1,725**

Locket, gold (14k yellow), decorated w/an applied cross design in black enamel & rose-cut diamonds (repair to back) **316**

Victorian Gold Locket

Locket, gold (14k yellow), shield shape decorated w/applied wiretwist & beaded accents, hinged top opens to reveal hidden locket, minor dents, Victorian (ILLUS.) **316**

Locket, gold (14k yellow), shield shape decorated w/applied wiretwist, seed pearl & blue stone accents, initialed locket compartment on reverse, Victorian **518**

Locket, gold (18k yellow), oval form, top set w/circular design of gold wire, prong-set pearls & rose-cut diamonds, wiretwist & beaded accents, Victorian... **805**

Locket, gold (18k yellow), the shield-form locket decorated w/applied wiretwist & seed pearl accents, suspended from a reeded fancy link chain, each link surmounted by a gold flowerhead, Victorian (minor discoloration to front & minor dents to back of locket).. **1,380**

Gold Pendant Locket

Locket, gold, an oval shape w/an applied design of gardening tools, a flower basket & a hat, engraved multicolor 18k gold, French hallmarks, in fitted box (ILLUS.)................ **2,185**

Locket, gold, Art Nouveau style, round shape depicting an American Indian accented by a diamond, repoussé & hand-chased, verso initialed **748**

Victorian Gold & Enamel Locket

Locket, gold & enamel, designed as a hand holding a moveable fan, oval frame w/shell & foliate motifs centered by red stones & a pearl, verso w/glass compartment, Victorian (ILLUS.) **1,495**

Locket, gold & enamel, tested 10k yellow gold & enamel-decorated diamond form folding out to eight compartments forming a large star, last quarter 19th c., closed 2" l., open 3 1/2" w. **575**

Gold Locket with Anchor

Locket, gold, oval form w/satin finish surmounted by a rose-gold anchor, wrapped in an 18k gold ropetwist cord (ILLUS.) **1,150**

Locket, onyx & diamond, mourning-type, surmounted by an old mine- & European-cut diamond & baroque pearl flower supported by faceted black onyx baton links highlighted w/seed pearl spacers, 26 1/2" l. **288**

Pearl & Ruby Portrait Locket

Locket, pearl & ruby, a circular design w/h.p. signed portrait of a child on porcelain, surrounded by a row of cushion-shaped, faceted Burmese rubies, framed by a row of natural half pearls that taper in size, seed pearl & ruby accents, hair compartment on reverse, circular bail decorated w/six additional pearls, mounted in 14k yellow gold, ca. 1810, together w/original fitted leather box (ILLUS.) **2,415**

Locket, ruby & diamond, oval w/three vertical rows bead-set w/eight round rubies & ten old mine-cut diamonds, 18k yellow gold mount, edge engraved "No. 2911" **1,380**

Antique Onyx & Diamond Locket

Locket & chain, gold (14k yellow), onyx, pearl & diamond, the barrel link chain set to the front w/six button-shaped natural pearls suspending a rose-cut diamond continuing to a rose-cut diamond bail, the oval locket set on the front & reverse w/oval black onyx tablets, the front w/a rose-cut diamond monogram & the reverse w/a Masonic emblem (ILLUS.) **977**

Locket pendant, enamel, the oval shape decorated w/transparent red Limoges enamel painted w/a putto within a foliate frame accented by seed pearls, mounted in silver & suspended from a silver link chain, Victorian, 26" l. (hairline to enamel) **575**

Art Nouveau Locket Pendant

Locket pendant, gold (18k yellow), Art Nouveau style, circular form depicting bust portrait of woman w/upswept hair & wearing a diamond melée choker, scrolled vine & floral border (ILLUS.) **1,380**

Locket pendant, gold, stylized shield shape, centered w/three seed pearls w/ropetwist & bead detailing throughout, the reverse w/hinged locket compartment, Victorian **345**

Locket/brooch, gold (18k yellow & rose), overall crest form, center framed open-winged bird on branch, reverse w/top-hinged compartment, lower watch hook & top circular opening for an additional loop, Victorian **578**

Locket/pendant, memorial-type, pavé-set turquoise w/Gothic Revival pearl initial, pavé turquoise terminals w/rose-cut diamond accents suspended from a bail w/simulated diamonds, gilt-metal mount, (solder evident), verso w/beveled glass compartment w/14k yellow gold trace link chain w/12 bezel-set light blue opaque glass beads, Victorian, 36" l. (bezels are gilt-metal, chipped glass) **920**

Lockets, gold, two heart lockets, each centered by an old mine-cut diamond in a star motif setting, verso engraved, gold bead chain, pr.... **403**

Victorian Mourning Bracelet

Mourning bracelet, hair & enamel, a wide braided hair bracelet joined by a 14k yellow gold tongue-in-groove locket clasp highlighted w/jet black enamel w/yellow gold floral chased work decoration, hinged lid opens to view a painted miniature of a young girl within a landscape, scratch from girl's hair down to her neck, ca. 1850, Victorian, 8 1/2" l. (ILLUS.).. **460**

Mourning locket/pendant/brooch, gold (14k yellow), enamel & diamond, circular design, the center w/a yellow gold & black enamel decorated hinged lid centered w/a floral motif set w/19 rose-cut diamonds opening to view a well compartment, leaf & scroll gold frame, ca. 1880, Victorian **518**

Mourning ring, gold (10k rose & green), centered by a swivel rectangular center glazed compartment containing a braided silver lock of hair surrounded by square-cut jet stones (one missing), the reverse in black, white & gold enamel w/the inscription "Heaven Has In Store What I Have Lost," the split shank inscribed "Mrs. Ann Beck obt. Feb. 1812 AE 65.," w/original red leather fitted box, ca. 1812 .... **1,035**

Necklace, amber & glass beads, 108 beads w/stations, amber glass beads as well as glass beads simulating lapis lazuli, jadeite & Imperial yellow glass, Mandarin, 19th c., China **1,200-1,800**

Necklace, amber & hardstone court necklace, 108 amber beads intersected by three jadeite foudou, a gourd-shaped fodouda supporting a large jadeite pendant, the silk cord intersected w/three small strands of coral beads w/a jadeite finial attached, 19th c., China **5,000-7,500**

Arts & Crafts Amethyst Necklace

Necklace, amethyst, Arts & Crafts style, designed w/graduating bezel-set oval amethysts & naturalistic links, completed by fancy links, attributed to Oakes, 16 1/2" l. (ILLUS.) **3,680**

Amethyst & Pearl Festoon Necklace

Necklace, amethyst, pearl & 14k gold, festoon-type, the pearl, amethyst, trace line & S-scroll chain suspending three pear-shaped amethysts hanging within pearl-set, shield-shaped drops, the center suspending a larger amethyst, Edwardian, 15 1/2" l. (ILLUS.) **1,610**

Amethyst & Seed Pearl Choker

Necklace, amethyst & pearl, choker-type, a 14k yellow gold single line necklace w/64 circular yellow gold links, each set w/a half seed pearl, the center w/five floral circular links, each set w/one half seed pearl surrounded by 12 smaller seed pearls suspending a removable 14k yellow gold floral pendant set w/a large oval faceted amethyst surrounded by 42 half seed pearls, joined by a 14k yellow gold rectangular box tongue-in-groove clasp set w/two half seed pearls, Europe, ca. 1900, 15 1/2" l. (ILLUS.) **1,840**

Necklace, amethyst & pearl, designed w/clusters of prong-set round amethysts suspending a fringe of five seed pearl-set chains terminating in amethyst briolettes, 14k yellow gold trace link chain, ca. 1900, 16" l. **805**

Necklace, aquamarine, centered by an oval aquamarine within a seed pearl & diamond frame, platinum-topped 18k yellow gold mount, completed by a platinum curb link chain, Edwardian, 18" l., ... **1,265**

Necklace, black onyx, gold & seed pearl, rectangular carved black onyx links connected by circular gold links w/a shield-shaped center pendant medallion overlaid w/delicate floral-shaped lily design in gold & seed pearls, the reverse opens w/a gold-mounted crystal door w/a velvet-lined compartment containing blond hair, in original silk-lined leather case, ca. 1865, medallion 1 1/2 x 2", overall 21" l........... **1,650**

Necklace, coral, carved in the Classical Revival style w/a female bust, flanked by cherubs & suspending pendant drops, fish & foliate motif links, 14k yellow gold findings, Victorian (minor damage to coral) **2,875**

Necklace, diamond & 18k white gold, the backchain designed as a series of diamond-set bows continuing to a front section designed as a line of graduated wreaths, each centered by a floret, the diamonds totalling approx. 8.50 cts., Edwardian... **6,325**

Exceptional Diamond Necklace

Necklace, diamond, Art Nouveau garland style, set w/rose-cut & old mine-cut diamonds, intricately decorated w/laurel leaf & lotus flower motifs, suspending several drops, the largest terminating in a pear-shaped old mine-cut diamond, mounted in silver & platinum, Russia, w/original fitted wooden box, approximately 16" l. (ILLUS.) **36,800**

Diamond Pendant Necklace

Necklace, diamond, floral & ribbon design, decorated w/old mine- & rose-cut diamonds, w/navette-shaped links, open oval links & small lozenge-shaped, diamond-set links, the detachable pendant w/brooch conversion attachment, mounted in silver-topped 18k yellow gold, 17 1/2" l. (ILLUS. of part).. **3,680**

Necklace, diamond & gold, the 14k yellow gold fine link chain necklace suspending five graduated buttercup blossom-form tassels each set w/one old mine-cut diamond weighing about .75 carats, late 19th c., 19" l....... **1,265**

Rose-cut Diamond Necklace

Necklace, diamond & ruby, the central element designed w/graduating rose-cut floral pendants, some ornaments highlighted w/collet-set rubies, suspended by a ruby & fancy link chain, 10k gold mount, 14 1/2" l. (ILLUS.).............................. **4,025**

Diamond and Silver Necklace

Necklace, diamond & silver-topped gold, scroll pattern w/collet-set rose-cut diamonds mounted in sterling silver, 14 1/2" l. (ILLUS. of part)................................... **5,750**

Necklace, diamond, the pendant designed as an articulated three-leaf clover w/four collet-set old European-cut diamonds & 46 bead-set old European-cut diamonds, platinum-topped 18k yellow gold mount, fine gold link chain, 18" l., Edwardian........ **3,335**

Necklace, dog collar-type, Art Nouveau style, three trace link chains spaced by freshwater pearls, separated by 14k gold elliptical-shaped plaques centered by collet-set peridots, hallmark for Perley Bros., 13 1/2" l. **1,955**

Plique-a-Jour Enamel Necklace

Necklace, enamel, Art Nouveau style, lavender & green iridescent enamel flowers w/green, pink & white plique-a-jour enamel leaves, accented throughout w/rose-cut diamonds & pearls, 18k yellow gold mount w/later faux pearl chain (ILLUS.)...... **1,265**

Necklace, enamel & pearl, Art Nouveau style choker, eight pansy links in translucent yellow, green & violet shaded enamel, the center motif suspending a flexible pendant designed w/a collet-set diamond & two freshwater pearls, edged by a fine trace link chain accented by freshwater pearls set a intervals, 13" l. (ILLUS. center page 23) **2,990**

Necklace, English paste riviere, the graduated collet-set white pastes mounted in silver-topped 18k yellow gold, ca. 1800.............................. **1,495**

Garnet & Diamond Necklace

Necklace, garnet & diamond, openwork pendant set w/a demantoid garnet, further set throughout w/rose- & old mine-cut diamonds, suspending a pear-shaped rose-cut diamond drop, completed by fine platinum chains accented w/rose-cut diamond trefoils, Edwardian (ILLUS.)... **6,038**

Necklace, garnet, fringe design w/oval crimped collet-set garnet links, suspending pear shaped faceted garnet drops, 10k gold mount, 13 3/4" l. **978**

Victorian Garnet Necklace

Necklace, garnet, single strand gilt metal necklace w/34 graduated floral links, each set w/seven round faceted garnets, the center w/four floral & scrolling garland-work pendants & drops set w/round faceted garnets, Victorian, 16 1/2" l. (ILLUS.) **1,093**

Necklace, gemstone & pearl, Arts & Crafts style, designed in the manner of an echelle w/descending faceted citrine drops framed by clusters of prong-set multicolored gemstones, pearls & carved emerald leaves w/similar citrine & gemstone clasp, silver mounts, completed by a strand of pearls linked w/twisted gold wire, by Dorrie Nossiter, England, 15" l.
.... **11,500**

Necklace, gold, 11strands of 14k. yellow gold beads, rigid gold bead spacers, Edwardian, 14" l. **1,725**

Gold Fringe Necklace

Necklace, gold (14k yellow), Archaeological Revival style, fringe design, trace link chain suspending graduated pendant drops, 15 1/2" l. (ILLUS.) **1,610**

Necklace, gold (14k yellow), braided link single line design, each end terminating w/a twisted wire, bead & hobnail shield form bails, Victorian, 17 1/2" l. (no clasp)...................................... **374**

Gold Victorian Festoon Necklace

Necklace, gold (14k yellow), diamond & enamel, festoon design, the snake chain w/five gold beads suspending four snake chain loops alternating w/three navette-shaped pendants decorated w/ribbon design at top & mounted w/rose-cut diamonds within an enamel starburst, ca. 1860, Victorian (ILLUS.)...................... **2,300**

Necklace, gold (14k yellow), Etruscan Revival style beads w/applied wiretwist decoration, clasp stamped "DC," 18" l. **1,093**

Necklace, gold (14k yellow), Etruscan Revival style, groups of elliptical & round beads w/overall applied wiretwist decoration spaced by amethyst roundels & gold beads, hallmark for Carter, Gough & Co., 17 3/8" l. **1,265**

Necklace, gold (14k yellow), fringe-type, graduated modified teardrops suspended from a trace link chain, 15 3/4" l. (one drop missing, minor dents).................... **1,093**

Necklace, gold (15k), composed of interlocking embossed & pierced fancy rectangular links, completed by a swivel clasp, 38" l.................. **3,450**

Necklace, gold (15k), Etruscan Revival style, pentagonal drops w/bicolor gold applied bead & wiretwist decoration spaced by triangular rose gold drops, 18" l. **3,565**

Necklace, gold (18k yellow), Etruscan Revival style, beads w/applied wiretwist decoration spaced by smaller plain gold beads, invisible clasp, 16 1/2" l. **1,725**

Necklace, gold (18k yellow) & Favrile glass, Arts & Crafts style, designed w/14 blue iridescent scarabs mounted on gold bases & edged by open scrolling frames, signed "Tiffany & Co.," 15" l. **40,250**

Necklace, gold (18k yellow) & garnet, a woven gilt chain suspending three foil-backed oval cabochon garnet drops in foliate frames, the center drop accented w/pale blue enamel, each w/a reverse locket compartment containing intricate hairwork, Victorian, 15 3/4" l. ... **690**

Necklace, gold (18k yellow) & pearl, fringe-type, the fine trace link chain suspending 72 graduated strands of pearl & gold links, Edwardian, overall 13 1/2" l. **1,610**

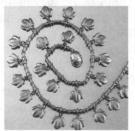

Etruscan Revival Necklace

Necklace, gold (18k yellow), Victorian Etruscan Revival style, barrel-shaped links suspending stylized ivy leaf drops threaded through a loop-in-loop chain, completed by a scarab clasp, 16" l. (ILLUS.) **3,450**

Necklace, gold (9k) & amethyst, festoon style w/graduating, collet-set oval-, round- & pear-shaped amethysts joined by a double trace link chain, 17" l. **1,495**

Necklace, gold, a tested 14k yellow gold twisted-wire & tubular-link form, crossed & joined at the bottom by a raised twisted-wire floral-decorated bail suspending a yellow gold tassel, the ends also suspending tassels, late 19th c., 15" l. **978**

Necklace, gold, enamel & diamond, 14k white gold setting, a center medallion of blue enameled white gold surrounding a relief of a leopard & surrounded by a circle of diamonds & flower-form petals set w/diamonds bordered by two flowerhead links on each side set w/diamonds & attached to a triple circular linked chain, signed on back center of medallion & clasp, 2.03 ctw. diamonds, 19th c. **1,120**

Necklace, gold, three twisted strands of pliable 18k yellow gold wire w/triple gold bead terminals & a hinged reeded circle clasp, 18 1/2" l. (minor dent) **1,380**

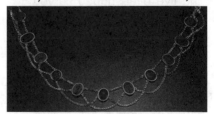

Classical Revival Intaglio Necklace

Necklace, hardstone intaglio, Classical Revival style, designed w/13 gem-set & hardstone oval intaglio seals depicting classical scenes & figures, suspended from a festooned 18k yellow gold chain, minor solder evident, ca. 1880 (ILLUS.) ... **2,530**

Jade & Enamel Necklace

Necklace, jade & enamel, Arts & Crafts style, elliptical-shaped jade within conforming enamel scrolled links joined by trace link chains, similarly-set pendant suspending three jade drops, 18k gold, some enamel loss, signed "Tiffany & Co.," 18" l. (ILLUS.)............................... **31,050**

Antique Jade & Seed Pearl Necklace

Necklace, jade & pearl, featuring five oval-shaped carved jadeite jade sections, bordered by a row of seed pearls & joined by a wire-wrapped bow-shaped link 14k yellow gold chain, 15" l. (ILLUS.)............................... **1,610**

Necklace, kunzite, negligee-type, the fancy link yellow gold-wash chain interrupted by collet-set faceted round kunzites, pear-shaped kunzite terminals, ca. 1900, 37 1/12" l. **1,150**

Necklace, lapis & 18k gold, Arts & Crafts style, designed w/ten slightly curved lapis plaques accented by floral vine motifs, 14 1/2" l. **6,325**

Micromosaic Necklace

Necklace, micromosaic & gold, depicting a dove on a branch w/pink & white flowers against a teal ground, within a 14k yellow gold frame w/wiretwist & beaded accents, later 14k box-link chain, damage to frame, 17" l. (ILLUS.)........................... **661**

Necklace, onyx & pearl, designed as a shield-form onyx plaque w/applied collet-set seed pearls suspended from a chain comprised of 14k rose gold trace links alternating w/onyx plaques centered by seed pearl floral accents, Victorian.............................. **748**

Necklace, onyx & pearl, designed as a shield-form onyx plaque w/applied collet-set seed pearls suspended from a chain comprised of 14k rose gold trace links alternating w/onyx plaques centered by seed pearl floral accents, Victorian.............................. **863**

Necklace, onyx & pearl, six onyx disks centered by collet-set split pearls, spaced by onyx beads, completed by a 14k gold & onyx baton link chain, Victorian, 15 1/2" l. **546**

Necklace, onyx & pearl, the pendant in a shield shape surmounted by a foliate design in seed pearls, black enamel bail, suspended from an onyx link chain w/pearl accents, 14k yellow gold mount, Victorian, 24" l. **920**

Edwardian Opal Matrix Festoon Necklace

Necklace, opal & 18k yellow gold, festoon style, set w/four cabochon-cut opals in matrix w/bead & wiretwist decoration, suspending seed pearl tassels, completed by a trace link chain, 16" l. Edwardian (ILLUS.)..... **1,725**

Necklace, opal & diamond, centered by an oval opal set within a navette-shaped platinum mount decorated w/old European- & single-cut diamonds, pierced gallery, millegrain accents, suspended from a fine trace link chain, Edwardian **863**

Necklace, pearl, a graduated mixture of natural, ten year & cultured pearls completed by a silver-topped gold clasp set w/an old mine-cut diamond, 18" l. **2,530**

Necklace, pearl, choker-type, six strands of natural pearls completed by a sapphire, ruby, emerald & rose-cut diamond clasp, w/GIA certificate, 13 3/4" l. **1,840**

Necklace, pearl & diamond, a graduated strand of 83 natural pearls completed by a modified octagonal clasp centered by a bezel-set marquise diamond surrounded by smaller round diamonds in a pierced & millegrained platinum mount, Edwardian, w/GIA report stating natural pearls **3,450**

Edwardian Festoon Necklace

Necklace, pearl & garnet, festoon-type, the floral center highlighted by seed pearls & bezel-set garnet & glass doublets, 10k gold mount, Edwardian, 15 1/2" l. (ILLUS.).. **403**

Victorian Gold & Pearl Necklace

Necklace, pearl & gold, pearl-set links w/a central fringe of floral motif drops, 14k yellow gold, later ropetwist chain, Victorian, 14 1/2" l. (ILLUS. of part).. **805**

Seed Pearl Necklace

Necklace, pearl, latticework seed pearl design suspending a seed pearl fringe pendant w/onyx terminals & cap, further highlighted by collet-set circular- & rose-cut diamonds, completed by a pierced & millegrained platinum clasp accented w/rose-cut diamonds, Edwardian, needs restringing, missing some pearls, 32" l. (ILLUS. of part)................................ **2,875**

Pearl & Spinel Necklace

Necklace, pearl & spinel, a strand of seed pearls suspending a fringe of mixed-cut oval red spinel drops surmounted by a prong-set pearl & further accented by three pearl drops, 18k yellow gold mount, 15" l. (ILLUS.).. **2,530**

Necklace, pearl, the single strand of 66 pearls measuring 3 1/2 to 6 1/2 mm., joined by a hallmarked 18k yellow gold & filigree platinum-topped floral tongue-in-groove clasp set w/24 rose-cut diamonds centered w/a botton pearl measuring 7.75 mm., last half 19th c., France, 14" l. (pearls possibly natural)..................... **1,100**

Cultured Pearl Necklace

Necklace, pearl, three strands of cultured pearls, the bow form 14k white gold clasp centered by an old European-cut diamond & edged w/30 single-cut diamonds, 17 3/4" l. (ILLUS. of part)...... **1,840**

Necklace, peridot & seed pearl, centered by an open heart-shaped frame accented w/seed pearl leaves suspending two collet-set peridots, completed by a 10k gold fine curb link chain, hallmark, Edwardian, 10 1/2" l.. **1,150**

Necklace, platinum & diamond, fringe design, the delicate platinum chain mounted at center w/five collet-set old European-cut diamonds joined by knife-edge bar links, each diamond suspending a knife-edge bar link & two collet-set old European-cut diamonds, Edwardian................. **4,025**

Necklace, sapphire & pearl, 14k yellow gold single line oval link necklace w/seven central floral motifs, six set w/split cultured pearls alternating w/five oval mixed-cut sapphires, the center sapphire surrounded by four split cultured pearls suspending garland tassels set w/split cultured pearls, ca. 1900, 16" l. **1,380**

Necklace, seed pearl & sapphire, Archaeological Revival, fringe style, seed pearl & sapphire pendants accented w/wiretwist & floral motifs, completed by a reverse hook pearl clasp, 18k gold, 15" l. (one pendant detached) **9,775**

Necklace, silver & glass, Arts & Crafts style, a purple glass drop w/silver foliate cap, completed by a fancy link silver chain, grape leaf & silver bead spacers, signed "H.B.F." for Hazel B. French, 25" l. **633**

Necklace, sterling silver, Art Nouveau style dog collar, the 13 figural plaques each depicting a different classical bust, hallmark for Shiebler, No. 1176, break to findings for one link, 13 1/2" l. **748**

Necklace, sterling silver & citrine, Art Nouveau style, sterling silver chain w/center designed w/collet-set cabochon citrines & citrine beads on double chain, the large center citrine flanked by a scrolled sterling frame & suspending multiple chains, two citrine beads & a center teardrop-shaped citrine **1,035**

Necklace, topaz & chrysoberyl, festoon style centered by a cushion-cut pink topaz surrounded by collet-set round- & rhomboid-cut green chrysoberyl, gold bead accents, completed by foxtail & curb link chains, ca. 1860, 15" l.. **2,185**

Arts & Crafts Gold & Tourmaline Necklace

Necklace, tourmaline, Arts & Crafts style, the center oval plaque set w/graduated tourmalines surrounded by Montana sapphires & edged w/various color natural pearls, joined by a triple strand of 18k yellow gold chains, clasp signed "Tiffany & Co.," together w/extra links, in original Tiffany box (ILLUS.)................................. **49,450**

Necklace & locket, gold (14k yellow) & pearl, single line necklace w/18 oval yellow gold relief bead & wire decorated links, each joined by yellow gold circular links, suspending a 14k yellow gold shield designed relief bead & wire decorated locket set w/five split seed pearls, verso a hinged compartment opening to view a well compartment, together w/original rosewood & satinwood inlaid & silk-lined fitted presentation box, ca. 1880, Victorian, 23 1/2" l. **863**

Necklace & pendant, citrine, the necklace designed as a band composed of 21 graduated oval faceted citrines, suspending a pendant of quatrefoil design center set w/a round citrine & surrounded by four large & four smaller oval citrines, the set **2,760**

Necklace & pendant, gold, pearl & coral, the tested 14k yellow gold wide circular & bar-link flexible choker-style necklace w/a removable 18k yellow gold pendant-brooch at the bottom, the pendant w/Florentine & bright-cut finish w/a grapevine design set w/freshwater pearls & centering a carved coral mask of Bacchus, last quarter 19th c., 1/2" w., 16" l. **1,265**

Necklace w/locket, jet & pearl, designed as a double strand of graduated faceted jet beads alternating w/semi-baroque pearls, suspending an oval locket pendant surmounted by a pearl-set bow w/a prong-set old mine-cut diamond, engraved 14k yellow gold clasp, Victorian, 15 1/2" l. (some minor chips) .. **863**

Pendant, cloisonné, gin bari, bird, flower & bud, set in new silver mount designed by Mike Kaye, ca. 1915, Japan **950-1,250**

Pendant, diamond, wreath design w/collet-set diamonds on a platinum grille, edged w/rose-cut diamond leaves & surmounted by a diamond-set bow, platinum & seed pearl fine link chain, Edwardian, 20" l. **1,495**

Pendant, enamel, circular form, the concave center de-

picting polychromed enamel griffins with guilloché enamel wings within an 18k yellow gold frame w/pearl & bead decorated border (lead solder evident on back, minor enamel loss) **863**

Etruscan Revival Portrait Pendant

Pendant, enamel & gilt, portrait-type, miniature, Etruscan Revival style, depicting two children in polychrome enamel, ropetwist, floral & beaded accents, locket back, gilt mount (ILLUS.) **1,725**

Art Nouveau Anemone Pendant

Pendant, enamel, pearl, diamond & 14k yellow gold, Art Nouveau style, depicting a shaded anemone, highlighted by a bezel-set circular diamond & suspending a flexibly-set baroque pearl, chips to enamel, hallmark (ILLUS.) **1,840**

Pendant, glass, Art Nouveau style, "Trefles" design of molded opalescent glass, arch shape decorated w/four-leaf clover retains some blue patina in recesses, signed "Lalique"...................... **431**

Lalique Molded Glass Pendant

Pendant, glass, Art Nouveau style, triangular-form molded glass depicting lily flowers against an opaque background in golden colors, attached to a knotted silk cord, minor crack near loop hole, signed "Lalique" (ILLUS.) **575**

Pendant, gold (14k yellow), top designed w/three marquise-shaped plaques, black enamel detail, applied beading & fleur-de-lis accents, suspending beaded tassels, Victorian.............................. **374**

Art Nouveau Eagle Circle Pendant

Pendant, gold (18k yellow), Art Nouveau style, circular form, one half w/relief-molded eagle depicted, detailed feathers & collet-set diamond highlights, openwork foliate design on other half, platinum-set rose-cut diamond & millegrain accents (ILLUS.)............................... **1,380**

Pendant, gold (18k yellow), diamond & enamel, Jerusalem cross set w/18 table-cut diamonds suspending a baroque pearl, the verso decorated w/champlevé enameling in green, gold, light blue & yellow (minor enamel loss) **13,225**

Pendant, gold (18k yellow) & enamel, Art Nouveau style, shield shape centering a woman in a blue guilloché enamel bonnet w/diamond necklace & earrings, against a background of polychrome plique-a-jour enamel squares, framed in diamond-accented flowers decorated w/en cabochon enameling, diamond-set bail, Swiss hallmarks **2,415**

Pendant, gold, octagon form, Art Nouveau style portrait of a woman w/flowers in hair, wearing a draped fringe shawl & rose-cut diamond necklace holding a tambourine, chased 18k yellow gold.. **345**

Pendant, komai, scenic motif in gold & silver, set in new silver mount designed by Mike Kaye, ca. 1915, Japan **1,000-1,500**

Pendant, micromosaic, depicting a beetle within an oval frame w/scroll & wiretwist accents, gilt mount & 23" l. trace link chain, later clasp, Victorian.............. **345**

Fine Early Lalique Glass Pendant

Pendant, molded glass, diamond & pearl, Art Nouveau style, a rectangular plaque of opalescent mold-blown glass w/a scene depicting a group of robed figures w/gold faces, within a frame of small rose-cut diamonds, the frame accented on each side w/a double rose-cut diamond, the diamond at the base suspending a natural pearl drop, mounted in silver-topped 18k yellow gold, signed by Lalique & w/French hallmark, w/original fitted box, ca. 1900 (ILLUS.)................................ **16,100**

Pendant, opal & enamel, Art Nouveau style, an oval bezel-set opal within a naturalistic openwork mount decorated w/guilloché enamel, further suspending an opal drop, hallmark for Henrich Levinger, silver gilt mount completed by a box link chain.................................... **1,265**

Art Nouveau Opal & Enamel Pendant

Pendant, opal & enamel, Art Nouveau style, centered by an oval opal within an openwork foliate design in pink jubilee enamel, diamond & opal accents, signed "Mrs. Newman, Goldsmith and Court Jeweller, 10 Savile Row," some damage to opals, in fitted box (ILLUS.). **2,875**

Pendant, opal & garnet, Arts & Crafts style, centered by an oval bezel-set fire opal set within an open circle w/four demantoid garnet highlights, 14k gold mount w/millegrain accents **1,840**

Pate de Verre Pendant

Pendant, pate de verre, Art Nouveau style, round medallion depicting a bouquet of hydrangea flowers, suspended by a sea green knotted silk cord, initialed "G. A-R." for Argy Rousseau ca. 1924 (ILLUS.)..................... **978**

Pendant, pate de verre, Art Nouveau style, round medallion depicting an Edelweiss flower w/graduating yellow to green colored leaves & pink stamen, suspended by a maroon knotted silk cord, initialed "G. A-R." for Argy Rousseau, ca. 1921 .... **1,093**

Pendant, pearl, Arts & Crafts style, centered by a winged cherub within a pearl frame, freshwater pearl drop, completed by a fancy knot link chain, boxed **3,910**

Pendant, pearl & diamond, circle set alternately w/a cluster of three seed pearls & a round-cut diamond, 14k yellow gold mount, Edwardian **891**

Edwardian Pearl & Diamond Pendant

Pendant, pearl & diamond, designed as a grape cluster w/seed pearls & diamond leaf accents, suspended from a platinum trace-link chain, platinum-topped gold mount, Edwardian, 8" l. (ILLUS.) **690**

Pendant, pearl & diamond, large baroque pearl set w/V-shaped band of rose-cut diamonds, cap w/tapered rows of rose-cut diamonds, French import assay marks, ca. 1900 .... **1,840**

Pendant, pearl & turquoise, shield form set throughout w/pearls & buff-top turquoise, 18k gold & silver mount, Victorian, together w/an 18k gold snake chain **633**

Pendant, photographic, oval, ambrotype portrait of a young man, gold frame w/initials, 1 1/2" l. **110**

Edwardian Diamond & Enamel Pendant

Pendant, platinum, enamel & diamond, quatrefoil form, centering a disk of cobalt blue guilloché enamel surmounted by a diamond quatrefoil accent, within a rose- & full-cut diamond filigree mount, suspended from a fine trace link chain w/pearl accent, Edwardian (ILLUS.) **3,220**

Pink Sapphire & Diamond Pendant

Pendant, sapphire & diamond, snowflake design centered by a cushion-cut pink sapphire, surrounded by prong-set round pink sapphires & collet-set diamonds, rose-cut diamond accents, suspended from a pinch-set diamond bail, silver-topped 14k yellow gold (ILLUS.).................. **4,025**

Pendant, Satsuma pottery, dragon & flames in gilt & colors, set in new silver mount designed by Mike Kaye, ca. 1910, Japan **900-1,200**

Imperial Topaz & Diamond Pendant

Pendant, topaz & diamond, bow form above oval mixed-cut Imperial topaz surrounded by old mine-cut diamonds, completed by a yellow diamond briolette, platinum-topped 14k yellow gold, minor abrasion, lead solder, one diamond missing, Edwardian (ILLUS.) **17,250**

Pendant, tourmaline, translucent & intense pink in color, carved w/a deer & two bats, approx. 40 mm. x 30 mm., late Qing Dynasty, China **5,000-7,500**

Art Nouveau Diamond Pendant Necklace

Pendant necklace, diamond, Art Nouveau highly stylized butterfly-shaped outline w/delicate openwork, intricately set w/round- & rose-cut diamonds, one free-hanging in the center, mounted in platinum-topped 18k yellow gold w/double wire loops on the back w/white gold chain attached on each side, 17 1/2" h. (ILLUS.) **4,830**

Persian Turquoise & Gold Pendant

Pendant, turquoise, gold & diamond, the openwork cartouche outline & foliate motif frame set w/an oval Persian turquoise cabochon & two old mine- & round rose-cut diamonds, suspending a teardrop-shaped turquoise cabochon (ILLUS.) **1,265**

Arts & Crafts Pendant Necklace

Pendant necklace, multi-stone & silver, Arts & Crafts style, a carved rose quartz pendant capped w/bezel-set opals & faceted pink & lavender stones within a berry & leaf motif, suspended from a trace link chain, one opal chipped, 23 1/2" h. (ILLUS.) ... **690**

Elegant Diamond Pendant

Pendant & chain, diamond, five free-hanging pear-shaped loops graduated in size & set w/round diamonds, centering a free-hanging pear-shaped diamond suspended from a row of round diamonds, the outer loop terminating in diamond-set fringe which tapers in size, mounted in platinum, on a 14k white gold chain, ca. 1915 (ILLUS.) **9,200**

Chalcedony Intaglio Pendant/Brooch

Pendant/brooch, chalcedony intaglio, depicting Marcus Aurelius or Commodus flanked by a snake, goddess & Apollo, mounted in an 1850s 18k yellow gold enameled frame w/foliate bail, ruby accents, some enamel loss to bail, ca. 1820 (ILLUS.)........................... **2,415**

Pendant/brooch, diamond & pearl, centered by a faceted collet-set diamond within a rose-cut diamond scroll motif frame suspending a natural pearl, silver-topped 14k yellow gold, Dutch hallmark...... **2,300**

Diamond Plaque Pendant/Brooch

Pendant/brooch, diamond, rectangular, centrally set w/three old European-cut diamonds & bordered by a filigree design pavé-set w/44 round, old European-cut diamonds, w/detachable diamond-set bail, mounted in platinum, ca. 1910 (ILLUS.) **4,600**

Pendant/brooch, diamond & silver, the silver openwork star-form mount set w/one old mine-cut diamond weighing about .80 carats surrounded by three tiers of forty smaller old mine-cut diamonds weighing about 4.10 carats, ca. 1850, 1 1/2" d............................. **1,955**

Pendant/brooch, glass & gold, centered by an oval plaque of engraved gold & green glass under mica, peacock motif, 18k yellow gold rosette border, from Pertabgarh, Northern India, ca. 1820-40 (some loss to gold on plaque).............. **316**

Pendant/brooch, platinum, diamond & sapphire, the modified rectangular shaped plaque of openwork design, set w/two old European-cut diamonds accented w/two curving bands set w/20 French-cut sapphires, cornered by four single-cut diamonds, mounted in platinum, completed by a delicate white gold chain, ca. 1920, 17 1/4" l. **1,610**

Pendant/brooch, tourmaline, garnet & diamond, centered by an oval mixed-cut pink tourmaline set within a diamond & demantoid garnet foliate & scroll frame, suspending a pear-shaped tourmaline drop, platinum-topped yellow gold mount, Edwardian.. **4,313**

Enamel Pendant/Compact

Pendant/compact, enamel & diamond, centered by a triangular neo-classical painted porcelain plaque depicting outdoor scene w/maidens, framed by single-cut diamonds, verso w/blue guilloché & white enamel decoration, opens to reveal two powder compartments, diamond set bail, platinum-topped yellow gold, Edwardian (ILLUS.).................. **3,738**

Victorian Gold Pendant/Locket

Pendant/locket, gold (18k yellow), a shield-form pendant locket w/applied wiretwist detail & pearl accent, completed by a double oval link chain of reeded design w/14k rose gold six-pointed star decoration, the pendant & chain 18k yellow gold, some dents to back of locket, Victorian (ILLUS.) **1,725**

Pillbox pendant, gold (18k yellow), Art Nouveau style, covered round hinged box w/repoussé foliate motif overall **633**

Pin, aquamarine & pearl, centered by an oval aquamarine surrounded by three rows of seed pearls, 14k yellow gold mount, Edwardian (one pearl damaged) **633**

Dyed Chalcedony Lily Pin

Pin, chalcedony (dyed), stylized lily designed w/purplish grey chalcedony petals & green chalcedony leaves, rose-cut diamond stem, 14k white gold, Austro-Hungarian assay mark (ILLUS.) **1,265**

Pin, cloisonné, gin bari w/lilies & foliage, ca. 1920, Japan, 3" d. **200-275**

Pin, diamond, a bow-shaped design of a serpent set w/rose-cut diamonds, green stone eyes, silver-topped gold mount **2,185**

Art Nouveau Circle Pin

Pin, diamond, Art Nouveau style, an open swirl motif design centered by a prong-set old European-cut diamond, surrounded by ten prong-set old European-cut diamonds, 18k yellow gold mount (ILLUS.) **1,725**

Edwardian Diamond Bow Pin

Pin, diamond bow design set w/28 bead-set old European-cut diamonds, open swirl accents, platinum mount, Edwardian (ILLUS.) **2,645**

Pin, diamond, bowknot design, set throughout w/71 old European-, mine- & rose-cut diamonds, silver mount (one diamond missing) **1,035**

Pin, diamond, circle design w/14 prong-set old European-cut diamonds, platinum-topped 18k yellow gold mount, signed "Tiffany" **3,680**

Pin, diamond, designed as a floral spray, silver-topped yellow gold base set w/42 assorted old mine-cut diamonds, total approx. 4 cts. **2,070**

Pin, diamond, floral spray design set w/rose-cut diamonds, the central flower set en tremblant, 18k gold-backed silver mount, ca. 1800, Georgian **2,645**

Pin, diamond & gemstone, a model of a lyre set w/rose-cut diamonds, rubies, emeralds & sapphires, silver-topped 18k yellow gold mount.............................. **1,150**

Pin, diamond, horseshoe nail shape set w/pavé rose-cut diamonds & centered by an old mine-cut diamond, silver-topped gold mount, Victorian .. **863**

Pin, diamond & pearl, star-burst design centered by an old European-cut diamond, surrounded by seed pearls, 14k yellow gold mount, Edwardian............................... **374**

Pin, diamond & ruby, four-leaf clover design, centered by a cushion-cut ruby, leaves set w/75 old European-cut diamonds, platinum mount, ca. 1910............................... **6,325**

Gold & Enamel Crown & Floral Pin

Pin, enamel & 18k gold, de-signed as three yellow enamel flowers w/old mine-cut diamond centers, sur-mounted by a crown set w/pearls, green & red enam-el accents, ca. 1900 (ILLUS.)............................... **920**

Pin, enamel, Art Nouveau grif-fin design set w/four dia-monds & a pearl, 14k gold (re-enameled, replaced clasp)............................... **316**

Pin, enamel, Art Nouveau style, designed as the head of a woman against an iri-descent pale blue enamel background, rose-cut dia-mond accents, circular 18k yellow gold mount w/scal-loped edge, signed "G. Charles"............................... **1,725**

Pin, enamel, Art Nouveau style, orchid design, light

pink & mauve enamel petals centering an old mine-cut di-amond, retractable bail (ILLUS. far left, pg. 23).......... **1,725**

Pin, enamel, centered by a prong-set old mine-cut dia-mond, surrounded by shad-ed pink enamel feathers, 14k yellow gold mount (losses to enamel)............................... **173**

Pin, enamel, designed as a trout w/basse taille greenish blue enamel fading into pink-ish white iridescent translu-cent enamel............................... **805**

Pin, enamel & diamond, clover design centered by an old mine-cut diamond, leaves decorated w/purple & white enamel & edged w/seed pearls, pearl-set stem, 14k gold, hallmark for Crane & Theurer, Edwardian............ **805**

Pin, enamel & gold, depicting an articulated girl w/painted enamel features & gold body seated upon a 15k yellow gold safety pin, fine safety chain, ca. 1910 (minor enamel loss)............................... **978**

Pin, enamel, pearl, & 14k yel-low gold, Art Nouveau style, modeled as an orchid w/light greenish yellow & purple openwork petals highlighted w/a baroque pearl & old Eu-ropean-cut diamond, retract-able bail............................... **1,265**

Pin, enamel & pearl, Art Nou-veau style, depicting a 14k gold stem of bleeding hearts in shades of opaque light to dark pink enamel, each bud accented w/single-cut dia-monds, translucent green enamel leaves, hallmark for Krementz & Co. (ILLUS. far right, pg. 23)............................... **1,495**

Pin, enamel & pearl, Art Nou-veau style pansy, yellow shading to purple enamel petals edged by seed pearls & centering an old Europe-an-cut diamond, retractible bail (ILLUS. bottom left, pg. 23)............................... **1,495**

Pin, enamel & pearl, oval shape w/cobalt blue guilloché enamel surmounted by an applied floral design of seed pearls set in silver, 14k yellow gold mount, locket compartment................................. **374**

Edwardian Demantoid Garnet Pin

Pin, garnet & diamond, a collet-set demantoid garnet w/diamond & pearl accents, further rose-cut diamond & platinum decoration, 14k yellow gold mount, Edwardian (ILLUS.)................................ **1,840**

Pin, garnet & diamond, designed as a turtle w/demantoid garnet shell & old European-cut diamond body, red stone eyes, platinum-topped 18k gold................................ **7,763**

Pin, garnet & diamond, rectangular openwork buckle form edged w/demantoid garnets spaced by old European-cut diamonds, silver-topped gold mount, Edwardian......... **1,380**

Pin, gold (14k), an old European-cut diamond within a domed foliate mount decorated w/green enamel suspended within a plaque decorated w/cream guilloché enamel, four pearl highlights, hallmark for Whiteside & Blank, Edwardian................. **1,035**

Art Nouveau Design Gold Pin

Pin, gold (14k), Art Nouveau design depicting a profile of a woman within a naturalistic motif, diamond & ruby accents (ILLUS.)............... **3**

Pin, gold (14k) & enamel, Art Nouveau style four-leaf clover shape, light shading to dark green leaves centering an old European-cut diamond, completed by a polished gold stem, hallmark for Crane & Theurer..................... **1,380**

Pin, gold (14k yellow), emerald & diamond, oval form centered by a cushion-cut emerald, surrounded by 11 round old mine-cut diamonds & enhanced w/black enamel (one diamond missing)................................ **3,450**

Pin, gold (14k yellow), modeled as an Airedale dog, hand-chased w/black enamel collar & red stone eye, hallmark for Sloan & Co., Edwardian....................... **316**

Pin, gold (14k yellow) & pearl, Art Nouveau style, designed as overlapping ginkgo leaves centered by a baroque pearl, diamond accent.. **633**

Pin, gold (18k yellow), a chased & engraved coiled serpent knot design.................... **863**

Pin, gold (18k yellow), Arts & Crafts style centered by a cabochon oval feldspar flanked by four seed pearls, naturalistic motif frame, signed "Tiffany & Co."............. **6,900**

Pin, gold, enamel & diamond, designed as a crescent moon decorated w/light blue enamel flowers w/white enameled leaves, framing a flowerhead w/applied purple & greenish yellow enamel petals, set w/one old mine cut diamond, mounted in gold, ca. 1890 .... **373**

Enamel & Diamond Butterfly Pin

Pin, gold, enamel & diamond, modeled as a butterfly w/body & wings set w/old European-cut diamonds, wings decorated in shaded orange guilloché enamel, black & white enamel accents (ILLUS.) **1,265**

Victorian Shell Pin

Pin, gold & pearl, designed as a rose & green gold pussy willow branch & sea grass surmounted by a natural shell & cultured pearl, 14k gold, Victorian (ILLUS.) **805**

Pin, gold, twist design w/three old European-cut diamonds & three sapphires set in a horseshoe, all prong-set, 18k yellow gold mount **403**

Pin, komai, round w/design of ladies & a flower cart, marked "S. Komai," ca. 1910, Japan **550-750**

Pin, multi-gem & 14k yellow gold, diminutive model of a flower basket, set w/seed pearls, rubies & demantoid garnets, diamond-set platinum leaves, wiretwist handle, Edwardian (minor lead solder) **1,265**

Pin, pearl, daisy design centered by an old European-cut diamond framed by freshwater pearl petals, 14k gold mount, Edwardian **546**

Pin, pearl, designed as a flower w/freshwater pearl petals centered by a diamond accent, 14k rose gold mount **431**

Pearl & Diamond Crown Pin

Pin, pearl & diamond, crown design, the points set w/two old European-cut diamonds & three white & grey pearls, the gallery in an alternating pattern of four old European-cut diamonds & three purple, rose & golden-pink pearls, edged by collet-set old mine- & rose-cut diamonds, 18k gold mount (ILLUS.) **4,025**

Pin, pearl & diamond, designed as a grape cluster set w/multicolored pearls & single-cut diamonds, platinum-topped gold mount, Edwardian **1,380**

Pin, pearl & diamond, designed as a pearl-set acorn w/diamond-set cap & leaves, platinum-topped 18k yellow gold mount, Edwardian **1,380**

Diamond & Natural Pearl Pin

Pin, pearl & diamond, oval form w/scalloped edge & scroll motif, center set w/natural pearl & numerous old mine-cut diamonds, millegrain & platinum mount, Edwardian (ILLUS.) **3,450**

Pin, pearl & diamond, seed pearl-set flower design centered by an old European-cut diamond, 14k yellow gold mount **403**

Pin, pearl & diamond, trefoil design w/four pearls within diamond-set leaves, silver-topped 14k gold mount **3,220**

Pin, pearl & sapphire, the oval shape set w/seed pearls in an openwork grillework design framed by a double row of pearls & accented at the top, bottom & both sides w/two prong-set sapphires, 14k yellow gold mount, Edwardian **978**

Pin, peridot & diamond, a rectangular peridot within an openwork mount, terminals decorated w/fleur-de-lis split pearls, old European-cut diamond highlight, 14k gold, hallmark for Crace & Theurer, Edwardian **460**

Pin, platinum & diamond, circular design w/collet-set old European-cut diamonds & single-cut diamonds within a pierced platinum mount, millegrain accents, Edwardian **2,990**

Pin, platinum, pearl & diamond, centered by an oval button pearl within an openwork platinum & rose-cut diamond mount **863**

Pin, sapphire & 14k yellow gold, Arts & Crafts circle pin, the openwork scroll motif highlighted by five collet-set apricot colored sapphires, 10k gold clasp **403**

Pin, zircon & onyx, a circular blue zircon set within an onyx, old mine- & rose-cut diamond frame, Edwardian **1,898**

Pin/pendant, diamond & pearl, designed as a bird w/outstretched wings & tail feathers, the silver-topped yellow gold base set throughout w/assorted rose-

cut diamonds, continuing to a foliate motif which suspends a freshwater blister pearl, set throughout w/rose-cut diamonds, French hallmarks **2,990**

Etruscan Revival Gold Pin

Pin/pendant, gold, Etruscan Revival style, centered by a carnelian scarab seal in a swivel setting w/ropetwist & beaded accents, 18k yellow gold mount, 14k clasp, ca. 1880, repair to bezel, boxed (ILLUS.) **1,150**

Pearl & Diamond Clover Pin/Pendant

Pin/pendant, pearl & diamond, modeled as a four-leaf clover, the leaves & stem pavé-set w/seed pearls, centered by an old European-cut diamond, 14k yellow gold mount, retractable bail, Edwardian (ILLUS.) **403**

Pin/pendant, pearl & enamel, Art Nouveau style, 16 pink, gold & white freshwater pearls in a grape cluster design, iridescent enamel leaves, 14k yellow gold vines, Krementz & Co. **748**

Ring, carnelian & gold, gentleman's intaglio-type, the tested 14k yellow gold bezel mount set w/an oblong carnelian intaglio depicting a satyr & cupid, last quarter 19th c., size 7............... **633**

Gentleman's Cat's Eye Ring

Ring, cat's eye, gentleman's, centered by a round double-sided cabochon chrysoberyl, 14k yellow gold dragon motif mount, ca. 1910 (ILLUS.)..... **9,200**

Ring, citrine, man's, Art Nouveau style w/center buff-top rectangular citrine, naturalistic 14k yellow gold mount, hallmark.............. **748**

Ring, diamond & 14k white gold, set w/an old mine-cut diamond beside smaller old mine-cut, round & round old European-cut diamond, surrounded by 30 single-cut diamonds............... **2,760**

Ring, diamond, 14k yellow gold & platinum-topped scrolled bypass design set w/20 old mine-cut diamonds, ca. 1900, Edwardian............... **978**

Ring, diamond, ballerina style centered by an old mine-cut diamond, surrounded by baguette-cut diamonds, platinum mount............... **4,140**

Ring, diamond, bypass design, the terminals set w/old mine-cut diamonds, platinum-topped yellow gold mount, further set w/eight old mine-cut diamonds **6,900**

Ring, diamond, bypass style centered w/three old European-cut diamonds set at an angle, 14k yellow gold palladium mount.............. **8,050**

Ring, diamond, bypass style twin stones, prong-set old mine-cut diamonds, engraved platinum mount, Edwardian................. **10,925**

Ring, diamond, centered by an old European-cut yellow diamond within a diamond-set platinum mount, Edwardian, accompanied by GIA report................. **37,950**

Ring, diamond, centering an old mine-cut diamond in a slightly domed square frame set w/round, single-cut diamonds, mounted in platinum **7,475**

Ring, diamond, cluster design w/a center old mine-cut diamond surrounded by six old mine-cut diamonds, 14k yellow gold mount............. **523**

Ring, diamond, decorated w/a row of three old mine-cut diamonds in the center & 12 small round diamonds in the sides & borders, mounted in platinum................. **1,380**

Ring, diamond, gentleman's, gypsy-set old European-cut diamond, approx. 1.56 cts., 14k yellow gold mount............. **5,175**

Ring, diamond, gentleman's, the 14k yellow gold shank w/a brushed finish, center set w/a round old mine-cut diamond, flanked by three small round diamonds............. **1,840**

Ring, diamond & gold, solitaire, a 14k yellow gold six-prong mount set w/one round old European-cut diamond weighing about 1.10 carats, ca. 1902, size 5 1/2. **2,530**

Ring, diamond & natural pearl, an oval baroque pearl surrounded by a narrow ring of rose-cut diamonds, mounted in a platinum-topped 18k yellow gold mount, ca. 1910 ..... **2,300**

Ring, diamond, old mine-cut diamond solitaire, set in platinum basket, 14k yellow gold shank.................................. **8,625**

Ring, diamond, old mine-cut diamond solitaire, shoulders set w/single-cut diamond melée, platinum mount.......... **6,900**

Ring, diamond & pearl, centered by an old European-cut diamond, flanked by a white pearl & a black pearl, 18k yellow gold mount, Victorian.................................. **2,185**

Ring, diamond & platinum, centered by a round old mine-cut diamond, approx. 1.71 cts. flanked w/six baguette-cut diamonds w/additional six round diamonds set above & below the center stone, approx. total .50 cts. **4,312**

Ring, diamond & platinum, the engraved mounting set w/a round European-cut diamond, accented w/12 round diamonds.................................. **6,037**

Twin Stone Diamond Ring

Ring, diamond, set w/two old European-cut diamonds, diamond-set platinum mount (ILLUS.)........................... **20,700**

Victorian Diamond Dinner Ring

Ring, diamond, silver & gold, dinner-type, the tested 14k yellow gold & silver top floral openwork mount set w/one old mine-cut diamond weighing about .50 carats surrounded by 48 smaller old mine-cut diamonds weighing about 2.25 carats, last quarter 19th c., size 7 1/2 (ILLUS.)............................. **1,150**

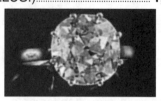

Diamond Solitaire Ring

Ring, diamond solitaire, an old mine-cut diamond weighing approx. 6 cts., mounted in platinum (ILLUS.)................... **16,675**

Ring, diamond solitaire, bezel-set old mine-cut diamond, textured frame, polished 14k white gold mount................ **575**

Ring, diamond solitaire, round old European-cut diamond flanked by two old mine-cut diamonds, platinum mount...... **805**

Three Stone Diamond Ring

Ring, diamond, three stone navette shape, centered by a cinnamon color circular-cut diamond, further enhanced w/similarly cut yellow & colorless diamonds, flanked by diamond trefoils & swags, platinum-topped 18k gold, obliterated hallmark, possibly for Tiffany & Co., Edwardian (ILLUS.).............................. **14,950**

Ring, emerald, centered by a rectangular-cut emerald within a platinum & diamond-set mount, foliate diamond-set shoulders, French hallmark, Edwardian (one diamond missing).............................. **3,795**

Ring, emerald & diamond, centered by an oval cabochon emerald, surrounded by 16 old mine-cut diamonds, 18k white gold mount (surface nicks & scratches).................................... **14,950**

Ring, emerald & diamond, centering a modified step-cut emerald of 1.25 cts. surrounded by 12 old mine-cut diamonds w/a total weight of 1.45 cts., applied coiled serpents in the shoulders, 14k yellow gold mount, ca. 1880 **2,185**

Ring, five old European-cut diamonds, white gold mount, w/finger guard.............................. **8,050**

Ring, garnet, centered by an oval demantoid garnet within a diamond-set navette-shaped 18k yellow gold mount, ca. 1900 .... **2,300**

Ring, garnet & diamond, three-stone design centered by an oval green demantoid garnet, flanked by prong-set old European-cut diamonds, 18k yellow gold scroll mount, English hallmark (repair to shank)................................ **4,888**

Ring, gold (10k yellow), Art Nouveau style, an oval cabochon stone, possibly a moonstone exhibiting a star, flanked by satiric figures, horns form prongs to hold the stone **748**

Ring, gold (14k), Art Nouveau style, centered by a green cabochon chalcedony framed by leaf & berry motifs, No. 111, hallmark for Georg Jensen (abrasion to stone)................................... **978**

Unusual Child's Face Ring

Ring, gold (14k bicolor), crystal, diamond & sapphire, the rose & yellow gold mount w/a carved frosted crystal depicting a young child's face wearing a bonnet set w/six old mine-cut & one round brilliant-cut diamond, ribbon below the child's chin set w/11 rose-cut diamonds, shank portion of ring is of a later date, ca. 1900 (ILLUS.) **1,265**

Ring, gold (14k yellow) & diamond, gentleman's, the gypsy mounting set w/a round old mine-cut diamond.............. **3,737**

Edwardian Diamond Filigree Ring

Ring, gold (14k yellow), platinum & diamond, filigree platinum reticulated mount set w/41 old mine- & old European-cut diamonds, ca. 1910, Edwardian (ILLUS.)................... **1,265**

Ring, gold (18k), triple coil snake design, head set w/five graduated old European-cut diamonds, hallmark for Birmingham, date letter for 1863, No. 285 .... **489**

Ring, gold (18k yellow) & diamond, Art Nouveau style, wide band w/molded foliate & scroll motif shoulders, centered by an old European-cut diamond **1,495**

Ring, gold (18k yellow) & diamond, Arts & Crafts style, centered by a cluster of collet-set old European-cut diamonds within an oval milgrain frame, scroll accents, flanked by two collet-set diamonds **2,530**

Ring, gold (18k yellow) & sapphire, set w/five oval graduated sapphires, diamond accents, hallmarks, Victorian **460**

Ring, gold, diamond & green hardstone, crossover design, set w/one old European-cut diamond & one round green hardstone, mounted in gold, ca. 1900 .... **805**

Ring, gold, diamond & split pearl, alternately set w/three split pearls & two old mine-cut diamonds within an incised openwork mounting, ca. 1900 .... **460**

Ring, gold, opal & diamond, the lozenge-shaped mounting centering one oval opal, set throughout w/20 rose-cut diamonds, engraving along the inside of the shank, mounted in gold, ca. 1900 .... **431**

Ring, gold & tourmaline, centered by a prong-set rectangular mixed-cut green tourmaline in an abstract 18k yellow gold mount, signed "Georg Jensen, No. 313" **1,610**

Ring, gold, turquoise & diamond, dinner-type, 18k yellow gold floral-designed mount set w/an oval cabochon turquoise stone measuring 5.6 x 7.2 mm surrounded by 14 old mine-cut diamonds weighing about .45 carats, ca. 1900, size 6 ...... **489**

Ring, moonstone & garnet, Arts & Crafts style design w/bezel-set carved moonstone & a faceted garnet, seed pearl accents **374**

Ring, moonstone & gold, Arts & Crafts style, collet set w/two cabochon-shaped moonstones in a floral motif, 14k yellow gold mount **230**

Ring, pearl & diamond, centered by an old European-cut diamond flanked by pearls, 14k gold mount, Edwardian **2,185**

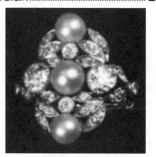

Pearl & Diamond Ring

Ring, pearl & diamond, the center vertically-set w/three pearls further set w/four collet-set diamonds & old European-cut diamond trefoils, platinum-topped 14k gold mount, Edwardian, w/finger guard (ILLUS.) **2,645**

Ring, pearl, garnet & diamond, Arts & Crafts style, bezel-set blister pearl surrounded by four old mine-cut diamonds & eight demantoid garnets, floral motif shoulders, 14k yellow gold mount (demantoids abraided)............................. **1,725**

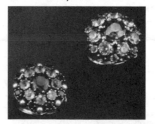

Arts & Crafts Jeweled Cluster Rings

Ring, peridot, citrine & aquamarine, Arts & Crafts style, the bombé design featuring a prong-set round peridot surrounded by seven prong-set citrines & seven smaller aquamarines, gold bead accents, silver gilt mount, by Dorrie Nossiter, England (ILLUS. right).................. **978**

Ring, platinum & diamond, pear-shaped table-cut diamond weighing approx. 3.80 cts., filigree mount w/diamond accents (some melée missing)............................. **25,300**

Ring, platinum & sapphire, centered by an oval faceted sapphire within a pierced platinum mount, diamond accents, Edwardian................. **1,380**

Unusual Art Nouveau Ring

Ring, ruby & diamond, Art Nouveau style floral design w/center-set ruby & three old mine-cut diamonds mounted in silver & 14k pink & green gold, Russian hallmark, ca. 1900 (ILLUS.)...................... **1,265**

Ruby & Diamond Ring

Ring, ruby & diamond, centered by a collet-set oval ruby framed by crimped collet-set old mine-cut diamonds, mounted in silver, surface scratches to ruby, later 14k white gold shank (ILLUS.)................. **5,750**

Ring, ruby & diamond, set w/three old mine-cut diamonds alternating w/two square-cut rubies & eight rose-cut diamonds, 18k yellow gold mount............... **1,840**

Sapphire & Diamond Ring

Ring, sapphire & diamond, a prong-set modified pear-shaped sapphire within a heart-shaped frame set w/old mine-cut diamonds in platinum, diamond-set shoulders, 18k yellow gold shank, European hallmarks (ILLUS.)................. **11,500**

Ring, sapphire & diamond, center set w/round faceted blue sapphire surrounded by eight old mine-cut diamonds, ca. 1900................. **1,725**

Ring, sapphire & diamond, centered by a cushion-cut intaglio sapphire within a framework of 24 rose-cut diamonds (later shank)............. **4,945**

Ring, sapphire & diamond, centered by an oval cabochon sapphire flanked by two gypsy-set old European-cut diamonds, engraved 18k yellow gold mount.................. **2,760**

Ring, sapphire & diamond, centered by intaglio sapphire depicting Leda & the swan, framed by rose-cut diamonds, silver closed-back mount w/engraved shank, signed in Greek letters possibly for Pichler **1,725**

Ring, sapphire & diamond, floral design center set w/round faceted blue sapphire surrounded by eight old mine-cut diamonds, platinum mount, ca. 1900........................ **1,840**

Ring, sapphire & diamond, pavé bead-set w/seven old mine-cut diamonds edged w/channel-set sapphires, platinum-topped 18k yellow gold mount.................................. **1,150**

Ring, sapphire, diamond, silver & gold, the 14k yellow gold & silver top floral-designed mount set w/one oval cabochon blue sapphire weighing about 1.50 carats & one round faceted blue sapphire weighing about .20 carats, the leaves set w/13 old mine- and European-cut diamonds weighing about .75 carats, Russia, last quarter 19th c., size 8 1/4 .... **690**

Ring, sapphire, pearl & aquamarine, Arts & Crafts style bombé design featuring a prong-set oval sapphire surrounded by eight prong-set round aquamarines & eight square-cut sapphires, seed pearl & gold bead accents, silver gilt mount, by Dorrie Nossiter, England (ILLUS. left, page 76).............................. **2,415**

Turkish Slave's Ring

Ring, silver & yellow gold, cat's eye & diamond, slave's ring set w/an oval cabochon cat's eye framed by ten rose-cut diamonds & flanked on shoulder by relief-molded Turkish slave wearing a belt set w/a rose-cut garnet, one garnet missing, ca. 1840 (ILLUS.)................................. **575**

Ring, spinel & diamond, set w/an oval prong-set red spinel & a crimped collet-set spinel, highlighted by seven collet-set old mine- & old European-cut diamonds, 14k gold openwork shield-form mount, ca. 1910........................ **1,840**

Turquoise & Diamond Ring

Ring, turquoise & diamond, centered by a marquise cabochon turquoise framed by 16 old mine-cut diamonds, 14k yellow gold mount (ILLUS.)............................... **863**

Ring, white gold, diamond & sapphire, 14k white gold filigree setting containing three mine-cut center diamonds bordered by one small round-cut diamond on each side & flanked by a small triangular sapphire above a band on each side, ca. 1900 ....**1,120**

Slide chain, diamond, enamel & gold, a tested 14k yellow gold mesh chain w/a tested 14k yellow gold slide w/two oval panels highlighted w/cobalt blue enamel, each centered by a white gold five-prong inset star set w/a rose-cut diamond, ca. 1900, 31" l................................. **748**

Stick pin, gold, pearl & diamond, 14k yellow gold birdform w/feather engraving on head, tail & wings, w/three graduated seed pearls in each wing & holding a prong-set diamond in its beak, ca. 1890, 6" l. **213**

Stickpin, carved labradorite, designed as an amusing devil's head w/rose-cut diamond eyes, Edwardian **431**

Stickpin, coral cameo three-dimensional carved bust of a man, gold stem, Victorian **575**

Stickpin, diamond & garnet, designed as a pavé-set diamond horse & demantoid channel-set horseshoe, platinum on 14k gold, Edwardian (one garnet missing) **1,265**

Stickpin, diamond, model of a butterfly, the body set w/old mine-cut diamonds, green stone eyes, silver-topped gold mount **345**

Stickpin, diamond, model of a trotting horse w/pavé-set round diamonds in platinum-topped 14k yellow gold, ruby eye accent, ca. 1910 .... **575**

Stickpin, enamel, Art Nouveau style in the form of a sweet pea blossom decorated w/lavender & white enamel, old European-cut diamond accent, 14k yellow gold **920**

Stickpin, enamel & diamond, designed as a pansy in shaded yellow & pale lilac, centered by an old mine-cut diamond, 18k yellow gold mount (minor enamel loss to edges) **345**

Stickpin, enamel & gold (14k), Art Nouveau style depicting the head of a Byzantine woman in polychrome guilloché enamel (minor enamel loss) **546**

Stickpin, gold, Art Nouveau style, tested 18k yellow gold mount depicting at the top

two embracing nude figures, Lalique, France, ca. 1900, 3 1/2" l. **4,370**

Stickpin, gold & diamond, 14k yellow gold buttercup-form mount set w/one old mine-cut diamond weighing about .60 carats, late 19th c., 2 1/2" l. **719**

Stickpin, moonstone & 14k gold, oval, carved moonstone of a gentleman's face, ca. 1900 .... **1,840**

Stickpin, moonstone, the circular design w/carved moonstone depicting the man in the moon & stars, surrounded by four faceted red stones, silver mount, ca. 1900 .... **259**

Stickpin, opal, carved as a scarab & set w/four modified fleur-de-lis prongs, 14k gold, Edwardian **633**

Stickpin, opal & diamond, centered by an oval opal surrounded by prong-set old European-cut diamonds, 14k yellow gold mount, in fitted Howard & Co., Paris box.. **460**

Stickpin, sapphire, bezel-set w/a pear-shaped sapphire mounted in 14k yellow gold, signed "Tiffany & Co.," Edwardian **978**

Belle Epoque Diamond Tiara

Tiara, diamond, Belle Epoque style, laurel leaf & ribbon garland design w/a large diamond free-hanging near the top & further decorated w/329 old mine- & rose-cut diamonds, mounted in silver-topped 18k yellow gold, gold-plated silver hair band, central portion is detachable, as well as the diamond drop, & can be worn as a ribbon & wreath designed brooch, ca. 1890, w/leather box (ILLUS.) **23,000**

Tiara, diamond, centered by a pear-shaped diamond flanked by old mine-cut diamond swags, platinum mount, on a metal frame, Edwardian...................................... **2,415**

Tiara, diamond & pearl, crescent forms framed by numerous diamonds, further set w/cultured pearls in a trellis pattern, 18k gold-topped platinum, metal frame, Edwardian.. **3,220**

Tortoiseshell & Diamond Tiara

Tiara, tortoiseshell, pearl & diamond, tortoiseshell band surmounted by swags of rose-cut diamonds & pearls, mounted in silver, Victorian (ILLUS.)...................................... **2,300**

Watch chain, gold (14k), interlocking fancy reeded links, Victorian, 14 3/4" l. **633**

Watch chain, gold (14k), oval gold ropetwist links alternating w/hammered nuggets suspending an "Alaska" fob, 23.3 dwt. **748**

Watch chain, gold (14k yellow), box cable link twin strand chain w/floral-etched yellow gold circular slide, each side w/a raised yellow gold & black enamel decorated floral motif set w/two seed pearls, hallmarked, last quarter 19th c., Europe, 26" l. **690**

Watch chain, gold (14k yellow), slide-type, rope chain, the heart-shaped slide set to center w/red stone, engraved detailing, 23" l. **518**

Watch chain, gold, scroll links spaced by pink & blue stones & joined by cartouche-shaped links, swivel clasp, 14k yellow gold, 59.7 dwt, 60" l. **1,380**

Watch chain, gold, the fancy link chain completed by a Victorian-style slide w/rose-cut diamond accents & black enamel tracery................................. **863**

Mixed Metal Watch Chain

Watch chain, mixed metal, four-sided flowerhead design links in four colors, Victorian, 51" l. (ILLUS.. of part) **2,185**

Watch chain, turquoise & 14k gold, trace link chain set w/ten bezel-set turquoise, swivel clasp, hallmark for Carter, Howe, Gough & Co., 25 1/4" l. **575**

Gold Watch Chain w/Intaglio Fob

Watch chain & fob, gold (14k yellow) & chalcedony, barrel & circular links, beaded accents, swivel hooks, chalcedony intaglio fob, Victorian (ILLUS.)................................. **805**

Watch chain & slide, gold & garnet, the 14k heavy yellow gold chain w/a shield-shaped slide centered by a large cabochon garnet w/black enameled decoration, w/14k gold swivel, ca. 1850, 64" l., the set.................. **1,624**

Watch chain w/fob, gold (14k yellow), w/T-bar & fob w/1909 U.S. five dollar gold coin in frame, 22" l. **440**

Watch chain w/locket, gold (18k rose), reeded tubular fancy link chain suspending an oval locket centered by a small round-cut diamond, ribbed slide, European hallmark, Victorian, 20" l. **920**

Watch fob, gold (14k yellow) & bloodstone, one side centered by an oval bloodstone plaque, the other side by an oval carnelian plaque, beaded accents **201**

Watch fob, gold (14k yellow), Egyptian Revival style, designed w/a sphinx suspended from four lily motif fancy links, ca. 1900 ...... **1,093**

Watch fob, gold (14k yellow & pink), Art Nouveau style, foliate-form top, suspended from foliate & trace links, swivel hook **431**

Watch fob, gold, four graduated round plaques depicting a dog's head in repoussé, largest on the end, suspended by trace link chains, swivel clasp, monogrammed, ca. 1900 ...... **575**

Watch fob, platinum, gold & diamond, the bar links of alternating platinum-topped & high karat gold-topped 14k yellow gold, suspending a bicolor reeded circle locket, highlighted by a collet-set old European-cut diamond, Austro-Hungarian hallmarks **1,150**

Watch fob, sterling silver, four graduated bulldog heads w/cabochon red eyes, suspended from a swivel hook, hallmark for Unger Bros. **748**

Watch fob/seal, bloodstone, rectangular bloodstone intaglio surmounted by a 14k gold foliate chased & engraved ring **276**

Watch fob/seal, gold (18k yellow) & citrine, rectangular faceted citrine set in a foliate chased & engraved mount w/similar ring, suspended on a grosgrain ribbon **863**

Watch fob/seal, gold, rectangular bloodstone lion intaglio surmounted by a 14k gold foliate chased & engraved ring **345**

Sets

Gold & Malachite Pin & Earrings

Bar pin & earrings, malachite & 18k gold, the three-dimensional pin enhanced w/wiretwist & bead terminals suspending a cube-shaped drop, together w/matching pair of earrings, Victorian, the set (ILLUS.) **546**

Etruscan Revival Gold Bracelet

Bracelet & brooch, gold, Etruscan Revival style, the bracelet w/five canatille starbursts joined by trace links, matching brooch, some discoloration to gold, solder evident to backs, the set (ILLUS. of bracelet) **1,035**

Bracelet & brooch, the bracelet w/brickwork links, coral bead flowerhead terminal, together w/brooch of flowerhead design suspending three teardrop-shaped coral drops, Victorian, bracelet 6 1/2" l., the set (chip to center drop) **460**

Berlin Iron Wirework Bracelet

Bracelet & brooch, woven wire, a braided bracelet w/floral & ruffled leaf design, together w/matching brooch, in original fitted box labeled "Berlin Ironwork 1845," earrings missing, 2 pcs. (ILLUS. of bracelet) **1,725**

Bracelet & earrings, opal, Arts & Crafts style bracelet designed w/two strands of opals, one a milky white color, the other bluish-grey, spaced by silver leaf-form links, together w/matching pair of earrings, signed "Curio Shop," bracelet 7 1/4" l., the set **431**

Bracelet & necklace, gold, a Victorian-style mesh slide bracelet together w/a matching necklace centered by a buckle w/fox tail chain tassel, bracelet 7" l., necklace 16 1/2" l., the set **1,035**

Brooch & bracelet, gold (14k yellow), the brooch decorated w/light blue enamel flowers, diamond accent, hallmark for Krementz, the curb link bracelet featuring similar pale pink & blue enamel flowers, heart padlock closure, Edwardian 6" l., the set (bracelet clasp missing) **489**

Brooch, bracelet & earrings, coral, a carved rose & foliate cluster brooch & bracelet, together w/a pair of coral acorn motif earpendants w/14k gold leaf accents, Victorian, the set (solder evident, one leaf missing, some chips) **1,610**

Victorian Coral Brooch

Brooch & earrings, coral, the brooch w/clusters of cabochon coral beads suspending three coral drops, 18k yellow gold mount w/applied gold bead decoration, matching pair of earrings, Victorian, fitted box, the set (ILLUS. of brooch) **1,495**

Brooch & earrings, enamel & diamond, the brooch designed as a floral spray in shaded light blue enamel, each flower centered by an old mine-cut diamond, matching pair of earrings w/screw backs, 14k yellow gold mounts, the set (some enamel loss) **374**

Brooch & earrings, enamel & gold, brooch modeled as a pansy w/shaded purple enamel petals, centered by a prong-set old mine-cut diamond, 14k yellow gold mount, matching earrings w/screw-backs, hallmark for A.J. Hedges & Co., the set (tiny chip to brooch & one earring) **1,380**

Enamel Pansy Brooch

Brooch & earrings, enamel, the brooch designed as a pansy w/shaded purple enamel petals, centered by a prong-set old mine-cut diamond, 14k yellow gold mount, together w/matching pair of earrings w/screw backs, hallmark for A.J. Hedges & Co., tiny chip to brooch & one earring, the set (ILLUS. of brooch) **1,380**

Victorian Gold Grapevine Suite

Brooch & earrings, gold (14k yellow), a grapevine design brooch w/gold repoussé leaves accented w/seed pearls, matching earrings, Victorian, repairs, the set (ILLUS. of part) **546**

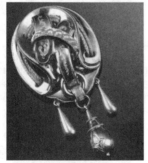

Victorian Gold Brooch

Brooch & earrings, gold (18k), the shield-shaped brooch designed w/overlapping gold sections accented w/seed pearls & amphora-shaped drops, matching earrings, Swedish import assay marks, Victorian, the set (ILLUS. of brooch) **1,265**

Micromosaic Scarab Brooch

Brooch & earrings, gold (18k yellow) & mosaic, the brooch a rectangular form w/scrolled & leaf design suspending a circular micromosaic plaque w/scarab design, together w/pair of matching earrings, ca. 1860, the set (ILLUS. of brooch) . **1,955**

Brooch & earrings, gold (18k yellow), the brooch designed as a cluster of seven filigree spheres, the earrings w/floral terminal suspending a teardrop & spherical pendant drop, in original fitted box w/note detailing origin of purchase in China, ca. 1850s (one small pendant missing) **690**

Gold & Amethyst Brooch & Earring

Brooch & earrings, gold, diamond & amethyst, Rococo Revival style brooch w/cabochon amethysts within scrolling 14k yellow gold mount w/collet-set old European-cut diamonds, matching earrings, the set (ILLUS. of part) **1,380**

Brooch & earrings, malachite, the brooch of pyramid shape accented by applied wiretwist & beaded gold designs suspending three malachite teardrops, 14k yellow gold mount, matching earrings, the set (minor chip to one earring) **920**

Brooch & earrings, onyx & 14k gold mourning jewelry, the brooch & earrings w/center hair compartment encircled by onyx, chased & engraved 14k gold mount, verso inscribed "Lorenzo Simmons, obt. Feb. 9th 1841, 18 yrs - Ann Simmons," earrings inscribed "LAS," together w/book entitled "The Ancestry of John Simmons" (This mourning jewelry belonged to Ann Simmons, wife of the founder of Simmons College in Boston), the set...................... **1,093**

Gold & Turquoise Brooch & Earring

Brooch/pendant & earrings, gold & turquoise, the brooch pendant an engraved scroll form surmounted by pavé-set turquoise & seed pearl decoration, fine link chain suspending scrolled gold drop w/two further cone-shaped drops, together w/pair of earrings of similar design, Victorian, the set (ILLUS. of part)................ **920**

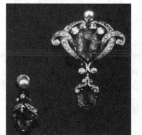

Sapphire & Diamond Brooch & Earring

Brooch/pendant & earrings, sapphire & diamond, the brooch centered by a prong-set pear-shaped mixed-cut sapphire within a diamond-set scroll design surmounted by a pearl, suspending a prong-set pear-shaped sapphire drop, retractable bail & detachable frame for brooch clasp, platinum-topped 14k yellow gold mount, together w/a matching pair of earrings, dated 1903, Edwardian, the set (ILLUS. of part) . **7,763**

Cameo brooch & earrings, agate, Classical Revival style, the brooch depicting female figures, gold scrollwork & seed pearl & rose-cut diamond accents set in silver, pearl drops, 18k yellow gold mount, together w/matching pair of earrings, the set.. **2,415**

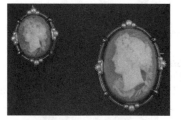

Victorian Cameo Brooch & Earring

Cameo brooch & earrings, carved agate brooch depicting the profile of a classical female w/a lyre, oval frame highlighted w/black enamel & seed pearls, 14k yellow gold, together w/matching earrings, Victorian, the set (ILLUS. of part)............................ **2,185**

Cameo brooch & earrings, coral & 14k yellow gold, the brooch centered by an oval carved coral cameo depicting a female head, polished gold frame w/wiretwist application & filigree top, coral cameo drop, together w/a matching pair of earrings, Victorian, the set (minor loss to foliate decoration).................... **748**

Victorian Cameo Pin

Cameo pin, necklace, earrings & hair comb, the pin w/four mythological figural oval & round cameos, a tortoiseshell hair comb w/six oval cameos & the necklace of oval cameos, depicting mythological scenes, the frames accented w/green & white enamel & ropetwist accents, 18k yellow gold, in original box together w/pair of cameo earrings, Victorian, the set (ILLUS. of pin) **7,475**

Dress set, gold (14k) & bloodstone, a pair of man's plaque cuff links & three similar shirt studs, 14k gold mounts, Victorian, the set **460**

Dress set, gold, diamond & enamel, pair of oval cuff links & three shirt & collar studs, decorated w/white enamel, all centered by collet-set diamonds, hallmark for Carter, Howe & Gough, ca. 1910, the set **374**

Diamond Earrings & Pendant

Earrings & pendant, diamond, the earrings each centrally set w/an old mine-cut diamond surrounded by ten smaller old mine-cut diamonds, the pendant-drop set w/an old mine-cut diamond solitaire attached to a fine curb link 16" l. chain, mounted in 18k & 14k white gold, the set (ILLUS.) **5,405**

Earrings & pin, paste, enamel & 14k yellow gold, earrings w/collet-set colorless pastes surrounded by black & white enamel ornamentation, matching pin, Victorian, the set **633**

Victorian Gold Locket

Locket & earrings, enamel & gold, an 18k yellow gold locket designed w/an enamel portrait of an angel, wings outlined in onyx & composed of rose-cut diamonds, the platinum-topped bail set w/two rose-cut diamonds, together w/pair of earpendants depicting an angel (originally cuff buttons), Victorian, the set (ILLUS. of locket) **1,840**

French Victorian Jewelry Ensemble

Necklace, bracelet & earrings, enamel, pearl & gold, consisting of French hallmarked 18k yellow gold serpent & leaf necklace, the leaves highlighted w/green enamel, alternating w/openwork serpent links suspending a removable serpent & leaf pendant-brooch w/four leaves highlighted w/green guilloché enamel centering a floral-designed set w/five baroque & one simulated pearl (one pearl missing), w/a matching bangle bracelet & earrings, last quarter 19th c., necklace 15" l., set of 4 (ILLUS.).. **1,840**

Necklace & ear clips, gold (14k yellow), a mesh necklace w/central buckle & foxtail fringe, black enamel tracery, matching pair of ear clips, the set (enamel loss) **920**

Edwardian Festoon Necklace

Necklace & earrings, citrine & pearl, festoon design set w/four pear-shaped buff-top citrines w/seed pearl & circular link chains, small diamond accents, 15" l., together w/matching earrings, platinum mounting, Edwardian (ILLUS. of necklace) **1,380**

Necklace & earrings, gold (14k yellow) & diamond, the necklace centered by an Edwardian diamond-set plaque of pierced openwork design, completed by a 14k yellow gold basketweave chain, together w/matching pair of earrings, together w/1 1/2" extra link extension, the set **1,495**

Necklace & earrings, onyx, the necklace w/shaped onyx links surmounted by seed pearl decoration suspending an oval pendant w/reverse hair locket, similar earrings, Victorian, the set (chips to glass, later findings)..................... **978**

Gold & Enamel Necklace, Buckle/Brooch & Earring

Necklace, earrings & belt buckle/brooch, gold (18k bicolor) & enamel, parure comprising a necklace w/detachable pendant, day/night earpendants & belt buckle/brooch, all matching pieces w/fruit & floral motif basse taille enameling w/acorn gold highlights, 18k yellow gold w/18k green gold inlay, French hallmarks, in original fitted leather box, the set (ILLUS. of part)............................ **8,625**

Necklace, earrings & ring, garnet, an 18" l. necklace w/graduated garnet clusters suspending foliate drops, two clustered pendant attachments, together w/teardrop earrings & a domed circle ring, gilt metal mounts, the set (two stones missing, one loose stone)............................. **690**

Garnet Necklace & Brooch/Locket

Necklace & locket/brooch, garnet, the necklace a single strand base metal design w/32 floral links set w/rose-cut garnets suspending a base metal pear-shaped locket set w/round & pear-shaped rose-cut garnets, verso an open-hinged compartment, together w/a base metal floral locket brooch set w/round & pear-shaped rose-cut garnets, verso an open compartment, Victorian, necklace 18" l., the set (ILLUS.) **1,380**

Necklace/brooch & earpendants, coral, a carved rose bouquet necklace w/bar links, detachable matching round brooch, both w/silver gilt findings, together w/matching earpendants w/modern 14k ball findings, Victorian, the set (repairs to necklace) **748**

Pendant/brooch & earrings, garnet, the teardrop-shaped brooch, tiered design set w/faceted clustered garnets, centered by large garnets & bordered by a row of tapering stones in gilt mounts, pair of matching earrings w/clustered terminals, the set **1,265**

Costume

Bar pin, Bakelite, carnelian color oval in brass chain frame, 1 x 3" **75-95**

Bar pin, felt & beads, braided cord w/multicolored beads suspending four colorful felt hats w/beaded trim, ca. 1943, 4" l. **75-95**

Bar pin, gold w/mother-of-pearl oval w/name "Babs" in silvertone, ca. 1940, 2" w..... **30-40**

Bar pin, gold-filled, Art Nouveau style attached scarf pin of leaves & swirls on 10" chain, ca. 1890 .... **110-125**

Bar pin, gold-filled, key design, Victorian, ca. 1890, 2 5/8" w... **65-90**

Bar pin, gold-plated w/pink art glass cabochon, hanging faux Roman coin, signed "Fendi," 3" w., 1 3/4" h........ **90-120**

Bar pin, plastic, white w/"La Conga" in red letters, hanging usable maracas w/etched multicolor designs, ca. 1943, 2 3/4"..... **65-85**

Bar pin, sterling silver, Art Nouveau style, openwork leaves w/large freshwater pearl, ca. 1900, 1 3/4" w...... **50-75**

Bar pin, white metal, set w/five filigree flowers, purple rhinestone centers, four hanging flowers, three leaves, 3 1/2" w., 3" h. **55-70**

Bar pin, wood & metal, black enamel & three white metal bands, ca. 1900, 1/2 x 2"..... **30-45**

Gold-plated & Faux Gemstone Bracelet

Bracelet, antique gold-plated links, four large ornate links set w/large faux gemstones & trimmed w/multicolor rhinestones, signed "Marino," 2 3/8" w. (ILLUS.) **80-100**

Bracelet, Bakelite, bangle-type, moss green carved leaves design, 3/4" w.......... **95-110**

Bracelet, bangle-type, 800 silver, hallmarked, plain w/raised pointed center.... **135-155**

Bakelite & Brass Bangle Bracelet

Bracelet, bangle-type, Bakelite, alternating sections of Bakelite & brass, 3 1/4" (ILLUS.).............................. **175**

Bracelet, bangle-type, Bakelite, butterscotch yellow, random set clear rhinestones, 1/2" w............. **150-175**

Bracelet, bangle-type, Bakelite, carved, brick red, 1/2" w. & thick................. **75-95**

Bracelet, bangle-type, Bakelite, carved, bright red, scalloped design, 3/4" w....... **80-100**

Bracelet, bangle-type, Bakelite, carved, carnelian color, leaves, flowers, 5/8" w.
.... **85-100**

Bracelet, bangle-type, Bakelite, carved flowers, moss green, 7/8" w.............. **115-135**

Bracelet, bangle-type, Bakelite, carved leaves, moss green mellowed to olive green, 3/4" w................. **115-135**

Bracelet, bangle-type, Bakelite, carved, shades of yellow marbling, 5/8" wide **125-150**

Bracelet, bangle-type, Bakelite, green & black, 1/2" w....................... **100-120**

Bracelet, bangle-type, Bakelite, green, two oval open designs, brass leaf designs on carvings on two sides, 1 1/8" w.......................... **270-295**

Bracelet, bangle-type, Bakelite, yellow, plain, 1" w... **65-85**

Bracelet, bangle-type, gutta percha, gold-filled inlay stripes design, ca. 1890.... **150-175**

Bracelet, bangle-type, hallmarked sterling, rose quartz stone set in silver bezel w/silver floral design in center of stone, flexible graduated closure, ca. 1880, 1 3/4" w.............................. **200-235**

Bracelet, bangle-type, hinged, black enameling on engraved design, marked "Lorna Gray 1883," 1/2" w. **150-175**

Bracelet, bangle-type, hinged, diagonal lines design, two purple cabochon stone ends, blue & red cabochon stone trim within single bands of clear rhonestones, signed in two places "Ciner" **65-85**

Bracelet, bangle-type, hinged, gold-plated, black snakeskin top, figural horse head end w/jockey cap end, signed "Oscar D'Argent," 3/4" w. **100-125**

Bracelet, bangle-type, hinged, gold-plated brass, very densely carved applied black Bakelite trim on sides, two large plain Bakelite circles in front, 1 1/8" w. at front
.... **170-195**

Bracelet, bangle-type, hinged, gold-plated, center shell cameo w/ornate leaf design, signed "Florenza," 1" w...... **85-110**

Bracelet, bangle-type, hinged, gold-plated, designed w/rows of lines, signed in two places "Ciner," 1/2" w... **55-75**

Bracelet, bangle-type, hinged, gold-plated, large rhinestone end ornaments can be removed & bracelet can be refitted w/black enamel & pearl ornaments, signed "Joan Rivers," mint condition in original box & velvet pouches................ **150-175**

Monet Bangle Bracelet

Bracelet, bangle-type, hinged, gold-plated, matte finish, squared top, purple marquise rhinestone designs, signed "Monet," 1 1/2" w. (ILLUS.)...................... **150-175**

Bracelet, bangle-type, hinged, gold-plated, narrow w/circle design, signed "Aldo Cipullo 1970 - Charles Revson Inc." **35-45**

Bracelet, bangle-type, hinged, gold-plated, pebble style textured finish w/openwork interlocked loops, center w/channel-set diamond-shaped purple stone, 3/4" w. **45-65**

Bracelet, bangle-type, hinged, gold-plated, plain smooth surface, signed "Bartek," 2 1/4" w................ **75-95**

Bracelet, bangle-type, hinged, gold-plated, raised textured surface, signed "KJL," 2 3/4" w................ **165-190**

Bracelet, bangle-type, hinged, gold-plated, textured "bark" style w/acorns & oak leaves center, signed "Freirich," 5/8" w.................. **65-85**

Bracelet, bangle-type, hinged, gold-plated w/applied furry leopard print strip, 5/8" w. **45-65**

Bracelet, bangle-type, hinged, sterling silver, plain, signed "JPN Mexico," 1" w................. **65-85**

Bracelet, bangle-type, hinged, white metal, applied pavé-set rhinestone set "ribbons," 5/8" w.................. **45-65**

Bracelet, bangle-type, hinged, white metal, sections of round clear rhinestones separated by brushed white metal curved designs, signed "Lisner," 1/2" w........... **50-65**

Bracelet, bangle-type, plastic, octagon shape, amber tortoiseshell color, white metal ball on each side, 3/4" w. **75-95**

Bracelet, bangle-type, plastic, plain, bright green, marbleized yellow, 1/2" w., 3/8" thick................... **40-55**

Bracelet, bangle-type, white metal, applied clear pavé-set rhinestones w/"Paris" written in purple rhinestones, signed "Idemaria," 1 1/4" w. **50-65**

Faux Gemstone Bangle Bracelet/Watch

Bracelet, bangle/watch, hinged, textured gold-plated finish, large faux emerald center w/marquise cabochon faux gemstones, opens to reveal watch under emerald center (ILLUS.).. **185-220**

Bracelet, bead, white metal expansion base w/multicolor art glass & silvertone beads in three-dimensional effect, 1 1/4" w. **65-85**

Bracelet, bead, woven white plastic bead base, white flowers w/blue & pink glass flowers hanging from the centers & the clasp, ca. 1955, 1 1/2" w...................... **50-75**

Bracelet, brass, hinged bangle-type, applied carved black Bakelite sides w/smooth circle design in front, 1 1/8" w...................... **165-185**

Bracelet with Rose Charms

Bracelet, charm, brass, chain w/six rose charms (ILLUS.) **55-75**

Bracelet, charm, celluloid chain w/carved leaf charms of brown wood w/multicolor plastic linings, multicolor clusters of beads on top of each leaf, ca. 1935................... **45-70**

Bracelet, charm, cuff style mesh bracelet w/gold-plated faux Elizabeth II coins attached to chain........................ **70-95**

Bracelet, charm, enamaled white metal w/five romantic motifs on original card, ca. 1930s **70-95**

Bracelet, charm, enamel on brass, assorted motifs, pitchers, pail, heart, etc. **45-65**

Bracelet, charm, enameled Pekinese type dog charm, ca. 1935...................... **50-75**

Bracelet, charm, gold-filled fancy link chain, swiveling oval agate charm, ca. 1890-1910............... **250-300**

Bracelet, charm, gold-plated chain w/multicolor glass fruit & berry charms........................ **50-70**

Bracelet, charm, gold-plated double link bracelet, snakechain tassel, signed "Valentino"...................... **75-95**

Bracelet, charm, gold-plated, enameled Christmas motif charms w/rhinestone accents, wreath, candy cane, Santa, etc................................ **55-70**

Vendome Charm Bracelet

Bracelet, charm, gold-plated multichain, filigree enclosed red beads, green "jade style" beads, basket style charm of green "jade" beads, red rhinestone trim, signed "Vendome" (ILLUS.)................ **65-90**

Bracelet, charm, gold-washed sterling, chain links w/15 assorted charms...................... **150-185**

Bracelet, charm, heavy sterling silver chain w/15 assorted motif charms **165-195**

Bracelet, charm, music box-type, chain links, figure of cat, plays "Beyond the Sea" **90-125**

Bracelet, charm, pearl w/mustard seed inside glass charm, ca. 1955................ **25-40**

Bracelet, charm, sterling silver chain w/cat charm.................. **50-75**

Bracelet, charm, sterling silver, five turquoise & enamel charms, one signed "Meka Sterling Denmark".................. **70-95**

Bracelet, child's, bangle-type, hinged, gold-plated, paisley-style designs, center initialed "JDR" & signed "DB&Co.," Victorian................................ **45-65**

Bracelet, child's, charm, gold-plated chain w/blue birds, pink heart & pearl plastic charms, signed "Disney Rosecraft Kids"........................ **15-25**

Bracelet, cuff-style, Bakelite, marbleized green, 3/4" w. **55-75**

Bracelet, cuff-style, Bakelite, yellow-orange, 3/4" w............ **55-75**

Bracelet, cuff-style, brass, enameled American flag motif, "USA 1776-1976," 1 3/4" w................................ **30-50**

Bracelet, cuff-style, gold-plated, domed w/two side hinges, signed "CoroCraft," ca. 1940s................................ **45-65**

Bracelet, cuff-style, gold-plated w/raised textured gold-plated center strip w/2 1/2" d., clear blown flat thick glass circle attached, signed "J. Hull, B-D, Denmark," 1 3/4" w.......................... **70-95**

Bracelet, cuff-style, nickel silver w/letters "ERA" cut out of center, signed "LWVUS," 1/2" w. **25-35**

Bracelet, cuff-style, sterling silver, hand-hammered asymmetric shape, signed "Mary Rita Padilla," 1 5/8" w. **135-165**

Bracelet, cuff-style, sterling silver, three openwork flowers w/raised centers, 1 1/2" w. **135-155**

Bracelet, cuff-style, white metal, marcasite openwork bow design, center blue faux lapis, matching accent beads, signed "Miriam Haskell," 1 1/8" w. **95-125**

Bracelet, enamel on sterling silver, aqua links, elephants, boats motifs, signed "Thai," 5/8" w. **70-90**

Bracelet, gold on brass links, center w/lock of hair inside glass frame, large crystal stone in middle links in back, ca. 1890, Victorian, 1 1/8" w. **165-185**

Bracelet, gold-filled links, five hinged links set w/oval shell cameos on circles, signed "Sammartino Bros.," ca. 1910, 1" w. **375-400**

Bracelet, gold-filled, Retro design, links w/three cabochon set topaz colored stones, hallmarked, signed "Doubte" **95-120**

Bracelet, gold-filled Retro style links alternating w/cabochon-set topaz, 3/8" w. ... **135-155**

Bracelet, gold-plated, chains, single crown charm w/"jade" beads, red rhinestones, signed "Vendome" **50**

Bracelet, gold-plated double kite-shaped links, pavé-set rhinestone top, signed "Hobé," 1 1/8" w. **90-115**

Bracelet, gold-plated, hinged bangle-type, applied oak leaves & acorns, signed "Freirich," 3/8" w. **50-75**

Bracelet, gold-plated, hinged bangle-type, diagonal stripe design, large blue, red & purple cabochon rhinestone ends, signed "Ciner" **55-75**

Bracelet, gold-plated, hinged bangle-type, large rhinestone ends interchangeable w/large pearl & black enamel designs, mint in box, signed "Joan Rivers" **95-125**

Bracelet, gold-plated, hinged bangle-type, ornate front w/center 1" shell cameo, signed "Florenza" **55-75**

Gold-plated & Art Glass Bracelet

Bracelet, gold-plated hinged links, large oval & octagonal purple art glass stones set on filigree & plain links, 1 1/8" w. (ILLUS.) **175-200**

Bracelet, gold-plated links, each hand-set w/faux gemstone, cameo or Victorian style motif, 3/8" w. **65-95**

Bracelet, gold-plated links, flowers w/rhinestone center, signed "Florenza" **45-65**

Bracelet, gold-plated links, pearl centers, rhinestone set connectors, 3/8" w. **35-45**

Bracelet, gold-plated links set w/green faux cabochon gemstones, green Aurora Borealis rhinestone accents, signed "Weiss," 1 1/4" w.... **95-125**

Bracelet, gold-plated links, square motif, Retro design center w/two rows of vertical baguettes, signed "Trifari," 1" w. **175-200**

Bracelet, gold-plated links, textured as tree bark, large cabochon turquoise stones, signed "Panetta," 7/8" w. ... **85-115**

Bracelet, gold-plated links w/openwork Scotties motif on each link, 1/2" w. **85-110**

Bracelet, gold-plated openwork links w/leaves, red baguette flowers w/clear pavé-set rhinestone center, signed "Trifari," 5/8" w. **125-150**

Bracelet, gold-plated openwork links w/three vertical textured cones hanging between each link, 1" w. **55-75**

Bracelet, gold-plated & pavé-set rhinestone diamond-shaped links, center black stone surrounded by clear rhinestones, 1 3/8" w. **50-75**

Bracelet, link, enamel on copper w/multicolor circles on white background, 1" w. **45-65**

Bracelet, link, four antique gold circles, each w/a heraldic symbol, set w/pearls & multicolored rhinestones, signed "Coro," 1 1/8" w. **65-90**

Bracelet, link, gold-filled circles alternating w/large emerald cut royal blue stones, 5/8" w. **95-115**

Bracelet, Lucite, bangle-type, clear w/applied black domes, 2" w. **50-70**

Bracelet, Lucite, hinged bangle-type, clear w/interior metallic blue glitter, 2" w. overlap in front **45-65**

Bracelet, matte gold-plated hinged cuff-style, grape-color marquise rhinestones leaves, signed "Monet," 1 1/2" w. **150**

Bracelet, pink gold on sterling links, Retro design, signed "Napier Sterling," 1" w. **75-100**

Bracelet, rhinestone, Art Deco style links set w/clear & blue stones, signed "TKF" (old Trifari mark), 1" w. **175-200**

Bracelet, rhinestone, Art Deco style white metal links w/red marquise center, clear baguette accents, 3/4" w. **85-115**

Bracelet, rhinestone, Aurora Borealis red large & small single row stones, signed "Karu," 3/8" w. **45-60**

Bracelet, rhinestone, clear center large marquise stones in small rhinestone-set white metal frames, 1/2" w. **60-80**

Bracelet, rhinestone, clear, channel-set in sterling silver, signed "Otis," ca. 1935, 3/8" w. **125-145**

Bracelet, rhinestone, clear, turquoise, flowers & leaves design, signed "Bogoff," 3/4" w. **125-150**

Bracelet, rhinestone, double row of large clear stones, center emerald-cut stones w/overlaid rhinestone-set ovals, signed "Eisenberg," 3/4" w. **150-175**

Bracelet, rhinestone, eight hand-set rows, clear stones, signed "Weiss," 1 3/8" w. **165-195**

Bracelet, rhinestone, expansion-type completely set w/large vertical emerald-cut clear rhinestones, 3/4" w. **60-80**

Bracelet, rhinestone, forest green cabochons alternating w/forest green art glass cabochons & forest green marquise stones, forest green Aurora Borealis accents, signed "Weiss," 1" w. **125-150**

Bracelet, rhinestone, handset clear openwork links, large oval red rhinestone centers, round red rhinestones accents, signed "Kramer," 1" w. **175-200**

Bracelet, rhinestone, individually set clear stones on white metal Art Deco links, ca. 1935, 3/8" w. **50-65**

Bracelet, rhinestone, large royal blue unfoiled square stones alternating w/double row clear baguettes, Art Deco style, ca. 1935, 3/8" w. **75-95**

Bracelet, rhinestone, triple row, handset unfoiled blue oval stones, Art Deco style clear rhinestone clasp, signed "Czechoslovakia," 5/8" w. **175-200**

Bracelet, silvertone links w/large cabochon "turquoise" stones, ornate 1 1/2" w. **65-85**

Bracelet, slide-style, circle, diamond-shaped links strung on gold-plated double chain, faux cabochon opal & other gemstones, signed "Pik NY," 3/4" w. **70-95**

Bracelet, slide-style, gold-plated, Victorian style motifs strung on double chain, pearl spacers, faux turquoise, jade & cultured pearl centers, thick oval clasp w/faux goldstone & three hanging chains w/pearls, 5/8" w. **70-95**

Bracelet, sterling silver, link-style, each link a handmade flower & leaf design, signed "Cini," ca. 1943, 1 1/8" w. **395**

Bracelet, sterling silver links, Art Deco style, four cabochon yellow glass motifs alternating w/wide openwork links, 1/2" w. **75-95**

Bracelet, sterling silver links, four large three-dimensional links w/very detailed flowers & leaves, signed "G. Cini," 1 1/8" w. **395-425**

Cini Floral Bracelet

Bracelet, sterling silver, links of flower & leaves motif, signed "G. Cini," 1" w. (ILLUS.) **250-275**

Bracelet, sterling silver links, six flower motifs w/red glass cabochon center, 3/4" w. .. **95-125**

Bracelet, white metal, ribbon style motif links w/one hanging as a charm, faux multi-color gemstones, 3/4" w. **75-95**

Bracelet, white metal, mesh design, six rows w/two applied oval Aurora Borealis rhinestone centers, same trim at ends, signed "Hobé," 1 1/8" w. **75-95**

Bracelet, woven hair, gold-filled fittings & center citrine in gold-filled frame, ca. 1875, 1" w. **175-215**

Bracelet watch, silver, cuff-style, gold ribbed, Alice Caviness, 1" w. **65-85**

Bracelets, bangle-type, gold-filled, black enameled buckle design on top, one marked "E.M. from W.M. Xmas 1888," pr. **295-325**

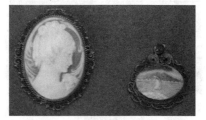

Carved Shell Cameo Pins

Cameo pendant, shell cameo carved w/a seascape w/a sailing boat, set in a scalloped openwork copper frame (ILLUS. right) **115-135**

Cameo pin, shell cameo carved w/a bust profile portrait of a pretty woman w/curly hair w/scroll-carved edges, set in an ornate sterling silver frame, 2" l. (ILLUS. left) **175-200**

Chain w/locket, gold-plated, 2 1/2" d. lion's head w/ring in mouth, signed "Judith Leiber," 18" l. **75-90**

Chain w/locket, sterling silver, Art Deco octagon shape w/stripes 18" l. **75-85**

Chatelaine w/Victorian-style Charms

Chatelaine, silver plate, Victorian motif charms suspended from two shell motif pins connected w/chains, ca. 1940s (ILLUS.) **100-125**

Chatelaine pin, pink gold-plated curved sword w/purple rhinestone trim, connected by double chain to clear rhinestone trimmed black enamel scabbard, can be worn as single pin w/sword inserted into scabbard, ca. 1943 .... **75-90**

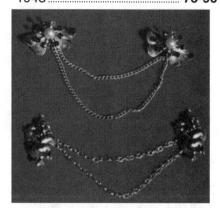

Butterfly and Clown Chatelaine Pins

Chatelaine pin, pink gold-plated, two butterflies w/center floral design of a pearl surrounded w/multicolored rhinestones, connected by double chain, ca. 1945 (ILLUS. top) **75-90**

Chatelaine pin, white metal, two figural clowns w/red rhinestone eyes, connected by double chain (ILLUS. bottom) **70-85**

Chatelaine pin, white metal, two figural does, connected by double chain **50-65**

Clip, Bakelite, Art Deco, red carved triangle, 2 1/4" **45-65**

Clip, Bakelite, Art Deco style carved dark brown inverted triangle, 1 5/8" **30-45**

Clip, Bakelite, Art Deco style carved red drop on large circle, 2 3/8" **40-60**

Clip, Bakelite, Art Deco style carved red spearhead shape, 2 3/8" **40-60**

Clip, Bakelite, Art Deco style shield shape, red over etched yellow, 2" **45-65**

Clip, Bakelite, black, carved three-dimensional leaves **45**

Clip, Bakelite, carved green leaves, 1 3/8" h. **35-50**

Clip, Bakelite, carved red shield shape, applied silver star & anchor, 2" **55-70**

Clip, Bakelite, carved red-brown inverted triangle, flower, leaves, scalloped top, 1 5/8" **35-50**

Clip, Bakelite, densely carved black oval, leaves design, 1 1/2" **45-65**

Clip, beads, rhinestone-set center flower, turquoise beads trim on sides, 2" **35-50**

Clip, celluloid, kite shape, center gold rose, textured background, 1 3/4" **20-30**

Clip, enamel, fur-type, black Teddy bear w/large pearl belly, rhinestone trim **65-80**

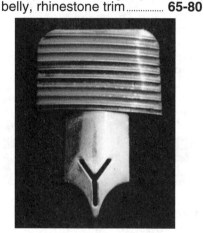

Unusual Art Deco Clip

Clip, enamel, gold-plated Art Deco style pen point, 2" (ILLUS.) **35-50**

Clip, enamel, red center Chinese character on textured gold background, 1 1/2" **30-40**

Clip, enamel, yellow leaves, gold flowers, rhinestone centers, 2" **25-35**

Clip, enameled black Teddy bear, pearl belly, pavé-set rhinestone face, 1 5/8" h. **65-85**

Clip, enameled ladybug on leaves, signed "Monet," 3" ... **35-45**

Teddy Bear Clip and Stork Pin

Clip, fur-type, model of a seated Teddy bear, black enamel, pave-set rhinestone face, large pearl "jelly belly," 1 1/2" h. (ILLUS. left) **85-115**

Clip, gold-plated, Art Deco style shield shape, openwork large enamel & rhinestone flower w/large red cabochon center, smaller flowers, blue centers, unsigned, attributed to Coro, 2 1/2 .... **130-150**

Clip, gold-plated, bird motif, movable wings w/clip on each wing, large snakechain tassel in mouth, tag marked "Claire McCardell," 4" **165-185**

Clip, gold-plated, fur-type, Retro ribbon motif w/eight large soft red tapered unfoiled open-set stones, 2 3/4" **75**

Gem-set Clips

Clip, gold-plated, fur-type, Retro style, tapering flat metal design w/coiled clip below large emerald cut topaz color stone, 2" (ILLUS. right) **50-65**

Clip, gold-plated, Retro style open fan style top, center blue baguettes, hanging tassel, signed "Kreisler," 2 3/4" **95-120**

Retro-style Clip

Clip, gold-plated, Retro style, very large center emerald-cut topaz stone, 2" (ILLUS.) **50-75**

Clip, gold-plated, six-sided shape w/floral medieval style design, 3" **40-55**

Clip, gold-plated, Victorian style w/raised acorns & leaves, 2" **30-45**

Clip, rhinestone, Art Deco style, large raised red center stone, pavé-set white metal, 2" **40-55**

Art Deco Style Clip

Clip, rhinestone, Art Deco style oval iridescent green art glass stones in inverted teardrop shape, large emerald green baguettes, trimmed w/clear square stones, 3" (ILLUS.)................ **90-120**

Clip, rhinestone, Art Deco style, pavé-set circle w/red marquise stone center, ribbon style drop, 1 3/4" **45-65**

Clip, rhinestone, Art Deco style pavé-set shield design, red oval center stone, 1 1/2" **45-60**

Grape Cluster Clip

Clip, rhinestone, Art Deco style w/red cabochon stones designed as a cluster of grapes, red & clear baguettes leaves & stem, 3 1/4" h. (ILLUS.) **90-120**

Clip, rhinestone, circular shape w/wheel design in red, blue & green cabochon stones, clear stones background, 1 1/4" d. **55-75**

Clip, rhinestone, flower & leaves design, large clear unfoiled emerald cut center stones, large marquise-set drop, pear-shaped & round stones trim, signed "Eisenberg Original," 2 1/2" w., 4 1/4" h. **375-425**

Clip, rhinestone flower w/turquoise bead trim, unusual design, 2" **30**

Leo Glass Ornate Filigree Clip

Clip, rhinestone, gold ornate inverted teardrop-shaped filigree set w/large cabochon amber stones, signed "Leo Glass," 2 1/4" (ILLUS.) **75-100**

Clip, rhinestone, gold-plated curved design set w/row of clear baguettes, signed "Corocraft," 1 1/2" **40-55**

Clip, rhinestone, gold-plated metal, bouquet of flowers design w/pink "moonstone" style cabochon stones, purple oval stones, pink enamel flowers w/pink rhinestone centers, 2 1/4 x 3" **40-60**

Clip, rhinestone, inverted teardrop shape w/pavé-set clear stones in Art Deco floral design accented w/blue baguettes, 2 1/2" **75-100**

Clip, rhinestone, large clear & emerald marquise stones in ribbon style Retro design, signed "Eisenberg Original," 3" **275-300**

Clip, rhinestone, large clear oval, emerald, marquise & round hand-set stones in openwork frame, 2 1/2" w., 3 1/2" h. **75-100**

Clip, rhinestone, large swirled feather motif, clear marquise stones, signed "Eisenberg Original," 3" h. **275-300**

Rhinestone Bow Clip

Clip, rhinestone, openwork bow design w/large oval pink, purple & aqua rhinestones, pavé-set clear stones on "ribbon," 2 1/4 x 3 1/4" (ILLUS.) **125-150**

Clip, rhinestone, pavé-set curved Art Deco ribbon design, signed "Creative," 1 3/8" **25-35**

Clip, rhinestone, pavé-set openwork graduated Art Deco design, 1 1/2"................ **25-40**

Clip, rhinestone, pavé-set w/clear marquise stones in openwork white metal, 2 5/8"... **75-100**

Clip, rhinestone, red cabochon-set oval stones on ornate filigree white metal, 2 1/4 x 2 5/8"............................. **60-85**

Shield-shaped Clip

Clip, rhinestone, shield shape design wthree large red cabochon marquise center stones & oval & diamond shaped red, green & blue stones, small clear stones trim, 2 x 2" (ILLUS.).............. **75-100**

Clip, rhinestone, shield-shaped gold-plated filigree metal w/citrine colored marquise, square & round stones, 2 3/4"............................ **80-100**

Clip, rhinestone, shield-shaped pavé-set openwork Art Deco design, signed "Goody," 1 3/4"........................... **40-55**

Clip, rhinestone, three large unfoiled blue crystal flowers, large clear rhinestone centers, 2 1/4"................................... **35-50**

Rosenstein Flower Design Clip

Clip, sterling & gold-washed, large openwork flower, cluster of green glass teardrops in center, w/clear rhinestones set in tips extending from center, signed "Nettie Rosenstein," 3 x 3 1/2" (ILLUS.)................................. **275-325**

Clip, sterling, pink, yellow gold-washed, Retro style, three ribbons over bar, signed "Monet," 2"................ **75-95**

Clip, sterling, scallop shape, marcasites set, center cabochon-set faux blue topaz, 1 3/4"................................ **95-125**

Clip, sterling silver set w/marcasite, ornate openwork leaves in coil design w/center cabochon-set faux aquamarine, 1 3/4" (ILLUS. left, page 95)................. **75-100**

Clip/compact, green enamel on chrome, opens to reveal compact w/puff, 1 5/8" d. **195-225**

Clip/locket, center black cameo in bead frame, 1 5/8"..... **80-100**

Clip/lorgnette, folded sterling silver lorgnette behind white metal marcasite set clip, Retro design, 1 1/4 x 2" when folded................................ **325-350**

Clip/pendant, gold-plated Retro style flower design, aqua pear-shaped stones flower, pink & clear stones trim, 2 1/4"............................... **60-80**

Clip/watch, black enamel, initials on one side, watch on other, 1 1/4"............................. **150-185**

Clips, Bakelite, carved orange leaves, 1 3/8", pr....................... **50-75**

Carved Bakelite Leaf Clips

Clips, Bakelite, marbleized butterscotch yellow circles, densely carved leaves, 1 3/4" d., pr. (ILLUS.).......... **85-110**

Clips, Bakelite, marbleized yellow w/light brown inlay design, 2", pr. **95-115**

Clips, beads, multicolor glass, flower motif, 1 1/4", pr. **40-55**

Clips, crystal, blue unfoiled rhinestones, three large oval crystals on each, pr. **55-75**

Clips, enameled, duette, blue enameled birds on floral branch, pavé-set rhinestone-set heads, signed "Coro Duette," 3 1/4" **265-300**

Clips, enameled, duette, red enameled Art Deco designs w/rhinestone accents, signed "Coro Duette," 2 3/4" **120-145**

Clips, glass & enamel, large red glass spheres w/red enameled ribbon style coils & clear rhinestone accents, signed "Coro Duette" **85-110**

Clips, gold finish, antiqued, wings motif set w/faux cabochon rubies, 2 1/2", pr. **70-85**

Clips, gold-plated, chatelaine style, pavé-set rhinestone keys on hearts, connected w/two chains **75-95**

Clips, gold-plated, sweater-type, leaf motif connected w/chain, pearls in center **20-25**

Clips, rhinestone, Art Deco bow motif, larger emerald, triangle rhinestone accents, 1" h., pr. **35**

Clips, rhinestone, bow motif, pavé-set rhinestones, 3/4", pr. **30-45**

Duette Rhinestone Clips

Clips, rhinestone, duette, large amber marquise stone flowers, 3" (ILLUS.) **100-125**

Clips, rhinestone, duette, pavé-set Art Deco sunburst style design, 2" **65-80**

Art Deco Rhinestone Duette Clips

Clips, rhinestone, duette, pavé-set openwork Art Deco design, signed "TKF (Trifari) Clipmates," 2 5/8" (ILLUS.) **175-200**

Clips, rhinestone, duette, pavé-set openwork Art Deco geometric design, 2 1/2" **75-95**

Clips, silver plate, openwork flowers & leaves in Art Nouveau style, 2 1/2", pr. **50-70**

Clips, sterling, sweater-type, circles connected w/chain links w/original flannel storage case, signed "Tiffany & Co." **95-125**

Earrings, crystal, drop-style, three small crystal beads, large crystal drop at bottom, ca. 1925, screw-on, 2 1/8" l., pr. **75-95**

Earrings, crystal & sterling, drop-style, two crystal beads on sterling chains hanging from Art Deco design, ca. 1930, screw-on, 2 1/8" l., pr **75-100**

Earrings, enamel on gold-plate, button style, purple glass center stones, pink accent stones, gold borders, purple enamel background, clip-on, signed "Michal Golan," 1 1/2" d., pr. **25-35**

Earrings, enamel on sterling, fan motif, blue, green, black enamel, Siam, 1 1/4" h., pr. **35**

Earrings, enameled, hoop drop-style, bright turquoise, ca. 1955, clip-on, 2", pr. **35-50**

Earrings, enameled, hoop-style, red, white & blue stripes, signed "Trifari," clip-on, 1", pr. **45-60**

Earrings, enameled & rhinestone, open basketweave design, clear rhinestones, black enamel, clip-on, 1" d., pr. **25-35**

Earrings, fresh water pearl ball drops, clip-ons, 1" l., pr. **25-35**

Earrings, glass beads, black beads wired to silver background, signed "Schiaparelli," clip-on, 1 1/4", pr. **150-175**

Earrings, glass beads, drop-style, swirled turquoise, black art glass, top made to resemble findings for pierced ears, screw-on, 1 1/2", pr. **35-50**

Earrings, glass, button-style, red art glass, screw-ons, 3/4" d., pr. **20-25**

Earrings, glass, button-style, swirled red art glass, screw-on, 3/4" d., pr. **30-40**

Earrings, glass, button-style, white w/raised scalloped side, 3/4" d., pr. **25-35**

Earrings, glass, button-tyle, white, raised scalloped arc design, screw-ons, 3/4" d. ... **15-20**

Earrings, glass, drop-style, large white ball, 1", pr. **25-35**

Earrings, glass stones, white free-form style shape, clear rhinestone background, signed "Jomaz," 1 1/8" d., pr. **75-95**

Earrings, gold-filled, drop-style, graduated oval forms w/center leaf designs, late Victorian, ca. 1890, pierced ear wires, 1 1/2", pr. **65-85**

Earrings, gold-plated, drop-style, gold-plated leaves connected w/rhinestone strips, large rhinestone center, one behind the other in three-dimensional effect, signed "Hobé," slip-on, 3 1/4" l., pr. **75-95**

Earrings, gold-plated drop-style hoops, textured finish, clip-on, 1 1/4", pr. **30-45**

Earrings, gold-plated hoop style, wide textured finish, signed "Avon," clip-on, 5/8" d., pr. **25-35**

Earrings, gold-plated, scallop shell motif, signed "Napier," clip/screw-on, 3/4", pr. **40-60**

Earrings, gold-plated, shell motif, clip/screw-ons, signed "Napier," pr. **30-45**

Earrings, goldtone, wide textured hoop style, clip-ons, signed "Avon," 3/4" w., pr. **35**

Earrings, large pearl ball drops below three baguette rhinestone links, screw-ons, 2" l., pr. **30-45**

Earrings, metal & plastic, nine multicolored plastic hoops which can be interchanged on gold-plated metal clips, signed "Kenneth Lane," together w/original black cylindrical box, also signed "Kenneth Jay Lane," 1 3/4" l., the set **150-175**

Earrings, pearl & Aurora Borealis beads, curved to fit outer ear, ca. 1955, clip-on, 1 1/2", pr. **35-50**

Earrings, pearl, freshwater cultured pearl finish, hanging ball, clip-on, 1 1/4", pr. ... **30-45**

Earrings, pearl, hanging teardrop, ca. 1950, screw-on, 1 1/4", pr. **30-45**

Earrings, pearl, large pearl ball hanging from short chain, ca. 1958, 1 1/2", pr. ... **40-55**

Earrings, pearl, large pearl ball hanging from three baguette rhinestone "chain," 2 1/4", pr. **45-65**

Earrings, pearl teardrops, screw-ons, 1 1/8" l., pr. **25-35**

Earrings, plastic, Christmas tree motif, screw-ons **10-15**

Earrings, rhinestone, Art Deco, clear rhinestones in white metal geometric design drops, screw-ons, 2 1/2" l., pr. **75-95**

Earrings, rhinestone, drop hoop-style, clear stones, ca. 1955, clip-on, 1 1/4", pr. **50-75**

Earrings, rhinestone, drop-style, diamond shape, clear stones, large center stone, clip-on, 2", pr. **45-65**

Pear-shaped Earrings

Earrings, rhinestone, drop-style, light blue top, large black pear-shaped drops w/Aurora Borealis finish, screw-on, 1 1/2", pr. (ILLUS.)........................ **45-65**

Earrings, rhinestone, drop-style, rhinestone-set balls on chains, signed "Napier," clip-on, 1 1/2", pr.............................. **35-55**

Earrings, rhinestone, flower design in clear pear-shaped stones, signed "A. Marango-ni," clip-on, 1 1/4" d., pr. **35-50**

Earrings, rhinestone, green, fleur-de-lis style, signed "Eisenberg," clip-on, 1", pr. **75-100**

Earrings, rhinestone, large to-paz & citrine colored stones, signed "Scaasi," clip-on, 1 1/4", pr. **45-70**

Earrings, rhinestone, pavé-set diamond-shaped drop, large center stone, 2 3/4" l., pr. **50-75**

Earrings, silver plate, fish mo-tif w/flexible segments, signed "DKNY" (Donna Ka-ran NY), 3 3/4" l., pr. **75-95**

Earrings, silver tone, fish mo-tif, entire body made mov-able by individual links, clip-ons, signed "DKNY (Donna Karen)," 4" l., pr. **55**

Earrings, silver tone shrimp motif in hoop style, clips, 3/4", pr............................ **30**

Fish-shaped Earrings

Earrings, silvertone fish drops, six flexible linked seg-ments, clip-ons, signed "DKNY" Donna Karen, New York, 4" l., pr. (ILLUS.)................................ **65-85**

Earrings, sterling marcasite set, bows, arc motif, clip-ons, 1 3/4" l., pr. **75**

Earrings, sterling silver, con-cave triangles, clip-ons, Mexico, pr.......................... **25-35**

Earrings, sterling silver, curved triangle motifs, Mexi-co, clip-on, 1", pr...................... **45-65**

Earrings, sterling silver, drop-type, marcasite-set graduat-ed crescents w/bow motif top, unsigned Alice Cavi-ness, clip-on, 1 3/4", pr...... **80-100**

Earrings, sterling silver, drop-type, marcasite-set heart motif, signed "KD," screw-on, 1 1/4", pr.............................. **60-75**

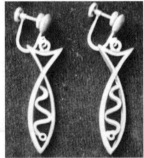

Sterling Fish Motif Earrings

Earrings, sterling silver, drop-type, openwork fish motif, screw-on, 1 3/4", pr. (ILLUS.)................................ **60-75**

Earrings, sterling silver flowers, screw-on, 1" d., pr. **60-75**

Earrings, sterling silver, half-hoop style, screw-on, 3/4", pr. **45-60**

Earrings, textured gold finish, hinged hoop-style, on original card, 7/8" d., pr. **20-30**

Earrings, white metal, hoop-style, screw-on, 1" d., pr. **25-35**

Earrings, white metal, hoop-style, shrimp design, clip-on, 1", pr. **25-35**

Earrings, white metal, mesh, drop-style, arrow on ends, screw-on, 1 3/4", pr. **25-35**

Earrings, white metal, pear-shaped, center grey iridescent pear-shaped stone in textured frame, clip-on, 1", pr. **25-35**

Hatpin, antiqued goldtone, figural butterfly in profile, 9" l. **95-115**

Hatpin, antiqued goldtone, figural cat's face w/amber rhinestone eyes, 9" l. **95-115**

Hatpin, clear rhinestone, round top, 12 3/4" l. **95-110**

Hatpin, figure of smiling man wearing derby hat, worn paint, 6 3/4" l. **95-120**

Hatpin, rhinestone, large purple stone in clear rhinestone frame, 8 1/2" l. **75-85**

Hatpin, silver plate, Art Nouveau woman w/long flowing hair reading book, 8" l. **85-100**

Hatpin, sterling silver, figural cat, hallmarked, England, 10" l. **175**

Hatpin, white metal, pavé rhinestone-set flying bird, 2" w., 10 1/2" l. **75**

Lapel pendant watch, 800 standard silver set w/marcasite, marcasite-set bow pin w/center swiveling drop to hold watch which can detach & be added to 30" marcasite accented chain, 17 jewel, w/original cylindrical box, signed "Bucherer" **350-400**

Lapel watch, chrome, clip-style, French, black enamel, back of watch marked "Deposé," front signed "Riviera" **75**

Lapel watch, chrome, clip-style, watch on one side, black enamel w/initial on reverse, signed "Riviera"...... **125-150**

Lapel watch, clear rhinestones in white metal frame suspended by four large rhinestone links attached to looped rhinestone-set bar pin, signed "Fidelity" **100-125**

Lapel watch, enameled beige flying duck on white metal, rhinestone half circle & rhinestone trim on wings & watch case, second hand, signed "Crawford," 1 1/2 x 2" **225-245**

Collectible Lapel Watch

Lapel watch, enameled cherries motif, hanging from brown bar pin, larger cherry contains watch by Clifford (ILLUS.)................................ **125**

Lapel watch, enameled, cloisonné, yellow background, pink roses & green leaves, watch suspended from bow motif by chains, watch swivels to read time, second hand, signed "Crawford," w/original blue velvet box, 2" l. **240-265**

Lapel watch, enameled, contemporary design of long-tailed tropical fish in yellow & green enamel, clear rhinestone trim, row of larger emerald-cut Aurora Borealis rhinestones on top fin, quartz movement watch suspended from tail, signed "Bonetto," 3 1/4"............ **65-85**

Lapel watch, enameled, red cherries w/green stems & leaves suspended from brown branch form bar pin, watch inserted into larger cherry, second hand, signed "Clifford," 2 1/2"............ **155-180**

Lapel watch, gold (12k yellow) on sterling silver, Retro style geometric rectangular watch on open rectangle suspended from bar pin, watch signed "Solex".......... **150-200**

Floral Design Lapel Watch

Lapel watch, gold-filled (12k yellow), floral spray pin w/watch set as a flower, signed "CA" pierced by an arrow (Carl-Art), 2 3/8" h. (ILLUS.)............ **150-200**

Lapel watch, gold-filled flower spray w/watch set as a flower on stem, second hand, watch signed "Louis," pin signed "Carl-Art," 2 1/2"... **200-225**

Lapel watch, gold-filled, heart-shaped watch suspended from Retro ribbon style pin, second hand, signed "Selbro," 2 1/2"...... **175-200**

Lapel watch, gold-filled on sterling silver, geometric design watch suspended from cylindrical bar pin, signed "Solrex," 1 1/2"............ **175-195**

Lapel watch, gold-filled, oval, openwork Retro style swirled bows w/center pearls, watch face w/jeweled numerals, signed "Banner," 2"............ **225-250**

Lapel watch, gold-filled, Retro style bow design suspending watch, signed "Pierce," 3"............ **185-225**

Lapel watch, gold-filled, ship's wheel-shaped watch suspended from Retro style bar pin, signed "Crawford" **175-200**

Lapel watch, gold-filled, square-shaped watch suspended from Retro style coiled ribbon form pin, jeweled numerals, signed "Monarch," 2 1/8" l. **155-175**

Lapel watch, gold-plated, flower w/pearl center suspending watch w/iridescent face, signed "Bercona," 2 1/4"............ **135-165**

Horse Head Form Lapel Watch

Lapel watch, gold-plated, Retro style horse head motif, watch w/works visible on reverse, signed "Monocraft" (old Monet mark), 2 1/4" (ILLUS.)............ **150-175**

Lapel watch, rhinestone, large red, green & blue pear-shaped frame, signed "Pedre," 1 1/2'" d. **160-185**

Lapel watch, rhinestone, watch framed w/clear rhinestones & suspended from rhinestone chain & bar pin, second hand, signed "Fidelity," 2" **150-170**

Lapel watch, rolled gold, 10k, scallop framed watch hanging by two bars from bow-motif bar pin **65**

Lapel watch, rolled gold (10k yellow), scalloped metalwork around watch suspended from Retro style bar pin, signed "Helbros" **125-150**

Lapel watch, rolled gold, watch inside scalloped frame suspending from Retro style ribbon design bar pin, second hand, signed "Helbros," 2" **150-175**

Lapel watch, sterling marcasite set, flower spray w/watch as a flower, watch is signed "Merit," 2 3/4" h. **155**

Lapel watch, sterling silver floral spray set w/marcasite, watch is set as a flower, signed "Merit," 3" h. **195-250**

Floral Spray Lapel Watch

Lapel watch, sterling silver & marcasite, floral spray design w/watch set as flower, second hand, signed "Merit," 3" (ILLUS.) **265-295**

Lapel watch, sterling silver & marcasite, Retro style swirled bar pin suspending leaf-framed watch face, signed "Croton," 2 1/2" **220-250**

Lapel watch/pendant, silver (800) & marcasite, bow pin w/swivel drop suspending detachable watch, attaches to matching 30" marcasite-set chain, signed "Bucherer," w/original box **400-425**

Necklace, antiqued gold, ethnic style openwork, three large circles on double swag design chains w/suspended drops, ca. 1935, 14" l. **50-65**

Necklace, antiqued goldplate, Renaissance style, purple marquise stone links & snakechain, ornate center moftif w/center purple stones, signed "Sandor," 16" l. **135-155**

Necklace, Bakelite, 2" black owl slide, white trim on 48" goldtone snakechain, ca. 1930 .... **165-190**

Necklace, Bakelite, graduated deeply-carved blue over ivory beads, 16" l. **75-95**

Necklace, Bakelite, green twisted leaves hanging from celluloid chain, 15" l. **145-170**

Early Collar-style Beaded Necklace

Necklace, beaded collar-style, all-black beaded openwork designs w/triple bead drops between each design, beaded button fastener, ca. 1900, 13 1/2" l. (ILLUS.).. **185-220**

Necklace, beads, agate, lavender & swirled purple, signed "Judith McCann NY, 1961," 26" l. **90-120**

Necklace, beads, Art Deco Native American style, black glass & crystal, 16" l. **75-100**

Necklace, beads, Aurora Borealis clear, faceted, graduated, 22" l., adjusts up to 25" l. **50-65**

Necklace, beads, black glass beads w/black beaded center medallion w/four long black bead drops, ca. 1890, 20" l., medallion 9" **100-125**

Necklace, beads, collar-style, clear, pink & violet frosted glass beads, five drops w/frosted leaves at ends, white metal chain, ca. 1940, 14" l. **75-100**

Collar Style Glass Bead Necklace

Necklace, beads, coral glass, collar style, hanging from gold-plated swag design chains, ca. 1955, 15" l. (ILLUS.) **100-150**

Necklace, beads, coral & pink w/gold-filled bead accents, 14" l. **180-220**

Necklace, beads, double row collar style, green glass teardrop-shaped beads on gold-plated chains, adjusts to 16" l. **85-115**

Hobe Beaded Necklace

Necklace, beads, double strand composed of red, black & clear beads separated by rhinestone rondells, multi-strand drop in center, signed "Hobé," adjusts to 15" (ILLUS.) **100-125**

Necklace, beads, double strand pink Aurora Borealis pale solid pink glass beads, gold filigree findings, 24" l. .. **65-95**

Ornate Glass Bead Necklace

Necklace, beads, double strand purple glass beads w/two very ornate overlaid beaded purple glass drops w/pink rhinestones & pink glass flowers, the center drop w/bow designs, custom made by Ian St. Gielar, 20" l. (ILLUS.) **1,200-1,500**

Necklace, beads, four strand, glass coral & gold designs, flat twist-style beads, gold spacers, adjusts to 15" l. **70-95**

Aurora Borealis Necklace

Necklace, beads, four strands, brown, yellow, green & yellow Aurora Borealis glass beads, rhinestone baguette ends, ca. 1955, adjusts to 17" l. (ILLUS.)............ **70-95**

Necklace, beads, four strands of flat glass Aurora Borealis beads, shades of green, ca. 1955, adjustable to 16" l. **50-75**

Beaded Fringe Collar Style Necklace

Necklace, beads, fringed collar -tyle consisting of multi-colored beads, ca. 1939 (ILLUS.)............... **170-200**

Necklace, beads, garnet, small, 31".............................. **55**

Necklace, beads, glass, Art Deco style, large red tear-drop-shape beads & oval faceted beads alternating w/small red & black beads, 33" l............................. **85-100**

Necklace, beads, glass carnelian colored beads w/double drops, enameled white metal, 16" l.............................. **50-75**

Necklace, beads, graduated amber, yellow & marbleized brown oval beads, 29" l. .. **135-155**

Necklace, beads, graduated coral & red beads on sterling silver chain, 16" l. **180-220**

Necklace, beads, graduated & faceted garnets, bead clasp, 16" l............................... **125-155**

Necklace, beads, green glass, ca. 1925, 32" l. w/5" tassel drop............................ **125**

Necklace, beads, green oval & round glass beads, eight-strand tassel, pearl finish teardrop bead accents, ca. 1925, 32" l. w/5" tassel..... **120-150**

Necklace, beads, long, round, wing-shaped maroon glass beads, center pendant w/silver leaves & flowers, signed "Czechoslavia," 16" l. **75-95**

Necklace, beads, rope of shaded blue & green art glass beads, round, cylindrical, oval & irregular shaped beads, 52" l. **50-75**

Necklace, beads, shades of blue, green & turquoise art glass beads, 52" l. **70-95**

Necklace, beads, white glass beads w/grey knots between each bead, signed "Les Bernard," 32" l. **65-85**

Necklace, beads, yellow art glass w/multicolored dots, long faceted beads alternating w/white metal spacers, double teardrop-shaped drops, ca. 1925, 25" l., drops 4 1/2" **150-175**

Necklace, blue rhinestone pendant w/flower on long chain, signed "Miriam Haskell".................................... **65**

Art Deco Carnelian & Enamel Necklace

Necklace, carnelian & enamel, Art Deco style, carved glass carnelians & enamel links w/Chinese writing, ca. 1930s (ILLUS.) **100-125**

Necklace, cloisonné enamel on green enameled links, pendant-style w/watch, 4" drop attached to Art Deco watch, ca. 1930.................... **125-150**

Necklace, enamel, cloisonné on sterling, green enamel links w/4" drop w/watch which reverses to yellow rose design, ca. 1930, chain 22" l. **155-185**

Necklace, enamel on brass, carved carnelian, four black & orange yellow enamel Far East motifs, ca. 1935, 16" l. **95-120**

Necklace, enamel on chrome, Art Deco style, plastic blue & chrome cylinder drop, ca. 1935, 20" l. **60-85**

Necklace, enamel on copper & turquoise, link style, signed "Matisse," adjustable **95-125**

Necklace, enameled collar-style, enameled links in red, forest green, signed "Lanvin Paris" **60**

Necklace, enameled red & forest green links, signed "Lanvin Paris," 15" l. **80-100**

Necklace, gold chain alternating w/pearls & art glass beads, six-part tassel drop, signed "Liz Claiborne," 34" l. w/4" l. drop **40-55**

Necklace, gold chain w/large black center circle, signed "Trifari," 16" l. **30-45**

Necklace, gold-filled, relief molded female face, rhinestone trim, ca. 1900 .... **115-135**

Necklace, gold-filled & rhinestone, Art Nouveau swirled design, ca. 1895 .... **175-190**

Necklace, gold-plated, bib-style composed of multiple chains w/ornate 6 1/2" pendant w/pink, fuchsia & moss green rhinestones, pink & blue art glass stones, pearl teardrop clusters on drop & bib portion, signed "Florenza" **125-175**

Necklace, gold-plated, black enamel purse pendant which opens, rhinestone trim, signed "World," 34" l. **30-45**

Necklace, gold-plated, carved red beads, large oval pearls alternating w/gold-plated chains, signed "Miriam Haskell," 31" l. **200-250**

Necklace, gold-plated chain alternating w/long clear art glass beads, glass perfume bottle pendant set in gold frame w/attached gold stopper, signed "YSL," Yves St. Laurent, 26" l. **65-85**

Necklace, gold-plated chain links, three larger links center set w/clear rhinestones, signed "Kenneth Lane," 14" l. **55-75**

Chain Necklace with Flower Drops

Necklace, gold-plated chain suspending six lacy green plastic flowers w/gold metal bead center, ca. 1935, 14" l. (ILLUS.).. **50-65**

Flower Motif Necklace

Necklace, gold-plated double chain suspending seven square-shaped enameled flower motifs w/center black oval stones framed by pearls, stone & pearl accents, signed "Hobé," 15" l. (ILLUS.).................................... **200-250**

Necklace, gold-plated, ethnic style, six rows of flexible flower design, signed "Matisse," 23" l. **40-60**

Necklace, gold-plated, four graduated chains, center three have Victorian style ornate pendants w/mesh fringes, ca. 1965, longest chain 40" **75-95**

Necklace, gold-plated, graduated gold leaves suspended from chain, ca. 1935, 15" l. .. **65-90**

Necklace, gold-plated, graduated triple row large link chains, each a different style, center circle w/large red stone, signed "Van S Authentics," 24" l. **60-80**

Jomaz Collar Necklace

Necklace, gold-plated, inverted triangular links, large center faux emerald on each, purple & clear rhinestone trim, signed "Jomaz," 14 1/2" l. (ILLUS.) **250-300**

Necklace, gold-plated large heart on large chunky gold-plated chain, signed "Erwin Pearl," heart 2" l., 32" l. **65**

Necklace, gold-plated, model of sword in scabbard, griffin head, trimmed w/multicolored cabochon glass stones, including three hanging stones, 5 1/4" w. sword can be removed from scabbard, 22" l. **40-55**

Necklace, gold-plated, nine graduated chain strands, star pendant, signed "Monet" **65-85**

Necklace, gold-plated, pendant style, textured 1 1/2 x 2 1/2" rectangle on cylindrical link chain, signed "Lanvin Paris," 27" l. **50-70**

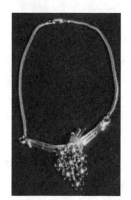
Corocraft Flower Spray Necklace

Necklace, gold-plated, red baguette rhinestone-set flower spray motif, green baguette stems on snake chains, short, signed "Corocraft" (ILLUS.) **125**

Necklace, gold-plated & rhinestone, Renaissance style design w/red rhinestones in center of two pearl links, pendant of red center stone w/pearl trim, two links leading to large oval stone in center of pearls & red stone motif w/three 4" hanging drops, signed "Ricarde of Hollywood," 16 1/4" l. **275-325**

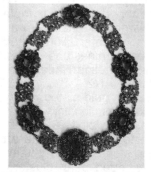
Filigree & Rhinestone Necklace

Necklace, gold-plated & rhinestone, wide filigree links alternating w/large royal blue oval & round unfoiled rhinestone flowers, large center flower on goldplated filigree, signed "Ricarde of Hollywood," 18" l. (ILLUS.) **275-325**

Rare Dior Necklace

Floral Mosaic Necklace

Necklace, gold-plated, six chains w/large four-part pink art glass stones drop, curved teardrop shapes, amber teardrop shapes, clear rhinestone trim, signed "Chr. Dior Germany," ca. 1970, 15" l w/5 1/2" l. drop, rare (ILLUS.)............................... **1,000-1,300**

Necklace, gold-plated snakechain w/carved gold marbleized Bakelite leaf & flower circular motif, 15" l..... **65-90**

Necklace, gold-plated triple chains alternating w/seated monkey motif, signed "Judith Leiber," 44" l............................ **170-195**

Necklace, gold-plated triple row large link chains, swag style w/center lion head w/green rhinestone eyes, signed "Pauline Rader," adjusts to 14 1/2" l......................... **70-95**

Necklace, gold-plated, very ornate multichain, 6 1/2" pendant w/pink & green rhinestones, pink & blue art glass stone, hanging teardrop-shaped pearl clusters, signed "Florenza," 17" l. at neck............................ **175-200**

Necklace, jade, black cord w/2 1/4" d. jade circle w/Chinese writing, adjustable slide, ca. 1925, 32" l............ **95-125**

Necklace, light gold-plated, pendant-type, spinning ballerina inside circle, 24" l........ **25-45**

Necklace, mosaic, rectangular red glass links w/multicolored mosaic floral design & larger floral decorated oval at center, white metal settings, 15" l. (ILLUS.)............ **125-150**

Necklace, pearl & bead, multistrand, pearls alternating w/red, blue & green glass beads, gold spacers, 3 1/2" beads drop, signed "deLillo," 18" l....................................... **150-175**

Necklace, pearl, double strand baroque pearls, ornate filigree drop w/center red marquise stone flower, signed "Miriam Haskell," adjusts to 15" l. **225-250**

Necklace, pearl, triple strand baroque pearls in shades of grey, ornate silvertone floral center, signed "Miriam Haskell," adjusts to 15" l. **185-225**

Necklace, pearls, choker-style, double strand small & medium baroque pearls, very ornate gold openwork center of seed pearl flowers, marquise emerald rhinestones, tiny blue, clear & maroon rhinestones, signed "Denbé," 12" l, adjusts 2 3/4" longer.............................. **85-110**

Necklace, rhinestone & antiqued gold metal, five center leaves, flowers w/large citrine color pear-shaped stones, smaller round accents, citrine color rhinestone chain, signed "Hattie Carnegie," 16 1/2" l. **275-300**

Fine Kramer Rhinestone Necklace

Necklace, rhinestone, clear w/emerald-cut & pear-shaped drop & matching green round accents, signed "Kramer of N.Y.," 17" l. (ILLUS.)..................................... **345-365**

Pearl, Crystal & Rhinestone Necklace

Necklace, rhinestone, crystal & pearl, single strand of pearls alternating w/purple crystal beads suspending a 5" l. triangular pendant set w/purple cabochons & centered by two large red oval rhinestones framed by clear rhinestones, three hanging baroque pearl drops, signed "deLillo," 20" l. (ILLUS.).... **700-800**

Necklace, rhinestone, double chains, gold metal pendant w/center blue, purple & citrine unfoiled stones, signed "Hobé," 16" l. **250-275**

Necklace, rhinestone, flower links w/clear round & marquise stones, signed "Trifari," adjusts to 14 1/2" l.. **100-125**

Necklace, rhinestone, "Fruit Salad" design w/red, blue & green stones in fruit motifs, pavé-set clear stone links, signed "Trifari," 16" l. **425-450**

Necklace, rhinestone, loop design links, signed "Bogoff," 14" l. **110-125**

Trifari Rhinestone Necklace

Necklace, rhinestone & metal, square-cut aquamarine rhinestones channel-set between bars of white metal, Trifari (ILLUS.) **150-175**

Necklace, rhinestone, very ornate complete rhinestone-set w/ornate sunburst drop of baguettes w/raised center, signed "Hollycraft 1957," adjusts to 17" l. **175-200**

Necklace, rhinestones set in sterling, single strand w/18 hanging pear-shaped rhinestone drops, signed "Coro Sterling," 13 3/4" l. **85-125**

Necklace, rhinestones set in white metal, Art Deco style center w/three marquise rhinestones, signed "Coro," 14" l. **40-65**

Necklace, shell cameo, profile of lady in 835 silver frame, 22" l. 835 silver chain, cameo 1".. **100-125**

Necklace, silver plated coiled chain, graduated crystal dangles in individual cups, ca. 1890, 16" l. **145-175**

Necklace, sterling, pendant-style, ornate openwork heart, 24" l. **65-85**

Egyptian Motif Pendant & Chain

Necklace, sterling, pendant-type, double chain w/Egyptian profile motif on textured background, 24" l. (ILLUS.) **100-150**

Necklace, sterling silver, Art Deco style 1 1/2" locket w/white enamel on chain w/pearls, ca. 1925, 36" l.. **145-175**

Necklace, sterling silver chain w/2" cut crystal drop, ca. 1935, 18" l. **50-75**

Necklace, sterling silver chain w/six heart charms, ca. 1900, 24" l. **140-165**

Necklace, sterling silver double chain w/2" pendant w/profile of Egyptian lady on rayed background, ca. 1935, 24" l. **135-165**

Necklace, sterling silver, double leaf link design, signed "Van Dell," 15" l. **55-75**

Sterling Silver Locket Necklace

Necklace, sterling silver heart-shaped locket, mother-of-pearl center w/sterling military insignia, ca. 1942, w/original velvet-lined box, 19" l. (ILLUS.) **100-125**

Necklace, sterling silver & jade, jade flowers on swag style center, 1 1/2" jade drop of Chinese monk, 16" l..... **150-175**

Necklace, sterling silver & marcasite, three blue cabochon-set gemstones alternating w/four ornate sterling & marcasite-set designs, ca. 1935, 15" l. **150-175**

Necklace, sterling silver, model of birds in nest pendant, garnet account, 21" l. **65-85**

Necklace, sterling silver w/oval pendant of 1920s lady wearing a locket, 16" l. **135-165**

Necklace, white metal, 1 3/4" open sardine can pendant w/tan plastic fish, signed "Hattie Carnegie," w/original tag & price, 24" l. **120-150**

Necklace, white metal, Art Deco style pendant w/marcasite & black stones, ca. 1935, 15" l. **55-75**

Necklace, white metal, faux Native American design set w/faux turquoise, adjusts to 20" l. **35-50**

Necklace, white metal & plastic, large plastic beads alternating w/chains, 3" white metal pendant w/ornate plastic design & red bead trim, 30" l. **50-75**

Faux Pearl Pin

Pin, antiqued gold metal large ornate hanging chain w/an iridescent top pearl & drop & rhinestone trim, 4 3/4" l. (ILLUS.)............................ **65-85**

Pin, Bakelite, bar-style, carnelian color, outer edge trimmed w/gold-plated chain, 1 x 3"..................... **70-85**

Pin, Bakelite, carved beige wood seahorse on brown wood, 3 1/8"............................ **100-125**

Carved Bakelite Pin

Pin, Bakelite, carved palm fronds & coconuts resembling acorns, dark green, ca. 1930s, 3 1/4" l. (ILLUS.)........... **175**

Pin, Bakelite, forest green carved leaves, 2 3/8"............. **70-95**

Pin, Bakelite, ivory color carved flower w/long leaves, made in France, 3"................ **75-100**

Pin, Bakelite, laminated, multicolored layers cut away to form striped design, maroon oval top, 1 1/2" w................ **150-175**

Pin, Bakelite, model of old fashioned camera, brown wood, 2".................................. **85-115**

Pin, Bakelite on wood, red on brown wood, 1 3/4"................ **40-55**

Pin, Bakelite, red carved scroll, 2"................................. **50-75**

Pin, Bakelite, very densely carved black raised flowers & leaves set in diamond shape, gold-plated twisted metal frame, 2 3/8"............. **175-200**

Pin, brass, bearded man wearing turban, signed "Joseph Hollywood," 2"........... **185-225**

Pin, brass, large oval turquoise center, ca. 1890, 2 1/2 x 3"............................... **70-95**

Pin, brass, man wearing Egyptian headdress, glass turquoise scarab, ca. 1900, 1 x 1 1/2"................................. **60-80**

Pin, brass, ornate dimensional openwork, large center cabochon purple stone, flowers w/purple stone center, ca. 1885, 2" w. **75-100**

Pin, brass, oval, openwork flowers, ca. 1935, 2 1/8 x 2 3/4"..................... **50-75**

Pin, brass, wishbone design, center knot w/rhinestone center, ca. 1910, 1 3/8"........ **30-40**

Pin, celluloid, figure of World War II sailor w/rope, marbleized beige, 2 3/4"................... **35-50**

Pin, celluloid, figure of World War II soldier in combat gear w/rifle, brown & beige, 2 3/4" **35-50**

Pin, ceramic on goldplate, figure of white Cupid w/arrows, Wedgwood blue jasper background, signed "Wedgwood Made in England," can also be worn as pendant, 1 3/8" d...................... **75-100**

Pin, ceramic on sterling, white cameo on deep blue jasper background, wide ornate silver filigree frame, signed "Wedgwood Made in England," w/original tag, in original gift box, 1 1/4" d...... **165-1850**

Pin, enamel, bird on branch, long tail, red glass "jelly belly" center, rhinestone trim, signed "Art," 3 1/4" h........ **120-150**

Enameled Bow & Daisy Pins

Pin, enamel, bow design in white enamel trimmed in gold, Trifari (ILLUS. bottom) **65-85**

Pin, enamel, Chinese style white lion, rhinestone trim, signed "Pauline Rader," 2 x 2 3/4".................................. **60-75**

Pin, enamel flower spray, iridescent amber, yellow & green pavé-set rhinestone trim, signed "Reja," 2 x 3" **175-200**

Pin, enamel, grey-white iridescent flower w/pearl center, signed "Kramer," 2 1/2" d..... **45-65**

Pin, enamel, model of a daisy, white enamel petals w/yellow center, unsigned (ILLUS. top, previous page) **35-50**

Pin, enamel, model of a red apple w/green leaves, beige worm w/pearl head, signed "Original by Robert," 2"......... **35-50**

Pin, enamel, model of black beetle w/pavé-set goldplated wings, "2000" in red enamel on wings, signed "Roman," 1 1/2"........................ **30-40**

Pin, enamel, model of yellow hat w/wreath of pink, blue & yellow flowers, orange ribbon, signed "My Fair Lady, BSK," 2".......................... **65-85**

Pin, enamel on copper, blue cloisonné flowers, ca. 1900, 2 3/4" w................... **35-50**

Pin, enamel on copper, green & yellow leaves on copper branch, signed "Martisse Renoir," 2 1/8"................... **60-85**

Pin, enamel on copper, model of whale, millefiori design in blue, white & lavender, 2 1/4" w................... **65-85**

Pin, enamel on goldplate, model of cockatoo on branch, red, blue & green, 3 1/8"........................... **35-50**

Pin, enamel on sterling, red w/green leaf center, ca. 1890, 2 1/4"...................... **145-175**

Russian Dancer Pin

Pin, enamel on sterling silver, figure of Russian dancer, red jacket trimmed w/gold, white hat & blue pants & boots, ca. 1940, 2 1/4" (ILLUS.)........ **150-175**

Pin, enamel on sterling silver, model of a butterfly, yellow rhinestone trim, signed "WB," ca. 1930, 1 1/2"......... **80-115**

Tiger and Leopard Pins

Pin, enamel & rhinestone, model of a black-enameled leopard w/pavé-set rhinestone trim, Carolee Limited Edition, 1992, 3 1/4" l. (ILLUS. bottom w/tiger) **100-125**

Christmas Lantern & Tree Pins

Pin, enameled metal, model of a carriage lantern w/Christmas trim including a red enameled bow & green holly, signed "Hollycraft," 2 1/4" l. (ILLUS. top w/Christmas tree pins) **40-50**

Pin, gold on sterling, butterfly set w/faux cabochon moonstones & rubies, pavé rhinestone trim on body & wing tips, signed "Trifari," 2 1/4" **220-250**

Pin, gold on sterling, curved Retro style flowers, pavé aqua rhinestone centers, pavé clear rhinestone trim, signed "Pennino," 2 1/4 x 2 3/4"............... **350-395**

Pin, gold on sterling, floral spray, three royal blue marquise stones in center, signed "Coro," 3 1/4" h. **70-90**

Pin, gold on sterling, flower w/very large emerald-cut red glass stone w/coiled leaves at sides, ca. 1940s, signed "Jolle," 2 3/4 x 3 3/4" **100-125**

Flower Spray Pins

Pin, gold on sterling Retro flower spray, two large red unfoiled open set stones in flowers, 3" (ILLUS. left) **125**

Pin, gold on sterling, Retro spray flower, leaves, unfoiled open set pink & light blue stones, old Boucher mark, 2 1/4" **250**

Pin, gold on sterling, small stars on top surrounding a center faux blue sapphire, clear rhinestone trim, signed "Nettie Rosenstein," 1 3/4" **100-145**

Pin, gold on sterling, two large Retro-style flowers, large turquoise rhinestone pavé-set centers, clear rhinestone trim, signed "Pennino," 2 7/8 x 2 3/8" (ILLUS. right) **395**

Pin, gold-filled, double rods coming from inner circle, Victorian, ca. 1890, 2 1/2" w. **80-100**

Pin, gold-plated, antiqued, filigreework, large diamond shape set w/pearls & red & green rhinestones hanging by seven chains from a matching rectangular design, 4 1/4" **100-125**

Ornate Gold-plated Pin

Pin, gold-plated, antiqued, large red center stone framed by grey stones, red & grey accent stones & scrolled & leaf-form border, multichains fringe, signed "Sandor," 4" (ILLUS.) **65-85**

Pin, gold-plated, antiqued, light blue stone, hanging matching mini purse w/blue stone, purse opens, 2 1/2" .. **45-55**

Pin, gold-plated, Art Nouveau style figure of nude on leaves w/vine background, ca. 1895, 2" **65-90**

Pin, gold-plated, basket w/three-dimensional pavé-set rhinestones, puppy leaning over edge, 1 1/4" h. **40-55**

Pin, gold-plated, centered by bust of lady wearing winged helmet, top set w/green, blue, red & violet oval stones, large ornate drop w/figure of Mercury in center, signed "Sathennic Arts," 3 1/2" **125-150**

Diamond-shaped Pin with Crystals

Pin, gold-plated & crystals, diamond-shaped openwork form w/rows of crystal Aurora Borealis finish hanging drops which move w/wearer, signed "Vendome," 2 1/2" (ILLUS.) **75-100**

Pin, gold-plated dimensional design Christmas tree, red, green & blue stones, clear baguette "candles," signed "Original by Robert," 2" **85-110**

Pin, gold-plated dimensional design Christmas tree w/red, green & clear rhinestone ornaments, signed "Art," 2 1/2" **65-85**

Pin, gold-plated, dimensional filigree work hand set w/large deep red & purple stones, signed "Czechoslo-vakia," 2 1/8" w. **65-90**

Pin, gold-plated & enamel, openwork gold-plated basket containing red flowers w/rhinestone center & green leaves, signed "Trifari," 2".... **55-75**

Pin, gold-plated figural chick, textured finish, amber rhinestone eye, signed "Trifari," 1 3/4" h............ **60-75**

Pin, gold-plated, figural lion head, large amber stone in mouth, mane made of chains, unsigned, designer quality, 3"........................ **75-95**

Gold-plated Stickpin & Holder Pin

Pin, gold-plated, five "stickpin" designs in ornate holder, pearls & colored rhinestone accents, unsigned designer quality (ILLUS.)........... **60-85**

Pin, gold-plated, freeform design set w/three large carved scarabs in pink, blue & olive green, 2 1/2 x 3 1/4"................ **55-80**

Pin, gold-plated, large three-dimensional flower w/green rhinestone center & clear rhinestone trim, unsigned designer quality, 2 3/4 x 4" **150-175**

Pin, gold-plated, leaf design set w/large red, white & blue opaque stones, signed "Pauline Rader," 2 x 2 1/2" **90-125**

Pin, gold-plated model of a Christmas tree w/red & green iridescent enameled balls, signed "Gerys," 2" h. (ILLUS. left w/lantern & tree, page 112)............... **25-35**

Pin, gold-plated, model of fish w/white metal body, cabochon moonstone eye, large top fin, unsigned designer quality, 2 1/4"...................... **40-55**

Pin, gold-plated, model of hinged treasure chest, lid opens to reveal "gold" & "precious stones" treasure, 1 3/4"............................ **30-45**

Pin, gold-plated, model of lady's hand holding heart-shaped locket, 2"...................... **50-65**

Figural Scottie Pin

Pin, gold-plated, model of Scottie dog, 1 3/4" w. (ILLUS.).. **35-50**

Pin, gold-plated, model of seated cat w/textured chest & paw, openwork green rhinestone eyes, 1 3/4".......... **35-50**

Pin, gold-plated, model of seated spaniel-type dog, red rhinestone eyes, 1 3/8".......... **35-50**

Pin, gold-plated, model of turtle w/openwork shell set w/clear, green & red rhinestones, tremblant head, signed "Lewis LTD," 2".......... **65-95**

Pin, gold-plated, open heart motif w/"Mother" in center, multicolored rhinestone trim, 1 1/2" **35-50**

Pin, gold-plated, openwork design of three balloons, 4" **35-50**

Pin, gold-plated, openwork design w/enameled blue & white flowers, center faux sapphire, blue rhinestone trim, five graduated dangles w/blue beads, signed "Czecho," 2" **75-100**

Ornate Gold-plated Pin

Pin, gold-plated, ornate scrolled top w/large pear-shaped blue stone accented w/pearls & blue rhinestones, suspending five chains w/blue art glass beads & pearls, ending in center starburst medallion set w/blue art glass bead surrounded by small pearls, signed "Coro," 2 1/4" w., 5" h. (ILLUS.) **125-150**

Victorian Revival Design Pin

Pin, gold-plated, oval Victorian revival design, center swings around to reveal photos of two 1940s film stars, 1 5/8 x 2" (ILLUS. closed) .. **65-95**

Pin, gold-plated, Retro-style, pink tone floral spray w/green rhinestone trim, ca. 1946, 3 1/2" **45-65**

Pin, gold-plated sterling silver, flower spray design w/large emerald-cut red glass stone, coiled leaves, signed "Jolle," ca. 1943, 2 1/4" w., 4" h. **165-195**

Pin, gold-plated sterling silver, model of old-fashioned bicycle w/a very large front wheel, very small rear wheel, hand-set w/aqua & clear rhinestones, 2 3/4" w., 3" h. **150-175**

Pin, gold-plated sterling silver, star motif w/center blue cabochon stone, small star accents, signed "Nettie Rosenstein," 2" **225-250**

Pin, gold-plated, woman wearing 1940s hat & suit carrying flower set w/purple rhinestone, signed "Coro," 2 1/2" **65-85**

Pin, goldplate w/black enamel & rhinestones, model of a tiger, signed "Hattie Carnegie," 3" l. (ILLUS. top w/leopard, page 112) **115-135**

Figural Cat & Cobra Pins

Pin, goldtone & glass, model of a standing modernistic cat w/white glass & "coralene" style design body, rhinestone collar & eyes, signed "Francoise" (ILLUS. right) **95-120**

Pin, goldtone & rhinestone, model of a hooded cobra, pave-set w/rhinestone & cabochon multicolored stones on the body & eyes (ILLUS. left w/cat pin) **85-115**

Pin, leather, model of cowboy-style hat in light brown w/hanging gold-plated guitar w/strings, matching leather back, ca. 1943, 2 x 2 1/2" **65-85**

Pin, Lucite, clear diamond shape w/red roses inside, hanging from gold-plated bow pin, ca. 1945, 2 1/2"...... **45-65**

Pin, Lucite, model of seahorse w/applied brown wood body, 2 7/8".............................. **45-65**

Pin, micromosiac, blue & white flower design w/red, white & black border, hallmarked, 1 1/2" d........................ **150-175**

Pin, mosaic, gold metal, oval w/roses in center on black background w/floral frame, Italy, 1 3/4"...................... **85-115**

Pin, pewter, figure of cocktail waiter carrying gold-plated tray w/drinks, 2 1/2" l. legs set on rings which move w/wearer, signed "Ultra Craft," 4 1/2" h. **35-50**

Pin, plastic, figure of Spanish dancer wearing long ruffled skirt, holding maracas, red, black & amber, 2 3/4" **40-60**

Pin, plastic, model of cartoon-style elephant, acid green, ca. 1965, 2"................. **35-50**

Pin, plastic, painted head of man wearing checkered cap & smoking a pipe, made in West Germany, 2 1/4"............ **35-45**

Rhinestone Bow Pin

Pin, rhinestone, bow motif completely set w/large pink & clear oval stones, clear square stone trim, signed "Coro," 2 3/4" w. (ILLUS.).. **85-110**

Pin, rhinestone, bow motif w/clear baguette borders, grey marquise openwork center, two hanging bottom "ribbons" are flexible & move w/wearer, signed "Vendome," 2 3/4 x 3"................. **125-150**

Rhinestone Pins

Pin, rhinestone, cabochon-set large oval glass stones in purple, faux agates, faux pink, red & purple gemstones, signed "Robert Original," 2 1/2 x 3" (ILLUS. left) **165-185**

Pin, rhinestone, Christmas tree w/clear baguette "candles" & trimmed w/red & green rhinestones, signed "Hollycraft," 2" h. **75-90**

Pin, rhinestone, clear coat hanger design w/row of baguettes on lower rung, pavé-set rhinestones on top, 2 3/4"............................... **25-35**

Pin, rhinestone, cluster of five flowers, individual petals set w/multicolored rhinestones in shades of blue & pink, signed "Vendome," 3" d. **125-150**

Pin, rhinestone, figural cat, entire body, head & ears completely covered w/hand-set amber Aurora Borealis rhinestones, signed "Warner," 1 3/4" h............................ **35**

Pin, rhinestone, figural cat w/ball, pavé-set w/lavender & red rhinestones, Alice Caviness, 1 3/4" **35-45**

Pin, rhinestone, floral motif, large aqua emerald-cut & round stones, clear trim, signed "Staret," 3 3/8" h.. **125-150**

Pin, rhinestone, flower all clear pavé-set w/large teardrop-shaped faux green emerald center, 2 1/4"............................ **40-55**

Pin, rhinestone & goldtone, figural cat, large red cabochon stones in body & head, clear rhinestone teardrop ears, baguette & round stone trim, signed "Trifari," 1 3/4"................................. **35**

Pin, rhinestone, head of cat motif, pavé hand-set pink stones, pink pear-shaped rhinestone ears, red marquise eyes, red round nose, signed "Weiss," 1 1/4" **25**

Floral Rhinestone Pin

Pin, rhinestone, large flower spray design set w/pink teardrop-shaped & emerald-cut rhinestones, large round pink stone in flower center surrounded by scalloped border set w/clear stones, stems set w/clear stones, leaves accented w/pink square-cut stones, signed "Staret," 3 x 5" (ILLUS.) .. **500-525**

Pin, rhinestone, layered snowflake design pavé-set w/aqua stones, signed "Sphinx," 1 1/4" d. **40-65**

Pin, rhinestone, metal openwork freeform S shape, gunmetal color w/faux center round & pear-shaped opals, hand-set deep blue, purple & pink stones in marquise & round shapes, signed "Austria," 4 3/4" w. **75-95**

Pin, rhinestone, model of a Christmas tree, ice blue stones on white metal, signed "Weiss," 2 1/4" h. (ILLUS. right, page 112) .. **90-120**

Pin, rhinestone, model of a peacock, clear pavé-set body, long tail of white metal w/hand-set faux sapphires at ends, 2 1/2" **95-125**

Pin, rhinestone, model of a stork w/multicolored stones, signed "Giorgio," 2 1/2" h. (ILLUS. right w/Teddy bear clip, page 95) **45**

Pin, rhinestone, model of butterfly w/pavé-set clear stone wings, faux ruby, sapphire & emerald gemstones, pearl antennae, 1 1/2 x 1 3/4" **70-95**

Pin, rhinestone, model of Dalmatian puppy, pavé-set clear stones w/black rhinestone "spots," gold stones on collar, 1 3/4 x 2 1/4" **55-75**

Pin, rhinestone, multicolored, large triangular, emerald-shaped, pear-shaped, marquise & round stones, designer quality, 2 1/2" **75-100**

Multicolored Rhinestone Pin

Pin, rhinestone, oval gold filigree metal set w/large topaz surrounded by green, red, blue & purple oval & marquise stones, 2 7/8" (ILLUS.) **125-150**

Snowflake-shaped Pin

Pin, rhinestone & pearl, gold-plated snowflake design, large center baroque pearl w/three-dimensional layered pearl drops & clear pear-shaped & round rhinestones, signed "DeMario NY," 3" d. (ILLUS.) **300-325**

Large Bow Design Pin

Pin, rhinestone, three-dimensional gunmetal finish bow design w/very large foiled & unfoiled multi-shaped rhinestones in shades of blue, purple, green, pink & citrine, signed "Lawrence Vrba," 4 x 4 1/2" (ILLUS.) **600-700**

Pin, rhinestone, three-dimensional openwork folded ribbon design w/large hand-set round & marquise stones, hanging rhinestone-set ball on one end, unsigned designer quality, 3" **45-60**

Pin, rhinestone, traditional design set w/clear pavé-set rhinestones, large clear center stones, 3 x 3 1/4" **90-120**

Pin, rhinestones, grape purple border of leaves around marquise-cut & custom made leaf-shaped dark purple & pale blue stones, Aurora Borealis rhinestone centers, 2 3/4" l. (ILLUS. right, page 116) **75-95**

Pin, shell cameo, classic female profile w/ornate frame, extended pin, ca. 1880, 1 3/4" **135-155**

Pin, shell cameo, oval w/800 silver frame, ca. 1900, can also wear as pendant, 1 5/8" **135-155**

Pin, silver, 830 grade, floral designs forming snowflake, ca. 1910, 2" d. **65-95**

Pin, silver, 840 Russian silver, dome center w/twisted & ball border, 2 1/2" d. **275-300**

Pin, sterling silver, marcasite set, exotic bird w/bluish green glass body, Alice Caviness, 2 3/4" h. (unsigned, originally had a tag) **100-145**

Figural Panther and Tiger Pins

Pin, sterling silver, Art Deco style figural black enamel panther, 1 3/4" (ILLUS. left) **75-100**

Pin, sterling silver, cat, 14k gold nose, sapphire eyes, original case & box, signed "Tiffany & Co.," 1 3/4" **125-150**

Pin, sterling silver, circle design, black enamel w/rhinestone trim, ca. 1910, 1 1/12" d.. **50-75**

Sterling Silver Cini Pins

Pin, sterling silver, floral spray design, Cini (ILLUS. left). **325-350**

Pin, sterling silver, marcasite & enamel tiger on top of large black onyx circle, 2 x 2" (ILLUS. right, with panther)................ **100-145**

Pin, sterling silver, model of a horseshoe, ca. 1900, English hallmarks, 1 1/8" **70-95**

Pin, sterling silver, model of a spoon, ca. 1947, 2 1/2" **40-65**

Pin, sterling silver, model of an open-winged bird feeding on a berry, signed "By G. Roupoli" & "Black, Starr & Gorham," 2 1/4" **175-200**

Pin, sterling silver, model of old-fashioned tennis racquet, 2 1/2" **60-80**

Pin, sterling silver, openwork design w/large green cabochon chrysoprase, smaller amethyst, amber & carnelian cabochons, Edwardian, 2 3/4" w., 1" h. **175-200**

Pin, sterling silver, rib-textured fabric-like Retro design, signed "Chr. Dior Germany," 2 3/8".......................... **150-175**

Pin, sterling silver, Rococo flower & leaf design set w/four large crystals, Cini (ILLUS. right, previous page) **325-350**

Pin, sterling silver, scallop shell design wflying bird inside, large real pearl, ca. 1910, 1 x 1 1/2"..................... **125-150**

Pin, sterling silver, three-dimensional cat w/movable face, signed "Beau," 2"................ **35**

Pin, sterling silver, two seated cats w/green cabochon stone eyes, one cat in matte gold-plated finish, signed "Gorham," 2 3/8".................... **125-150**

Pin, Vulcanite, bust profile of lady, ca. 1890, 1 1/2" d. **70-95**

Pin, white metal, blue & white glass cameo w/rhinestone trim, Victorian watch-style locket hanging from fleur-de-lis motif, when locket is opened, four photo spaces pop up, signed "Coro," 2 1/4" **45-65**

Figural Pin with Turquoise

Pin, white metal, face of native w/hanging turquoise ball earrings, ivory plastic horn headdress w/turquoise trim, signed "Alexander Konda," 3 1/4" h. (ILLUS.)................. **150-175**

Marcasite Christmas Tree Pin

Pin, white metal, model of a Christmas tree, scalloped branches set w/marcasites & red stones, signature illegible, 2 1/8" (ILLUS.) **55-75**

Pin, white metal, model of a sword, cabochon turquoise stone trim, head of bird on hilt, signed "Coro," 5" w. **90-120**

Circle Pin with Multicolored Stones

Pin, white metal, ornate openwork metal circle design, 1 3/8" d. raised faux topaz center, cabochon oval multicolored "agate" border, signed "Miracle," 3 1/4" d. (ILLUS.)................................... **195-225**

Reinad Rhinestone Orchid Pin

Pin, white metal & rhinestone, modeled as an orchid w/curved petals & leaves set w/grey & clear rhinestones, Reinad, 4" h. (ILLUS.) **250-275**

Pin, white metal, three musical instruments, two hands, word "JAMMIN" suspended in individual letters, 3 x 3 1/2" **65-75**

Pin, wood, brown carved wood leaves w/large brown hanging beads, multicolored wood button accents, ca. 1943, 3 3/4" l. **65-90**

Pin, wood, carved cat head w/painted eyes, red bow on neck, 2" **45-55**

Novel Wooden Pin

Pin, wood, carved leaf motif, three hanging celluloid chains w/brown nuts, each w/h.p. face, ca. 1935-40 (ILLUS.) **110-135**

Figural Chinese Man Pin

Pin, wood, h.p. figure of Chinese man carrying two wooden buckets on chains hanging from yoke, ca. 1935, 3" (ILLUS.) **125-150**

Pin/pendant, glass, seven intaglio cut topaz color glass circles, classic lady profile in circle arrangement, 2 1/2" d. **65-90**

Pin/pendant, gold-filled, snowflake motif set w/pink baguettes, marquise & diamond-shaped stones, 2" d.. **65-85**

Pin/pendant, gold-plated, antiqued, ornate snowflake set w/large topaz stones at center & each point, made in France, 3 1/2" d................... **100-125**

Pin/pendant, gold-plated, antiqued, oval red marquise center, smaller clear & red rhinestone frame, looped edge, signed "Hobé"............... **65-85**

Pin/pendant, Lucite, model of elephant, amber w/gold-plated ears, blanket & trim, 3 1/4".. **65-85**

Openwork Pin w/Purple Stones

Pin/pendant, rhinestone, rectangular openwork white metal setting w/assorted stones in shades of purple, alternating large pearl & glass drops in shades of purple, signed "Schreiner NY," 3 x 3 1/2" (ILLUS.)............. **275-300**

Pin/pendant, sterling, Art Nouveau style swirled ornate paisley design, ca. 1900, 1 3/4" d............. **50-75**

Pin/pendant, sterling silver, Art Nouveau style, bust of woman w/long hair, swirling flowers & vines, ca. 1890, 1 1/2".. **95-125**

Pin/pendant, sterling silver, design w/two horses facing each other over large oval black cabochon stone, 1 3/4 x 2".................. **100-125**

Pin/pendant, sterling silver, handmade abstract design w/polished grey shell center, signed "A. Idan." 2 1/4"..... **100-125**

Pins, enamel, h.p. figures of a girl & a boy publicizing movie "The 5000 Fingers of Dr. T," Columbia Pictures, set of two................ **125-150**

Ring, gold on sterling, dome style, blue & green enamel border, clear rhinestone-set diamond design, signed "Jomaz"................ **85-115**

Ring, gold-filled, large emerald-cut purple stone, 1"...... **75-100**

Ring, gold-plated & rhinestone, high dome style, latticework design w/amber rhinestones in each section, signed "Trifari"............ **30-45**

Ring, sterling silver, cabochon amethyst & marcasites, 1" w. **75-100**

Ring, sterling silver, cigar band style w/large ruby red center cabochon stone, two wide citrine color cabochons, applied curved designs on dark background, 1" w. **40-55**

Ring, sterling silver, filigree design w/large marquise crystal stone............ **80-100**

Ring, sterling silver, raised oval blue topaz center, tiny sapphires at sides............... **125-150**

Ring, sterling silver, shell cameo framed w/rhinestones, signed "Martelli," 1" w., adjustable **65-95**

Art Nouveau Sash Pin

Sash pin, enamel on sterling, Art Nouveau style, shaded enamel leaf motif (ILLUS.) **225-250**

Sets

Art Deco Style Bracelet & Clip

Bracelet & clip, rhinestone, Art Deco style, the wide bracelet center set w/blue & clear rhinestones, together w/matching shield-shaped clip, gold metal mount, McClelland, the set (ILLUS.) **575-600**

Bracelet, clip & pin, copper, cuff style bracelet & clip w/three-leaf design, matching screw-on earrings, signed "Rebajes," the set **175-200**

Bracelet & Earrings w/Amethyst

Bracelet & earrings, metal, ornate gold metalwork links, center link set w/faux amethyst, matching pair of 1 1/2" l. drop earrings w/center-set faux amethyst, the set (ILLUS.) **75-95**

Festoon Style Necklace

Bracelet & necklace, gold-plated, festoon style necklace w/multi-row chains, antiqued center circular motif w/large green stone, matching 1 5/8" w. bracelet, unsigned designer quality, necklace 17 1/2" l., the set (ILLUS. of necklace) **250-275**

Bracelet, necklace & earrings, rhinestone, necklace w/two rows of stones w/fancy gold chain between, matching 3/4" w. bracelet & pair of 1 1/2" screw-on earrings, adjustable necklace 14" l., the set **65-90**

Clip & earrings, rhinestone, scalloped shell design set w/baguette rows of rhinestones, matching pair of 1" w. shell earrings, clip 1 1/2", the set **65-85**

Clip & necklace, gold-plated & rhinestone, Retro style diamond-shaped motif necklace set w/green diamond-shaped rhinestones on snakechain, matching pair of 2 3/4" clip-on earrings, signed "Trifari," the necklace 15" l., the set **175-200**

Earrings & pin, Bakelite, amber circles, 1 1/2" d. w/gold metal seahorses in center, matching 3/4" d. clip-on earrings, signed "JHP Paris, Made in France," the set **75-100**

Earrings & pin, gold-plated & plastic, dome style openwork pin, large coral cabochon in center of three rows of individually set coral & white plastic dome-shaped cabochons w/matching pair of 1" clip-on earrings, signed "KJL," the pin 2 3/4" d., the set **100-125**

Earrings & pin, gold-plated, Retro style ribbon circle motif w/"flying" ends, blue rhinestone trim, matching pair of 1" clip-on earrings, the pin 2 1/4", the set **50-75**

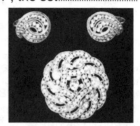

Rhinestone Pin & Earrings Set

Earrings & pin, metal & rhinestone, the pin in ornate gold metal openwork lacy circle design, together w/matching pair of 1" d. clip-on earrings, signed "Trifari," pin 1 3/4" d., the set (ILLUS.) **70-95**

Earrings & pin, pearl & red marquise stones, wreath design w/pair of matching clip-on 1" earrings, signed "B. David," on signed card, pin 1 3/4" d., the set **50-75**

Earrings & pin, rhinestone, earrings w/red square & round individual cabochons, red Aurora Borealis accents, matching pair of 1 1/8" clip-on earrings, signed "Weiss," pin 1 7/8", the set **100-125**

Earrings & pin, rhinestone, model of American flag set w/red, clear & blue rhinestones, matching 2" screw-on rhinestone earrings, pin 3/8" l., the set **30-45**

Earrings & pin, rhinestone, ornate pin w/green, blue & turquoise stones, cabochon turquoise, matching 3" drop, w/matching pair of matching 1" clip-on earrings, signed "Art," the set **135-165**

Earrings & pin, rhinestone, Retro style coiled ribbon motif pin w/baguette-set flowers, matching pair of 1 1/2" d. clip-on earrings, signed "Corocraft," pin 2" d., the set.............. **90-120**

Necklace & bracelet, gold-plated swirled Retro style openwork links, signed "Monet Jewelers," bracelet 7" l, necklace 16" l., the set.......... **65-90**

Eisenberg Rhinestone Set

Necklace, bracelet & drop earrings: rhinestone, hand-set royal blue rhinestones w/clear rhinestone trim, necklace w/central large stones & drops, the bracelet w/double row of stones & a center design, matching clip-on earrings, signed "Eisenberg," earrings 1 3/4" l., necklace adjusts to 16", the set (ILLUS.) **565-600**

Necklace, bracelet & pin, gold-plated & rhinestone, matching set w/raised center floral motif set w/multicolored rhinestones, unsigned designer quality, necklace 15" l., bracelet 1 1/4" w., pin 2" d., the set.............. **375-400**

Necklace & earrings, bead, large & small green art glass beads & filigree white metal beads, 3" l. double green bead drop, matching pair of 1" l. teardrop screw-on earrings, necklace 28" l., the set **70-95**

Necklace & earrings, bead, the necklace w/double strand of red & clear faceted beads, large round red beads at center, w/pair of matching earrings, ca. 1940s, necklace 20" l., the set **60-90**

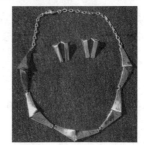

Renoir Copper Necklace & Earrings

Necklace & earrings, copper, Retro-style, 1950s, Renoir, the set (ILLUS.).............. **115-135**

Necklace & earrings: glass "jade" inside openwork gold, rhinestone pendant, green bead trim, matching clip earrings, signed "Kramer," necklace 24", the set **85**

Necklace & Earrings with Green Stones

Necklace & earrings, gold-plated chain composed of circular ropetwist & rectangular textured links, some set w/green rhinestones, five drops set w/large teardrop-shaped green art glass & amber & green rhinestone accents, ropetwist frame, the center drop further decorated w/three ropetwist links set w/small green stones, together w/matching pair of 2 3/4" l. drop earrings, necklace adjusts to 17" l., the set (ILLUS.).............. **250-300**

Necklace & earrings, gold-plated & rhinestone, adjustable necklace w/leaf-shaped links, pavé-set rhinestone trim, matching pair of 1" l. clip-on earrings, signed "Carnegie," the set **140-165**

Necklace & earrings, metal & glass, oval design set w/green iridescent art glass, hand-set silver stones on chain together w/pair of 2" l. matching drop earrings, unsigned designer quality, necklace adjusts to 16" l., the set **150-175**

Necklace & earrings, rhinestone, bib style w/large multicolored stones in oval center, earrings match oval center, clip-ons, 2", necklace 16" l., the set (unsigned, designer quality) **85-115**

Necklace & earrings, rhinestone & glass, necklace w/center mottled green cabochon art glass motif under gold filigreework w/center emerald green rhinestones, light green marquise cabochon trim, matching 1" pair of large green art glass clip-on earrings, unsigned designer quality, necklace 15" l., the set........................... **100-125**

Necklace & earrings, sterling silver, Retro-style baguettes, openwork design w/drop, pair of 1 1/2" l. matching drop earrings, signed "Carl-Art," necklace 16" l., the set **90-120**

Aurora Borealis Necklace, Brooch & Earrings

Necklace, earrings & brooch, rhinestone, the necklace composed of Aurora Borealis beads suspending a round pendant w/center-set large rhinestone surrounded by smaller stones, the 1 1/2" brooch & 3/4" d. earrings match the drop, necklace 20" l., the set (ILLUS.)................................ **300**

Necklace & fur clip, gold-plated, 14" snake chain necklace w/diamond-shaped center set w/emerald green diamond-shaped rhinestones, raised gold centerpiece leading to chain, matching 2 3/4" clip, signed "Trifari," the set...................... **150-165**

Rhinestone Necklace and Pin

Necklace & pin: rhinestone, faux cabochon sapphire links w/hand-set clear rhinestone borders, the necklace w/a single row of the sapphires & the pin w/five drops, signed "Kramer," necklace adjusts to 15", pin 3" h., the set (ILLUS.) **425-450**

Gold & Enamel Turtle Set

Necklace & pins, enamel on gold, 3" l. white figural turtle on 17" chain, matching scatter pins 1 1/2" l., signed "Miriam Haskell," the set (ILLUS.)................................. **295-365**

Pendant necklace & pins, gold-plated metal & enamel, pendant modeled as a turtle w/white enamel shell w/two matching 1 1/2" turtle scatter pins, ca. 1950, signed "Miriam Haskell," pendant 2 3/4" l., chain 18" l., the set **385-425**

Pin & earrings, brushed gold, sunflower centered w/large open-set topaz glass stone, matching clip-on earrings, 1" d., pin 3" d., the set (unsigned, designer quality) **75-95**

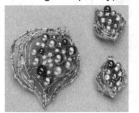

Goldplate and Faux Pearls Set

Pin & earrings, goldplated metal, a design of openwork branches, the center w/a design of blue & grey pearls w/rhinestone trim, signed "Gasty Paris," manufactured by Grosse, dated "1969," earrings 1" w., pin 2" d., the set (ILLUS.) **100-125**

Amber Glass Pin & Earring Set

Pin & earrings, metal & glass, the pin designed as a flower w/swirled detailed gold metal petals centered w/a large amber glass stone, together w/pair of matching earrings, unsigned, the set (ILLUS.) **120-145**

Pin & fur clips, pink gold on sterling silver, flying birds motif w/rhinestone trim on body & wings, signed "Sterling Coro-Craft," pin 2", clips, 1 1/2", the set...........................**275-300**

Pins, gold & rhinestone, antiqued figures of musicians, one playing flute & the other a mandolin, clear, blue & green rhinestone trim, signed "Hobé," 2 1/2" h., pr. **120-145**

Modern (1920-1960s)

Bar brooch, diamond, Art Deco style, bow design w/one collet-set round diamond & 18 bead-set round diamonds, platinum mount, signed "Tiffany & Co."..............**2,645**

Jasper Bar Pin

Bar pin, carved jasper & 14k gold, depicting the profile of a Native American Indian chief, headdress composed of finely engraved rose & yellow gold feathers & highlighted by seven rose-cut diamonds, a single seed pearl suspended from his collar, w/original box (ILLUS.)...........**1,840**

Bar pin, diamond, Art Deco style, an openwork platinum mount w/pointed ends set w/old mine-cut diamonds, beaded accents, signed "Tiffany & Co."......................................**4,600**

Art Deco Diamond & Onyx Bar Pin

Bar pin, diamond, black onyx & platinum, Art Deco style, the narrow rectangular platinum mount w/a central shield-form openwork design set w/two old mine-cut diamonds each weighing about .75 & .60 carats alternating w/four rectangular & one calibré-cut onyx stones, flanking the central design are 14 square scissor-cut black onyx stones, ca. 1930, 3" l. (ILLUS.) **1,840**

Bar pin, diamond & gold, Art Deco style, 14k white gold filigree openwork mount set w/one old mine-cut diamond weighing about .55 carats, ca. 1930, 2 1/2" l. **489**

Bar pin, diamond, platinum & 14k white gold, Art Deco style, filigree openwork form set w/nine round old European-cut diamonds, ca. 1930, 2 1/2" l. **403**

Bar pin, diamond & platinum, Art Deco style, bead-set w/three old mine-cut diamonds in a geometric mount, further enhanced by bead-set round diamonds, millegrain accents (dents to gallery) **1,380**

Bar pin, diamond & platinum, Art Deco style, reticulated filigree design set w/five old mine- & old European-cut diamonds, ca. 1920-30, 2 1/4" l. **748**

Bar pin, diamond & platinum, Art Deco style, the filigree openwork mount centered by one old mine-cut diamond weighing about .50 carats flanked by 21 graduated old mine-cut diamonds weighing about .85 carats, ca. 1930, 3 1/2" l. (repairs to mount) **748**

Bar pin, diamond & sapphire, Art Deco style, narrow lozenge shape centrally set w/a sugar loaf cabochon sapphire weighing 1.5 cts. within a background of round, single- cut diamonds, the borders decorated w/faceted calibré-cut sapphires, mounted in platinum, France (replaced 14k yellow gold clasp)................................. **5,060**

Bar pin, platinum & diamond, Art Deco style, a curved tapering design set w/105 old European- & single-cut diamonds, filigree mount w/millegrain accents, yellow gold pin stem **3,565**

Art Deco Diamond Bar Pin

Bar pin, platinum & diamond, Art Deco style, central diamond-shaped motif set w/an old mine-cut diamond, surrounded by 54 graduated old mine- & rose-cut diamonds, ca. 1920-30, 3 1/4" l. (ILLUS.)...................... **2,185**

Bar pin, platinum & diamond, Art Deco style, set w/round diamonds within an openwork platinum mount w/millegrain accents, 14k yellow gold clasp **863**

Ruby & Diamond Bar Pin

Bar pin, ruby & diamond, yellow gold & silver scrolled openwork design alternately set w/five rubies & four round diamonds (ILLUS.) **920**

Bar pin, sapphire & diamond, Art Deco style, 12 square sapphires set in groups of three spaced by six old European-cut diamonds, platinum mount w/millegrain accents (one sapphire missing) .. **920**

Bar pin, sapphire & diamond, Art Deco style, 12 square sapphires set in groups of three spaced by six old European-cut diamonds, platinum mount w/millegrain accents (one sapphire missing).. **920**

Sapphire & Diamond Bar Pin

Bar pin, sapphire & diamond, Art Deco style, centered by a transitional-cut diamond flanked by calibré-cut sapphires within a diamond-set mount w/millegrain accents, missing two diamonds (ILLUS.)... **863**

Art Deco Sapphire & Diamond Bar Pin

Bar pin, sapphire & diamond, Art Deco style, long narrow form set in the center w/three old European-cut diamonds, accented w/four French baguette-cut sapphires w/diamond-set flower heads, flanked by 12 French baguette-cut sapphires, mounted in platinum w/a 14k yellow gold pin, ca. 1930s (ILLUS.)................................. **4,485**

Bar pin, sapphire & pearl, Art Deco style set w/nine round faceted blue sapphires alternating w/eight baroque pearls, 14k yellow gold mount, ca. 1935............................ **431**

Belt buckle, silver, chased w/blossoms, center inlaid w/malachite, 19th c., Tibet, 3" l. **100-150**

Belt buckle, silver, oval, decorated w/plum blossoms, ca. 1920, Japan **175-225**

Belt buckle, silver w/turquoise stones, filigree scrolls, Nepal, 6" d.......................... **375-450**

Sterling Silver & Amethyst Bracelet

Bracelet, amethyst quartz & sterling silver, nine bezel-set pear-shaped amethyst cabochons mounted on sterling silver "X" links, partially obliterated Mexican hallmark, 7 1/2" l. (ILLUS. of part)............. **288**

Bakelite Cuff Bracelet

Bracelet, Bakelite & faux pearl, cuff-style, hinged design w/an abstract foliate motif of carved green Bakelite set w/faux golden pearls (ILLUS.) **2,185**

Bakelite "School Days" Charm Bracelet

Bracelet, Bakelite "School Days" charm-type, the links designed as rulers suspending seven plastic, Bakelite or felt school-related charms (ILLUS.).. **345**

Bracelet, bangle-type, Bakelite, hinged & surmounted by a green Bakelite & brown wood turtle **316**

Diamond & Sapphire Bangle Bracelet

Bracelet, bangle-type, diamond, sapphire & enamel, centered by a collet-set diamond flanked by eight diamonds w/sapphire terminals, further set w/old European-cut diamonds framed w/blue enamel, hinged platinum-topped 14k yellow gold mount, solder evident. ca. 1966 (ILLUS.)... **3,220**

Bracelet, bangle-type, garnet, hinged design set w/three rows of faceted garnets, gilt-metal mount **288**

Bracelet, bangle-type, gold (14k yellow), pearl & amethyst, the top portion of the bracelet set w/five oval faceted amethysts alternating w/eight graduated cultured pearls, ca. 1950 .... **374**

Bracelet, bangle-type, jadeite, mottled apple green, interior measurement 60 mm. ca. 1920, China (cracked)
.... **4,500-6,500**

Bracelet, bangle-type, onyx & diamond, Art Deco style, channel-set alternating pattern of French-cut onyx & old European- & single-cut diamonds, platinum-topped 18k yellow gold mount, 7" d. (out of round, solder evident due to sizing) **2,300**

Bracelet, bangle-type, onyx, emerald & diamond, onyx bangle surmounted by a geometric design of calibré-cut emeralds & old European-cut diamonds set in platinum, millegrain accents, signed "Ghiso," accompanied w/statement that bracelet was made by Alberto Ghiso (one emerald missing, some abraided) **5,463**

Bracelet, bone & jade, six expandable disks of petrified whalebone spaced by jade saddles, signed "Bakers, Nome, AK.." ca. 1950 .... **690**

Musical Instrument Charm Bracelet

Bracelet, charm-type, gold, the oval link chain suspending seven musical instrument charms, two marked "Italy" & two signed "Tiffany & Co.," all in 14k yellow gold, 7" l. (ILLUS.) **805**

Bracelet, crystal, sapphire, diamond, gold & platinum, Art Deco style, the 14k yellow gold & platinum top flexible mount w/five square links each w/a sunburst-etched frosted crystal panel & set w/one round old European-cut diamond weighing about .08 carats alternating w/five oval openwork links each set w/one square French-cut blue sapphire weighing about .10 carats, ca. 1930, 7 1/2" l **1,840**

Bracelet, diamond, Art Deco style, centered by a row of calibré-cut synthetic sapphires, flanked by two rows of round-cut diamonds, platinum mount **3,795**

Bracelet, diamond, Art Deco style, composed of ten circular links, each set w/old European-cut diamonds, separated by ten bezel-set old European-cut diamonds w/a total weight of 5 cts., signed by Cartier, France, ca. 1930s, 7 1/2" l **18,400**

Bracelet, diamond, Art Deco style, composed of three large rectangular segments each centering a marquise-shaped brilliant-cut diamond weighing .75 ct. & flanked by straight baguette diamonds surrounded by round diamonds w/round-cut diamonds forming the borders, each segment separated by an open diamond-set link, total weight of marquises 2.25 cts., baguettes 1.10 cts. & round diamonds 11.50 cts., mounted in platinum, 7" l. **11,500**

Bracelet, diamond, Art Deco style, segmented, flexible strap w/a repeating design centering a single marquise-shaped brilliant-cut diamond weighing approx. 0.75 ct. & bead-set w/217 round-cut diamonds weighing approx. 9.0 cts., mounted in platinum, 6 1/4" l. (two small diamonds missing) **11,500**

Art Deco Style Diamond Bracelet

Bracelet, diamond, Art Deco style, wide design w/three repeated rectangular-shaped sections, each centrally set w/an old European-cut diamond having a total weight of approx. 2.0 cts., each section pavé-set w/round diamonds, including open, rectangular-shaped links & barrel-shaped connectors, the diamonds having a total weight of approx. 18 cts., mounted in platinum, two small stones missing, 7 3/4" l. (ILLUS. of one section) **16,675**

Bracelet, diamond & emerald, flexible, strap-type having a repeated eye-shaped motif set w/round diamonds & bordered by round diamonds, separated by two pairs of baguette-cut emeralds, mounted in platinum, ca. 1920, 7" l. (two of the 14 emeralds are simulated) **5,290**

Bracelet, diamond & emerald, flexible, w/a repeating motif composed of two triangle-shaped, faceted emeralds set base to base on a slightly bombé background of pavé-set old European-cut diamonds, mounted in platinum, ca. 1925, 7 1/2" l. (three emeralds replaced w/emerald simulants) **4,830**

Bracelet, diamond, emerald & platinum, Art Deco style, center plaque set w/a marquise diamond, flexibly-set throughout w/72 single- & full-cut diamonds, calibré-cut emerald accents, 7" l. (one emerald missing) **5,463**

Art Deco Filigree & Diamond Bracelet

Bracelet, diamond & gold, Art Deco style, slender 14k filigree white gold openwork flexible mount, the center portion set w/five single & two old European-cut diamonds weighing about .65 carats, ca. 1930, 6 3/4" l. (ILLUS.) **633**

Bracelet, diamond, onyx & platinum, Art Deco style, centered by an old European-cut diamond flanked by flexibly set geometric plaques decorated w/72 diamonds, edged w/calibré-cut onyx, millegrain accents, 6 5/8" l. (one onyx missing) . **8,338**

Bracelet, diamond & platinum, Art Deco design w/28 squares set w/single-cut diamonds, black enamel diagonal pattern, French hallmarks, numbered 50504, 7" l. (some enamel missing) **24,150**

Art Deco Diamond Bracelet

Bracelet, diamond & platinum, Art Deco style, centered by a bead-set round diamond, accented w/46 round diamonds in a pierced, square link bracelet w/29 bead-set round diamonds, one diamond missing (ILLUS.) **3,738**

Bracelet, diamond & platinum, Art Deco style, designed w/three modified rectangular sections, each centering three marquise-cut diamonds connected by rectangular diamond-set links, ca. 1920 .... **5,750**

Bracelet, diamond & platinum, Art Deco style flexible design composed of rectangular links alternating w/oval links set w/three round old European-cut & 176 smaller round old European-cut diamonds & joined by 12 baguette diamonds, ca. 1930, J.E. Caldwell & Co., 7" l. **9,200**

Bracelet, diamond & platinum, Art Deco style line design w/43 brilliant-cut slightly graduated diamonds set in engraved box links, 6 3/8" l. **7,475**

Bracelet, diamond & platinum, Art Deco style, line-type w/34 box-set circular-cut diamonds, divided into three segments by two French-cut synthetic sapphire accents, engraved gallery, 6 1/2" l. **2,645**

Diamond & Platinum Bracelet

Bracelet, diamond & platinum, centered by a spray of eight marquise & bead-set diamonds framed by straight baguettes, flanked by an openwork, graduated flexible band set throughout w/bead-set diamonds, ca. 1950, 6 1/4" l. (ILLUS.) **3,335**

Bracelet, diamond, ruby & platinum, Art Deco style, designed w/geometric plaques set w/round diamonds, enhanced by channel-set ruby links, together w/two extra plaques, in fitted box for Cartier, 6 1/2" l. **12,650**

Bracelet, diamond, sapphire & platinum, Art Deco style, centered by an old European-cut diamond & approximately 140 full-cut diamonds & 22 calibré-cut sapphires in flexible geometric plaques, fancy engraved gallery, 6 1/2" l. **5,463**

Bracelet, emerald & diamond, the central portion containing a square emerald-cut Columbian emerald, flanked on each side w/a row of tapering, calibré-cut emeralds bordered by round single-cut diamonds w/a single row of old mine-cut diamonds on either side, mounted in platinum, 6 3/4" l. **11,500**

Bracelet, gold (14k rose & yellow), Retro style, wide abstract rose gold links, yellow gold reeded spacers, signed "Tiffany & Co." **2,990**

Bracelet, gold (14k yellow), Retro style, wide honeycomb link design w/buckle motif closure set w/diamonds & sapphires **2,300**

Bracelet, gold (18k pink) & diamond, Retro style, flexible double row of articulated tread design, the 18 square-shaped links set w/round brilliant-cut diamonds, French hallmarks, 7 1/2" l. **3,220**

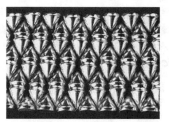

Retro Style Gold Bracelet

Bracelet, gold (18k yellow), Retro style, wide fancy link design, 14k gold tongue, hallmark, 84.30 dwt. (ILLUS. of part)............................... **2,070**

Bracelet, gold & aquamarine, 14k white gold oval links alternating w/prong-set faceted cushion-cut aquamarines, 8" l............................ **575**

Bracelet, gold & garnet, Retro style, belt-form, the 14k yellow gold braided & curb-link band w/a polished yellow gold buckle design, set w/four round faceted garnets weighing about .40 carats, ca. 1940, 1" w., 7 1/4" l. (repairs to two garnet mounts)......................... **518**

Bracelet, gold, Retro style, 18k polished yellow gold belt & buckle style w/buckle-form clasp, adjustable, ca. 1940, 3/4" w., 8" l......................... **575**

Large Gold Retro Bracelet

Bracelet, gold, Retro style, composed of large 14k yellow gold faceted arched rectangular flexible links, ca. 1940, 1 1/4 x 7 1/4" (ILLUS.).. **316**

Bracelet, gold, Retro style consisting of center row of domed rectangular 18k yellow gold links flanked by a row of triangular 18k yellow gold links, French import marks, 105.6 dwt....................... **2,760**

Bracelet, gold, ruby & sapphire, alternating oval & rectangular 14k yellow gold plaques set w/square-cut rubies & faceted oval sapphires, gold bead accents, stamped "BH" **345**

Bracelet, gold, wide strap-form, 14k florentine & polished finish yellow gold flat flexible band, ca. 1960, 3/4" w., 7 1/2" l. **403**

Bracelet, hemitite & gold, Art Moderne design w/cut-corner 18k yellow gold square plaques centered by domed hematite cabochons, alternating w/reeded white gold rectangular links, French gold mark & maker's mark, signed "G. Fouquet, No. 20461," ca. 1930, 7 1/2" l. (rectangular links show minor evidence of gold solder, probably from original construction)................................. **35,650**

Art Deco Jade Bracelet

Bracelet, jade & enamel, Art Deco style, comprised of three carved jade plaques separated by openwork red & black enamel spacers, mounted in 14k yellow gold, hallmark for Carter, Gough & Co., Newark, inscribed & dated 1932, very minor enamel loss, 7" l. (ILLUS. of part)...............................**2,415**

Bracelet, komai, set w/seven rectangular medallions, plain silver links, each medallion w/a floral design in gold & silver, ca. 1930, Japan **700-900**

Bracelet, onyx & lapis, round onyx links, buff-top lapis spacers set in silver, French hallmark, 7 3/4" l. **1,725**

Bracelet, platinum & diamond, flexible mount w/14 rectangular links joined by 14 arched links set w/58 round old European- & single-cut diamonds, ca. 1920-30, 6 3/4" l. **4,850**

Platinum & Diamond Bracelet

Bracelet, platinum & diamond, hinged, flexible geometric plaques set throughout w/transitional-cut diamonds, spaced by plaques centered by square-cut diamonds & straight baguettes, ca. 1940, 6 1/2" l. (ILLUS.) **18,400**

Bracelet, platinum, sapphire & diamond, Art Deco style line type, designed w/an alternating pattern of four round brilliant-cut diamonds & five channel-set sapphires, engraved gallery **8,050**

Bracelet, platinum, sapphire & diamond, flexible design, the center eight tapered plaques set w/graduated oval sapphires alternating w/old European-cut diamonds, completed by an integral diamond-set band, 7" l. **4,715**

Bracelet, reverse intaglio crystal, equestrian theme consisting of a horse head, fox head & dog head links attached by stirrup & horseshoe motif links, 14k yellow gold, dated 1924, 6" l. **863**

Art Deco Ruby & Diamond Bracelet

Bracelet, ruby & diamond, Art Deco style, designed w/five cushion-cut rubies within diamond-set links, French platinum & gold hallmarks & maker's mark, No. 57938 (ILLUS.) **18,400**

Art Deco Ruby & Diamond Bracelet

Bracelet, ruby & diamond, Art Deco style, flexible bracelet w/two oval links center set w/oval cabochon rubies, framed by round old European-cut diamonds & flanked by links set w/round old European-cut, baguette & square-cut diamonds & alternating w/two sections of links set w/round old European-cut diamonds bordered by a total of 48 ruby beads, ca. 1920-30, J. E. Caldwell & Co., 7" l. (ILLUS.) **20,700**

Bracelet, ruby, diamond & platinum, the oval links connected by three square-cut rubies alternating w/a bead-set round diamond within a square mount, ca. 1930s, 7" l. **3,105**

Bracelet, silver, hinged-form, three rows of pierced rosettes & two large clusters of plain silver beads attached to the terminals, India **450-600**

Bracelet, silver & sodalite, an oval cabochon stone set in silver, marked "Mexico Sancho," mid-20th c., 8" l. **115**

Bracelet, sterling silver, cuff-type, a spiral form w/rows of lapped leaves highlighted w/beaded decoration, impressed mark "HL 925 Sterling Mexico - Taxco" w/an eagle & 3, 2 1/4" d. **173**

Bracelet, sterling silver, design w/three Harlequin masks decorated w/blue stone eyes, signed "Flato" **431**

Sterling Silver Bracelet

Bracelet, sterling silver, flexibly set scrolled & shaped plaques, signed "Spratling," ca. 1940s, 7 1/4" l. (ILLUS. of part) **920**

Art Deco Paste Band Bracelet

Bracelet, sterling silver & paste, Art Deco style, a floral motif w/multiple hinged plaques set w/colorless pastes, highlighted by a geometric design of green & black stones, French hallmarks, 7" l. (ILLUS.)............... **1,725**

Bracelet, sterling silver, seven rows of lozenge-shaped links w/beaded edge between links on first & last rows, No. 86, designed by Harald Nielsen, signed "Georg Jensen," Denmark, ca. 1945, together w/bill of sale from Georg Jensen, 1 1/4" w., 7 1/2" l.... **2,645**

Bracelet, sterling silver & shell, cuff-style, two ridged bands of silver surrounding a leaf-shaped insert of dark brown shell, decorated w/nine silver rivets, impressed "WS" script hallmark & 925, Spratling, Mexico, design created in 1958, 2 1/2" l... **1,840**

Sterling Silver Dove Bracelet

Bracelet, sterling silver, square form leaf & bead decorated links alternating w/openwork oval links centering a model of a dove, No. 14, signed "Georg Jensen," Denmark, 7" l. (ILLUS.).......... **1,035**

Bracelet, sterling silver, three domed links & three floral links, hallmark for Georg Jensen, No. 28 .... **633**

Gold Bracelet/Ring

Bracelet, Bakelite, "Philadelphia Bracelet," hinged bangle-type, amber w/multicolor spiky teeth **3,565**

Bracelet/ring, gold & gemstone, eight hinged engraved circular links that convert from a bracelet to a ring, the clasp forming the top of the ring w/two interchangeable gemstones, one a blue zircon, the other a citrine, French hallmarks (ILLUS.).. **805**

Bracelets, Bakelite, tapered rectangular links of overlapping carved Bakelite, each bracelet w/one green & brown link, the other 12 links all green, pr. **690**

Modern Wood & Ivory Bracelets

Bracelets, wood, ivory & 18k gold, hinged contemporary style, one w/a nephrite bar, the other w/a hematite bar, signed "Amalia del Ponte," numbered "2/50" & "3/50" & dated "1967," in original felt & leather box from Sculpture to Wear, New York, pr. (ILLUS.).. **2,415**

Brooch, aquamarine & diamond, Art Deco style, centered by an emerald-cut aquamarine encompassed by bead-set & baguette-cut diamonds within an openwork platinum frame **5,463**

Brooch, citrine & gold, Retro style, centered by a prong-set emerald-cut citrine highlighted by five round diamonds & eight round rubies within a bicolor 14k yellow gold scroll design **1,150**

Brooch, coral, gold & enamel, the 18k yellow gold mount set w/a large carved angel-skin coral rosebud above two green enameled-decorated leaves, ca. 1960, 2 1/2" l. **518**

Brooch, crystal, diamond & onyx, Art Deco style bow design w/etched crystal center, edged in calibré-cut onyx & diamonds, set in platinum, gold pin stem (two onyx missing) **2,070**

Brooch, diamond & 14k white gold, ribbon design centered by an old European-cut diamond, further set w/single-cut diamonds, three ribbon terminals set w/old European-cut diamonds, ca. 1940 .. **3,335**

Brooch, diamond & 18k bicolor gold, daffodil flowerhead design in pink gold, the leaves in green gold & the stamens & stem w/37 bead-set diamonds set in silver **1,093**

Brooch, diamond, angel-skin coral, gold & enamel, an 18k yellow & white gold star-shaped mount set w/a round angel-skin coral half-bead measuring 12.2 mm surrounded by 12 round brilliant-cut diamonds weighing about .60 carats, surrounded by 12 marquise cabochon lapis stones, the lower tier set w/six pear-shaped cabochon coral stones alternating w/six cobalt blue enamel decorated petals, ca. 1960, 1 1/4" d. **1,495**

Brooch, diamond, Art Deco style, filigree wing design set w/three large round old European-cut diamonds surrounded by 106 smaller round old European- & sin-

gle-cut diamonds & two baguette diamonds, ca. 1930, 2 1/2" w. **7,475**

Art Deco Diamond Plaque Brooch

Brooch, diamond, Art Deco style, oblong plaque-form, centering an old European-cut diamond weighing 1 ct. flanked by straight baguette-cut diamonds within an intricate frame of round & baguette-cut diamonds w/a total weight of 10.80 cts. for the round diamonds & 3.90 cts. for the baguettes, mounted in platinum w/an 18k white gold catch, French hallmarks (ILLUS.) **6,900**

Brooch, diamond, Art Deco style, rectangular pierced design forming stylized ribbon & bow motifs, set w/old mine-cut diamonds mounted in platinum, w/additional safety pin & chain, French hallmarks **2,185**

Brooch, diamond, Art Deco style, set throughout w/31 old European-cut diamonds in an openwork geometric mount w/millegrain accents . **1,495**

Art Deco Brooch

Brooch, diamond, coral & onyx, Art Deco style, a brilliant-cut diamond-set open geometric design centering an oval-shaped black onyx topped w/a cabochon-cut coral w/two half-moon-shaped coral designs each accented w/a narrow band of onyx, the diamonds having a total weight of approx. 1.30 cts., mounted in platinum w/a 14k white gold pin (ILLUS.) **2,530**

Diamond & Enamel Lily Brooch

Brooch, diamond & enamel, designed as a lily w/two pavé-set diamond leaves, polychrome guilloché enamel leaves & stem, further accented by 16 diamond stamen, 18k yellow gold, some loss to enamel, marked "Italy" (ILLUS.) **3,220**

Brooch, diamond, modeled as a bicycle w/movable parts & set w/128 round diamonds, 18k yellow gold mount, maker's mark **1,150**

Brooch, diamond & onyx, Art Deco style, centered by a collet-set European-cut diamond, flanked by an onyx & diamond-set tapering design, platinum mount w/millegrain accents, French hallmark (one onyx missing, minor solder to gallery) **8,050**

Brooch, diamond & platinum, Art Deco style, the oblong platinum filigree mount set w/one round old European-cut diamond weighing about .60 carats surrounded by 70 graduated round old European-cut diamonds weighing about 1.50 carats, ca. 1930, 3/4 x 2" **1,955**

Brooch, diamond & platinum, Art Deco style, the platinum openwork mount centered w/one round brilliant-cut diamond weighing about .40 carats set w/60 round brilliant-, old European- and single-cut diamonds weighing

about 2.50 carats suspending three teardrop tassels, the center of each suspending a fancy light to fancy brownish-yellow natural-colored briolette-cut diamond weighing about two carats surrounded by 49 round brilliant-cut diamonds weighing about 1.05 carats, 1 1/4 x 2" **9,200**

Brooch, diamond & sapphire, Art Deco style, lozenge-shaped bow design mounted w/old European-cut diamonds & calibré-set French-cut sapphires, ca. 1925 .... **3,220**

Diamond & Sapphire Brooch

Brooch, diamond & sapphire, Art Deco style, platinum oval reticulated filigree ribbon design set w/54 round old European- & single-cut diamonds & 22 square & rectangular cut sapphires, ca. 1930, 3/4 x 2" (ILLUS.) **3,220**

Art Deco Citrine Brooch

Brooch, diamond, sapphire & citrine, Art Deco style, the lozenge shape centered by a pear-shaped citrine flanked by three collet-set round citrines, w/French-cut sapphire terminals & round sapphire accents, within an openwork platinum mount bead-set w/old mine- & single-cut diamonds (ILLUS.) **3,450**

Brooch, diamond, sapphire & platinum, Art Deco style, the clipped-corner geometric plaque set w/approx. 127 old European- & full-cut diamonds, calibré-cut sapphire accents, pierced mount w/millegrain accents, French hallmarks **3,565**

Brooch, diamond, synthetic sapphire & 14k white gold, Art Deco style, oval filigreee w/sides tapering to a point, center set w/three round old European-cut diamond flanked by 16 square-cut synthetic blue sapphires, ca. 1930, 1 1/2" w. **575**

Brooch, emerald & diamond, Art Deco style, model of a small 1930s automobile centered by a slabbed emerald crystal, surrounded by round brilliant-cut diamonds on the body of the auto & tires, on a thin black onyx pavement, mounted in platinum, France **1,380**

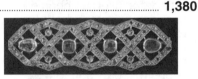

Emerald & Diamond Brooch

Brooch, emerald & diamond, two rectangular & two pear-shaped collet-set emeralds within an openwork geometric design set throughout w/rose-cut diamonds, silver-topped 14k yellow gold mount (ILLUS.) **690**

Gem-set Clip Brooch

Brooch, emerald, ruby & sapphire, clip-type, set w/cabochon emerald surrounded by cabochon rubies & carved sapphires, ca. 1940s, French assay & hallmark "H.L," Cartier, Paris (ILLUS.) **8,625**

Starburst Design Brooch

Brooch, gold (14k bicolor), aquamarine & ruby, designed as a rose & yellow gold starburst centered by a step-cut aquamarine, enhanced by six round-cut rubies (ILLUS.) **546**

Retro-style Butterfly Brooch

Brooch, gold (14k bicolor) & gemstone, designed as a butterfly w/diamond & colored gemstone accents, rose & yellow gold openwork mount, hallmarked (ILLUS.) **1,380**

Brooch, gold (14k bicolor), ruby & moonstone, Retro-style foliate & scroll design set w/three oval moonstones, ruby accents, signed "Trabert & Hoeffer, Mauboussin" **1,150**

American Painted Porcelain Jewelry

Watch chatelaine with portrait of woman, $115. Courtesy of Dorothy Kamm, Port St. Lucia, FL.

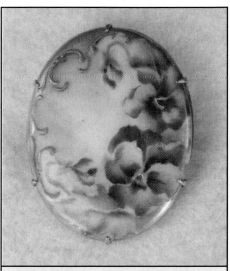

Brooch decorated with purple pansies, $75. Courtesy of Dorothy Kamm, Port St. Lucia, FL.

Shirt waist buttons decorated with roses, the set, $70. Courtesy of Dorothy Kamm, Port St. Lucia, FL.

Brooch decorated with forget-me-nots, $35. Courtesy of Dorothy Kamm, Port St. Lucia, FL.

Brooch & cuff links decorated with forget-me-nots, the set, $250. Courtesy of Dorothy Kamm, Port St. Lucia, FL.

Antique Jewelry

Edwardian Kashmir sapphire & diamond slide/brooch, $88,300. Courtesy of Skinner, Inc., Bolton, MA.

Elegant diamond pendant, ca. 1915, $9,200. Courtesy of Antiquorum Auctioneers, New York, NY.

Ruby & diamond ring, $5,750. Courtesy of Skinner, Inc., Bolton, MA.

Arts & Crafts jeweled brooch by Dorrie Nossiter, $3,680. Courtesy of Skinner, Inc., Bolton, MA.

Arts & Crafts coral & jeweled earrings, $2,070. Courtesy of Skinner, Inc., Bolton, MA.

Antique Jewelry

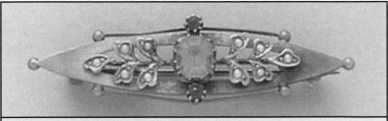

Victorian navette-shaped gold bar pin, $1,035. Courtesy of William Doyle Galleries, New York, NY.

Sapphire & diamond ring in heart-shaped frame, $11,500. Courtesy of Skinner, Inc., Bolton, MA.

Arts & Crafts moonstone & sapphire brooch, $2,645. Courtesy of Skinner, Inc., Bolton, MA.

Arts & Crafts jeweled wreath brooch by Dorrie Nossiter, $8,625. Courtesy of Skinner, Inc., Bolton, MA.

Art Nouveau plique-a-jour brooch, $18,400. Courtesy of Skinner, Inc., Bolton, MA.

Antique Jewelry

Exceptionally fine Belle Epoque diamond necklace, $36,800.
Courtesy of Antiquorum Auctioneers, New York, NY.

Tiffany antique jeweled
pendant/brooch, $63,000. Courtesy of
Skinner, Inc., Bolton, MA.

Diamond corsage brooch, ca. 1830,
$6,900. Courtesy of Antiquorum
Auctioneers, New York, NY.

Antique micromosaic necklace, $661. Courtesy of Skinner, Inc., Bolton, MA.

Natural pearl & ruby portrait locket, ca. 1810, $2,415. Courtesy of Antiquorum Auctioneers, New York, NY.

Art Nouveau figural dragonfly brooch, $2,645. Courtesy of Skinner, Inc., Bolton, MA.

Edwardian "Three Graces" cameo pendant/brooch, $325. Courtesy of DuMouchelle's, Detroit, MI.

Heart-shaped opal & fine diamond brooch/pendant, $1,840. Courtesy of Skinner, Inc., Bolton, MA.

Antique Jewelry

Antique natural pearl bee pin, ca. 1890, $1,725. Courtesy of Antiquorum Auctioneers, New York, NY.

Russian Art Nouveau ruby & diamond ring, ca. 1900, $1,265. Courtesy of Antiquorum Auctioneers, New York, NY.

Gold & amethyst cross, $1,035. Courtesy of Antiquorum Auctioneers, New York, NY.

Antique citrine, diamond & enamel bangle bracelet, $3,450. Courtesy of Antiquorum Auctioneers, New York, NY.

Antique Jewelry

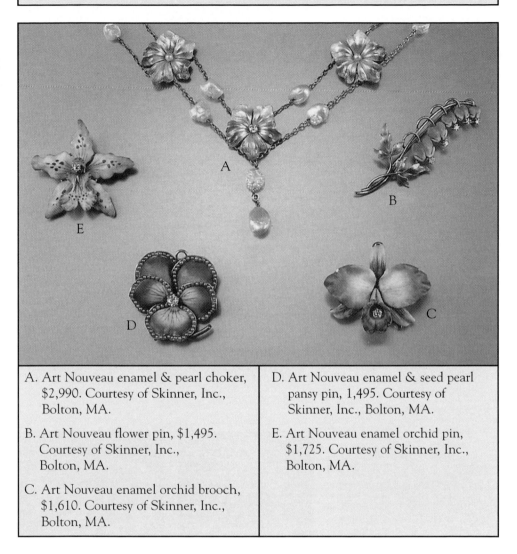

A. Art Nouveau enamel & pearl choker, $2,990. Courtesy of Skinner, Inc., Bolton, MA.

B. Art Nouveau flower pin, $1,495. Courtesy of Skinner, Inc., Bolton, MA.

C. Art Nouveau enamel orchid brooch, $1,610. Courtesy of Skinner, Inc., Bolton, MA.

D. Art Nouveau enamel & seed pearl pansy pin, 1,495. Courtesy of Skinner, Inc., Bolton, MA.

E. Art Nouveau enamel orchid pin, $1,725. Courtesy of Skinner, Inc., Bolton, MA.

Costume Jewelry

Carved wooden leaf pin suspending nuts with painted faces, $110-135. Courtesy of Marion Cohen, photo by Robert Cohen.

Hand-painted wooden figural pin of Chinese man carrying buckets, $125-150. Courtesy of Marion Cohen, photo by Robert Cohen.

Enamel on sterling Russian dancer pin, $150-175. Courtesy of Marion Cohen, photo by Robert Cohen.

Rhinestone & pearl pin/pendant by Schreiner of New York, $275-300. Courtesy of Marion Cohen, photo by Robert Cohen.

Rhinestone flower spray design pin by Staret, $500-525. Courtesy of Marion Cohen, photo by Robert Cohen.

Openwork bow design rhinestone clip, $125-150. Courtesy of Marion Cohen, photo by Robert Cohen.

Costume Jewelry

Rhinestone & art glass necklace & earring set, $250-300. Courtesy of Marion Cohen, photo by Robert Cohen.

Necklace with multiple gold-plated chains suspending elaborate four-part drop of pink art glass & amber stones with rhinestone accents, $1,00-1,200. Courtesy of Marion Cohen, photo by Robert Cohen.

Gold-plated filigree link & blue rhinestone necklace, $275-325. Courtesy of Marion Cohen, photo by Robert Cohen.

Art Deco style clip with rhinestones & iridescent green art glass stones, $90-120. Courtesy of Marion Cohen, photo by Robert Cohen.

Ornate white metal openwork pin set with faux topaz & multicolored "agate" stone border, $195-225. Courtesy of Marion Cohen, photo by Robert Cohen.

Three-dimensional bow design with large multicolored rhinestones by Lawrence Vrba, $600-700. Courtesy of Marion Cohen, photo by Robert Cohen.

Costume Jewelry

Gold-plated hinged link bracelet set with purple art glass stones, $175-200. Courtesy of Marion Cohen, photo by Robert Cohen.

Charm bracelet with six figural rosebud charms, $55-75. Courtesy of Marion Cohen, photo by Robert Cohen.

Gold metal filigree pin decorated with multicolored rhinestones, $125-150. Courtesy of Marion Cohen, photo by Robert Cohen.

Bangle bracelet decorated with purple rhinestones by Monet, $150-175. Courtesy of Marion Cohen, photo by Robert Cohen.

Gold-plated Flowerpot pin with five "stickpin" designs, $60-85. Courtesy of Marion Cohen, photo by Robert Cohen.

Bakelite clips with carved leaf design, $85-110. Courtesy of Marion Cohen, photo by Robert Cohen.

White metal openwork Christmas tree pin with red rhinestone & marcasite decoration, $55-75. Courtesy of Marion Cohen, photo by Robert Cohen.

Modern Jewelry

Art Deco & ruby diamond brooch, $10,120. Courtesy of Antiquorum Auctioneers, New York, NY.

Art Deco diamond & black onyx lapel watch, $8,050. Courtesy of Antiquorum Auctioneers, New York, NY.

Unusual sapphire & diamond ring, ca. 1930, $6,325. Courtesy of Antiquorum Auctioneers, New York, NY.

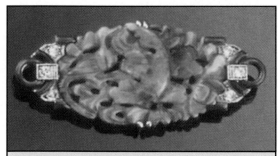

Art Deco jade brooch, $1,380. Courtesy of Skinner, Inc., Bolton, MA.

Natural pearl ear pendants, ca. 1930, $57,500. Courtesy of Antiquorum Auctioneers, New York, NY.

Modern Jewelry

Art Deco jade, moonstone & diamond double clip brooch & earclips, the set, $8,338. Courtesy of Skinner, Inc., Bolton, MA.

Art Deco diamond, coral & onyx brooch, $2,530. Courtesy of Antiquorum Auctioneers, New York, NY.

Art Deco jadeite jade & diamond brooch, $13,800. Courtesy of Antiquorum Auctioneers, New York, NY.

Art Deco ruby & diamond double clip brooch, $6,325. Courtesy of Skinner, Inc., Bolton, MA.

Art Deco sapphire, ruby & diamond double clip brooch, $4,600. Courtesy of Skinner, Inc., Bolton, MA.

Modern Jewelry

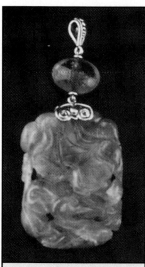

Carved jade & pink tourmaline pendant, $2,070. Courtesy of Skinner, Inc., Bolton, MA.

Retro-style gold & sapphire spray pendant, $1,380. Courtesy of Skinner, Inc., Bolton, MA.

Art Deco emerald & diamond pendant $9,200. Courtesy of Skinner, Inc., Bolton, MA.

Diamond & enamel figural brooch, $3,220. Courtesy of Skinner, Inc., Bolton, MA.

Art Deco tourmaline & diamond pendant, $9,200. Courtesy of Skinner, Inc., Bolton, MA.

Estate Jewelry

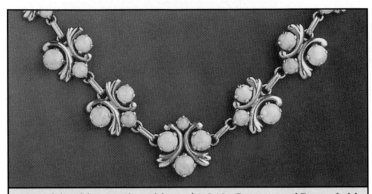

Beautiful gold & opal necklace, $1,840. Courtesy of Butterfield & Dunning Auctioneers, San Francisco, CA.

Large diamond double clip brooch, $14,950. Courtesy of Antiquorum Auctioneers, New York, NY.

Amusing aquamarine, ruby & diamond fish clip brooch, $3,200. Courtesy of Antiquorum Auctioneers, New York, NY.

Cultured freshwater pearl, tourmaline & peridot choker/clip brooch, $4,025. Courtesy of Antiquorum Auctioneers, New York, NY.

Estate Jewelry

Opal brooch design of birds in flight, $1,035. Courtesy of Butterfield & Dunning Auctioneers, San Francisco, CA.

Ruby & diamond cross-over design ring, $13,800. Courtesy of Antiquorum Auctioneers, New York, NY

Ribbon design diamond, emerald & sapphire clip brooch, $3,910. Courtesy of Antiquorum Auctioneers, New York, NY.

Ruby, diamond & gold bow pin with drop, $6,325. Courtesy of Skinner, inc., Bolton, MA.

Gold, ruby, emerald & diamond berry brooch, $3,738. Courtesy of Skinner, Inc., Bolton, MA.

Watches

Gold & enamel watch with horse portrait, $5,750. Courtesy of Antiquorum Auctioneers, New York, NY.

Cloisonné enamel floral decorated watch, $4,255. Courtesy of Antiquorum Auctioneers, New York, NY

Longines gold & garnet-set fob watch with matching clip, $1,380. Courtesy of Antiquorum Auctioneers, New York, NY.

Sterling silver & marcasite lapel watch, $265-295. Courtesy of Marion Cohen, Albertson, NY.

Antique enamel & diamond portrait pocket watch by Longines, $2,875. Courtesy of Skinner, Inc., Bolton, MA.

Brooch, gold (14k rose & green), Retro-style three loop bowknot design, ca. 1940, Larter & Sons, Newark, New Jersey............... **633**

Brooch, gold (14k rose), ruby & diamond, the flower design set w/round rubies & diamonds, 14k rose gold foliate mount, ca. 1940 .... **1,265**

Brooch, gold (14k tricolor) & zircon, openwork floral motif set w/two faceted blue zircons, ca. 1930s (minor abrasions)............................ **86**

Crown & Stickpin Brooch

Brooch, gold (14k yellow), crown design w/seven points, each set w/a cultured pearl w/seven stickpins protruding from crown, variously set w/rose-cut diamonds, paste baroque & seed pearls, a large buff-top amethyst & a round faceted aquamarine, ca. 1950 (ILLUS.)............................ **460**

Brooch, gold (14k yellow), Retro style, twisted ribbed ribbon design, gold bead terminals **546**

Brooch, gold (18k yellow), designed as an owl on a branch, detailed & textured feathers, green stone eyes, Italy (ILLUS.) **345**

Gold Abstract Bow Brooch

Brooch, gold (18k yellow), modeled as an abstract bow, the terminals bead-set w/round diamonds & channel-set w/emerald baguettes, French hallmarks (ILLUS.)............................. **748**

Brooch, gold (18k yellow), platinum & diamond, Art Deco style, openwork floral design set w/two large round old European-cut diamonds, the leaves set w/49 smaller round old European-cut diamonds, ca. 1930, Tiffany & Co., 1" w., 2" l. **3,220**

Brooch, gold (bicolor) & gemstones, Retro style butterfly design set w/diamonds & colored gemstone accents, 14k rose & yellow gold openwork mount, American hallmark................................ **1,380**

Brooch, gold & coral, designed as an 18k yellow gold branch w/four coral acorns (solder evident) **805**

Gold & Dendrite Agate Brooch

Gold Owl Brooch

Brooch, gold & dendrite agate, the landscape agate bezel-set in an abstract rectangular 18k yellow gold frame w/diamond accents, ca. 1955, Russian hallmarks (ILLUS.)............................... **920**

Gold & Diamond Floral Brooch

Brooch, gold & diamond, floral circle design, prong set w/seven round brilliant-cut diamonds, 14k yellow gold mount, hallmark (ILLUS.) **978**

Brooch, gold, Egyptian Revival style, the naturalistic-type faience scarab dating to the Egyptian Late Period, ca. 500 B.C., mounted in a winged 18k yellow gold frame flanked by cobras, signed "Blanchard, Cairo" **1,380**

Brooch, gold, Etruscan Revival style, bar pin top designed as the chariot of the sun w/lion's head terminals, suspending a capped tassel w/bead, palmette & ovoid drops, overall granulation & millegrain accents, signed "Giacinto Melillo, Napoli" (designed w/two figures of Victory, one missing, one detached)................................ **8,050**

Brooch, gold "figure 8," bicolor 14k gold concentric loops centered by rose gold bars, hallmarked for Lester **374**

Brooch, gold, jade, pearl & ruby, butterfly-form, a 14k yellow gold mount, the wings set w/two carved green jadeite panels, the body set w/two large cultured pearls

measuring 7.8 & 8.7 mm., the eyes set w/two round faceted rubies, ca. 1950, 2 1/4" w. **230**

Flowerpot Brooch

Brooch, gold, pearl & ruby, designed as a baroque pearl planter surmounted by spiky 18k yellow gold leaves, accented w/four prong-set round rubies (ILLUS.) **920**

Retro Style Gold Double Clip Brooch

Brooch, gold, Retro style double clip-type, in an abstract bird's wing & scroll motif, 14k yellow gold, hallmark for Larter (ILLUS.) **863**

Egyptian Revival Scarab Brooch

Brooch, hardstone & enamel, Egyptian Revival design of two polychrome enamel falcon wings centered by a collet-set hardstone scarab & flanked by two serpent heads, collet-set diamond accents, 14k yellow gold mount, signed "Schumann Sons" (ILLUS.) **2,070**

Art Deco Brooch

Brooch, hematite, crystal & marcasite, Art Deco style, rectangular sterling silver & marcasite frame center set w/quartz crystal & flanked by hematite, hallmarks for Theodor Fahrner (ILLUS.) **1,035**

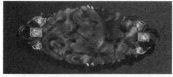

Art Deco Jade Brooch

Brooch, jade, Art Deco style, the oval jade plaque in a carved & pierced foliate design w/red & green enamel & diamond terminals, 14k white gold mount (ILLUS.)... **1,380**

Lily of the Valley Brooch

Brooch, jade, diamond & quartz, lily of the valley design w/carved jade leaf, flowers of carved quartz suspending prong-set round diamonds, 14k gold mount, marked "Made in Austria" (ILLUS.).............................. **1,495**

Jade & Diamond Brooch

Brooch, jadeite jade & diamond, Art Deco style carved jade plaque bordered on both ends w/old mine-cut diamonds, weighing approx. 3.75 cts., mounted in platinum-topped 18k white gold w/14k white gold pin (ILLUS.)............................ **13,800**

Water Lily Brooch

Brooch, mixed metal, modeled as a waterlily w/beaded center & leaves, chased & engraved 18k yellow gold, hammered silver leaves & lilypads, signed "Janiyé" (ILLUS.)............................ **345**

Brooch, moonstone & diamond, Retro-style, stylized floral spray set w/ten moonstones, 20 prong-set sapphires & 31 bead-set diamonds, platinum-topped 14k yellow gold mount, signed "Trabert & Hoeffer Mauboussin, Reflection, No. 4383" **5,175**

Onyx & Diamond Brooch

Brooch, onyx & diamond, Art Deco style, a calibré-cut onyx set in an openwork design edged w/37 round diamonds, platinum mount (ILLUS.)............................ **3,450**

Brooch, onyx & diamond, Art Deco style, onyx circle w/diamond-set 14k white gold bow accent............................ **518**

Art Deco Opal Brooch

Brooch, opal, garnet & ruby, Art Deco style, centered by an oval bezel-set opal within platinum & diamond open-work mount w/millegrain decoration set w/demantoid garnet & ruby florets, repair to back (ILLUS.)............................ **4,600**

Pearl Brooch

Brooch, pearl & silver, circular form set w/11 grey & cream pearls, flanked by an additional pearl at each end & alternating w/engraved leaves, scrolled vine holding center pearl, signed "S.I." w/hallmark for Mikimoto, ca. 1950s (ILLUS.).............................. **1,725**

Brooch, platinum & diamond, Art Deco style, oval form set w/graduated old European-cut diamonds, rectangular terminal centered by an old mine-cut diamond surrounded by diamonds, platinum mount... **2,875**

Double Clip Bird Brooch

Brooch, platinum & diamond, double clip-type, designed as two birds w/long curled tail feathers, encrusted w/single-cut diamonds, perched on a baguette diamond branch, red stone eyes, ca. 1940s (ILLUS.)...... **1,475**

Handcrafted Quartz Brooch

Brooch, quartz & 14k yellow gold, handcrafted large nugget-textured mount set w/a large quartz crystal rough set w/a blue/grey Baroque cultured pearl, marked "NKT.BRUYN," 2" w., 3 1/4" l. (ILLUS.)............................. **431**

Art Deco Double Clip Brooch

Brooch, ruby & diamond, Art Deco style, double clip-type, designed w/eight oval cabochon rubies & set throughout w/bead-set circular-cut diamonds, 12 baguette diamond accents, platinum mount (ILLUS.)............................. **6,325**

Art Deco Ruby & Diamond Brooch

Brooch, ruby & diamond, Art Deco style w/a center sugar loaf cabochon-cut ruby within a finely worked open frame decorated w/rose-cut diamonds, each end w/an old European-cut diamond, all within a border of small old European- and old mine-cut diamonds, two diamonds missing, mounted in platinum & 18k yellow gold (ILLUS.) **10,120**

Ruby & Diamond Flower Brooch

Brooch, ruby & diamond, designed as a flower bud highlighted by four circular-cut rubies & one circular-cut diamond, 18k yellow gold, Cartier (ILLUS.).................................. **1,150**

Retro Style Flower Brooch

Brooch, ruby & diamond, Retro style, designed as two flowers w/smooth gold petals & stem, the flowerhead accented w/prong-set rubies & diamonds, 14k yellow gold, Tiffany & Co. (ILLUS.) **1,380**

Brooch, sapphire & 14k yellow gold, designed as a Scottie dog, the body covered w/a coat of blue sapphires in various shapes, sizes & colors, collar & eye accented w/diamond melée **2,645**

Sapphire & Diamond Floral Brooch

Brooch, sapphire & diamond, floral bouquet design set w/21 round faceted blue sapphires & 18 round brilliant-cut diamonds, the stems set w/35 straight baguette diamonds, tied by a white gold knot set w/nine single-cut diamonds, platinum mount, ca. 1950, 1 1/4 x 2" (ILLUS.) **4,600**

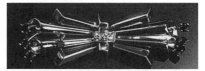

Retro Bicolor Sapphire Brooch

Brooch, sapphire & gold, Retro style stylized 14k yellow & rose gold bow centered by three bead-set diamonds mounted in platinum, circular & calibré-cut sapphire terminals, inscription on back (ILLUS.).. **1,725**

Art Deco Double Clip Brooch

Brooch, sapphire, ruby & diamond, Art Deco style, double clip-type, set w/marquise shield, round & baguette diamonds, ten carved oval cabochon sapphires & eight cabochon rubies, platinum & 18k gold mount (ILLUS.) **4,600**

Abstract Design Brooch

Brooch, silver glazed earthenware & fused glass, abstract design in shades of green & blue glaze, ceramic backing, abstract silver mount, impressed on reverse "Elsa" for Elsa Freund, ca. 1960 (ILLUS.)............................ **1,093**

Brooch, star sapphire & diamond, Art Deco style, bezel-set center star sapphire framed in old European-cut diamonds, platinum mount, signed "M. & Co." for Marcus & Co. **9,200**

Brooch, sterling silver, an abstract three dimensional multi-plaque butterfly designed by Nanna Ditzel, signed "Georg Jensen No. 335," ca. 1950s............................ **431**

Brooch, sterling silver, designed as a bird within a rectangular foliate & bead motif frame, hallmark for Georg Jensen, No. 204.............. **259**

Brooch, sterling silver, designed as a deer & squirrel on a square foliate border, signed "Georg Jensen, No. 318".. **374**

Sterling Silver Brooch

Brooch, sterling silver, designed as two leaves attached to a scrolling vine w/four round bead accents,

stamped "USA, No. 108," L.P. hallmark for Alphonse LaPaglia (ILLUS.)........................ **144**

Brooch, sterling silver & enamel, open amorphic form accented w/cobalt blue enamel, No. 323, by Henning Koppel for Georg Jensen **633**

Brooch, sterling silver & lapis, designed as a flower centered by a collet-set round lapis, three curving leaves & bead accent, hallmark for Georg Jensen, No. 71.............. **403**

Sterling Silver Deer Brooch

Brooch, sterling silver, model of a deer decorated w/an ivy vine, signed "Georg Jensen, No. 311" (ILLUS.)........................ **489**

Brooch, sterling silver & moonstone, designed as a dove within an openwork foliate circular frame, moonstone highlights, No. 123, signed "Georg Jensen" **546**

Silver & Moonstone Fuchsia Brooch

Brooch, sterling silver & moonstone, the fuchsia flower designed w/five flexibly set cabochon moonstone drops, signed "Sterling by Cini" (ILLUS.).................................. **748**

Sterling Silver Butterfly Brooch

Brooch, sterling silver, open round design depicting two butterflies & a flower, Georg Jensen, Denmark, No. 283 (ILLUS.)... **403**

Brooch, sterling silver, oval, scalloped & beaded edge w/openwork center decorated w/abstract grapevine design, No. 177, signed "Georg Jensen".. **546**

Silver Kingfisher Brooch

Brooch, sterling silver, rectangular frame decorated as a Kingfisher perched on a leafy branch, impressed "M" with a circle "Sterling Denmark 390," 1 3/4" d. (ILLUS.).. **460**

Brooch, sterling silver, the openwork design w/two acorns & an oak leaf, signed "Georg Jensen Inc. USA" & "L.P." for LaPaglia, No. 105..... **431**

Brooch, sterling silver, three curved bars below a small round silver bead surmounting a geometric form, signed "Ed Wiener," ca. 1950s **173**

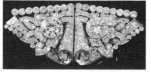
Diamond Brooch Clips

Brooch clips, diamond, a scrolled ribbon & floral motif, each clip centering a transitional old European- to round brilliant-cut diamond weighing approx. 3.75 cts., the leaves, scrolls & borders decorated w/124 round diamonds having a total weight of approx.7 cts., mounted in platinum w/18k white gold clip backs & brooch attachment, brooch attachment w/maker's mark, ca. 1930, Rome, pr. (ILLUS.)................ **25,300**

Art Deco Diamond Brooch/Pendant

Brooch/pendant, diamond, Art Deco style, bead-set w/old mine-cut diamonds within pierced platinum mount, retractable diamond bail (ILLUS.)................................. **3,105**

Brooch/pendant, diamond & pearl, pinwheel design centered by a prong-set round brilliant-cut diamond weighing approx. 0.26 cts., surrounded by 24 full-cut diamonds w/approx. total diamond weight of 1.36 cts., further enhanced by 56 seed pearls, mounted in 14k yellow gold, retractable bail, verso dated "1947"..................... **1,380**

Art Deco Brooch/Pendant

Brooch/pendant, diamond & platinum, Art Deco style, rectangular form centered by five circular-cut diamonds surrounded by 80 diamonds, further highlighted by a band of 32 calibré sapphires (ILLUS.).............................. **2,645**

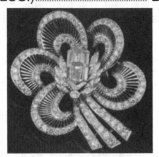

Diamond Brooch/Pendant

Brooch/pendant, diamond & platinum, designed as a flower, the center set w/two bullet-shaped, eight baguette-cut & nine marquise-cut diamonds, petals & stem set w/141 circular-cut diamonds, ca. 1950 (ILLUS.)................................. **5,520**

Retro-style Brooch/Pendant

Brooch/pendant, gold (14k yellow), diamond & ruby, Retro style, a domed circle bead-set w/six round rubies in a star motif w/a ribbon design at center highlighted by seven round diamonds, pendant loop, 22.9 dwt. (ILLUS.).. **690**

Brooch/pendant, gold & opal, large center opal surrounded by eight round opals on a shield-shaped filigree mounting, ca. 1940....................... **420**

Brooch/pendant, jade & diamond, Art Deco style, pierced & carved jadeite in the form of a gourd surrounded by an oval platinum frame set w/round diamonds & channel-set faceted onyx, diamond-set bail & slide, suspended from a black cord, w/box, 19" l. **5,463**

Sapphire & Diamond Brooch/Pendant

Brooch/pendant, sapphire & diamond, centered by a square sugarloaf sapphire suspended within a geometric & openwork platinum grille set throughout w/single & old European-cut diamonds, 14k white gold pin stem, ca. 1920s (ILLUS.)....... **1,380**

Buckle, enamel & sterling silver, Egyptian Revival, polychrome enameled openwork design based on pectoral from the tomb of Egyptian pharaoh Sesostris III, engraved on reverse, ca. 1920s... **431**

Cameo Bracelet

Cameo bracelet, shell, mother-of-pearl & onyx, eight oval cameos depicting classical female busts in 14k yellow gold wiretwist mounts spaced by textured roundels (ILLUS. of part)................................. **920**

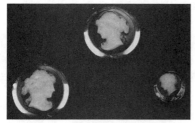

Hardstone Cameo Shirt Set

Cameo cuff buttons & shirt studs, hardstone, the cuff buttons & three shirt studs depicting the profile of a classical female, 14k yellow gold mount, stamped "S.L. & Co." for Savage, Lyman & Co., Montreal, w/original fitted box (ILLUS. of part)............. **805**

Art Deco Cameo Pendant/Brooch

Cameo Pendant/brooch, shell, Art Deco style, 14k yellow gold scalloped latticework decorated pentagonal mount set w/a large cameo depicting a seated classical woman w/a young child within a garden landscape, ca. 1930, 3 x 3 1/4" (ILLUS.) **316**

Cameo ring, hardstone, finely carved profile of a classical warrior surrounded by graduated collet-set diamonds, 18k yellow gold mount **460**

Chain, gold (14k yellow), double curb link, Tiffany & Co., ca. 1960, 20" l. **1,725**

Chain, gold (18k yellow), double-sided oval links w/fishhook clasp, 80" l. **920**

Choker, sterling silver, breast plate style, flat rectangular links in a graduating form, Mexico **1,265**

Art Deco Flower Basket Clip

Clip, diamond, emerald, ruby & sapphire, Art Deco style, designed as a flower basket encrusted w/circular & baguette diamonds, cabochon sapphire, carved emerald & ruby highlights, platinum mount (ILLUS.) **4,313**

Fine Diamond 'S' Clip

Clip, diamond & platinum, stylized 'S' form, the platinum mount set w/14 round brilliant-cut diamonds weighing about 4.90 carats, six emerald-cut diamonds weighing about 4 carats, two pear-shaped & four marquise-cut diamonds weighing about 2.90 carats, ca. 1960, 1 1/2 x 2" (ILLUS.) **5,750**

Clip, enamel & diamond, Art Deco style, designed as a sailboat w/light blue enamel sails, the hull set w/ten graduated single-cut diamonds, dark blue enamel sea, platinum mount (chips to enamel) **518**

Gold, Ruby & Diamond Christmas Tree Clip

Clip, gold (18k yellow), ruby & diamond, modeled as a stylized Christmas tree, the base set w/11 graduated old mine- & old European-cut diamonds, the body composed of circular swirls set w/42 round faceted rubies,ca. 1950, 1 1/2" w., 3" h. (ILLUS.) **1,495**

Clip, moonstone & tourmaline, Art Deco style, the geometric design surmounted by carved moonstone flowers w/collet-set diamond accents & carved green tourmaline leaves, 14k white gold, hallmark for Krementz (chip to one leaf) **575**

Turquoise & Aventurine Clip

Clip, turquoise & aventurine, flower design w/collet-set turquoise petals framing a round matrix turquoise completed by a carved aventurine leaf, 18k yellow gold mount, stamped "AVI Spain" (ILLUS.) **978**

Clip brooch, diamond, Art Deco style circular design w/a cascade motif, decorated w/two large old mine-cut diamonds w/a total weight of approx. 2.5 cts., w/old mine-, old European- & a few rose-cut diamonds, pavé-set within the circle & old mine single-cut diamonds bead set in the cascade, pin on back which allows it to be worn in two directions together w/hinged pendant bail, mounted in platinum w/18k white gold pin, accompanied w/thin neck chain, French hallmarks **4,255**

Retro Style Diamond & Ruby Clip/Brooch

Clip brooch, diamond, ruby & platinum, Retro style, pavé-set & circular-cut diamond-set caps surmounted by a similarly set swag, suspending a spray of 18 square-cut rubies & eight tapered baguette-cut ribbons, Austrian import assay marks, hallmark (ILLUS.) **4,715**

Retro Style Gold Clip Brooch

Clip brooch, gold (14k) & diamond, Retro style, rectangular form arranged w/contrasting rose & yellow gold in a stepped pattern, surmounted by circular & baguette-cut diamonds, signed "Cartier" (ILLUS.) **2,645**

Clip brooch, pearl & diamond, Art Deco style double clip, each half having a stylized scroll motif decorated w/seed pearls (several missing) & old mine-cut diamond accents, mounted in platinum & 14k white gold **3,220**

Clip brooch, ruby & diamond, Art Deco style double clip designed w/eight oval cabochon rubies & set throughout w/bead-set circular-cut diamonds, 12 baguette diamond accents, approx. total weight 2.85 cts., platinum mount **5,175**

Art Deco Double Clip Brooches

Clip brooches, emerald, sapphire, ruby & diamond, Art Deco 'tutti frutti' style, two-part rectangular form set in the center w/carved emeralds, sapphires, rubies & baguette-cut diamonds within a double row of round diamonds, diamonds total weight 2.2 cts., mounted in platinum w/18k white gold clip backs & brooch attachment, pr. (ILLUS.) **6,900**

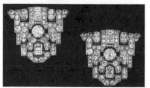

Art Deco Diamond Clips

Clips, diamond & platinum, Art Deco style, designed as chevrons centering a large round-cut diamond & enhanced w/numerous round brilliant-cut & emerald-cut diamonds, approx. 8.00 cts., pr. (ILLUS.) **21,850**

Clips, diamond & platinum, ribbon & scroll design set w/146 bead- & collet-set round brilliant- & single-cut diamonds, ca. 1940, pr. **4,025**

Compass pendant, gold & clear crystal, a 14k yellow gold mount set w/crystal front & back enclosing the compass movement, ring handle, outer casing inscribed "To Find Your Way Home, Maurice," England, ca. 1940, 1 1/2" d. ... **776**

Cuff links, diamond, enamel & platinum, Art Deco style, centered by four French-cut diamonds, framed by calibré-cut onyx & single-cut diamonds in a geometric design, millegrain accents, pr.. **7,763**

Gold Pistol Cuff Link

Cuff links, gold (14k yellow), modeled as a pistol w/revolving barrel, stamped "Jost," pr. (ILLUS. of one) **748**

Cuff links, gold (14k yellow), "Tragedy/Comedy," oval design depicting a frowning head & a smiling head on either side, pr. **1,035**

Cuff links, gold (15k) & moonstone, designed w/bezel-set oval moonstones, ca. 1920, pr. **575**

Cuff links, gold (18k yellow) & enamel, ball-shaped w/a center circle of yellow enamel, signed "Georg Jensen, No. 1099A," in original box, pr. **1,093**

Cuff links, gold (18k yellow), hollow circle centered by a bar, oblong monogrammed T-bar, signed "Georg Jensen, No. 1091," pr. **690**

Cuff links, gold, an 18k yellow gold scaly fish w/tiny ruby eyes suspended from a bamboo-form gold bar, Tiffany & Co., by Jean Schlumberger, ca. 1960, 1" l., pr. **1,495**

Cuff links, gold, moonstone & enamel, Art Deco style, a 14k yellow gold twin-oval mount set w/two oval cabochon moonstones measuring 7 x 10 mm, within a green to white enameled border, ca. 1935, pr. **1,093**

Cuff links, mother-of-pearl & enamel, the circular disk centrally set w/a cabochon blue stone, edged in cobalt blue enamel, mounted in 14k yellow gold, hallmark for Krementz, pr. **345**

Cuff links, Satsuma pottery, round, each set w/Satsuma design of a bamboo tree in green & gilt, ca. 1925, Japan, pr. **200-300**

Cuff links, silver, bird & berry motif, hallmark for Georg Jensen, No 43, ca. 1933-44, pr. **374**

Cuff links, sterling silver, domed rectangular form w/cut-out fish motif & copper eye accent, signed "Ed Wiener," pr. **345**

Cuff links, sterling silver, modeled as a zeppelin, No. 121, signed "Georg Jensen," pr. **345**

Dress clips, platinum & diamond, Art Deco style, set throughout w/100 old European-cut diamonds & ten baguettes in a pierced & millegrain mount stamped "N 9689" **5,463**

Ear studs, diamond & gold, Art Deco style, 14k white gold octagonal floral-deco-

rated mount set w/one round old European-cut diamond weighing about .45 carats, ca. 1930, pr. **1,840**

Earrings, agate & 14k yellow gold, Revival style, banded agate teardrop w/ropetwist & bead cap suspended from a gold roundel centered by a ropetwist flowerhead, 2 5/8" l., pr. **345**

Earrings, amethyst & diamond, Art Deco style, a faceted & fluted amethyst teardrop suspended from a platinum & diamond link chain, screw-on, signed "Tiffany & Co.," pr. **2,185**

Earrings, aquamarine & diamond, Art Deco style, oval aquamarine tops suspending a row of bead & collet-set diamonds in millegrain & platinum mounts terminating in claw-set pear-shaped aquamarines, pr. **3,565**

Earrings, diamond, Art Deco style pendant-type, each w/old mine-cut diamonds consisting of a center stone held in a geometrically designed diamond-set frame, suspending five rows of freehanging diamonds & attached to a tapered diamond-decorated bar which is joined to a diamond-set ear pad, mounted in platinum w/added 14k white gold posts, w/box, pr. **5,060**

Earrings, diamond & platinum, Art Deco style, centering a bezel-set braided form frame suspended from a bezel-set diamond, pr. **2,300**

Emerald Earring

Earrings, emerald, diamond & platinum, designed w/bezel-set circular old mine-cut diamond tops, suspending diamond-set trefoils & similarly styled caps terminating in tumbled pear-shaped emerald beads, ca. 1920s, missing end finials on terminals, in original S.J. Phillips fitted box, pr. (ILLUS. of one)...... **16,100**

Gold Dogwood Earrings

Earrings, gold (18k yellow), designed as dogwood blossoms, center w/gold bead decoration, French clip-back, Tiffany & Co., together w/original box, pr. (ILLUS.) **978**

Elegant Art Deco Jade Earrings

Earrings, jade & diamond, Art Deco style, a large carved mottled green & white jadite jade disk accented w/rose-cut diamonds in scrolled designs, suspended from round & rose-cut diamonds, mounted in platinum & 18k yellow gold, jade has some hairline cracks, ca. 1926, w/maker's mark, w/leather box, pr. (ILLUS.) **5,060**

Earrings, jade & diamond, Art Deco style, old European-cut diamond tops suspending elongated pear-shaped jade drops from a link chain, 14k yellow gold mount, screw-backs, boxed, 2 1/4" l., pr. **1,265**

Earrings, moonstone & ruby, center set w/a prong-set round moonstone, surrounded by round rubies, 14k yellow gold mount, pr. **633**

Earrings, onyx, carnelian & marcasite, Art Deco style, the marcasite-set terminals suspending a rectangular carnelian plaque & ovoid onyx drop w/marcasite accents, sterling silver mount, pr. **403**

Fine Natural Pearl Ear Pendants

Earrings, pearl, large pear-shaped natural pearl drops, each topped w/a round brilliant-cut diamond attached to a button-shaped pearl ear pad surrounded by round diamonds, can be worn independently without the detachable drops, mounted in 14k white gold, ca. 1930, w/original leather box & EGL report stating the pearls are saltwater natural pearls, pr. (ILLUS.) **57,500**

Earrings, platinum & diamond, designed as abstract bowknots set w/82 full-cut & baguette diamonds, ca. 1950, pr. **2,875**

Sapphire & Diamond Earrings

Earrings, sapphire & diamond, designed as a stylized bowknot, centered by an oval faceted sapphire w/channel-set sapphire & bead-set diamond highlights, 18k white gold, ca. 1940s, signed "Kutchinsky," pr. (ILLUS. of one) **2,875**

Hair comb, tortoiseshell, six long teeth, pierced & carved w/an oval panel of figures in a boat, 19th c., China, 4" w. **600-900**

Hat brooch, silver, a feather placed in an engraved pin designed as a bird, decorated w/swag inscribed "Virtutem Coronat Honos," hallmarks for Edinburgh, Scotland, ca. 1935, w/original box **104**

ID bracelet, gold & diamond, man's, a solid 14k yellow gold curb link mount centered by an arched panel w/raised white gold initials set w/a pavé of 21 round old mine-, European- and brilliant-cut diamonds weighing about 5 carats & joined by a tongue-in-groove clasp w/a thumb-pressure release set w/five old mine-cut diamonds weighing about .25 carats, ca. 1940, 9" l. **2,415**

Art Deco Jabot Arrow Pin

Jabot pin, onyx & diamond, Art Deco style, designed as an arrow w/calibré-cut onyx & rose-cut diamonds set in platinum mount (ILLUS.) **1,380**

Lapel pin, silver, rectangular form featuring two clasped hands over the continents of North & South America, impressed marks of Spratling of Mexico, mid-20th c., 3/4 x 1" **374**

Lavaliere, onyx & diamond, Art Deco style, three graduating bezel-set old European-cut diamonds within black onyx & platinum frames, suspended from a fine trace link chain (chain & pendant bail needs repair) **920**

Locket, gold (18k yellow), rectangular w/applied monogram, Austria **1,150**

Diamond & Crystal Lorgnette

Lorgnette, diamond & crystal, Art Deco style, the reverse intaglio depicting a dancer within a diamond & frosted crystal frame, diamond-set bail, completed by a platinum & collet-set diamond chain, 28" l. (ILLUS.) **8,625**

Art Deco Lorgnette

Lorgnette, diamond & platinum, Art Deco style, beadset round & rose-cut diamonds, French platinum mark (ILLUS.) **2,415**

Art Deco Diamond Lorgnette

Lorgnette, diamond & platinum, Art Deco style, filigree platinum openwork mount set w/28 round old European-cut diamonds, a hinged release opens to hinged eyeglasses, together w/a platinum chain set w/eight round old European-cut diamonds, ca. 1920, 19 1/2" l. (ILLUS.) **2,875**

Necklace, amber, 51 graduated ovoid honey colored beads, China **600-800**

Necklace, amber, comprised of butterscotch colored "rock" amber alternating oval & elliptical beads, purchased in 1922, 39" l. (some cracks) .. **316**

Art Deco Necklace

Necklace, aquamarine & platinum, Art Deco style large teardrop-shaped aquamarine pendant suspended from a platinum-topped 14k gold floral engraved box & rectangular link chain, hallmark for Allsopp & Allsopp, 15 1/2" l. (ILLUS.) **3,738**

Necklace, coral & jade, a carved urn-shaped jade suspended from jade links, attached to a cord w/coral rondelle spacers & seed pearl terminals, accented by two carved coral beads, ca. 1920s, 30" l. **546**

Art Deco Diamond & Ruby Necklace

Necklace, diamond & ruby, Art Deco style featuring a slightly graduating row of square-cut calibré rubies & round brilliant-cut diamonds, 18k white gold mounting, approx. diamond wt. 3.00 cts. (ILLUS.) **2,185**

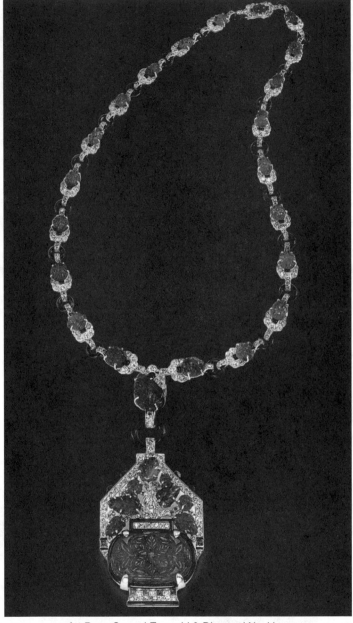

Art Deco Carved Emerald & Diamond Necklace

Necklace, emerald & diamond, Art Deco style, a large pendant in the Oriental flower vase motif designed from carved Columbian emeralds & round diamonds, w/black enamel & cabochon-cut emerald accents, joined by a black enamel loop to a similarly designed emerald, diamond & black enamel chain, mounted in platinum, numbered, w/French hallmarks & maker's mark, ca. 1925, Mauboussin, Paris (ILLUS.).. **167,500**

Necklace, gold (14k yellow), choker-type, gold bead & oval link design suspending 47 floral & arrowhead tassels joined by a yellow gold tongue-in-groove clasp, w/extra 1 1/4" l. links, ca. 1950, 14 1/2" l. **1,610**

Gold & Diamond Necklace

Necklace, gold (18k yellow) & diamond, designed w/an open circle & oval drop w/prong-set diamonds suspended from a pavé-set terminal, completed by a double barrel link chain w/collet-set diamonds, approx. total diamond wt. 2.40 cts., obliterated signature for Cartier, ca. 1950s (ILLUS.). **4,025**

Necklace, gold & cultured pearl, choker-type, 14k yellow gold twisted rope of gold wrapped w/a band of cultured pearls, ca. 1950, 15" l.... **489**

Necklace, jade, a strand of graduated jade beads, rose design clasp w/prong-set diamond center accent, 14k yellow gold, 25" l. **633**

Necklace, jade, lariat-type, oval-shaped jade within 14k gold & enamel frame suspending two teardrop-shaped jade drops suspended by a black cord, ca. 1930 .. **920**

Necklace, jadeite, diamond & seed pearl, Art Deco style, composed of delicately woven seed pearls w/four oval pierced & carved green jadeite plaques & suspending another larger elongated oval pierced & carved jadeite pendant w/a floral design, accented w/small round brilliant- and rose-cut diamonds, mounted in platinum, 17" l. **10,580**

Necklace, lapis lazuli beads flecked w/gold, 14k yellow gold clasp, 20" l. **546**

Necklace, pearl, 81 cultured pearls measuring approx. 8.40 to 8.90 mm., 14k gold clasp, 32" l. **805**

Necklace, pearl, choker-type composed of four strands of pink button-shaped pearls spaced by gold bars & clasp .. **748**

Necklace, pearl, double strand of 124 semi-baroque pearls measuring approx. 9.1 mm., completed by an Art Deco platinum, diamond & black opal clasp, later 14k white gold back & findings, 24" l. **6,325**

Necklace, ruby & diamond, Art Deco design featuring an oval link of square-cut rubies & a prong-set old mine-cut diamond linked w/two loops of rose-cut diamonds, millegrain accents, mounted in platinum w/yellow gold gallery, completed by a 14k white gold ropetwist chain, 15" l. (repairs) **805**

Necklace, silver-gilt, turquoise & coral, star-form w/deity in low relief in center, Nepal.. **50-100**

Abstract Design Necklace

Necklace, sterling silver, abstract open form links, designed by Henning Koppel, hallmark for Georg Jensen, ca. 1947, 15 1/2" l. (ILLUS. of part)............................ **1,150**

Necklace, sterling silver & amethyst, designed w/overlapping silver arcs suspending teardrop cabochon amethyst, signed "Antonio, Taxco, Mexico".. **920**

Necklace, sterling silver, curved row of ten stylized flowerhead links, No. 145, signed "La Paglia," 15" l............ **460**

Necklace, sterling silver, designed w/graduated convex disks accented by flat circular plaques, stamped "Taxco, Mexico"...................................... **230**

Necklace, sterling silver, elliptical form links, No. 171, signed "Georg Jensen," 15 3/8" l. **690**

Art Deco Sterling Marcasite Necklace

Necklace, sterling silver, quartz & marcasite, Art Deco style, designed w/marcasite-set hinged silver links centered by an abstract knot terminating in a faceted fancy shape smoky quartz, green stone accents, hallmarks for Theodor Fahrner (ILLUS.) ... **6,900**

Pearl enhancer, gold (18k yellow) & diamond, the stamped polished triangular form mount w/scalloped edge & set w/52 round brilliant-cut pavé-set diamonds **1,035**

Art Deco Style Crystal Pendant

Pendant, crystal, diamond & platinum, Art Deco style, the crystal reverse intaglio depicting a dancer within an openwork frame w/bead-set round diamonds, diamond-set bail (ILLUS.)........................... **2,990**

Art Deco Pavé Diamond Ball Pendant

Pendant, diamond, Art Deco style, pavé-set diamond ball, diamond bail, platinum mount (ILLUS.) **5,980**

Pendant, diamond & gold, solitaire, the 14k yellow gold four-prong A-Box mount set w/one round old European-cut diamond weighing about 1.40 carats.................................. **5,060**

Pendant, diamond & pearl, Art Deco style, designed as an openwork bell-shaped cap bead-set w/old European- and full-cut diamonds & a row of channel-set square-cut sapphires, diamond-set bail, platinum mount, suspending a multi-strand seed pearl tassel, Tiffany & Co. partially obliterated signature.. **3,220**

Pendant, diamond & platinum, Art Deco style, an old European-cut diamond within an onyx circular frame, further enhanced by three collet-set old European-cut & 36 rose-cut diamonds within a pierced & millegrain mount, suspended from a trace link chain, 16" l. **2,300**

Art Deco Diamond & Sapphire Pendant

Pendant, diamond & sapphire, Art Deco style, elongated flared design composed of four moveable sections decorated w/round diamonds w/baguette-cut, triangular-shaped & calibré-cut sapphires set in geometric designs, attached to a fine link chain w/rectangular-shaped, barrel clasp decorated w/two small diamonds, two triangular-shaped & two baguette-cut sapphires, platinum mounting & chain, approximately 21 1/2" l. (ILLUS.) **4,830**

Emerald & Diamond Pendant

Pendant, emerald & diamond, Art Deco style, a collet-set old mine-cut diamond suspending a cut-corner square-cut emerald set in 18k yellow gold within a quatrefoil frame of bead-set old mine-cut diamonds, platinum mount, surface nicks to emerald, completed by a rectangular trace link platinum chain, 17" l. (ILLUS.)..... **9,200**

Art Deco Style Pendant

Pendant, enamel & onyx, Art Deco style, navette-shaped silver, ivory & black enamel plaque centered by a sugarloaf onyx, marcasite highlights, suspended from a black cord, French hallmarks, signed "Batik" (ILLUS.)................................ **805**

Pendant, gold, designed as a standing lion w/chased & repoussé detail, 20k gold **1,840**

Pendant, jade & diamond, Art Deco style, the jade carved & pierced in a floral design, accented w/collet-set diamonds & surmounted by a diamond-set cap, cabochon sapphire accent, suspended from a rose-cut diamond bail & black cord w/rose-cut diamond terminals, pendant signed "Cartier New York," clasp signed "Cartier," numbers obliterated, 27" l. **8,050**

Pendant, jade & diamond, Art Deco style, the platinum & white gold mount having twin bails set w/two round old European-cut diamonds, suspending a platinum bell-capped tassel set w/six rose-cut diamonds & one teardrop apple green jadeite jade stone, together w/a 14k white gold chain of a later date, ca. 1920-30, 18 1/2" l. .. **604**

Carved Jade Pendant

Pendant, jade & gold (18k yellow), foliate carved jade plaque, surmounted by a gold scrolled cap, topped by a tumbled oval pink tourmaline, beaded gold bail (ILLUS.) **2,070**

Pendant, jadeite, white, rectangular w/dragon & cloud decoration on both sides, 36.1 mm. x 29.3 mm., China **1,000-1,500**

Art Deco Pendant

Pendant, onyx, diamond & platinum, Art Deco style, centered by an old European-cut diamond within an onyx circular frame, further enhanced by three collet-set old European-cut & 36 rose-cut diamonds within a pierced & millegrain mount, suspended from a trace-link chain, 16" l. (ILLUS.) **2,300**

Pendant, platinum & diamond, Art Deco style, waisted rectangular form, old European- & single-cut diamonds within an openwork platinum mount, green stone accents, engraved & millegrain accents (minor solder) **1,840**

Pendant, ruby, sapphire & diamond, Art Deco style circular abstract design set w/calibré-cut rubies, sapphires & round diamonds, platinum mount, completed by a 14k white gold trace link chain, 17" l. **690**

Sapphire & Diamond Pendant

Pendant, sapphire & diamond, Art Deco style, flexible bail suspending a lozenge shape plaque set throughout w/old European- & single-cut diamonds, calibré-cut sapphire accents, millegrain & platinum (ILLUS.) **3,565**

Gold & Sapphire Spray Pendant

Pendant, sapphire & gold, Retro style, the 14k yellow gold bow edged w/a row of prong-set oval light blue, violet & golden sapphires, suspending a ruby-set accent spray, pin stem from brooch removed, signed "KS" (ILLUS.) **1,380**

Pendant, sterling silver, abstract geometric form suspended from a torque, signed "Ed Wiener," ca. 1949 .... **2,990**

Pendant, sterling silver & amethyst, centered by an oval faceted amethyst within a circular foliate frame, hallmark for Theodor Fahrner, completed by a twisted curb link silver chain, 28" l. **374**

Sterling Silver & Amethyst Pendant

Pendant, sterling silver & amethyst, designed w/graduated concentric circles, intersected by a sterling bar w/a cabochon amethyst terminal, No. 143, signed "Georg Jensen" (ILLUS.) **1,495**

Pendant, sterling silver, circular form w/thin molded rim, decorated w/abstract figural design on blackened silver background, suspended by a black cord attached to two rings off center of pendant, signed "Janiyé" **400**

Pendant, sterling silver, domed top suspending nine tubular drops, No. 142, designed by Bent Gabrielsen Pedersen, signed "Georg Jensen" **546**

Art Deco Tourmaline & Diamond Pendant

Pendant, tourmaline & diamond, Art Deco style, centering a pinkish-purple tourmaline carved in a three-dimensional floral design w/a small diamond pistil, in a frame of old mine-cut (one replaced w/an old European-cut) & baguette-cut diamonds mounted in platinum & 18k white gold (ILLUS.) **9,200**

Pendant, tourmaline, pink stone carved on the front w/a fish & on the underside w/a lotus, 14k gold bail, post-1950, Hong Kong, China **500-700**

Stone-set Pendant & Chain

Pendant & chain, gold & semi-precious stone, egg-form, tested 18k yellow gold mount set w/eight oval cabochon multi-colored & lace agate stones each measuring 9 1/2 x 13 mm, together w/an 18k yellow gold rope chain, ca.1950, 20" l. (ILLUS.)................................ **230**

Art Nouveau Style Pendant/Brooch

Pendant/brooch, citrine, pearl, coral & gold, Art Nouveau style, the 18k yellow gold delicate scrolling leaf mount set w/a large heart-shaped scotch-colored citrine weighing about 50 carats flanked by two leaping silver panthers, the top set w/four freshwater pearls, the bottom suspending a yellow gold, orange coral & baroque pearl tassel, ca. 1960, 2 x 4" (ILLUS.).......................... **1,265**

Art Deco Pendant/Brooch

Pendant/brooch, diamond, Art Deco style, the elongated hexagonal shape set w/old mine-cut diamonds, pierced platinum-topped 14k white gold mount w/millegrain accents, one diamond missing, hallmarked F.N. (ILLUS.)...... **1,495**

Pendant/brooch, diamond & platinum, Art Deco style, the platinum rectangular openwork mount set w/77 graduated old European- and mine-cut diamonds weighing about 5 carats, ca. 1930, 1 x 2 1/4".. **4,600**

Figural Bakelite Pin

Pin, Bakelite, figural articulated design, black body & arms, brown legs, painted face, red topknot, holding a white stick & orange shield, ca. 1930 (ILLUS.).......... **805**

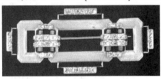

Art Deco Coral & Onyx Pin

Pin, coral, onyx & diamond, Art Deco style geometric buckle design of coral w/onyx & diamond highlights, platinum mount (ILLUS.)....... **2,990**

Pin, diamond, designed as a narrow tapering circle of pavé-set round brilliant- & single-cut diamonds w/an attached floral ornament, pavé-set w/single-cut diamonds, having a total weight of approx. 1.5 cts., mounted in platinum, ca. 1930............... **1,035**

Pin, diamond & enamel, fish w/pierced body decorated w/blue-green enamel scales & yellow-orange fins, diamond-set mouth, ruby eye, 18k yellow gold mount, hallmark (minor enamel loss)........ **633**

Pin, diamond, open circular design w/22 old European-cut diamonds weighing 1.54 cts., mounted in platinum w/a 14k white gold catch...... **1,150**

Pin, diamond, pearl & platinum, Art Deco style, 'S'-form, the platinum mount in the form of an elongated S set w/seven round old European- and mine-cut diamonds weighing about 1.05 carats alternating w/12 rose-cut diamonds, the ends set w/two oblong pearls, one natural, the other cultured & added at a later date, together w/the original fitted box, dated 1922, 1 1/2" l................. **1,265**

Pin, diamond & sapphire, Art Deco style, bow design centered by a collet-set old European-cut diamond surrounded by smaller bead-set old European-cut diamonds, edged w/channel-set calibré-cut sapphires, silver mount, gold pin stem, European hallmarks.......................... **2,415**

Pin, enamel, butterfly design, the silver-topped wings set w/pearls, opals, colored gemstones & diamond accents, bordered by orange guilloché enamel, 19k yellow gold mount, Portuguese hallmarks............................ **633**

Pin, gold & pearl, "Golden Mink," designed as a textured 14k yellow gold mink w/sapphire eye accents, surmounting three baroque pearls, signed "Rotter"............... **259**

Pin, gold & pearl, mistletoe design w/pearl berries, brushed 18k yellow gold leaves & branches, numbered & signed "Buccellati" **863**

Pin, gold, Retro style bow of 14k pink & green gold, stamped "H.S.B."............................ **374**

Pin, gold & silver, sterling silver eagle surmounting a shield atop two crossed anchors in 14k yellow gold, signed "Tiffany & Co.".................. **460**

Art Deco Moonstone Pin

Pin, moonstone, sapphire & platinum, Art Deco style, centered by a sugarloaf moonstone, flanked by square-cut sapphires, edged w/rectangular moonstones, all channel-set, oval moonstone terminals, wiretwist filigree accents, yellow gold pin stem, signed "Tiffany & Co.," 3" l. (ILLUS.) **24,150**

Art Deco Circle Pin

Pin, onyx, diamond & ruby, Art Deco style, onyx circular plaque w/round diamond & calibré-cut ruby terminals, platinum mount, minor chip to onyx, signed "J.E. & Co." for J.E. Caldwell & Co., No. K-5045 (ILLUS.)......................... **9,775**

Pin, pearl, onyx & diamond, Art Deco style bow design centered by a cultured pearl w/collet- & bead-set pavé-set diamond accents, engraved platinum mount............. **978**

Art Deco Circle Pin

Pin, ruby & diamond, designed as a circular band of channel-set rubies & single-cut diamonds surmounted by a diamond floret, platinum & millegrain mount (ILLUS.) **2,760**

Pin, sterling silver, modeled as a pansy, hand-hammered w/beaded accents, signed "Georg Jensen, No. 113" **374**

Amethyst Heart-shaped Pin

Pin/pendant, amethyst & diamond, heart-shaped amethyst surrounded by 20 prong-set round diamonds, 14k yellow gold mount (ILLUS.) **862**

Diamond & Sapphire Pin/Pendent

Pin/pendant, diamond & sapphire, center set round diamond w/rose-cut diamonds in the circular white gold openwork design & framed by 12 round sapphires (ILLUS.) **1,840**

Ring, amethyst & 14k yellow gold, hinged lid set w/an amethyst scarab, opens to view a well compartment, ca. 1950 .... **1,100**

Ring, amethyst & diamond, Art Deco style, an oval buffed top amethyst flanked by 14 single-cut & two baguette diamonds, palladium four-prong mount, ca. 1935 .... **460**

Ring, aquamarine & diamond, Art Deco style, 18k yellow gold & platinum four prong A-box set w/a rectangular scissors-cut pale aquamarine flanked by four round old European-cut diamonds, ca. 1930 .... **748**

Ring, aquamarine & diamond, Art Deco style, the filigree platinum four-prong A-box mount set w/a rectangular cut aquamarine flanked by six round old European- & single-cut diamonds, ca. 1920-30 .... **1,380**

Ring, aquamarine & diamond, center set w/an oval faceted aquamarine surrounded by 15 round brilliant-cut diamonds, flanked by additional six round brilliant-cut diamonds set in triangular design, ca. 1950 .... **633**

Ring, aquamarine, diamond & platinum, Retro-style, dinnertype, the platinum four-prong A-box mount set w/one rectangular emerald-cut aquamarine weighing about 6.35 carats flanked by three round brilliant-cut & two baguette diamonds weighing about .35 carats, J.E. Caldwell, Philadelphia, ca. 1940, size 9 .... **1,725**

Ring, aquamarine & platinum, dinner-type, Retro style, the platinum mount set w/one rectangular emerald-cut aquamarine weighing about 9.70 carats, ca. 1940, size 5 3/4 .... **1,725**

Ring, cat's-eye & diamond, Art Deco style, center cabochon cat's-eye chrysoberyl w/single-cut diamonds mounted in a scalloped border, set in platinum, obliterated hallmarks (surface abrasions to chrysoberyl) **1,840**

Ring, citrine & silver, a square sugarloaf citrine set within a stepped, ribbed shank, decorated w/18k yellow gold geometric shoulders, signed "Hermes," ca. 1940 .... **1,955**

Ring, coral & diamond, Art Deco style, carved coral scarab surmounted by three rose-cut diamonds, triangular onyx & rose-cut diamond shoulders, signed "Koch" **218,500**

Ring, coral, enamel & diamond, Art Deco style, a sugarloaf coral within a black enamel bezel, foliate-motif diamond shoulders, mounted in platinum & 18k yellow gold (enamel loss, coral reglued) **2,760**

Ring, diamond & 14k white gold, floral design, the stamen set w/a round old European-cut diamond, the surrounding six petals set w/a cluster of 42 single-cut diamonds, ca. 1950 .... **575**

Edwardian Diamond Ring

Ring, diamond, 14k yellow gold & platinum-topped oval mount set w/three round old European-cut diamonds framed by 20 old mine-, old European- & single-cut diamonds, ca. 1910, Edwardian (ILLUS.) **1,035**

Ring, diamond, Art Deco style, 14k yellow & 18k white gold topped mount set w/three old mine- & old European-cut diamonds, ca. 1930 .... **518**

Ring, diamond, Art Deco style, center fancy color diamond flanked by two old European-cut diamonds in a pierced platinum mounting set w/diamonds in the gallery, hallmark for Jung & Klitz **28,750**

Ring, diamond, Art Deco style, center set w/one round old European-cut diamond flanked by two smaller old mine-cut diamonds, 14k white gold marquise-shaped mount, ca. 1930 .... **1,725**

Ring, diamond, Art Deco style, centered by a bead-set old European-cut diamond, accented by six bead-set old European-cut diamonds, pierced platinum mount **2,415**

Ring, diamond, Art Deco style, centered by a bead-set old European-cut diamond in a square platinum mount, surrounded by bead-set round & marquise-cut diamonds, engraved foliate detail (sizing evident) **3,910**

Ring, diamond, Art Deco style, centered by a round old European-cut diamond flanked by six single-cut diamonds, platinum triple four-prong mount, ca. 1920-30 .... **920**

Ring, diamond, Art Deco style, centered by an old European-cut diamond flanked by two round brilliant-cut diamonds, ca. 1930 .... **1,955**

Art Deco Diamond Ring

Ring, diamond, Art Deco style, geometric design centered by a collet-set old European-cut diamond surrounded by 12 baguette round diamonds accented w/12 blue stones in a platinum mount (ILLUS.).. **863**

Ring, diamond, Art Deco style, rectangular plaque set w/ten old European-cut diamonds, pierced & engraved 18k white gold mount, millegrain accents... **1,265**

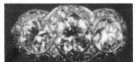

Art Deco Ring with Diamonds

Ring, diamond, Art Deco style, set w/three European-cut diamonds, pierced platinum & diamond mount (ILLUS.).... **14,950**

Ring, diamond, Art Deco style three-stone, the center stone a round fancy yellow diamond, flanked by two round diamonds, within a pierced white gold mount..... **1,093**

Art Deco Style Diamond Ring

Ring, diamond, Art Deco style, twin stone design, set w/two old European-cut diamonds, separated by baguettes in stepped geometric design, platinum mount (ILLUS.).... **23,000**

Ring, diamond, Art Deco style, two collet-set old European-cut diamonds, each within a black enamel & platinum bezel, engraved platinum & 14k yellow gold mount............ **6,900**

Art Deco Diamond Dinner Ring

Ring, diamond & gold, Art Deco dinner-type, tested 18k white gold filigree mount set w/11 round old European-cut diamonds weighing about 1 carat, ca. 1930, size 6 3/4 (ILLUS.)................................. **690**

Ring, diamond & gold, Art Deco style, solitaire, the 18k white gold mount set w/one round old European-cut diamond weighing about .75 carats, ca. 1930, size 6 3/4 . **1,035**

Ring, diamond & gold, Art Deco-style, cluster-type, the 18k yellow & white gold floral-design mount set w/a cluster of nine round old European-cut diamonds weighing about 1 carat, ca. 1920-30, size 4 3/4................................ **633**

Ring, diamond & gold, gentleman's solitaire, the 14k white gold gypsy mount set w/one round brilliant-cut diamond weighing about 1.55 carats, ca. 1940, size 7.......... **1,725**

Ring, diamond & gold, tested 18k yellow & white gold mount centered by one oval old mine-cut diamond weighing about 2.75 carats flanked by two smaller old mine-cut diamonds each weighing about 1.30 & 1.50 carats, size w/ball spacers 5 3/4.... **14,950**

Ring, diamond & platinum, Art Deco dinner-style, the platinum octagonal three-tiered mount set w/one round old European-cut diamond weighing about .40 carats surrounded by two tiers of 40 smaller round old European-cut diamonds weighing about 1 carat, ca. 1930, size 4 1/4 .... **1,610**

Ring, diamond & platinum, Art Deco eternity band-style, the platinum fishtail-designed mount set w/25 round old European-cut diamonds weighing about .75 carats, ca. 1920-30, size 6 1/4 .... **863**

Ring, diamond & platinum, Art Deco solitaire, the platinum four-prong mount set w/one round old European-cut diamond weighing about 1.25 carats flanked by two marquise & ten single-cut diamonds weighing about .40 carats & three straight baguette emeralds weighing about .15 carats, ca. 1920-30, size 6 (one emerald missing)............... **3,680**

Ring, diamond & platinum, Art Deco solitaire, the platinum mount set w/one round old European-cut diamond weighing about .55 carats, surrounded by ten old mine- and old European-cut diamonds weighing about .30 carats, ca. 1920-30, size 4.. **1,610**

Ring, diamond & platinum, Art Deco style, centered w/old European-cut diamond, flanked by single- & baguette-cut diamond shoulders............... **5,290**

Ring, diamond & platinum, Art Deco style filigree diamond-set mount centering a round old-European-cut diamond.. **1,840**

Ring, diamond & platinum, Art Deco style, set w/two round old European-cut diamonds surrounded by six straight baguette- & 16 smaller round old European-cut diamonds, ca. 1920-30.......... **6,900**

Ring, diamond & platinum, solitaire, the platinum six-prong mount set w/a fancy vivid yellow pear-shaped diamond weighing exactly 6.31 carats flanked by two tapered baguette diamonds weighing about .50 carats, J.E. Caldwell & Co., ca. 1940, size 8 1/4 .... **232,250**

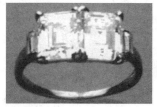

Two-stone Diamond Ring

Ring, diamond & platinum, two-stone, the platinum four-prong mount set w/two square-cut diamonds each weighing about 1.75 carats flanked by four straight baguette diamonds weighing about .40 carats, ca. 1940, size 6 1/2 (ILLUS.) **8,050**

Ring, diamond, Retro style, centering two round diamonds, one old European- and one round brilliant-cut w/a total weight of 1.50 cts., decorated on one side w/five round & six baguette-cut diamonds & on the opposite side w/four baguette-cut diamonds within a frame of eight round-cut diamonds w/a total weight of 1.30 cts. for the baguettes & .60 cts. for the rounds, mounted in platinum............... **4,370**

Ring, diamond & ruby, Art Deco style wide platinum band set w/round diamonds & carved ruby cabochons, millegrain detail............... **2,645**

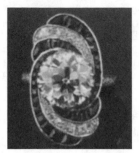

Yellow Diamond & Sapphire Ring

Ring, diamond & sapphire, centered by an old European-cut yellow diamond, further set w/14 diamonds & 33 calibré-cut Burmese sapphires in a swirl design, platinum mount, ca. 1940 (ILLUS.)................................. **8,625**

Retro Style Diamond Ring

Ring, diamond solitaire, gentleman's, Retro style, 18k white gold box illusion mount set w/one old mine-cut diamond (ILLUS.)............................ **2,760**

Gentleman's Diamond Solitaire Ring

Ring, diamond solitaire, gentleman's, Retro style centering a round old European-cut diamond, 14k yellow gold mount, ca. 1940 (ILLUS.) **4,830**
Ring, emerald & diamond, Art Deco style set w/an octagonal square-cut emerald flanked by 18 single-cut diamonds, platinum mount, ca. 1920-30................................. **1,840**

Ring, emerald & diamond, centered by a marquise-cut diamond framed by calibré-cut emeralds, within a diamond-set rectangular plaque, diamond shoulders, silver-topped 18k gold mount, Austrian hallmarks, ca. 1930................. **1,495**
Ring, emerald & diamond, set w/five round faceted emeralds alternating w/ten single-cut diamonds, 14k yellow gold mount, ca. 1950 .... **604**
Ring, gold (14k white) & diamond, Art Deco style bypass design set w/two round old European-cut diamonds flanked by ten single-cut diamonds, ca. 1935................. **805**

Art Deco Diamond Dinner Ring

Ring, gold (14k white) & diamond, Art Deco style, set w/one round old European-cut diamond approx. 1.05 cts., flanked by two smaller old mine- & European-cut diamonds, approx. .40 cts., ca. 1930 (ILLUS.)............ **1,495**
Ring, gold (14k yellow), cat's eye & diamond, bypass style w/clipped flared edges, three central prong-set round chrysoberyls, offset w/four small brilliant-cut prong-set diamonds, the stones accented w/central ropetwist detailing......................... **690**
Ring, gold (18k yellow), surmounted by a concave elliptical disk, sinuous tapering shank, signed "Georg Jensen, Denmark" & "Torun, No. 929"................. **431**

Ring, gold & amethyst, Retro style, tested 18k yellow gold four-prong A-box mount set w/one large emerald-cut amethyst weighing 26 carats, ca. 1940, size 5 1/2..... **460**

Ring, gold & diamond, man's, 14k yellow gold gypsy mount set w/three old mine- and European-cut diamonds weighing about .65 carats, size 9 1/2 .... **403**

Ring, gold & elephant hair, woven design of alternating elephant hair & 18k yellow gold, marked "France," size 5 1/2 .... **288**

Ring, gold, platinum, diamond & ruby, Retro style, 14k yellow gold band w/platinum top mount set w/a cluster of ten oval cabochon rubies weighing about 2.5 carats flanked by 28 round brilliant- and single-cut diamonds weighing about .8 carats, ca. 1940, size 6 1/2................ **1,150**

Ring, gold, ruby & sapphire, domed 18k yellow gold coiled wire design surmounted by prong-set ruby & sapphire flowerheads, bordered by bead-set diamonds set in platinum **748**

Ring, jade, Art Deco style, set w/an oval jade mounted w/baguette- & circular-cut diamonds w/black enamel accents, platinum mount (chips & wear to enamel)................ **4,600**

Ring, jadeite, set w/oval-shaped cabochon of mottled apple green, approx. 14.7 mm. x 10.8 mm. x 5.9 mm., 14k gold mount, post-World War II, China................ **1,000-1,500**

Ring, moonstone & 18k yellow gold, the abstract organic form surmounted by a bezel-set oval moonstone, tapering shank, signed "Georg Jensen, Denmark" & "Torun, No. 915"................ **863**

Ring, moonstone & pearl, Retro-style, a round cabochon moonstone surrounded by natural seed pearls, 14k tricolored gold mount, ca. 1940................ **633**

Ring, opal & diamond, Art Deco style, an oval opal edged by four collet-set old European-cut diamonds, eight diamond accents, platinum mount w/engraved & chased shoulders (minor scratches to opal)................ **1,495**

Ring, opal & diamond, center oval opal cabochon surrounded by 18 round diamonds, 14k yellow gold mount................ **1,035**

Ring, opal, diamond & gold, dinner-type, the 14k yellow & white gold floral-designed mount set w/three oval cabochon white opals weighing about 2.25 carats & 16 single-cut diamonds weighing about .30 carats, ca. 1960, size 6................ **403**

Art Deco Opal & Garnet Ring

Ring, opal & garnet, Art Deco style, centered by an oval opal framed w/28 channel-set demantoid garnets, 18k white gold mount w/diamond shoulders, French hallmarks (ILLUS.)................ **2,185**

Ring, pearl & diamond, Art Deco style, centered by a mabé pearl in a pierced platinum mount set w/rose-cut diamonds, millegrain accents, French assay mark (two diamonds missing)......... **1,265**

Ring, pearl & diamond, Art Deco style w/center prong set old European-cut diamond flanked by pearls, platinum & diamond basket setting....................................... **14,950**

Ring, pearl & diamond, two large vertically set cultured pearls surrounded by 16 single-cut diamonds, 14k white gold mount, ca. 1950.................. **690**

Ring, pearl & emerald, Art Deco style, centered by a cultured pearl flanked by table-cut emeralds, diamond shoulders, pierced & millegrain platinum mount (one emerald cracked)...................... **3,450**

Ring, platinum & diamond, Art Deco bypass design set w/a circular colorless & light yellow diamond, further highlighted w/a geometric pattern of baguette-cut diamonds (shank out of round) **11,500**

Ring, platinum & diamond, Art Deco style, bezel-set old European-cut diamond within a domed pierced platinum mount, engraved gallery, millegrain accents **633**

Ring, platinum & diamond, Art Deco style, centered by a collet-set old European-cut diamond flanked by a row of calibré-cut sapphires within a pierced diamond-set platinum mount (abrasions to sapphires) **1,495**

Art Deco Diamond Dinner Ring

Ring, platinum & diamond, Art Deco style, dinner-type, platinum braided design mount centered by a bezel-set round old European-cut diamond surrounded by 34 round old mine- & old European-cut diamonds, ca. 1930 (ILLUS.) **2,415**

Ring, platinum & diamond, Art Deco style, set w/an old European-cut diamond within a later openwork diamond-set mount w/engraved shoulders, millegrain accents, expandable shank (one diamond missing)............................. **2,990**

Ring, platinum & diamond, Art Deco style, set w/two old European-cut diamonds in a diamond-set openwork geometric platinum mount, millegrain accents **8,625**

Ring, platinum & diamond, Art Deco style, the platinum mount set w/one round old European-cut diamond weighing about .80 carats flanked by six single-cut diamonds weighing about .15 carats, ca. 1930, size 6 1/2 . **1,955**

Ring, platinum, diamond & emerald, Art Deco style, set w/a circular-cut diamond encircled by calibré-cut emeralds, further enhanced by 16 old mine- & European-cut diamonds, diamond-set scrolled shoulders **6,325**

Ring, platinum & star sapphire, Art Deco style, centered by a star sapphire flanked by bead-set & tapered baguette-cut diamonds... **4,025**

Ring, ruby & diamond, Art Deco style, centered by a collet-set oval ruby, flanked by graduating calibré-cut rubies, platinum scroll mount, millegrain & engraving detail (one diamond missing)........... **4,140**

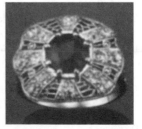

Art Deco Ruby & Diamond Ring

Ring, ruby & diamond, Art Deco style, centered by a prong-set round ruby surrounded by bead-set old mine-cut diamonds in a filigree platinum mount, surface scratches & nick to collct of ruby, repronged (ILLUS.) **1,610**

Ring, ruby, diamond & gold, Claddach-style, the tested 14k yellow gold mount set w/a pear-shaped diamond weighing about .50 carats & one pear-shaped ruby weighing about .35 carats surrounded by 30 old mine-cut diamonds weighing about .75 carats, ca. 1930, size 4 3/4 .... **2,530**

Ring, ruby, diamond & gold, man's Retro style, tested 14k yellow gold gypsy mount set w/an oval mixed-cut ruby weighing about .75 carats flanked by two old mine-cut diamonds weighing about .25 & .30 carats, ca. 1940, size 7 .... **690**

Ring, ruby, diamond & platinum, Art Deco eternity band-style, the platinum channel mount set w/21 single-cut diamonds weighing about .35 carats alternating w/21 square-cut rubies weighing about .70 carats, ca. 1920-30, size 6 1/2 .... **1,035**

Retro Style Ruby & Diamond Ring

Ring, ruby & diamond, Retro style, centered by a cabochon ruby framed by a scroll of 22 circular -& pavé-set diamonds, platinum mount (ILLUS.) **1,035**

Ring, ruby & diamond, Retro style, designed w/a cluster of rubies & a cluster of round-cut diamonds, wide reeded bypass 14k yellow gold mount **1,955**

Ring, sapphire, Art Deco style, centered by an oval sapphire within a single-cut diamond-set platinum mount, millegrain accents (solder evident, two small diamonds missing) **5,750**

Ring, sapphire, Art Deco style, emerald-cut sapphire within an engraved platinum & diamond mount **4,715**

Art Deco Sapphire & Diamond Ring

Ring, sapphire & diamond, Art Deco style, centered by a sugarloaf sapphire surrounded by 76 old mine-cut diamonds & 16 French-cut sapphires, platinum mount (ILLUS.) **10,063**

Ring, sapphire & diamond, Art Deco style, centering an emerald-cut sapphire weighing 1.10 cts. flanked by smaller sapphires & rose-cut diamonds, mounted in platinum **1,955**

Ring, sapphire & diamond, Art Deco style, centering an emerald-cut sapphire weighing 3.70 cts. decorated on each end w/two small triangular sapphires, within a frame of old round single-cut diamonds w/three additional diamonds in each shoulder, mounted in platinum **3,680**

Ring, sapphire & diamond, Art Deco style eternity band, 18 single-cut diamonds alternating w/18 square-cut sapphires channel-set in platinum mount, ca. 1920 .... **403**

Ring, sapphire & diamond, Art Deco style, three-stone design centered by an old mine-cut diamond, flanked by oval sapphires, engraved foliate platinum mount **3,105**

Art Deco Sapphire & Diamond Ring

Ring, sapphire & diamond, Art Deco style w/center prong-set cushion-shaped sapphire surrounded by 13 old European-cut diamonds, platinum mount, 14k white gold shank (ILLUS.) **4,830**

Ring, sapphire & diamond, centered by a cabochon sapphire, flanked by 12 channel-set baguette-cut diamonds, weighing approx. 1.05 cts., 18k yellow gold mount **978**

Unusual Sapphire & Diamond Ring

Ring, sapphire & diamond, centrally designed w/two rows of faceted calibé-cut sapphires w/a row of round brilliant-cut diamonds forming a border on each side, having an approx. total diamond weight of 0.50 ct., mounted in platinum, numbered & signed "Cartier," ca. 1930 (ILLUS.) **6,325**

Ring, sapphire & diamond, designed w/stepped bars of channel-set square sapphires & round diamonds, platinum mount, ca. 1940s... **2,760**

Ring, star sapphire, centering a round cabochon-cut star sapphire weighing approx. 17 cts., mounted in platinum, ca. 1935, signed "Tiffany & Co.," w/original leather box................ **3,680**

Ring, star sapphire & diamond, Art Deco style, filigree platinum mount set w/round cabochon star sapphire surrounded by four triangular-cut synthetic blue sapphires & 46 old mine-cut diamonds, ca. 1920-30........... **1,035**

Retro Style Man's Star Sapphire Ring

Ring, star sapphire, diamond & platinum, gentleman's, Retro style, the platinum gypsy mount set w/one large round cabochon blue star sapphire weighing about 21.85 carats flanked by two trillion-cut diamonds weighing about 1 carat, ca. 1940, size 6 1/2.. **1,380**

Ring, star sapphire & diamond, set w/an oval high cabochon star sapphire flanked by four round brilliant-cut diamonds, platinum mount, ca. 1950.............................. **518**

Art Deco Diamond Ring/Watch

Ring/watch, diamond & platinum, Art Deco style, silvertone dial w/black Arabic numerals, 18-jewel movement, five adjustments, diamond-set bezel & foliate shoulders, signed C.H. Meylan, No. 33739, case hallmarked for Cresaux, No. 1453, Tiffany & Co. (ILLUS.) **3,565**

Seal ring, Egyptian Revival style, centered by an oblong double-sided faience seal, lily motif shank, 18k yellow gold mounting, European import mark.............................. **575**

Shoe buckles, komai & gilt metal, rectangular, marked w/trademark in Japanese, label w/Komai trademark, ca. 1920, w/original box, pr..... **375-575**

Animal Stickpins

Stickpin, crystal & gold, depicting a reverse-painted crystal portrait of a bridled horse's head, 14k yellow gold, marked "JEC & Co., N4732" for J.E. Caldwell Co. (ILLUS. left) **288**

Emerald & Diamond Stickpin

Stickpin, emerald & diamond, Art Deco style, cushion-cut emerald in a pierced & platinum millegrain mount edged w/12 old mine-cut diamonds (ILLUS.).............................. **1,495**

Stickpin, enamel, designed as a beagle head, diamond eye, 14k yellow gold engraving & chasing, hallmark (ILLUS. right).............................. **575**

Stickpin, platinum & sapphire, three calibré-cut sapphires surmounted by a marquise-shaped sapphire, European hallmarks.............................. **518**

Stickpin, sapphire & diamond, Art Deco style, circular form set w/29 channel-set sapphires & 35 rose-cut diamonds, the inner rings swivel to reveal opposite color combination, maker's mark on pin stem, French assay marks, signed "Cartier Paris Londres, No. 2432".............................. **4,140**

Watch fob, gold (18k) & enamel, Egyptian Revival style, depicting the bust of a pharaoh, blue enameled hood, diamond accents (enamel loss) **489**

Egyptian Revival Watch Fob

Watch fob, hardstone, Egyptian Revival style, suspending a faience scarab & two engraved 14k yellow gold frames, hardstone cylinder seals, solder evident (ILLUS.).............................. **978**

Sets

Bracelet & brooch, Bakelite, the bangle-type bracelet, red w/heavily carved leaf design, the brooch in a leaf & berry design, the set.................................. **374**

Art Deco Bracelet & Brooch

Bracelet & brooch, gold (18k yellow), Art Deco style, flexible belt design w/three rectangular & oval interlocking links, together w/matching brooch converted from one of the bracelet links, ca. 1930, bracelet 6" l., the set (ILLUS.).............................. **1,380**

Bracelet & necklace, gold (14k yellow), a floral & scroll link necklace together w/a bracelet of similar design, No. 251, signed "Georg Jensen," necklace 19 1/2" l., bracelet 7 1/2" l., the set....... **3,738**

Citrine & Diamond Brooch & Earring

Brooch & earrings, citrine & diamond, the brooch designed as a four-leaf clover w/heart-shaped citrine leaves centered by a circular-cut diamond w/a bead-set diamond stem, 14k yellow gold mount, matching earrings, the set (ILLUS. of part)... **546**

Brooch & earrings, gold (18k yellow), orchid design in textured gold w/seed pearl accent, w/matching pair of earrings, the set.......................... **316**

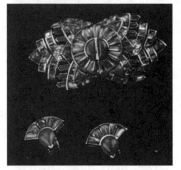

Art Deco Brooch & Earrings

Brooch & earrings, jade, moonstone & diamond, Art Deco style, a double-clip brooch (one moonstone missing) & matching pair of clip earrings, platinum mounts, signed "Seaman Schepps," the set (ILLUS.).. **8,338**

Brooch & earrings, sterling silver, the brooch of asymmetric design w/bead accents, No. 235, signed "Sigi, Taxco," together w/pair of matching earrings designed w/asymmetric pendant drop decorated w/two beads & suspended from round silver bead, screw-on, the set **460**

Dress set, mother-of-pearl, a pair of cuff links w/center pearl accent, together w/four matching vest buttons & three shirt studs, platinum-topped 14k gold mount, the set.. **633**

Earrings & pendant, aquamarine, prong-set emerald-cut aquamarine earrings & similar pendant suspended from a 20" l. 14k white gold box-link chain, 14k white gold mounts, the set **403**

Garnet & Seed Pearl Necklace

Necklace & earrings, garnet & seed pearl, the necklace set w/faceted garnet clusters, the center three accented by seed pearls, together w/a matching pair of clip earrings, gilt silver mounts, ca. 1950s, hallmark, the necklace 14" l., the set (ILLUS. of part) **1,035**

Opal & Diamond Necklace

Necklace & earrings, opal & diamond, the necklace centered by an opal suspended within a blue enamel engraved plaque w/diamond accents, further suspending a similar drop, the fine 10k yellow gold chain w/old mine-cut diamond floral links spaced by opal-set plaques, together w/silver-topped gold mount earrings, the set (ILLUS. of necklace) **2,300**

Necklace & earrings, sterling silver & enamel, the necklace designed w/stylized links & light blue enamel, w/matching earrings, No. 5372, signed "Margot de Taxco," the set **403**

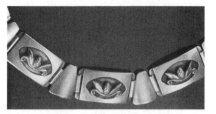

Sterling Silver Necklace

Necklace & earrings, sterling silver, the necklace of hinged rectangular plaques decorated w/an applied foliate design, together w/matching earrings, signed "USA Georg Jensen Inc.," earrings No. 419B, necklace No. 429B, the set (ILLUS. of part) **633**

Necklace & earrings, sterling silver, the necklace w/rectangular links w/oval floral cartouche spaced by trapezoid shape links, signed "Georg Jensen, No 60B," together w/clip earrings designed as round balls set within open circles, signed "Georg Jensen, No 91," the set **633**

Estate (1960-present)

Bar pin, diamond & 14k white gold, five collet-set diamonds, approx. total wt. 0.95 cts., within a millegrain floral mount set w/14 diamonds **518**

Bar pin, diamond & 14k yellow gold, five bezel-set old European-cut diamonds, approx. total wt. 4.42 cts., highlighted by 74 diamond melée, approx. 1.03 cts., w/bead & millegrain mount **5,175**

Bar pin, diamond & platinum, designed as three open sections of scrolling design set throughout w/158 small round diamonds, total approx. 4 cts., approx. 10.2 dwt. **4,312**

Bar pin, diamond & sapphire, bowknot design in 18k white gold set w/a square-cut & 18 baguette blue sapphires weighing approx. 1.65 cts. surrounded by 56 round brilliant-cut diamonds weighing approx. .25 cts., 2 1/4" l.............. **403**

Bar pin, gold (14k yellow), sapphire, ruby & diamond, centrally set w/an oval-shaped cabochon-cut sapphire weighing approx. 2.50 cts., the ends oppositely oriented & set w/two round diamonds, four square-cut & four cabochon-cut rubies, signed "J.E. Caldwell"................. **805**

Bar pin, moonstone & diamond, centered by an oval cabochon moonstone & accented by six rose-cut diamonds set on platinum top, gold mount............... **633**

Bar pin, pearl & diamond, centered by a golden pearl measuring approx. 11.70 mm., round & baguette-cut diamond-set 14k yellow gold mount, approx. total diamond wt. 1.14 cts., signed "Manning"................. **748**

Bar pin, ruby & diamond, a center oval faceted ruby weighing approx. 1 ct. surrounded by 12 round brilliant-cut diamonds weighing approx. 0.22 ct., flanked by 12 round faceted rubies w/total weight of approx. 1 ct., mounted in 18k yellow gold, maker's mark................. **1,725**

Bar pin, sapphire & diamond, centered by a cushion-cut sapphire, measuring approx. 10.01 x 9.23 x 4.49   mm., flanked by four square-cut sapphires & four old European-cut diamonds, approx. total diamond wt. .96 cts., platinum mount, signed "Cartier Paris/Londres No. 9372," French platinum mark............. **7,475**

Turquoise & Sapphire Bar Pin

Bar pin, turquoise, sapphire & diamond, centered by a row of square-cut sapphires flanked by two small round brilliant-cut diamonds w/navette-shaped cabochon-cut turquoise surrounded by calibré-cut sapphires at each end, one sapphire missing, mounted in 18k white gold (ILLUS.) ... **1,150**

Barrette, gold, abstract butterfly openwork design in 18k yellow gold, signed "Tiffany & Co.," 8.4 dwt. **1,035**

Bracelet, bangle-type, 14k gold, hinged, hammered pattern, the interior w/honeycomb design, 52.4 dwt. **1,093**

Bracelet, bangle-type, 14k white gold & diamond, hinged design set w/round diamonds............................... **2,070**

Bracelet, bangle-type, diamond, sapphire & enamel, the hinged bangle centered by a collet-set diamond flanked by eight diamonds, sapphire terminals, further set w/old European-cut diamonds framed w/blue enamel, platinum-topped 14k yellow gold mount, ca. 1966 (solder evident) **3,220**

Bracelet, bangle-type, gold (14k), emerald & diamond, oval hinged design, the top set w/a raised channel of square-cut emeralds, flanked by rows of 20 channel-set square-cut diamonds, approx. total wt. 1.20 cts. **1,150**

Cuff Bangle-style Gold Bracelet

Bracelet, bangle-type, gold (14k yellow), beryl, garnet & diamond, cuff style centered w/an oval-shaped green beryl, approx. 12.50 x 10.00 x 7.70 mm. & enhanced by triangular-shaped rhodolite garnets accented by full-cut diamonds, approx. 5 1/2" (ILLUS.)............................. **690**

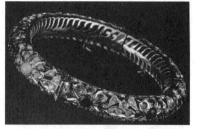

Jeweled Bracelet

Bracelet, bangle-type, gold (14k yellow) & gemstone, hinged tubular reticulated form set w/clusters of colored gemstones, including ruby, sapphire, emerald, turquoise, carnelian & pearl, India, 33.4 dwt. (ILLUS.).............. **863**
Bracelet, bangle-type, gold (18k) & diamond, narrow hinged design, top set w/21 round brilliant-cut diamonds in partial collet mountings, approx. total weight 1.86 cts., pierced scrolled gallery **1,035**
Bracelet, bangle-type, gold (18k) & gems, wide band set w/faceted stones of various shapes & sizes, including peridot, tourmaline, citrine, garnet & sapphire in high collet mountings, hand-chased, signed "Ed Wiener," ca. 1980.................. **3,738**

Bangle Bracelet with Lion's Head

Bracelet, bangle-type, gold (18k), surmounted by a gold wire lion's head, diamond eyes, cabochon ruby nose, signed "Lalaounis" (ILLUS.) **2,070**
Bracelet, bangle-type, opal & diamond, hinged design top-set w/an alternating pattern of round opals spaced by round-cut diamonds, 14k white & yellow gold mount (solder evident)................ **230**
Bracelet, bangle-type, opal & diamond, the hinged top set w/eight graduated oval opals & accented w/24 bead-set diamonds set in 14k white gold, 14k yellow gold bangle **1,840**
Bracelet, bangle-type, opal & sapphire, hinged design set w/five graduating opals & four sapphire-set scroll motifs, 14k yellow gold mount (one sapphire missing).............. **460**
Bracelet, bangle-type, pearl, diamond & 14k yellow gold, abstract design set w/multi-colored baroque pearls & two prong-set multicolor round diamonds, signed "King," 68.50 dwt.................. **1,725**

Pearl & Gem-set Cuff Bracelet

Bracelet, bangle-type, pearl, ruby, sapphire, emerald & diamond, cuff-style, flexible design w/five rows of cultured pearls measuring approx. 5.50 mm. each, separated by spacers set w/cabochon rubies, sapphires, emeralds & cluster of round brilliant-cut diamonds, 18k yellow gold mount (ILLUS.).................................. **1,840**

Bracelet, bangle-type, platinum & diamond, hinged & brushed, bezel-set w/15 diamonds, some w/yellow gold "halos," designed by Rudolph Erdling............................ **920**

Bracelet, bangle-type, sapphire & yellow gold, set w/alternating tapered cushion-cut pale yellow & blue sapphires, hinged........................... **1,610**

Bracelet, charm-type, 14k gold curb link chain, signed "Tiffany & Co.," 7 1/4" l.............. **690**

Coral & Diamond Bracelet

Bracelet, coral & diamond, flexible, designed w/ten fluted, oval-shaped, cabochon-cut corals, each separated by a section of four ribbed gold petals & five round brilliant-cut diamonds, total approx. weight for the 50 diamonds, 3.75 cts., mounted in 18k yellow gold, approx. 7 1/2" l. (ILLUS. of part)......... **5,750**

Bracelet, crystal & 14k gold, three reverse-painted crystals depicting a bridled horse & equestrian scenes, stirrup form clasp, 7 1/4" l. (scratches to crystal)................................ **633**

Reverse-painted Crystal Bracelet

Bracelet, crystal & 14k yellow gold, two reverse-painted fox heads & a bridled horse's head, gold spacers designed as coiled crops, gold link horse bits & buckles, Raymond Yard, 7 1/4" l. (ILLUS.)............................. **2,185**

Reverse-painted Crystal & Gold Bracelet

Bracelet, crystal, consisting of four round reverse-painted crystals of birds, a hummingbird, a robin, a cardinal & a woodpecker, 14k yellow gold mount, the crystals alternating w/chain links centering figural gold designs, a tree, a flower & a birdhouse, American hallmark, fitted box marked "Hancocks & Co." (ILLUS.)............................. **3,105**

Bracelet, cultured pearl & diamond, the double strand w/48 pearls measuring 7 to 7 1/2 mm. w/two 14k yellow gold spacer bars joined by a 14k yellow & white gold openwork box clasp set w/four single-cut diamonds, 8" l................................ **920**

Bracelet, cultured pearl & gold, the triple strand w/96 pearls measuring 4 to 4 1/2 mm. alternating w/15 14k polished yellow gold spacer bars joined by a 14k Florentine-finish box tongue-in-groove clasp, 1/2" w., 7" l........ **920**

Bracelet, cultured pearl, ruby & diamond, a triple strand w/60 pearls measuring 6 to 6.5 mm. alternating w/two 14k yellow gold spacer bars set w/ten round faceted rubies weighing about .70 carats joined by a 14k yellow & white gold tongue-in-groove box clasp set w/12 round faceted rubies weighing about 1.50 carats surrounded by 12 round brilliant-cut diamonds weighing about .20 carats, 1" w., 7" l.............. **2,530**

Bracelet, diamond & 14k white gold, line-type, set w/18 brilliant-cut diamonds, alternating w/36 straight baguettes, approx. total wt. 6.00 cts., 7 1/4" l. **3,738**

Bracelet, diamond & 14k yellow gold, designed as a hinged cuff w/applied dragon's head & tail, terminals set w/four old mine-cut diamonds, applied wire & bead decoration, 30.7 dwt. **1,380**

Bracelet, diamond & 18k gold, designed w/four hinged brushed gold sections edged w/numerous circular-cut diamonds, 44.8 dwt. **2,415**

Bracelet, diamond & 18k yellow gold, 156 prong-set round brilliant-cut diamonds in flexible links, approx. 6.00 cts. **3,565**

Bracelet, diamond & 18k yellow gold, flexible design composed of two horizontally-set baguette-set diamonds alternating w/one round brilliant-cut diamond, approx. 6.15 cts. **4,025**

Ornate Diamond Design Bracelet

Bracelet, diamond, a central swirled design w/an off-center large round brilliant-cut diamond surrounded by a mixture of smaller round brilliant- & baguette-cut & pear-shaped diamonds attached to a flexible strap composed of round brilliant-cut, baguette-cut & pear-shaped diamonds having a total weight of approx. 16 cts., baguette-cut diamond clasp, mounted in platinum, 6 1/2" l. (ILLUS.) **10,350**

Bracelet, diamond & cultured pearl, open seed pearl & platinum mesh interspersed w/four open wreath designs, each centering a round brilliant-cut diamond weighing .40 ct., encircled w/laurel leaves set w/round, brilliant-cut diamonds weighing 3 cts., mounted in platinum w/an 18k gold tongue, 7 1/2" l. **6,210**

Bracelet, diamond, emerald & 14k gold, composed of five rows of full-cut diamonds & square-cut emeralds set in a checkerboard design, approx. 3.90 cts. diamonds, approx. 6 7/8" l. **1,380**

Diamond & White Gold Bracelet

Bracelet, diamond, flexible, the center set w/a marquise-shaped, brilliant-cut diamond weighing approx. 0.40 ct., flanked by straight baguette- and round brilliant-cut diamonds, w/a double row of round single-cut diamonds decorating the bracelet & catch ends, having approx. 3.60 cts. total weight, mounted in 14k white gold, w/maker's mark, approx. 7" l. (ILLUS.) **2,760**

Bracelet, diamond & gold, a wide hinged cuff design of reeded 18k yellow gold w/Greek key motif in bead-set round diamonds mounted in white gold, approx. total diamond wt. 2.00 cts., 55.60 dwt, signed "Tiffany" .. **2,875**

Bracelet, diamond & gold, cocktail-style, the 18k white gold floral & leaf designed flexible mount set w/136 single-cut diamonds weighing about 2.60 carats, 6 1/4" l. ... **2,760**

Bracelet, diamond & gold, cuff-style, encrusted w/clusters of ten small diamonds, abstract textured 18k yellow gold mount, 77.6 dwt, signed "Webb" for David Webb **3,738**

Bracelet, diamond & platinum, flexible design of alternating barrel & oval links set w/253 round brilliant-cut diamonds weighing approx. 1.25 cts., 7 1/4" l.. **2,300**

Diamond & Platinum Bracelet

Bracelet, diamond & platinum, flexibly-set w/17 circular-cut diamonds in open circles alternating w/diamond-set openwork geometric links, 6 3/4" l. (ILLUS.)........................ **1,610**

Bracelet, diamond & platinum, line-type, set w/44 old European-cut diamonds set in box links, approx. total wt. 7.04 cts., 6 3/4" l....................... **6,900**

Unusual Diamond Bracelet

Bracelet, diamond, repeated sectional, wide, open & intertwining links set w/round brilliant-cut diamonds having an approx. total weight of 7 cts. & further decorated w/pairs of square-cut diamonds, the 28 diamonds having an approx. total weight of 10 cts., mounted in platinum, signed "Koch," 7 1/2" l. (ILLUS.) .. **11,500**

Bracelet, diamond, ruby & gold, bangle-type, 14k yellow gold mount, the top portion set w/15 round brilliant-cut diamonds weighing about 2.25 carats alternating w/28 round faceted rubies weighing about .85 carats.... **2,300**

Diamond & Sapphire Bracelet

Bracelet, diamond, sapphire & platinum, designed w/22 pear-shaped & ten round brilliant-cut diamonds, approx. total weight 13.4 cts., alternating w/ten sugarloaf sapphires, 7" l. (ILLUS. of part).. **14,950**

Bracelet, diamond & sapphire, rectangular center set w/a square-cut blue sapphire, weighing approx. .95 cts., flanked by triangular-shaped links tapering to flexible 18k white gold links all set w/round faceted brilliant-cut diamonds, weighing approx. 1.65 cts., 7" l. (converted from a watch) **1,035**

Diamond Bracelet

Bracelet, diamond, seven sections w/repeated open design set w/baguette & round diamonds, total weight of approx. 14.50 cts., mounted in platinum, measuring approx. 6 3/4" l. (ILLUS.)................................. **9,200**

Bracelet, diamond, tennis-style, 14k yellow gold flexible mount set w/47 round brilliant-cut diamonds weighing approx. 4.70 cts., 7" l............. **1,150**

Bracelet, diamond & tourmaline, platinum Florentine finish oval & box link design set w/ten multicolored oval faceted tourmalines, weighing approx. 19.60 cts., alternating w/ten arched square links set w/210 round brilliant-cut diamonds weighing approx. 2.70 cts., 7 1/4" l..... **4,140**

Bracelet, emerald, diamond & 18k yellow gold, bypass-style in a hinged design, the terminals set w/26 round brilliant-cut diamonds, approx. total diamond wt. 1.04 cts., & two pear-shaped emeralds, Italian hallmarks........................ **1,495**

Emerald, Pearl & Diamond Bracelet

Bracelet, emerald, pearl & diamond, centered by an oval cabochon emerald weighing approx. 19.67 cts., framed by pearls & diamonds, suspended within a bracelet designed w/four strands of cultured pearls measuring 6 1/2 to 7 mm. w/diamond set terminals & plunger clasp, approx. total wt. 1.26 cts., platinum mount, 7 1/2" l. (ILLUS.).. **4,600**

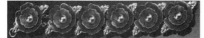

Gold & Enamel Flowerhead Bracelet

Bracelet, enamel & 14k gold, flowerhead design, each flower link w/a central rose gold bead & exterior petals colored w/red enamel, hallmark for Sloan & Co., 7" l. (ILLUS.).. **518**

Garnet Bracelet

Bracelet, garnet, graduated shaped hinged plaques set throughout w/faceted garnets, together w/extra link, gilt-metal mount, solder evident, some stones missing, 6 1/4" l. (ILLUS.)............................ **489**

Bracelet, gemstone & 18k yellow gold, cluster links set w/four prong-set oval colored gemstones, in box marked "Amsterdam Saver, Rio" **920**

Bracelet, gold (14k), braided basketweave design, signed "Tiffany & Co.," 7 3/4" l.......... **1,725**

Bracelet, gold (14k), eight fine rope chains completed by a Florentine finish box clasp surmounted by rose-cut diamond & pearl florets, 14.6 dwt., 6 1/2" l.............................. **345**

Bracelet, gold (14k), rectangular mesh links w/sapphire & diamond buckle terminals, adjustable.................................... **805**

Bracelet, gold (14k white & yellow) & aquamarine, centered by an oval aquamarine, approx. 20.35 x 14.37 x 9.21 mm., within a platinum filigree & diamond applied plaque, fancy link white gold bracelet w/yellow gold foxtail border................................ **805**

Bracelet, gold (14k yellow), abstract shell motif, flat hinged links, 8.9 dwt. **144**

Bracelet, gold (14k yellow), crystal & enamel, designed w/four reverse-painted crystals depicting dogs set on an oval link bracelet w/black & light green enamel decoration (crack to one crystal, minor enamel loss)........................ **1,265**

Bracelet, gold (14k yellow) & diamond, tennis-style, stylized S link flexible mount set w/44 round brilliant-cut diamonds weighing approx. 3 cts., 7" l.................................. **633**

Bracelet, gold (14k yellow), double curb links, 37.00 dwt. **1,035**

Bracelet, gold (14k yellow), double row of fluted twisted links bordered by single rows of rope links, 35.0 dwt.... **403**

Bracelet, gold (14k yellow), flexible braided design w/twisted rope border, one end suspending two yellow gold bell-capped tassels, the other end w/a hinged clasp to adjust length from 6 1/2 to 7 1/2" l., ca. 1960, 46 dwt........ **633**

Bracelet, gold, 14k yellow gold in a wide flexible design of repeating large curled repoussé floral blossoms, Tiffany & Co., New York, 8 1/2" l.. **2,760**

Bracelet, gold (18k), brushed & curved arched links, signed "M. Buccellati," 7 1/2" l.. **3,450**

Gold Cuff Bracelet with Lions

Bracelet, gold (18k) cuff-type, facing lions in repoussé, signed "Webb" (ILLUS.)......... **4,370**

Bracelet, gold (18k) & diamond, a flexible row of curved ribbed rectangular links alternating w/small rounded links & flanked by similar flexible rows of 140 bead-set diamonds, approx. 6.04 cts., signed "Tiffany & Co.," 7" l. **6,325**

Bracelet, gold (18k) & enamel, ruffled design w/textured gold links w/blue & green enamel (some enamel loss).... **431**

Bracelet, gold (18k), flexible design of wide, faceted square links spaced by gold half balls, 7 3/4" l........................ **489**

Bracelet, gold (18k), fluted & shaped curved links, brushed finish, 8" l........................ **575**

Bracelet, gold (18k) & sapphire, wide, hinged rectangular plaques set w/66 mixed-cut sapphires, approx. total wt. 43.0 cts., separated by chased abstract gold branches, 7 1/4" l........... **3,105**

Textured Gold Bracelet

Bracelet, gold (18k), textured woven links, signed "Buccellati," 7 3/4" l. (ILLUS.)............. **2,875**

Bracelet, gold (18k tricolor), comprised of three asymmetrical yellow, white & rose gold braided wire bangles, 24.70 dwt. (minor gold solder).. **431**

Bracelet, gold (18k tricolor), wide flexible mesh design of polished honeycomb links engraved in a geometric & floral pattern, 7 1/2".................. **1,380**

Bracelet, gold (18k white) & diamond, flexible design of round links set w/221 round brilliant-cut diamonds, weighing approx. 1.50 cts., 7" l..**1,100**

Bracelet, gold (18k yellow), amethyst & turquoise, designed as a wide bangle w/six prong-set amethysts & turquoise accents, flanked by twisted & solid bands of gold, partially obliterated hallmarks for Andre Poirier, Paris (one turquoise bead missing).................................... **805**

Bracelet, gold (18k yellow), buckle design, mesh w/pierced scroll motif buckle clasp, 33.00 dwt........................ **1,150**

Gold "Chaine d'Ancre" Link Bracelet

Bracelet, gold (18k yellow), "chaine d'ancre" links w/toggle clasp, signed "Hermes," 36.20 dwt. (ILLUS.)................. **7,186**

Tiffany Coral & Diamond Bracelet

Bracelet, gold (18k yellow), coral & diamond, a semi-rigid design constructed from seven fluted coral-set sections, each separated by a heavy gold wire-designed flower set w/a round brilliant-cut diamond having a total weight of approx. 1.15 cts., signed "Tiffany & Co.," 7" l. (ILLUS.)............................ **5,060**

Bracelet, gold (18k yellow), designed in an alternating pattern of open rectangular & modified knot links, one link inscribed, hallmarked & signed "Cartier, Inc.," Swiss, 55.9 dwt., 7 1/2" l. **3,220**

Bracelet, gold (18k yellow), designed w/H-shaped hinged links, suspended from a chain a round gold charm enclosing a gold ball, European hallmark, 6 1/4" l.... **546**

Gold & Diamond Bracelet

Bracelet, gold (18k yellow) & diamond, 3/4" wide band w/twisted gold wire design, set throughout w/256 small round diamonds, total approx. 13.50 cts., signed "Tiffany," approx. 53 dwt. (ILLUS.)............................ **19,550**

Bracelet, gold (18k yellow) & diamond, buckle style, centered by a platinum plaque w/collet- & bead-set round diamonds, approx. 3.68 cts., 6.00 mm. cultured pearl & channel-set French-cut sapphires, completed by a brick-style bracelet w/diamond & sapphire accents, adjustable length **2,875**

Bracelet, gold (18k yellow) & diamond, cuff-type designed as two panther heads enhanced w/22 small round diamonds & four small round emeralds, further enhanced w/a brushed finish, approx. 62.2 dwt............................. **1,955**

Bracelet, gold (18k yellow) & diamond, the reeded curb links centered by round diamonds, approx. total wt. 1.96 cts. **2,300**

Unusual Diamond & Gold Bracelet

Bracelet, gold (18k yellow) & diamond, wide hinged cuff-style decorated along centerline w/a detachable, flexible platinum bracelet decorated w/marquise-, baguette- & round brilliant-cut diamonds set in a ribbon motif, total approx. diamond weight 9.30 cts., cuff signed, platinum bracelet numbered, each approx. 6 1/2" l. (ILLUS.).............. **7,475**

Enamel & Diamond Bracelet

Bracelet, gold (18k yellow), enamel & diamond, a flexible, fluid, reptilian design decorated w/blue & green enameling & two rows of equispaced round brilliant-cut diamonds w/total approx. weight of 3 cts., approx. 7" l. (ILLUS.)............................. **2,875**

Enamel Snakeskin Bracelet

Bracelet, gold (18k yellow) & enamel, snakeskin-style design w/alternating rows of black & green enamel, approx. 6 5/8" l. (ILLUS.)................ **863**

Bracelet, gold (18k yellow), flexible design w/four rows of domed links accented by gold half beads, 68.20 dwt.. **1,380**

Bracelet, gold, 18k yellow gold ropetwist design w/white gold chain link accent, 7 1/4" l., 16.7 dwt. **575**

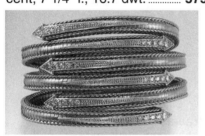

Unusual Gold & Diamond Bracelet

Bracelet, gold (18k yellow), platinum & diamond, hinged at the base w/three rows of gold on each side that separate & interlock at the top, the six rows each terminating in an arrow design set w/round brilliant-cut diamonds that have a total weight of approx. 1.50 cts., the gold having a parallel tile design decorated on the sides w/foxtail borders, number, French hallmarks & signed "Sterlé, Paris," 6 1/4" (ILLUS.) **6,325**

Gold & Ruby Bracelet

Bracelet, gold (18k yellow) & ruby, flexible design of openwork coiled links mounted throughout w/small round-cut rubies, signed "Tiffany & Co." (ILLUS.) **4,025**

Gold, Sapphire & Diamond Bracelet

Bracelet, gold (18k yellow), sapphire & diamond, the flexible tapered band centered by an oval section set w/an oval sapphire approx. 1 ct. & eight round full-cut diamonds, total approx. .75 cts., the band further adorned w/18 graduated small round sapphires, approx. 38.8 dwt. (ILLUS.)...**2,185**

Bracelet, gold (22k yellow) & gems, designed w/ten collet-set gemstones in various cuts, accented by applied gold beads & wiretwist, signed "Luna"................................... **805**

Ornate Gold & Amethyst Bracelet

Bracelet, gold, amethyst & turquoise, centering an openwork oval set w/a faceted amethyst, further decorated w/turquoise & ruby florets, flanked by flexible, hinged oval openwork links w/similar decoration, 6 3/4" l. (ILLUS.).................................. **863**

Bracelet, gold, designed as overlapping golf tee links in 18k yellow gold, signed "Gucci Italy," 23.7 dwt., 7" l. **1,380**

Bracelet, gold & diamond, an 18k yellow gold floral-decorated polished & cylindrical bead flexible mount, suspending from one bead a large 18k yellow & white gold floral-decorated bead tassel set w/16 single-cut diamonds weighing about .20 carats & 16 round faceted green chalcedony stones, 8 1/2" l.. **920**

Tricolor Rolling Bangle Bracelet

Bracelet, gold & platinum, rolling bangle w/rose gold, yellow gold & platinum bangles, French assay marks, numbered "25409" & signed "Cartier Paris," 67.0 dwt. (ILLUS.)............................ **6,009**

Bracelet, gold, sapphire & diamond, flexible mesh design coated w/textured gold grains, highlighted w/clusters of circular-cut sapphires & diamonds, 7 1/2" l. (some grains).............................. **2,415**

Bracelet, hawk's eye, designed w/rectangular cabochon hawk's eye links, measuring approx. 28.00 x 15.23 x 6.22 mm., 9k gold mounts, English hallmarks, boxed................................ **518**

Moonstone & Sapphire Bracelet

Bracelet, moonstone & sapphire, oval moonstones & collet-set sapphires mounted in fancy 14k yellow gold links, signed "Yard" for Raymond Yard, 6 3/4" l. (ILLUS.)............................. **2,300**

Bracelet, onyx & 18k yellow gold, alternating sugarloaf green onyx w/open rectangular onyx links, French hallmarks **1,725**

Bracelet, pearl & 14k gold, flexible tennis-style gold bracelet set w/30 4 1/2mm. cultured pearls **748**

Bracelet, pearl & diamond, four rows of cultured pearls spaced w/four knife-edge bars set w/diamonds, completed by a scroll motif clasp w/channel-set baguette-cut diamonds, prong- & bead-set round diamonds & prong-set marquise-cut diamonds, approx. total wt. 2.35 cts., 14k white gold mount, 7 1/2" l. **4,025**

Pearl & Diamond Bracelet

Bracelet, pearl & diamond, four strands of pearls measuring approx. 7.70 mm., separated by spacers set w/four round brilliant-cut diamonds, diamond-set domed shell motif clasp centered by a row of baguette-cut diamonds & bordered by baguette-cut diamonds, approx. total wt. 7.00 cts., platinum clasp, 14k white gold spacers (ILLUS. of part) **6,900**

Baroque Pearl Bracelet

Bracelet, pearl & diamond, hinged openwork top set w/baroque pink & grey pearls, diamond accents, 14k yellow gold mount (ILLUS.)............................... **920**

Cultured Pearl Bracelet

Bracelet, pearl, the single knotted strand w/21 egg-shaped freshwater cultured pearls measuring 13.5 x 9 mm., joined by a 14k yellow gold ring & bar clasp, each end of bar set w/a pearl measuring 6 1/2 m.., 8" l. (ILLUS.)............................ **431**

Bracelet, pearl, the triple strand w/84 cultured pearls measuring 6 1/2 to 7 mm., alternating w/two 14k yellow gold spacer bars joined by a 14k yellow gold cylindrical tongue-in-groove clasp, 7 1/2" l.................................... **748**

Peridot & Pearl Bracelet

Bracelet, peridot & pearl, designed w/graduated collet-set oval & rectangular peridots, twisted seed pearl links, silver-topped 18k yellow gold mount, boxed (ILLUS.).................................. **1,380**

Bracelet, platinum & diamond, designed as three rigid brushed tubular segments, the center section highlighted w/19 bezel-set diamonds, some w/yellow gold "halos," designed by Rudolph Erdling... **2,300**

Elegant Ruby & Diamond Bracelet

Bracelet, platinum, diamond & ruby, designed w/three diamond-set flowers, the middle flower centered by a round brilliant-cut diamond, approx. 2.10 cts., the two side flowers centered by an old European & an old mine-cut diamond, approx. total wt. 1.50 cts., round & French-cut diamond links, approx. total 11.00 cts., diamond flower clasp, round ruby highlights, one small diamond missing, accompanied by a letter of authenticity from Oscar Heyman (ILLUS.)............................... **25,300**

Bracelet, platinum, sapphire & diamond, line-type designed w/an alternating pattern of six round-cut diamonds, approx. 3.60 cts. & five channel-set sapphires, engraved gallery, signed "Tiffany & Co.," boxed **8,625**

Reverse-painted Crystal Bracelet

Bracelet, reverse-painted crystal, rectangular plaques depicting four different scenes, a woodcock, a grouse, a quail & a pheasant in flight, spaced by alternating gold leaf-shaped & crossed shotgun-shaped links, 14k gold frame, hallmark (ILLUS.)............................... **920**

Bracelet, ruby & diamond, flexible 18k white gold circular links set w/round brilliant-cut diamonds, alternating w/floral links center set w/round brilliant-cut diamonds flanked by four marquise rubies, total of 92 diamonds, weighing approx. 1.30 cts. & 48 rubies weighing approx. 4 cts., 7" l. **1,035**

Bracelet, ruby & diamond, line-type set w/35 cabochon rubies, each measuring approx. 4.00 x 2.20 mm., further highlighted by 68 diamond melée, 14k white & yellow gold, 6 3/4" l. (minor blemishes to some rubies) ... **1,265**

Sapphire and Diamond Bracelet

Bracelet, sapphire & diamond, a flexible design set w/seven emerald-cut blue sapphires alternating w/seven emerald-cut yellow sapphires, having a total weight of approx. 103 cts., accented between each sapphire w/a small round brilliant-cut diamond flanked by two tapered baguette diamonds, mounted in platinum, numbered & signed "Oscar Heyman," 7" l. (ILLUS.) **23,000**

Sapphire & Diamond Leaf Bracelet

Bracelet, sapphire & diamond, alternating pavé-set diamond & sapphire leaves, channel-set baguette stems, the 240 diamonds w/approx. total wt. of 21.95 cts., the 175 Burmese sapphires w/approx. total wt. of 18.00 cts., platinum mount, signed "Tiffany & Co.," w/original Tiffany box, 6 3/4" l. (ILLUS.) **41,400**

Bracelet, sapphire & diamond, designed as an alternating pattern of graduating round diamonds & emerald-cut sapphires, approx. total diamond wt. 2.09 cts., prong-set 18k white gold & collet-set platinum mount, millegrain & engraving accents **1,840**

Bracelet, silver & gold, trace link chain suspending a heart-shaped pendant wrapped in an 18k gold arrow, signed "Tiffany & Co.," 7" l. **202**

Bracelet, star sapphire & diamond, a hinged bangle, top centered by a cabochon star sapphire flanked by old mine-cut diamonds, set in 18k yellow gold w/black & white enamel detail, hallmarks for Carlo Giuliano **5,750**

Bracelet, sterling silver & lapis, hinged design of twisted sterling silver wire, cabochon lapis terminals, 14k yellow gold accents, signed "D. Yurman" **518**

Bracelet, tanzanite & 14k gold, line-type w/French-cut tanzanite stones weighing approx. 19.00 grams, approx. 7" l. **1,093**

Bracelet/ring, gold, zircon & citrine, eight hinged engraved circular links which convert from a bracelet to a ring, the clasp forming the top of the ring w/two interchangeable gemstones, a blue zircon & a citrine, French hallmarks **805**

Bracelets, bangle-type, round, hinged, w/saddles of green Peking glass within a gilt silver-chased & engraved mount, Chinese hallmarks, pr. **259**

Bracelets, gold (18k yellow) & diamond, hinged cuff style w/a brickwork design w/pavé-set diamond terminals, the 20 round diamonds totalling approx. 1 ct. each, signed "Webb," approx. 52.3 dwt., pr. **6,325**

Brooch, amethyst, an oval bezel-set faceted amethyst flanked by fan-shaped amethysts within an engraved platinum-topped 14k yellow gold openwork mount **748**

Amethyst & Diamond Brooch

Brooch, amethyst & diamond, a carved & faceted oval amethyst cameo depicting the profile of a classical female within an openwork diamond-set foliate platinum-topped 14k yellow gold mount (ILLUS.) **1,725**

Amethyst Grape Cluster Brooch

Brooch, amethyst & diamond, designed as a cluster of grapes set w/oval, faceted amethysts accented w/round brilliant-cut diamonds, the leaves pavé-set w/round single-cut diamonds, having a total weight of approx. 33 cts. for the amethyst & approx. 2.50 cts. for the diamonds, mounted in 18k yellow gold & 14k white gold (ILLUS.) **2,530**

Brooch, amethyst & pearl, centered by a collet-set oval amethyst, measuring approx. 15.98 x 12.20 x 7.69 mm. within a freshwater pearl & gold wire frame, millegrain & wiretwist accents, 14k yellow gold mount **431**

Brooch, anodized steel & pearl, designed as a spray of lilies-of-the-valley, curved & swirled anodized steel stems w/flexibly-set cultured pearls & diamond accents set in white gold & platinum, retailed by Marsh's **1,840**

Brooch, aquamarine, diamond & 18k white gold, abstract curvilinear design set w/an oval aquamarine measuring approx. 19.8 x 15.5 x 9.0 mm., further set w/full- & single-cut diamonds **1,265**

Brooch, aquamarine & diamond, openwork design of a flower & bud, faceted aquamarine petals w/diamond-set stems, platinum mount .. **2,105**

Fish Brooch

Brooch, aquamarine, ruby & diamond, a three-dimensional blow fish w/an oval-shaped, cabochon-cut aquamarine mouth, round faceted ruby eyes, set w/various hues of fancy champagne-colored diamond scales, diamond accents in the gills & mouth, mounted in 18k yellow gold, aquamarine weighs approx. 12 cts., the 111 diamonds approx. 6.50 cts. total weight, signed, numbered & w/hallmark, Vantichelen (ILLUS.) **3,220**

Brooch, citrine intaglio, carved in the profile of a man, possibly Rev. William Mason (1724-1797), within an 18k yellow gold oval frame w/applied wiretwist & grapevine decoration, intaglio signed "Burch," boxed (chip to citrine) **633**

Brooch, diamond & 14k yellow gold, designed as a turtle, the shell centering a fancy brown 3.00 ct. diamond, surrounded by pavé-set diamonds & emerald-set eyes.. **1,035**

Star-shaped Brooch

Brooch, diamond & 18k gold, nine graduating layers of gold wire in a star-shaped form surmounted by a diamond floret (ILLUS.) **489**

Brooch, diamond, a free-form stylized wing design, pavé-set w/90 round diamonds & 37 baguette-cut diamonds, total weight of approx. 7.5 cts., mounted in 14k white gold **4,600**

Diamond Bow Brooch

Brooch, diamond, bow design pavé-set w/round brilliant-cut diamonds & bordered by baguette diamonds, 360 diamonds approx. 4.20 cts., 18k white gold mount (ILLUS.)... **3,450**

Brooch, diamond, design of three flowers on curved stems tied w/bow, set throughout w/numerous circular, marquise- & baguette-cut diamonds, highlighted by yellow diamond petals, 18k gold **2,760**

Brooch, diamond & enamel, modeled as a beetle, the wings in green guilloché enamel, body, antennae & feet w/round diamonds set in silver, cabochon emerald eyes, sapphire accents, 14k yellow gold mount, Russian hallmarks **1,725**

Diamond Floral Brooch

Brooch, diamond, floral design set w/145 round brilliant-cut diamonds, stem set w/24 tapered baguette diamonds, weighing approx. 3.10 cts., 18k white gold mount, 2 1/4" h. (ILLUS.)...... **3,910**

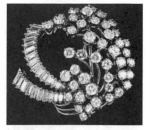

Diamond Floral Spray Brooch

Brooch, diamond, floral spray design set w/round brilliant-cut diamonds, stems set w/straight baguette-cut diamonds, approx. total weight 4.75 cts., mounted in platinum (ILLUS.)................................. **2,530**

Fancy Colored Diamond Floral Brooch

Brooch, diamond, floral spray design w/seven round colored diamonds ranging in color from fancy yellow to brown yellow to light grey, completed by a rectangular-cut fancy yellow diamond, approx. total wt. 7.68 cts., pavé-set diamond leaf, 14k white gold mount (ILLUS.) **10,350**

Brooch, diamond, openwork flower design, petals set w/old European-cut diamonds, approx. 2.90 cts. & decorated w/gold scrollwork, platinum-topped 14k yellow gold mount **1,955**

Brooch, diamond & pearl, bumble bee design, the platinum upper body & wings pavé-set w/81 round brilliant-cut diamonds, weighing approx. 1.40 cts., the lower body set w/one baroque Tahitian black pearl measuring 12.7 mm., 1 1/2" w., 1" l........ **1,725**

Diamond Ribbon Brooch

Brooch, diamond & platinum, designed as a spray of pear & marquise-shaped diamonds surmounted by baguette-set ribbons, approx. total 6.63 cts., numbered 186 (ILLUS.)............................... **6,900**

Diamond & Platinum Filigree Brooch

Brooch, diamond & platinum, European-cut diamonds weighing a total of approx. 2.50 cts. set in a filigree design, completed by a 14k gold bail & pin stem (ILLUS.) **2,185**

Diamond Leaf Brooch

Brooch, diamond & platinum, leaf design w/center diamond weighing approx. 1.00 cts., pavé-set w/245 old European-cut diamonds, approx. total wt. 9.80 cts. (ILLUS.).. **11,500**

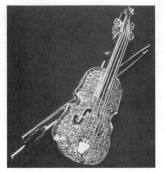
Diamond & Ruby Violin Brooch

Brooch, diamond, ruby & 14k yellow & white gold, designed as a violin, the body pavé-set w/50 round faceted diamonds weighing approx. .50 cts., the neck of the violin set w/11 square-cut rubies weighing approx. .40 cts. (ILLUS.)... **805**

Brooch, diamond & sapphire, abstract design of two slender crescent shapes, one platinum set w/27 round diamonds, total approx. 1.23 cts. & the other 18k yellow gold set w/24 calibré-cut sapphires, total approx. 2.58 cts., signed "Tiffany & Co. 13879".. **4,600**

Brooch, diamond & sapphire, circle design set w/20 round brilliant-cut diamonds weighing approx. .80 cts., alternating w/16 square-cut blue sapphires weighing approx. 1.60 cts., platinum mount...... **1,265**

Gem-set Floral Spray Brooch

Brooch, diamond, sapphire, ruby & emerald, floral spray design set on the stems w/a large oval faceted sapphire weighing approx. 3.50 cts., 22 smaller round faceted sapphires weighing approx. 2.15 cts., 24 round faceted rubies weighing approx. 2.25 cts., seven round faceted emeralds weighing approx. 1 ct. & 62 round brilliant- & single-cut diamonds weighing approx. 5.50 cts., platinum mount, ca. 1950 (ILLUS.)............................ **2,300**

Brooch, diamond, spray design w/three central leaves, pavé-set w/round brilliant-cut diamonds from which extend clusters of round brilliant-cut diamonds w/stems of baguette-cut diamonds, total diamond weight of approx. 9.5 cts., mounted in platinum............................... **5,520**

Brooch, emerald & diamond, a crescent-shaped design set w/old mine-cut diamonds alternating w/round cushion- & emerald-cut emeralds, mounted in 18k yellow & white gold.............................. **1,495**

Emerald & Diamond Frog Brooch

Brooch, emerald & diamond, modeled as a leaping frog, the body set w/an oval-shaped carved emerald, pavé-set round single-cut diamonds in the legs & head w/round cabochon-cut emerald eyes, mounted in 18k white & yellow gold, w/hallmarks (ILLUS.)...................... **4,140**

Emerald & Diamond Spray Brooch

Brooch, emerald & diamond, spray design set w/marquise, baguette & round diamonds, approx. total wt. 7.43 cts., suspending two flexibly-set square emerald-cut emeralds weighing approx. 1.44 cts. & 1.37 cts., platinum mount (ILLUS.) **10,925**

Floral Bouquet Brooch

Brooch, enamel, 18k yellow gold & diamond, designed as a bouquet of three flowers & textured leaves, the flowers of orange enamel w/gold trimmed petals & centered by a cluster of three diamonds, approx. 0.80 cts. (ILLUS.)............................... **1,380**

Sunflower Brooch

Brooch, enamel & 18k yellow gold, sunflower design in orange & yellow enamel, dated "1992" & signed "Cummings" for Angela Cummings (ILLUS.)............................... **1,610**

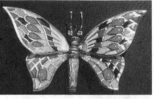

Unusual Cartier Butterfly Brooch

Brooch, enamel, a three-dimensional butterfly design w/moveable wings which open & close, decorated w/lavender, yellow, green, black, orange & white enameling in a geometric pattern on both sides, round brilliant-cut diamond eyes & ribbed 18k yellow gold body, numbered & signed "Cartier" (ILLUS.)............................ **3,450**

Brooch, enamel, designed as a parrot on a branch, green & red enamel w/diamond eye accent, 18k yellow gold mount.................................... **748**

Figural Enamel & Diamond Brooch

Brooch, enamel, diamond & 18k gold, designed as a winged woman holding a diamond-set double star, decorated w/pale pink & green guilloché enamel, some enamel loss (ILLUS.).................... **920**

Brooch, enamel & diamond, flower design w/blue plique-a-jour enamel petals, prong-set diamond pistils, diamond-set leaf in a platinum-topped 18k yellow gold mount (minor discoloration to metal of leaf)........................... **1,150**

Enamel & Diamond Turtle Brooch

Brooch, enamel & diamond, modeled as a turtle, the shell in shaded brown enamel set in 18k yellow gold, w/pavé-set diamond head, feet & tail in 18k white gold (ILLUS.) **1,610**

Dragonfly Brooch

Brooch, enamel, modeled as a dragonfly, cabochon emerald & rose-cut diamond body decorated w/green to blue shaded plique-a-jour enamel, wings set en tremblant & highlighted by rose-cut diamonds, platinum-topped 14k gold (ILLUS.)................................. **4,140**

Tsavorite & Diamond Orchid Brooch

Brooch, garnet & diamond, designed as an orchid w/tsavorite garnet petals, the stamen & stem enhanced by numerous circular-cut diamonds & a marquise-cut diamond, blackened 18k white gold mount (ILLUS.).............. **13,800**

Brooch, gemstone & 14k yellow gold, designed as a flower w/articulated yellow gold petals & pistils set w/rubies, sapphires, diamonds & emeralds, signed "Robert Altman, Inc." **805**

Brooch, gold (14k yellow) & aquamarine, centered by a heart-shaped aquamarine, measuring approx. 24.00 x 29.00 x 12.10 mm. within an ornate yellow gold frame **1,725**

Figural Crab Brooch

Brooch, gold (14k yellow), coral & diamond, model of a crab w/coral cabochon body & full-cut diamond eyes (ILLUS.) **690**

Brooch, gold (14k yellow), diamond & ruby, designed as a spray of daisies centered by box-set rubies & tied w/a diamond-set ribbon, signed "Tiffany & Co." **1,380**

Brooch, gold (14k yellow), model of a chased gold eagle engraved "Mikie" on back, partially obliterated mark for Tiffany & Co. **1,093**

Brooch, gold (14k yellow), Retro-style, designed as a bow tied w/a yellow gold center w/an applied row of collet-set diamonds & a spray w/diamond accented terminals **690**

Brooch, gold (14k yellow) & ruby, modeled as a bee, the eyes & body set w/20 round faceted rubies weighing approx. 3 cts., detailed honeycomb design wings, 1 x 1" **978**

Diamond Floral Brooch

Brooch, gold (18k bicolor) & diamond, floral design, the yellow & white gold mount center set w/63 round brilliant-cut pavé-set diamonds, approx. .95 cts. & the surrounding eight petals set w/146 round faceted & brilliant-cut fancy brown diamonds, approx. 6.60 cts. (ILLUS.) **1,725**

Brooch, gold (18k) & diamond, a curving gold feather plume design w/diamond highlights set in platinum, French hallmarks **3,450**

Brooch, gold (18k) & diamond, flower design w/eight large curved petals, each w/clipped edges & highlighted w/prong- & bead-set diamond melée, No. Z660, signed "J.E.C." for J.E. Caldwell & Co. **1,035**

Gold & Diamond Wire Spray Brooch

Brooch, gold (18k) & diamond, gold wire spray design centered by a cluster of old mine-cut diamonds w/diamond accents, approx. total 1.55 cts., signed "Mauboussin Paris no. P5024" (ILLUS.) **1,093**

Brooch, gold (18k) & diamond, the domed design comprised of woven 18k gold wire surmounted by a swirl of prong-set round diamonds, French hallmarks..... **2,185**

Brooch, gold (18k) & enamel, modeled as a racing panther w/black & brown enamel & pavé-set diamond accents, French hallmark.......................... **2,300**

Brooch, gold (18k), owl on branch, designed w/finely detailed matte finish feathers accented w/blue stone & diamond eyes **431**

Brooch, gold (18k), ruby & diamond, horse chestnut design, the articulated outer shell opens to reveal a prong-set ruby & diamond center, signed "Tiffany & Co." **1,725**

Brooch, gold (18k), textured knot design w/four ropetwist tassel terminals, signed "Tiffany & Co.," Italy **2,760**

Brooch, gold (18k white), diamond & emerald, designed as a stalking leopard, the body set w/172 round brilliant-cut pavé-set diamonds, approx. 1.10 cts. & 74 round faceted emeralds, approx. .70 cts., 1 3/4" l. **690**

Brooch, gold (18k yellow), amethyst & turquoise, designed as a bouquet w/prong-set amethyst petals w/turquoise accents & gold stems w/textured gold leaves, hallmarks for Andre Poirier, Paris **3,335**

Brooch, gold (18k yellow) & diamond, designed as a chrysanthemum w/open loop twisted gold petals centered by a cluster of round brilliant-cut diamonds, approx. 1.70 cts., signed "H.B." for Hammerman Bros............. **1,840**

Cartier Gold & Diamond Flower Brooch

Brooch, gold (18k yellow) & diamond, flower design, the center articulated petals set w/round diamonds, platinum collet settings, approx. total diamond wt. .70 cts., signed "Cartier Paris, No. 00584 or 06584" (ILLUS.) **5,750**

Brooch, gold (18k yellow), diamond & ruby, designed as a bee w/detailed gold wings, full-cut diamonds & round-cut rubies on body, ruby eyes, signed "Rosenthal" **489**

Brooch, gold (18k yellow), diamond & ruby, designed as a flowerhead w/a wide undulating Florentine finish border surrounding the white gold stamen set w/a cluster of round brilliant-cut diamonds weighing approx. .40 cts., surrounded by 12 round faceted rubies weighing approx. .35 cts., 1 1/2" d............... **920**

Brooch, gold (18k yellow), diamond, ruby, sapphire & emerald, textured openwork gold wire knot design, set w/cabochon round rubies, sapphires & emeralds, faceted round brilliant-cut diamonds, approx. total diamond wt. 1.20 cts. **978**

Diamond Bar Brooch

Brooch, gold (18k yellow) & diamond, stylized vertical bar design tapering to a point, two rows of baguette-cut diamonds, approx. 3.40 cts. (ILLUS.) **3,450**

Brooch, gold (18k yellow) & diamond, textured gold bow design w/diamond highlights, approx. total diamond wt. 2.06 cts., European hallmark **2,070**

Gold & Enamel Clown Brooch

Brooch, gold (18k yellow) & enamel, designed as an enameled yellow gold clown sitting in a textured white gold crescent moon w/diamond accents (ILLUS.) **4,600**

Cartier Figural Native American Brooch

Brooch, gold (18k yellow gold), the figure of a Native American, bow slung over his back, finely textured feathered headdress w/ruby trim, turquoise-set shawl w/textured fringe, sapphire eyes, numbered, maker's mark, signed "Cartier," w/leather Cartier box (ILLUS.) **3,450**

Figural Fly Brooch

Brooch, gold (18k yellow gold), turquoise, ruby & diamond, designed as a fly, featuring one oval-shaped Persian turquoise cabochon enhanced by one oval-shaped ruby cabochon, eyes & wings w/full-cut diamonds (ILLUS.) **1,380**

Brooch, gold (18k yellow), model of a koala, brushed gold w/ruby eyes, hallmark **460**

Brooch, gold (18k yellow), opal & diamond, modeled as two violets, the larger flower-head set en tremblant, w/prong-set black opals & pavé bead-set round diamond petals mounted in 18k yellow gold, the leaf also pavé diamond-set, signed "W.T. Ltd.," hallmarks, w/fitted box **2,185**

Brooch, gold (18k yellow) & pearl, designed as a twisted wire freeform knot, pearl accents, platinum-topped 18k yellow gold mount **518**

Gold & Pearl Fish Brooch

Brooch, gold (18k yellow) & pearl, model of a fish, the flexible tail set w/eight round brilliant-cut diamonds, weighing approx. .20 cts., the head set w/an irregularly shaped mabé pearl, the eye set w/a round faceted emerald weighing approx. .15 cts., two pearl-shaped rubies weighing approx. .30 cts. set at the mouth, marked "GK," 1" w., 2 1/2" l. (ILLUS.) **805**

Brooch, gold (18k yellow) & ruby, modeled as a hummingbird, the textured bird perched on a flowering branch, the flowerhead centered by a cluster of five round rubies, diamond accent, 9.10 dwt. **633**

Stylized Leaf Design Brooch

Brooch, gold (18k yellow), sapphire & diamond, stylized leaf on a branch accented w/round-cut sapphires, approx. 0.95 cts. & round-cut diamonds, approx. 0.50 cts. (ILLUS.)................................. **863**

Brooch, gold (18k yellow), two swans w/necks crossed, textured wings & body, emerald eyes (one missing), 15.1 dwt. **805**

Dogwood Tree Brooch

Brooch, gold, aquamarine & ruby, 18k yellow gold openwork dogwood tree-form mount, each stamen set w/one faceted ruby weighing about .40 carats, surrounding each stamen are four oval faceted aquamarines each weighing about 1 carat, 2 x 2 1/2" (ILLUS.) **575**

Brooch, gold (bicolor), model of an eagle, 18k white gold head, textured 18k yellow gold body, diamond accent & ruby eyes, hallmark **518**

Gold Leaf Brooch

Brooch, gold, designed as two wind-blown leaves attached to a vine accented w/three circular-cut diamond accents, approx. total wt. 0.24 cts., 14k yellow gold mount, stamped "Laykin etc. at. I. Magnin & Co.," 23.1 dwt. (ILLUS.)................................. **748**

Brooch, gold, diamond & turquoise, floral-shaped, an 18k yellow & white gold mount, the stamen set w/one round brilliant-cut diamond weighing about .10 carats surrounded by six turquoise half-beads, the stems & curled leaves set w/ten single-cut diamonds, Italy, 1 1/2" w., 2 1/4" h. **604**

Brooch, gold, dragonfly design, tips of the openwork wings set w/single-cut diamonds, tail set w/square-cut emeralds to delineate segments, diamond terminal, emerald eyes **259**

Hummingbird Brooch

Brooch, gold & enamel, hummingbird design w/brown enamel body & textured gold feathers, highlighted w/sapphires (ILLUS.) **489**

Brooch, gold, modeled as a bison, textured 18k yellow gold w/red stone eyes & round brilliant-cut diamond accents, signed "Cartier, No. 20577," 13.0 dwt. **863**

Brooch, gold, modeled as a panther, textured 18k yellow gold w/diamond eye accent, marked "Italy, No. 237AL," 11.6 dwt. **518**

Brooch, gold & silver, spray of three textured yellow bicolored gold leaves & pods surmounted by silver wire thistles, signed "M. Buccellati" .. **2,588**

Hematite, Dyed Jasper & Pearl Brooch

Brooch, hematite, jasper, pearl & 18k yellow gold, center set w/a large dyed jasper tablet surrounded by various shaped hematite & cultured pearls set in ribbed cone-shapes, additionally enhanced w/seven small round diamonds, approx. .30 cts. (ILLUS.) **2,185**

Brooch, jade, a rectangular form of carved & pierced variegated green jadeite jade in a foliate design, mounted in a frame of 14k yellow gold **518**

Jade & Diamond Brooch

Brooch, jade & diamond, centered by an oval foliate carved jade plaque, diamond-set ends, 18k white gold mount, millegrain accents (ILLUS.) **1,380**

Abstract Form Jade & Diamond Brooch

Brooch, jade & diamond contemporary style openwork abstract frame set w/three bezel-set jades & two baguette-cut diamonds, textured 18k yellow gold, signed "Janiye" (ILLUS.) **920**

Jade & Pearl Brooch

Brooch, jade, gold & pearl, centered by a round jade plaque edged w/seed pearls within a 14k yellow gold oval frame w/applied bead & wiretwist decoration (ILLUS.) **633**

Lapis Lazuli Butterfly Brooch

Brooch, lapis lazuli & diamond, model of a butterfly w/spread carved lapis lazuli wings accented w/three small round brilliant-cut & single-cut diamonds, mounted in 14k yellow gold, signed "Gump" (ILLUS.) **575**

Brooch, moonstone & 14k yellow gold, textured gold sailboat highlighted by moonstones depicting waves, diamond & sapphire accents .. **633**

Brooch, moonstone & sapphire, center carved moonstone face framed in sapphires & rose-cut diamonds further surrounded by moonstones & small sapphires, 14k yellow gold mount **1,093**

Moonstone & Sapphire Floral Spray Brooch

Brooch, moonstone & sapphire, curved design of a foliate branch set w/pear-shaped moonstones & round faceted sapphires, 14k yellow gold mount (ILLUS.) **805**

Moonstone & Sapphire Crescent Brooch

Brooch, moonstone, sapphire & diamond, crescent design centered by a sugarloaf moonstone, enhanced by marquise shape yellow sapphires, freshwater pearls & eight circular-cut diamonds, 18k white gold mount, signed "Luscher" (ILLUS.).... **2,070**

Opal & Diamond Brooch

Brooch, opal & diamond, foliate design set w/cabochon opals, rose-cut diamonds & demantoid garnet accents, silver & 14k yellow gold mount (ILLUS.) **1,265**

Black Opal Doublet & Diamond Brooch

Brooch, opal & diamond, the oval black opal doublet surrounded by a platinum foliate framework set w/20 round & 70 small round diamonds, total approx. 2.10 cts. (ILLUS.) **3,737**

Brooch, opal, emerald & garnet, butterfly design, opal body, emerald head, green garnet eyes, the wings set w/rubies, emeralds & diamonds in an 18k gold & silver-top mounting **2,645**

Opal Birds Brooch

Brooch, opal, ruby, diamond & 18k yellow gold, designed as three birds in flight, featuring full-cut diamonds enhanced by triangular-shaped opal wings, accented by calibré-cut rubies (ILLUS.) **1,035**

Pearl & Diamond Swan Brooch

Brooch, pearl, diamond & 14k white gold, model of a swan, the body composed of a freshwater pearl, the neck & head accented w/round diamonds & a cabochon ruby-set eye (ILLUS.) **1,610**

Brooch, pearl & diamond, flower design, the petals & leaves composed of baroque pearls centered by a grey pearl surrounded by five prong-set round brilliant-cut diamonds, the stem set w/nine tapered baguette-cut diamonds, platinum mount **20,700**

Brooch, pearl, model of a pussy willow, 14k textured gold branch mount, freshwater pearl pussy willows (one pearl missing) **978**

Cultured Pearl & Diamond Brooch

Brooch, pearl, platinum & diamond, centered by a cultured pearl measuring approx. 18.30 mm., further designed w/44 round brilliant-cut diamonds & 14 straight baguettes, approx. total wt. 4.88 cts., terminal set w/cut-corner triangle-cut diamonds, approx. total weight 2.03 cts., signed "Winston" for Harry Winston, original leather pouch (ILLUS.) **20,700**

Diamond Heart & Arrow Brooch

Brooch, platinum & diamond, double heart & arrow design, set w/round brilliant-cut diamonds, approx. 2.50 cts. (ILLUS.) **2,415**

Comtemporary Diamond Brooch

Brooch, platinum & diamond, triangular openwork design set w/three large round old European-cut diamonds & 48 smaller old European- & single-cut diamonds, K. Uyedoe, Tokyo, Japan, total diamond weight 6.50 cts. (ILLUS.) **5,750**

Platinum & Diamond Flower Brooch

Brooch, platinum & diamond, two bell-form flowers w/baguette- & pavé-set diamonds, the smaller flower also w/buff top amethyst & ruby accents (ILLUS.) **12,650**

Brooch, reverse-painted crystal, depicting a standing boxer dog wIthIn an oval 14k gold frame, signed "W.F. Marcus" **920**

Rock Crystal & Diamond Brooch

Brooch, rock crystal & diamond, designed as a leaf accented w/21 circular-cut diamonds, platinum-topped 14k yellow gold, minor chips to crystal, Tiffany & Co. (ILLUS.)... **2,070**

Ruby & Diamond Brooch

Brooch, ruby & diamond, designed as two tapered rows of bead-set round brilliant-cut diamonds intertwined w/curved gold wires terminating in three rows of prong-set round, faceted rubies, mounted in platinum & 18k yellow gold, Güblin, numbered w/hallmarks (ILLUS.)... **1,380**

Ruby & Diamond Bee Brooch

Brooch, ruby & diamond, figural bee, the body pavé-set w/rubies, the wings w/pavé-set diamonds, cabochon emerald eyes, 18k yellow gold mount (ILLUS.)................ **4,830**

Ruby & Emerald Berry Brooch

Brooch, ruby, emerald, diamond & 18k gold, designed as a cluster of strawberries w/cabochon rubies & emeralds on curved stems w/diamond-set caps, pierced & textured   diamond-set leaves, approx. total wt. 2.01 cts., French assay marks, 28.2 dwt., together w/Raymond Yard box (ILLUS.)....... **3,738**

Brooch, ruby & gold, horse chestnut design, the articulated outer shell opening to reveal a prong-set diamond & ruby center, 18k yellow gold mount, signed "Tiffany & Co.".................................... **2,645**

Brooch, sapphire & 14k gold, flowerhead & leaf design, centered by an oval sapphire approx. 1.20 cts., signed "BB&B" for Bailey, Banks & Biddle, together w/original box (nick to sapphire)................ **805**

Brooch, sapphire, diamond & bicolor gold, designed as three textured yellow gold birds perched on a brushed rose gold branch, bodies & eyes set w/blue sapphires, emerald plumes, pavé-set & marquise-cut diamond accents, 18k gold............................ **2,990**

Brooch, sapphire & diamond, centered by a foliate cluster of round sapphires & diamonds set in platinum, reeded 18k yellow gold mount, French hallmarks............................ **863**

Sapphire & Diamond Circle Brooch

Brooch, sapphire & diamond, circular w/20 channel-set sapphires & 20 circular-cut diamonds, 14k white gold mount (ILLUS.) **748**

Floral Spray Brooch

Brooch, sapphire, diamond & platinum, floral spray design w/clusters of 11 circular-cut diamonds each centered by an oval sapphire, baguette set stem surmounted by a floret accent, approx. total diamond wt. 3.00 cts., hallmark for McTeigue (ILLUS.) **4,313**

Sapphire, Emerald & Diamond Brooch

Brooch, sapphire, emerald & diamond, a spray design featuring pear-shaped sapphires, approx. 5.00 cts., pear-shaped emeralds, approx. 2.00 cts. & pear-, marquise-, oval- & baguette-cut diamonds, approx. 10.50 cts., platinum mounting (ILLUS.) **15,525**

Brooch, sapphire, emerald & diamond, designed as a parrot perched on a branch, the body w/cabochon sapphires & diamonds, coral beak, emerald & diamond eyes, 18k yellow gold mount, 20.1 dwt. **1,265**

Brooch, silver, 14k yellow gold & enamel, designed as an engraved gold lion encircled by a green enameled serpent in a twisted silver branch frame w/gold leaves & enameled berries, red stone eye accents **863**

Brooch, sterling silver & chrysoprase, shield form w/purplish blue enamel surmounted by a buff top pyramid-shaped chrysoprase, suspending three chrysoprase teardrops, hallmarks for Theodor Fahrner & Patriz Huber, imported by Murrie/Bennet & Co. (minor enamel loss) **2,070**

Flowerhead Brooch

Brooch, tourmaline & diamond, flowerhead design, the petals set w/pink tourmaline, highlighted by diamonds, set in platinum & 18k yellow gold, signed "Tiffany & Co." (ILLUS.) **8,625**

Large Diamond Double Brooch Clip

Brooch clip, diamond, double, a spray of flowers, designed from triangular-, hexagonal-, square-, lozenge-, round-, marquise- & straight & tapered baguette-cut diamonds, approx. total weight 25 cts., mounted in platinum, one small round diamond missing, both clips fit into a 14k white gold brooch attachment, w/maker's mark (ILLUS.)... **14,950**

Diamond Floral Brooch Clip

Brooch clip, diamond, floral design w/round, pear-shaped & marquise-shaped brilliant-cut & baguette-cut diamonds, approx. 15.50 cts., one small marquise diamond missing, mounted in platinum w/18k white gold clip (ILLUS.) **10**

Floral Spray with Diamonds & Emeralds

Brooch/clip, diamond, emerald & 18k yellow gold, designed as a floral spray w/pavé diamond petals outlined in gold wiretwist, centered by emerald clusters, diamond-set stem, approx. total weight 12.5 cts., signed "Tiffany & Co.," France (ILLUS.)............................... **11,500**

Carved Emerald Brooch/Pendant

Brooch/pendant, carved emerald & diamond, central hexagon emerald surmounted by rose-cut diamonds, the reverse carved w/foliate motifs within a framework of circular-cut diamond swags, cabochon emeralds & pearls suspending a removable rose-cut capped emerald drop, 18k gold (ILLUS.)....... **10,350**

Diamond & Pearl Butterfly Brooch

Brooch/pendant, diamond & pearl, designed as a butterfly, the wings highlighted w/seed pearls & old European-cut diamonds set in platinum, approx. total wt. 2.90 cts., missing fore leg, 14k gold (ILLUS.)................................. **3,565**

Brooch/pendant, emerald & diamond, pavé-set diamond 18k white gold bow edged in yellow gold w/channel-set calibré-cut emeralds **1,093**

Brooch/pendant, mixed metal, abstract shakudo design in 11k & 18k gold, palladium & sterling silver, centering a biwa pearl, signed "LDW" **403**

Reverse Intaglio Brooch

Brooch/pendant, quartz, ruby, diamond & emerald, centered by a large reverse intaglio carved oval-shaped smokey quartz depicting a female profile, square-cut rubies set above & below w/full-cut diamonds at the sides centered by an emerald cabochon, 18k gold frame (ILLUS.) **2,070**

Pink Sapphire Brooch/Pendant

Brooch/pendant, sapphire & 10k yellow gold, a sunburst design, enhanced by round-cut pink sapphires, retractable bail (ILLUS.)...................... **1,265**

Cameo bracelet, lava & stone cameos & silver, links depicting various chariot scenes, approx. 7 1/2" l............. **288**

Shell Cameo Brooch

Cameo brooch, carved shell, depicting winged female figures leading a group of prancing horses within a horizontal oval 14k yellow gold frame, applied wiretwist detail (ILLUS.).. **748**

Sardonyx Cameo Brooch

Cameo brooch, sardonyx, depicting the bust of a male in profile within an 18k yellow gold laurel & berry motif frame, signed "M. & Co." for Marcus & Co. (ILLUS.) **1,725**

Cameo earrings, carved shell & jet, designed as a jet ball suspending pendant teardrop-shaped drops inset w/shell cameos w/woman's profile, pr. (minor wear to cameos) **259**

Cameo earrings, carved shell & tortoiseshell, oval tops suspending an openwork scrolled tortoiseshell frame centered by an oval cameo, pr. **316**

Cameo pendant/brooch, agate, depicting Diana, goddess of the hunt, within an 18k yellow gold scroll motif frame set w/ten seed pearls, retractable bail, cameo signed "E. Girardet," together w/box (hairline to agate, minor lead solder to back of frame) **1,265**

Cameo ring, carved shell, depicting classical woman's profile, 18k yellow gold ropetwist oval mount.................. **374**

Stone Cameo Ring

Cameo ring, rectangular shape set w/a deeply carved & detailed carnelian cameo of a soldier's profile, mounted in 14k yellow gold (ILLUS.)................................. **403**

Chain, crystal, garnet & gold, eight faceted garnets & crystal roundels w/seed pearl accents joined by a 18k yellow gold trace link chain, garnet floret clasp, 45 1/2" l.................. **489**

Chain, gold (14k yellow) & diamond, diamond-set curb link chain, approx. total wt. 7.00 cts., 66.60 dwt., 30" l. **6,498**

Chain, gold (14k yellow) & diamond, flat curb links, front links w/pavé-set diamonds, obliterated signature for Tiffany & Co., 43.20 dwt............. **1,725**

Chain, gold (18k bicolor) & pearl, a cable link chain designed w/alternating engine-turned engraved bars & cultured pearls, pink & green gold, toggle clasp, w/hallmark, 41 1/2" l............................. **1,610**

Chain, gold (18k), yellow gold stirrup-form links spaced by oval white gold links, signed "Gucci," 31" l. **575**

Chain, turquoise & 14k yellow gold, ten collet-set stones set at intervals, joined by a trace link chain w/swivel clasp, 29" l. **575**

Enamel & Diamond Medallion & Chain

Chain & pendant, enamel & diamond, the chain w/alternating gold & blue enameled links suspending a blue enameled plaque depicting the astrological sign of Gemini, centering the "twins" surrounded by five diamond stars & framed by waves of gold, 33 1/2" l. (ILLUS.).......... **1,265**

Charm bracelet, gold (14k yellow), open rectangular & circle links suspending five charms including an Asian medallion, a reeded gold disk centered by a diamond, a picture charm & a gilt cuff link charm, 31.40 dwt................ **413**

Charm bracelet, gold (14k yellow), the double circular link band suspending assorted pendants designed as sea shells, approx. 10.4 dwt... **143**

Diamond Choker

Choker, diamond, seven stylized lozenge-shaped sections, tapering in size, each decorated w/three marquise-shaped diamonds flanked by round brilliant-cut diamonds w/round brilliant-cut diamonds forming the borders, approx. total weight 8.75 cts., attached to snake chain, approx. 13 1/2" l. (ILLUS.)................................. **5,750**

Choker, peridot, designed w/faceted flower-shaped & round beads, 17" l. **2,185**

Clip, diamond & 18k gold, three flowers w/pavé-set diamond petals, each centered by an old European-cut diamond, approx. total wt. 1.35 cts., 188 pavé-set diamonds, French assay marks, approx. total wt. 9.40 cts... **5,175**

Clip, gold (18k yellow), diamond & sapphire, the fluted swirl design set to the center w/a small round diamond & flanked by two small round sapphires, hallmarked for Preformed Parts & signed "Tiffany & Co.," approx. 7.4 dwt. **862**

Diamond, Emerald & Sapphire Brooch

Clip brooch, diamond, emerald & sapphire, an open ribbon design w/random clusters of 40 round, brilliant-cut diamonds, approx. 4.50 cts., 50 round faceted emeralds, approx. 4.50 cts. & 34 round faceted sapphires, approx. 3.25 cts., mounted in 18k yellow gold & platinum (ILLUS.)............................... **3,910**

Clip brooch, diamond & sapphire, double, centered by two trapezoid-cut diamonds, weighing approx. 2.10 cts. & 1.91 cts., surrounded by round-, square- & baguette-cut diamonds, approx. total wt. 10.46 cts., w/carved foliate sapphire in a buckle motif setting, 18k white gold mount............................... **17,250**

Gold Circle Clip Brooch

Clip brooch, gold (14k), ruby & diamond, circular form w/overall reeded pattern highlighted w/channel-set rubies & bead-set diamonds within an arch-shaped element (ILLUS.)............................... **1,380**

Clip/brooch, gold (18k) & gems, stylized openwork design of two leaves joined by a diamond melée band, leaves set w/various colored stones, including amethysts, sapphires, citrines, aquamarines & emeralds, Gübelin....... **863**

Clip/brooch, gold (18k), sapphire & diamond, designed as a bouquet w/four flower-head clusters, the stems tied w/a plaque stamped "Forget me not," No. 3431, French assay marks, signed "Van Cleef & Arpels" **1,840**

Emerald & Diamond Clips

Clips, emerald, diamond & platinum, the pair suspending a cascade of 34 pear-shaped emeralds, approx. total wt. 8.00 cts., surface fissure to one emerald, encircled by 18 pear-shaped & undulating baguette diamonds, approx. total wt. 15.50 cts., pr. (ILLUS.) **17,250**

King & Queen Enamel Clips

Clips, gold & enamel, red, white, blue & black enamel king & queen figures w/diamond-set crowns, reverse w/French, English & American registry numbers, damage to enamel, signed "Cartier, Paris," pr. (ILLUS.) **9,775**

Cocktail ring, amethyst, diamond & garnet, set w/a modified cushion-cut amethyst framed in 14 diamonds, approx. total wt. .70 cts. & bordered w/round garnets, 18k yellow gold mount **1,380**

Diamond & Ruby Cocktail Ring

Cocktail ring, diamond, ruby & platinum, the modified oblong top set to the center w/a round diamond, approx. .66 cts. surrounded by two scrolling bands of 28 square-cut rubies, total approx. 1.50 cts., the shoulders pavé-set w/26 small round diamonds, total approx. .60 cts. (ILLUS.) **4,312**

Cocktail ring, platinum & diamond, the twisted wire domed design set w/a rectangular-cut diamond, approx. 3.38 cts., surrounded by 104 round diamonds, total approx. 5 cts., signed "Webb" **17,825**

Cocktail ring, platinum, emerald & diamond, centered by a cluster of round brilliant-cut diamonds & round emeralds, within a baguette-set diamond bypass platinum mount, approx. total diamonds wt. 2.00 cts **2,070**

Silver Cross w/Moonstone & Amethysts

Cross, silver, moonstone & amethyst, centered by an oval moonstone, cabochon amethyst terminals, collet-set diamond & silver bead accents, signed "FG Hale," together w/a fancy link chain, 22" l. (ILLUS.) **1,265**

Cross pendant, diamond & 18k gold, contemporary brushed gold design, centered by an old European-cut diamond weighing approx. 0.45 cts., further enhanced by multicolored cabochon gemstones, the reverse centered by a chrysocolla, suspending an amethyst bead & freshwater pearl gold chain, 23 3/4" l. **863**

Amethyst & Gold Cross Pendant

Cross pendant, gold & amethyst, a delicate gold beading & floral design, decorated w/six round, faceted amethyst, mounted in 9k yellow gold w/15k overlay (ILLUS.).............................. **1,035**

Cross pendant & chain, diamond, the cross form set w/17 round brilliant-cut diamonds & rose-cut diamond accents having a total weight of approx. 3.20 cts., mounted in a platinum frame, 14k white gold chain 18" l............. **2,530**

Cat's Eye Chrysoberyl Cuff Links

Cuff links, chrysoberyl & 14k yellow gold, each centering an oval-shaped cabochon-cut cat's eye chrysoberyl, having a total weight of approx. 3.30 cts., set in oval-shaped domed disks engraved w/a florentine finish, pr. (ILLUS.) **2,415**

Citrine & Diamond Cuff Links

Cuff links, citrine & diamond, pyramidal-shaped design, faceted citrine, the top of which is studded w/a small round brilliant-cut diamond, attached to a flexible chain & rigid bar back, mounted in 18k yellow gold, pr. (ILLUS.)
.... **1,035**

Cuff links, diamond & 18k yellow gold, circular form, surmounted by baguette diamonds in a geometric design, French hallmarks, pr. **1,265**

Cuff links, diamond & gold, stirrup design in bicolor 18k gold w/a collet-set round brilliant-cut diamond accent on the side, squeeze bar clasp, signed "Cartier, No. 250515"
.... **1,495**

Cuff links, emerald, double ball form, pavé bead-set w/faceted emeralds, rose gold mount, pr. **748**

Gold & Enamel Cuff Links

Cuff links, enamel & 18k yellow gold, blue & white enamel stripes surrounding an oval blue enamel center, minor chips & scratches to enamel, signed "Webb," pr. (ILLUS.)............................... **2,185**

Cuff links, enamel & 18k yellow gold, irregular shape accented w/green plique-a-jour enamel, a raised engraved gold snake design forming the edge, hallmarked "MR," pr. **1,380**

Cuff links, enamel, coral & pearl & 18k yellow gold, figure of a man w/pearl head & coral body, black enameled jacket & pants riding a broomstick-handle horse, pr. .. **920**

Cuff links, enamel, designed as a rectangular blue & white enamel postal stamp, possibly South African, trace link chain & barbell fastener, 9k gold, pr. **201**

Cuff links, gold (14K), circular form w/applied head of a boxer dog w/diamond eyes, 16.3 dwt., pr. **489**

Cuff links, gold (14k), one w/etched design of a bull, the other of a bear, fixed bar link, pr. **546**

Cuff links, gold (14k yellow), depicting the Prince of Wales feathers against a light blue porcelain background, pr. **288**

Cuff links, gold (14k yellow) & malachite, designed w/malachite button, beaded gold "X" accent, signed "Cartier no. 27964," pr. **633**

Cuff links, gold (14k yellow) & sapphire, double-sided square shape w/criss-cross design w/a round, faceted sapphire set in center of X in each corner, pr. **748**

Cuff links, gold (14k yellow) & star sapphire, designed w/a collet-set oval star sapphire, one measuring approx. 9.89 x 7.99 mm., the other 9.35 x 8.71 mm., yellow gold T-bar, pr. **403**

Cuff links, gold (18k) & diamond, depicting a demon's face, old mine-cut diamond-set mouth, hallmark for MR, pr. **920**

Cuff links, gold (18k), enamel & diamond, designed as black spades centered w/a collet-set rose-cut diamond, pr. **460**

Cuff links, gold (18k yellow), double-sided links designed as an owl perched on a bar of calibré-cut rubies & decorated w/rose-cut diamond eyes, pr. **2,070**

Cuff links, gold (18k yellow) & enamel, double-sided octagonal shape, decorated w/a border of blue enamel, pr. **460**

Gold Cuff Links with Enamel Stripes

Cuff links, gold (18k yellow) & enamel, oval-shaped design enhanced by alternating stripes of blue & reddish brown enamel, each signed "Tiffany & Co.," pr. (ILLUS.) ... **403**

Earring/brooches, gold, ruby & cultured pearl, each 14k textured gold openwork floral-design mount set w/13 round & oval faceted rubies weighing about 2 carats suspending a baroque cultured pearl tassel measuring 9 mm., earrings may be worn as pins, 2 1/2" l., pr. **316**

Amethyst & Mabe Pearl Earring

Earrings, amethyst & mabe pearl, designed w/interchangeable centers & framed w/circular- & graduating baguette-cut diamonds, 14k white gold mount, clip-on, pr. (ILLUS. of one) **2,185**

Earrings, aquamarine, prong-set oval studs, mounted in 14k white gold, pr............................. **633**

Earrings, coral & diamond, textured 18k yellow gold ribbon form centered w/a small oval-shaped cabochon-cut coral suspending a fluted pear-shaped coral drop w/a small round brilliant-cut diamond accent, pr. **450**

Coral & Turquoise Earrings

Earrings, coral, diamond & turquoise, centering a large round fluted coral cabochon surrounded by 12 round brilliant-cut diamonds, approx. 1.50 cts., w/a border of 12 oval-shaped cabochon-cut turquoises, mounted in 18k yellow & white gold, clip-on, pr. (ILLUS.) **2,760**

Coral & Emerald Earrings

Earrings, coral, emerald & diamond, centering an oval-shaped cabochon-cut emerald surrounded by two round brilliant-cut diamonds & bor-

dered by ten oval-shaped cabochon-cut corals, each separated by a heavy gold wire w/a twisted wire scalloped border, 18k yellow & white gold mount, approx. 4.50 cts of emerald & 2.50 cts. diamonds, clip-on, pr. (ILLUS.)........................... **2,760**

Earrings, diamond & 14k white gold, "huggies" style w/reversible pavé-set diamond front & plain gold back, the 84 round diamonds approx. 1.70 cts........ **1,495**

Earrings, diamond & 18 k. gold, pavé-set diamond stylized bean shape, signed "Elsa Peretti" for Tiffany & Co., pr... **3,220**

Earrings, diamond & 18k yellow gold, half-hoop design w/ten prong-set round diamonds & 80 channel-set tapered baguettes, approx. total wt. 3.11 cts., posts w/omega clip-backs, hallmark, pr.................................... **1,725**

Earrings, diamond, a long scrolling floral design decorated w/marquise-, baguette, emerald-, pear- and round brilliant-cut diamonds w/a total weight of 17 cts. total, mounted in platinum, pr. **5,750**

Earrings, diamond, circular-cut stud-type, each weighing approx. 0.85 cts., mounted in gold, pr.. **4,600**

Earrings, diamond, designed as cluster of eight rose-cut diamonds, 14k gold mount, Russian hallmarks, pr............. **1,380**

Earrings, diamond, designed as pavé-set natural pink diamond hoops highlighted by an emerald-cut diamond, 18k yellow gold mount, signed "Cartier No. 51630," French hallmarks, boxed, pink diamonds accompanied by Gem Testing Laboratory of Great Britain certificate, pr. **12,650**

Diamond Earrings

Earrings, diamond, designed as two concentric rows of round brilliant-cut diamonds having a total weight of approx. 5.40 cts., each earring suspending five marquise-shaped brilliant-cut diamonds having a total weight of approx. 1.20 cts. for the ten stones, mounted in platinum, pr. (ILLUS.) **4,140**

Earrings, diamond, designed w/a diamond stud terminal w/knife-edge bar suspending a larger prong-set round brilliant-cut diamond, approx. total diamond wt. 1.39 cts., 14k white gold mounts, pr. **1,725**

Earrings, diamond, drop design set w/a round brilliant-cut tapering baguette completed by a pear-shaped diamond, approx. 2.61 cts., platinum mount, pr. **6,900**

Elegant Diamond Earrings

Earrings, diamond, each set w/a round brilliant-cut diamond weighing approx. 3.0 cts., suspended from a row of three hexagonal-cut diamonds having a total weight of approx. 0.50 ct., free-hanging from an old mine-cut diamond weighing approx. 0.50 ct., having a total weight of approx. 8.0 cts., mounted in platinum w/18k white gold posts, French hallmarks, pr. (ILLUS.) **21,850**

Earrings, diamond, egg-shaped drops pavé-set w/round brilliant-cut diamonds enhanced w/interwoven swirls of black enamel, suspended from a round ear pad by a double stirrup link, also set w/round diamonds & black enamel, in 14k white & yellow gold, w/Russian hallmarks & fitted wooden box, pr. **2,760**

Earrings, diamond & emerald, the top in a spray of round-, marquise- & pear-shaped diamonds, further enhanced by round- & pear-shaped emeralds, flexibly supporting a smaller spray of diamonds & a pear-shaped emerald drop, approx. total diamond weight 2.58 cts., platinum & 18k yellow gold mount, pr. ... **3,450**

Pavé-set Diamond Earrings

Earrings, diamond, foliate-set diamond tops, silver-topped gold mounts suspending spheres set w/approx. 336 round pavé-set diamonds, pr. (ILLUS.) **7,475**

Diamond & Gold Earrings

Earrings, diamond & gold, (18k yellow & white gold), a diamond-set floral design w/ribbed petals suspending a detachable spray of ribbed gold leaves & diamonds, total weight of approx. 3.42 cts., pr. (ILLUS.) **2,990**

Earrings, diamond & gold, hoop-style, each 14k yellow gold channel mount set w/11 round brilliant-cut diamonds weighing about .90 carats, 1" d., pr. **978**

Earrings, diamond, heart-shaped studs weighing approx. 1.70 cts. & 1.58 cts., 14k white gold mount, pr. **6,785**

Earrings, diamond & pearl, bezel-set old European-cut diamond tops suspending a fall of four bezel-set & seven bead-set diamonds terminating in a South Sea pearl drop measuring approx. 14.90 x 13.80 mm., platinum mount, pr. **2,530**

Elaborate Diamond Earrings

Earrings, diamond, platinum & 18k gold, each centered by an old mine-cut diamond approx. 10.98 x 10.37 x 6.40 & 10.95 x 10.30 x 6.42 mm., set in an 18k gold basket design & surrounded by diamond & platinum trefoils, flanked by pavé-set diamond leaves, designed by Jean Schlumberger for Tiffany & Co., pr. (ILLUS.) **90,500**

Earrings, diamond & platinum, each prong-set w/one round brilliant-cut diamond, suspending four marquise-cut diamonds & five round brilliant-cut diamonds, approx. total wt. 4.30 cts., & ending in two round brilliant-cut diamonds, approx. wt. 2.40 & 2.68 cts., 14k white gold findings, pr. (chip to one large stone) **14,950**

Earrings, diamond & platinum, hoop style, channel-set w/baquette-cut diamonds, approx. total wt. 2.28 cts., hallmark, pr. **2,530**

Earrings, diamond, ruby & 18k yellow gold, oval half-hoop design alternating round-cut rubies & diamonds, approx. 2.20 cts. diamond wt., approx. 6.75 cts. ruby wt., pr. **4,600**

Earrings, diamond & silver, each set throughout w/pavé single-cut diamonds, brown diamond accent, rose-cut ruby eyes, 18k yellow gold posts, pr. **1,725**

Earrings, diamond, snowflake design set w/round brilliant-cut diamonds, approx. 1.40 cts., set in platinum & gold findings, pr. **1,380**

Earrings, emerald & diamond, a pavé-set diamond snake coiled around a cabochon emerald, approx. total diamond wt. 0.72 cts., approx. total emerald wt. 3.45 cts., flexible tail, red stone eyes, 18k white & yellow gold mount, clip-back posts, pr. **920**

Emerald & Diamond Earrings

Earrings, emerald & diamond, each centering a pear-shaped, faceted emerald surrounded by pavé-set round brilliant-cut diamonds, two small emerald accents at top, mounted in 18k yellow gold, approx. 1.30 cts. emeralds & 9.90 ct. diamonds, pr. (ILLUS.)............... **2,760**

Earrings, gold (14k yellow) & diamond, loveknot design set w/40 assorted round diamonds, approx. .50 ct., pr........ **402**

Earrings, gold (14k yellow) & enamel, comprising three flexible links suspended from a foliate top, all accented w/enameled flowers, 2 1/2" l., pr............................ **748**

Earrings, gold (14k yellow), open loop clover-leaf design centered by a cross, 6.9 dwt., pr. **201**

Earrings, gold (14k yellow) & ruby, designed w/a wiretwist gold knot suspending a reeded pear-shaped ruby drop within a wiretwist gold frame, signed "Cartier," pr... **2,530**

Earrings, gold (14k yellow) & ruby, wrapped bouquet design in gold, round ruby flowers, stamped "Tiffany & Co.," pr.. **805**

Earrings, gold (18k bicolor) & diamond, designed w/three graduated tiers of foliate links, each centered by a cluster of diamonds, approx. .92 cts.................................. **805**

Earrings, gold (18k) & lapis, round gold dome set w/lapis beads, gold bead stems, pr. **1,035**

Earrings, gold (18k), round slightly domed, textured & engraved w/foliate designs, clip-type, signed "Buccellati," pr................................ **1,495**

Earrings, gold (18k) & ruby, half circle design w/overlapping, textured leaves w/cabochon ruby highlight, signed "Tiffany & Co.," clip-on, pr.... **1,093**

Earrings, gold (18k), sapphire & diamond, each w/two textured matte yellow gold flowers w/twisted white gold stems, diamond & sapphire accents, clip-on, pr. **546**

Earrings, gold (18k) & silver, textured bicolor gold leaves surmounted by silver wire thistles, signed "Buccellati," pr.. **2,300**

Earrings, gold (18k yellow), designed as textured pineapples, round ruby accents, pr.. **920**

Gold Leaf Design Earrings

Earrings, gold (18k yellow) & diamond, carved ribbed leaf center-set w/seven round brilliant-cut diamonds in a floral design w/diamond accents along leaf edge, diamond total approx. 1.70 cts., clip-on, pr. (ILLUS.)................. **2,070**

Earrings, gold (18k yellow) & diamond, doorknocker design w/a fluted & hammered finish, each arched top set w/19 round diamonds, total approx. .50 ct. each, signed "Webb," approx. 33.3 dwt., pr. **3,220**

Earrings gold (18k yellow), diamond & emerald, designed as hoops, alternately set w/bands of small round diamonds & emeralds, the 48 diamonds totalling approx. 1.47 cts., the 60 emeralds total approx. 2.33 cts., signed "SDG Cartier 30326," approx. 13.2 dwt., pr. **4,025**

Earrings, gold (18k yellow) & diamond, flowerhead design, each centered by a round brilliant-cut diamond surrounded by textured gold petals, diamond accents, signed "Cartier Paris," pr. **2,530**

Earrings, gold (18k yellow), diamond & pearl, four loop bow design set w/26 round brilliant-cut diamonds suspending a yellow gold cone-shaped pendant set w/16 round brilliant-cut diamonds & a pearl measuring 8.9 mm., total diamond weight .70 cts., 1" l., pr. **863**

Earrings, gold (18k yellow), diamond & pearl, gold ribbon design set w/two round brilliant-cut diamonds, .06 cts., suspending a yellow & white gold tassel set w/ten round brilliant-cut diamonds, approx. .10 cts., ending w/a 10 mm. Tahitian black pearl, pr. .. **863**

Earrings, gold (18k yellow) & diamond, sculptured floral design enhanced w/36 round brilliant-cut diamonds, approx. 3.00 cts., signed "Kuchinsky," pr. **3,220**

Earrings, gold (18k yellow), ruby & diamond, ribbed square design mounted w/calibré-cut square rubies & diamonds, pr. **803**

Earrings, gold (18k yellow), textured gold leaf design w/ruby accents, signed "Tiffany & Co.," pr. **546**

Contemporary Gold Earrings

Earrings, gold (18k yellow), textured swirl design, signed "Lalaounis," clip-on, pr. (ILLUS.) **1,380**

Earrings, gold (22k) & emerald, collet-set pear-shaped cabochon emeralds, applied bead & ropetwist mount, clip-on, signed "Tracy Dara Kamenstein," pr. **978**

Earrings, gold (bicolor), designed as a 14k pink gold heart w/a yellow gold padlock, hallmark for Larter & Sons, pr. **259**

Earrings, gold & diamond, a 14k yellow gold knot-form mount set w/27 round brilliant-cut diamonds weighing about 1 carat, pr. **805**

Starburst Earrings

Earrings, gold, pearl & diamond, starburst design, one centered by a cultured white pearl measuring approx. 10.27 mm., the other by a cultured black pearl measuring approx. 10.15 mm., surrounded by prong-set round diamonds mounted in 18k white gold, clip backs w/retractable posts, pr. (ILLUS.) **6,325**

Earrings, gold, sapphire & cultured pearl, a 14k yellow gold corrugated crescent-shaped mount set w/one cultured pearl at the tip meausuring 9.2 & 9.1 mm. above a band of six square-cut blue sapphires weighing about 35 carats, pr. **633**

Earrings, gold (yellow), honeycomb half-hoop design, 8.30 dwt., pr. **288**

Earrings, malachite, centered by round malachite spheres, fluted 14k yellow gold mount, pr. **259**

Earrings, moonstone & 14k rose gold, day/night style, set w/marquise-cut moonstones & faceted round sapphires, detachable moonstone & sapphire-set drop, pr. **1,380**

Earrings, morganite & pearl, center morganite measuring approx. 13.60 mm. framed by cultured pearls, measuring approx. 3.00 mm. each, 18k yellow gold mount, pr.... **1,840**

Earrings, morganite & pearl, centered by a round faceted morganite surrounded by seed pearls, 18k gold mount, pr. **2,185**

Earrings, opal & diamond, centered by a heart-shaped opal, measuring approx. 13.10 x 11.49 x 3.95 mm. surrounded by single-cut diamonds, 14k white gold mount, clip-on, pr. **1,265**

Earrings, pearl, 11 cultured pearls separated by small gold spacers, mounted in 14k yellow gold, pr. **690**

Earrings, pearl & 14k gold, designed as a spray of cultured pearls surmounted by etched gold leaves, clip type, pr. **230**

Earrings, pearl & 14k yellow gold, cultured grey pearl cluster, hallmark, pr. **288**

Earrings, pearl & diamond, 11.40 mm South Sea pearl & diamond top suspending a 11.20 mm. pearl drop, 14k white gold mount, pr. **1,495**

Earrings, pearl, diamond & 14k gold, starburst design centered by an old European-cut diamond weighing approx. 0.15 cts., further set w/seed pearls, screw-back findings, pr. **345**

Earrings, pearl, diamond & 14k white gold, centered by a 7 mm. pearl w/a diamond spray top, suspending a foliate diamond drop, pr. **316**

Earrings, pearl & diamond, a collet-set diamond top suspending three diamond-set drops completed by a cultured pearl measuring 8.00 mm., platinum mount, European hallmarks, pr. **2,185**

Earrings, pearl & diamond, centering a cultured pearl measuring approx. 6.9 mm., surrounded by a scalloped 18k white gold design set w/eight round brilliant-cut diamonds approx. 0.80 cts., pr. **920**

Earrings, pearl & diamond, designed as a cascade of hinged geometric plaques bead-set w/round diamonds, approx. total wt. 0.50 cts., suspending a black Tahitian pearl drop, measuring approx. 10.90 mm., platinum mount, pr. **2,530**

Pearl & Diamond Earring

Earrings, pearl & diamond, designed as a cluster of feathers surrounding eight bead-set diamond melée & a pearl approx. 10.00 mm., platinum-topped 18k yellow gold mount, pr. (ILLUS. of one) **920**

Pearl & Diamond Earrings

Earrings, pearl & diamond, designed w/a cultured pearl measuring approx. 8.90 mm., suspended from three tiers of diamond & emerald caps, two collet-set diamond terminals, platinum mount, pr. (ILLUS.) **2,415**

Earrings, pearl & diamond, each set w/a semi-baroque grey Tahitian pearl measuring approx. 11.8 mm. suspending a diamond-capped oval-shaped pearl measuring approx. 13.4 x 11.0 mm., signed "KW" for Kurt Wayne, pr. **1,265**

Earrings, pearl & diamond, each set w/a South Sea pearl, one measuring approx. 14.40 mm., the other 14.90 mm., surmounted by a baguette diamond bow, 14k. yellow gold mount, pr. **2,300**

Earrings, pearl, each containing a large 12.25 mm. cultured pearl, mounted on 14k yellow gold post, pr. **1,150**

Earrings, pearl & gem, centered by an oval amethyst, surrounded by an alternating pattern of oval amethyst, aquamarine, citrine, peridot & pearls, 14k yellow gold mounts, pr. **1,035**

Diamond & Pearl Earrings

Earrings, pearl & platinum, the tops composed of 15 fancy-cut diamonds suspending a South Sea cultured baroque pearl w/pavé-set diamond caps, pearls measure approx. 12.3 mm., approx. diamond wt. 15.00 cts., pr. (ILLUS.) **21,850**

Earrings, ruby, diamond & 14k yellow & white gold, floral design, each w/center set round faceted ruby weighing approx. .65 cts., the petals set w/eight round brilliant-cut diamonds weighing approx. .20 cts., pr. **374**

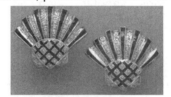

Shell-shaped Ruby & Diamond Earrings

Earrings, ruby, diamond & 18k yellow gold, designed as shells & alternately set throughout w/bands of small round diamonds & calibré-cut rubies, approx. 16.8 dwt., pr. (ILLUS.) **2,300**

Earrings, ruby & diamond, a triple-tiered, oval-shaped outline w/an oval cabochon-cut ruby in the center top, surrounded by 36 round brilliant-cut diamonds having a total weight of approx. 5 cts. for rubies & approx. 3.75 cts. for the diamonds, mounted in 18k yellow gold, signed, pr. **2,300**

Earrings, ruby & diamond, button-form, pavé-set diamond center within three rows of bead-set rubies, 18k white gold mount, clip-on, pr. **1,840**

Earrings, ruby & diamond, centered by an oval ruby weighing approx. 4.00 cts. & edged w/two rows of single-cut diamonds, approx. total 2.00 cts., millegrain accents, 18k white gold mount, pr. **4,715**

Earrings, ruby & diamond, channel-set square-cut rubies in a chevron pattern w/pavé-set diamond edge & prong-set diamond accent, 18k yellow gold mount, pr.... **1,840**

Earrings, ruby & diamond, four graduated bezel-set circular-cut diamonds, approx. total wt. 1.00 cts. suspending seven marquise-cut & pear-shaped ruby drops, approx. total wt. 4.50 cts., within a platinum-topped 18k yellow gold openwork mount w/diamond accents, pr. **4,025**

Earrings, sapphire, diamond & 18k white gold, designed as hearts, centering invisibly set square-cut sapphires, approx. 5.80 cts., within a diamond-set frame, approx. 0.20 cts., pr. **2,415**

Sapphire & Diamond Earrings

Earrings, sapphire & diamond, a rectangular heavy ribbed gold design top & a circular design at the base which is set w/five round faceted sapphires weighing a total of approx. 6 cts. & four round billiant-cut diamonds w/a total weight of approx. 0.60 ct., mounted in 18k yellow gold, signed "Webb," pr. (ILLUS.)... **5,750**

Earrings, sapphire & diamond, each set w/an oval faceted sapphire cradled by four round brilliant-cut & three marquise-cut diamonds w/a total weight of 1.60 cts., total weight of sapphires 7 cts., mounted in 18k white gold, pr. **5,750**

Earrings, sapphire, diamond & pearl, butterfly design centered by a marquise-cut sapphire & a cultured pearl w/single-cut diamond-set wings & bail, silver-topped 18k yellow gold mount, pr. ... **1,495**

Prong-set Sapphire & Daimond Earrings

Earrings, sapphire & diamond, prong-set oval blue sapphires & bead- & prong-set round diamonds, approx. total diamond wt. 3.19 cts., sapphire wt. 17.88 cts., 18k white gold mount & bicolor findings, pr. (ILLUS.) **4,888**

Sapphire & Diamond Pear-shaped Earrings

Earrings, sapphire & diamond, stylized pear-shaped outline centering an oval-shaped faceted sapphire framed by round brilliant-cut diamonds free hanging from a diamond decorated ear pad, mounted in 14k white gold-topped pink gold, approx. total sapphire weight 3.40 cts., pr. (ILLUS.).............. **2,875**

"The Nile" Earrings by Erte

Earrings, sterling silver, 14k yellow gold & sapphire, "The Nile" design of sterling silver wings w/14k yellow gold feathered terminals set w/a round cabochon sapphire, signed "Erte No. 226/250," accompanied by a Circle Fine Art Corp. certificate of authenticity, pr. (ILLUS.) **690**

Earrings, sterling silver & 18k yellow gold, buckle form, the center of woven silver w/gold buckle frame, French hallmarks, "Hermes, Paris" **805**

Contemporary Sterling Silver Earring

Earrings, sterling silver, rectangular w/irregular edges, accented w/folds, textured silver & 14k gold filings & Biwa button pearls, designed by Maria Fredriksen, pr. (ILLUS. of one) **230**

Earrings, tourmaline, agate & gold, a carved pale green tourmaline top surmounting an oval cabochon agate dyed blue-green, applied gold bead accents, 22k yellow gold mount, signed "Luna," pr. **1,093**

Earrings, tourmaline & diamond, scroll design, each set w/a round green tourmaline, measuring approx. 8.69 x 5.27 mm. within a diamond-set platinum mount, pr. **978**

Turquoise & Sapphire Earrings

Earrings, turquoise, sapphire & diamond, centering an oval-shaped, cabochon-cut sapphire, approx. 4.60 cts., surrounded by ten round brilliant-cut diamonds, approx. 2.50 cts., bordered by ten oval-shaped cabochon-cut tuquoises, each separated by a heavy gold wire, twisted wire scalloped border in 18k yellow & white gold, clip-on, pr. (ILLUS.) **2,875**

Engagement ring, diamond & platinum, centered by a marquise-cut diamond, approx. 5.57 cts., flanked by two tapered baguette-cut diamonds, total approx. 1 ct., accompanied by GIA certificate... **40,250**

Engagement ring, diamond & platinum, centered by an azure-cut diamond, approx. 3.65 cts., flanked by two baguette-cut diamonds............. **25,300**

Engagement ring, diamond & platinum, centered by an octagonal-cut diamond, approx. 3.83 cts., flanked by two tapered baguette-cut diamonds...... **19,550**

Engagement ring, diamond & platinum, the rectangular tablet set to the center w/a round diamond, approx. 1.20 cts., flanked by four baguette & 22 round diamonds, total approx. .85 cts., approx. 4.9 dwt............. **4,600**

Engagement ring, diamond solitaire & 14k yellow gold, a round diamond, approx. 1.35 cts. in a six-prong setting.............. **2,737**

Engagement ring & enhancer, diamond & 14k white gold, the fishtail mounting set w/a round diamond, approx. .90 cts., flanked by two tapered baguette-cut diamonds, the enhancer set w/assorted small round diamonds, the set **2,760**

Hatpin, gold & diamond, designed as a blue guilloché egg w/a platinum floral overlay set w/assorted rose-cut diamonds (stem is not gold).... **805**

Identification bracelet gold (18k yellow), the wide semi-rigid bracelet w/engraved decoration to the edges & an inscription on the central panel, approx. 123.2 dwt...... **1,150**

Jabot pin, gold & gem, set w/cabochon-set emeralds & sapphires, fancy shape & circular-cut diamonds, signed "A. Molinari"............. **2,875**

Jabot pin, opal & diamond, collet-set cabochon opal terminals surrounded by rose-cut diamonds, platinum-topped 18k yellow gold mount........... **345**

Key chain, sterling silver, designed as three stirrups connected by trace links, signed "Tiffany & Co." **316**

Lavaliere, aquamarine, centered by a collet-set oval aquamarine, measuring approx. 14.55 x 12.10 x 7.46 mm. suspending a collet-set pear-shaped aquamarine measuring approx. 14.20 x 9.10 x 5.36 mm., seed pearl & red stone accents, 14k yellow gold mount, completed by a fine 18k yellow gold chain, 17" l. **1,265**

Gold, Pearl & Sapphire Lavaliere

Lavaliere, gold (14k yellow), pearl & sapphire, designed w/a shield-form pendant centered by a round sapphire measuring approx. 9.45 x 8.86 mm. surrounded by a foliate & seed pearl frame, suspending a freshwater pearl drop, completed by a 14k yellow gold fancy link chain, enamel & seed pearl spacers, toggle clasp, 16" l. (ILLUS.)............. **1,150**

Gold Maltese Cross Pin

Maltese cross pin, gold (18k yellow), the design composed of small textured round forms & polished linear forms, signed "Tiffany & Co. Italy," approx. 23.9 dwt. (ILLUS.)............. **2,300**

Necklace, amber, a single strand of graduated black amber beads ranging in size from approx. 1.50 to 3.25 mm., 36" l. **259**

Necklace, amber, oval faceted cherry amber beads graduating in size from approx. 11.50 to 29.00 mm., 19 1/2" l. **431**

Necklace, amber, pendant designed as a grape cluster of amber beads suspended by a sterling silver filigree cap, black cord accented w/seed pearls & amber beads, 18 1/2" l. **403**

Amethyst, Pearl & Gold Necklace

Necklace, amethyst, 14k yellow gold & pearl, collet-set oval amethyst links, centered by two amethyst link drops, seed pearl accents (ILLUS.) **1,495**

Necklace, amethyst beads, a strand of fluted amethyst beads graduating in size from 15 mm. to 20 mm., spaced to the front by glass rondelles, 19" l. **575**

Amethyst & Diamond Necklace

Necklace, amethyst & diamond, shield-shaped pendant centered by a modified heart-shaped cabochon amethyst measuring approx. 33.99 cts. framed within an openwork floral pattern accented w/29 collet-set circu-lar-cut diamonds weighing approx. 1.50 cts. & 13 circular-cut amethysts, minor chip to back of cabochon amethyst, one amethyst missing, silver-topped 14k yellow gold mount, suspended from a 14k yellow gold chain of amethyst flowerheads spaced by figure-eight links (ILLUS.) **3,105**

Necklace, amethyst, pearl & 18k gold, designed w/graduated oval amethyst links in textured gold & seed pearl frames, seed pearl foliate spacers, 14 1/2" l. **1,495**

Necklace, amethyst & pearl, oval amethyst carved w/a classical bust centered within a seed pearl choker, 14k gold clasp (needs repair) **805**

Necklace, amethyst, the platinum baton link chain set a intervals w/ten natural pearls, suspending a large pear-shaped amethyst topped by a diamond-set bail, the diamonds totalling approx. .55 ct. **1,610**

Necklace, carnelian, a strand of graduated faceted cylindrical beads, 22k gold clasp, 29" l. **460**

Necklace, coral beads & cameo, bib-type, triple strand of graduated orange coral beads measuring 8 to 12 1/2 mm. joined by a 14k yellow gold tongue-in-groove clasp set w/a carved shell cameo depicting a classical woman sitting on a cloud feeding a bird, 20" l. **805**

Necklace, cultured pearl, tourmaline & diamond, the single strand w/74 pearls measuring 8 to 8 1/2 mm suspending an 18k white gold floral pendant set w/a large oval purplish red tourmaline surrounded by 40 round melée diamonds weighing about .60 carats joined by an 18k white gold fishhook clasp, 26" l. **1,265**

Necklace, diamond & 14k white gold, designed w/bead-set diamond elliptical links w/collet-set diamond terminals, clasp set w/two straight baguettes flanked by triangular diamonds, 15" l. **1,610**

Necklace, diamond & 18k gold, diamond-set chevron, approx. total weight 2.82 cts., suspended from a baton link chain, signed "Webb," in blue silk envelope **2,530**

Necklace, diamond & 18k white gold, choker-type Florentine finish button-shaped bezel link mount set w/88 round brilliant-cut diamonds weighing approx. 3 cts., 16" l. **3,680**

Necklace, diamond, centered by a bezel-set pear-shaped diamond, approx. 1.50 cts., completed by a 14k yellow gold snake chain, 15" l. **2,300**

Diamond Choker

Necklace, diamond, choker-type, designed as a continuous row of gradually tapering baguette-cut diamonds w/an approx. total weight of 32 cts., mounted in platinum, numbered, 16" l. (ILLUS.) . **29,900**

Diamond and Gemstone Bib Necklace

Necklace, diamond, emerald, ruby & sapphire, bib-style 18k yellow gold chain set w/12 round brilliant-cut diamonds w/total weight of approx. 3.60, 13 round faceted sapphires weighing approx. 4.50 cts., nine round faceted rubies, approx. 3.25 cts. & ten round faceted emeralds weighing approx. 2.50 cts., chain approx. 39.5 cm., 15 1/2" l. (ILLUS.) **5,750**

Necklace, diamond & gold, 14k yellow gold snake link chain w/three diamond cluster slides, approx. total wt. 3.00 cts., 18k yellow gold mount, signed "Jabel," 15" l. **1,840**

Diamond & Chrysoprase Choker

Necklace, diamond, green chrysoprase & platinum choker-type, the double chain alternating 62 collet-set round- & 62 marquise-cut diamonds totallying approx. 11.50 cts., centering a modified oval openwork section w/a marquise-cut diamond, approx. 2.50 cts., & two square-cut, eight baguette-cut & two half-moon-shaped diamonds, total approx. 2.60 cts., defined by carved green chrysoprase accents, approx. 26.1 dwt. (ILLUS.) **16,675**

Necklace, diamond & platinum, a repeated design of lozenge-shaped sections that alternate w/small navette-shaped sections, each decorated w/round brilliant- and single-cut diamonds w/a weight of 6 cts., mounted in platinum, 14" l. ... **4,370**

Diamond & Platinum Necklace

Necklace, diamond & platinum, set w/59 baguettes in a cross-over design, suspending 31 circular & 30 marquise-cut diamonds, joined by 56 baguette-cut diamond links, completed by a barrel clasp, approx. total weight 32.6 cts., 16" l. (ILLUS.) **31,050**

Tiffany Diamond Riviere Necklace

Necklace, diamond Riviere, 80 graduated prong-set round brilliant-cut diamonds ranging in size from approx. 1.59 to 0.16 cts., approx. total wt. 33.50 cts., mounted in platinum, signed "Tiffany & Co.," ca. 1960s, in original fitted Tiffany box, 15 1/2" l. (ILLUS.) **91,600**

Necklace, diamond Riviere, set w/81 graduated round brilliant-cut diamonds ranging in size from 0.16 to 1.54 cts., total wt. 30.0 cts., platinum mount, accompanied by seven GIA certificates... **51,750**

Necklace, diamond, step collet-set heart-shaped diamond weighing approx. .64 cts. within a bicolored 18k gold bezel, marked "K.M." for Karina Mattei, suspended from a 14k yellow gold snake chain, 15 1/2" l. **863**

Diamond Ribbon Design Necklace

Necklace, diamond, suspending a stylized ribbon motif set w/round & baguette-cut diamonds, terminating in a free-hanging drop set w/a marquise-shaped, brilliant-cut diamond weighing approx. 0.36 ct., surrounded by & topped w/round diamonds, mounted in platinum & attached to an open link, platinum chain, approximately 17" l. (ILLUS.) **3,680**

Necklace, emerald, a graduated strand of 58 tumbled emerald beads ranging from 4.50 to 15.30 mm., platinum navette clasp set w/five round diamonds, 20" l. **633**

Necklace, emerald beads, the triple strand w/approx. 450 graduated emerald beads measuring 3 to 7 mm., joined by a 14k white gold fishhook clasp set w/four round brilliant-cut diamonds, 19" l. **863**

Necklace, emerald beads, triple strand of graduated oval emerald beads ranging from 2.70 to 8.10 mm., diamond-set 14k white gold clasp w/faceted emerald accent, 21" l. **1,093**

Necklace, emerald & diamond, set w/257 prong-set round diamonds suspending five drops set w/pear-shaped emeralds, approx. total wt. 6.00 cts., surrounded by two rows of prong-set round diamonds, foliate marquise-cut diamond caps, approx. total wt. 16.50 cts., platinum mount, 14" l. **14,950**

Necklace, glass & metal, silver & gold-plated scrolling leaf design chain set w/foiled blue glass stones....................... **1,035**

Necklace, gold (14k white), pearl & diamond, a graduated cultured pearl circle pendant w/a pearl drop in the center, diamond-set 14k white gold foliate accents, completed w/a 14k white gold rope chain, 29" l.................... **230**

Necklace, gold (14k yellow), charm-type, the oval link chain suspending assorted charms including a pair of dice & a roulette wheel, total approx. 26 dwt................ **287**

Necklace, gold (14k yellow), choker-type, wide gold snake chain band w/a groove to the center, approx. 64.9 dwt., 14 to 16" l. **2,760**

Necklace, gold (14k yellow), comprised of three chains, a foxtail link, a box link & a curb link, interrupted by gold beads & roundels, signed "FBM," 28.00 dwt., 31" l............. **518**

Necklace, gold (14k yellow), contemporary style, five rows of flexible, lozenge-shaped staggered links, 16 1/2" l.. **1,035**

Elegant Gold & Diamond Necklace

Necklace, gold (14k yellow) & diamond, a braided lock design chain w/front closure suspending a bezel-set round diamond, approx. 4.85 cts. (ILLUS. of part)...... **8,625**

Unique Diamond Necklace

Necklace, gold (14k yellow) & diamond, a four section tube style necklace, the lower curved sections set w/graduated round diamonds & suspending a bezel-set light brown shield-shaped diamond, approx. 11.70 cts., surrounded by graduated round brilliant-cut diamonds, approx. 3.65 cts. (ILLUS.). **12,075**

Necklace, gold (14k yellow), diamond & ruby, choker-type, 3/8" wide snake band set to the front w/a scrolling device adorned w/ten small round diamonds, total approx. 1.50 cts. & calibré-cut rubies, approx. 57.4 dwt....... **2,300**

Necklace, gold (14k yellow), triple herringbone links joined by a yellow gold lobster-spring clasp, Italy, 40 dwt., 21" l. **978**

Necklace, gold (18k bicolor) & diamond, the semi-rigid band designed as cluster of acorns & oak leaves, some leaves in white gold & set w/small round diamonds, approx. 81 dwt. **3,105**

Necklace, gold (18k), flat rectangular panther link design, signed "Cartier," 39.0 dwt., 15 1/2" l. **2,185**

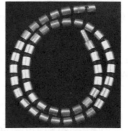

Gold & Lapis Necklace

Necklace, gold (18k) & lapis, tubular gold links spaced by lapis rondelles, hallmark, 15 3/4" l. (ILLUS.)........................ **1,955**

Necklace, gold (18k), lozenge-form links w/center column motif, signed "Kieselstein-Cord," 16" l. **5,463**

Necklace, gold (18k) & sapphire, snake link chain centered by an oval cabochon sapphire accented by two bands of square-cut diamonds, 16" l. **1,093**

Necklace, gold (18k white) & diamond, openwork leaf design bezel-set w/52 round-cut brilliant-cut diamonds, approx. 4.25 cts. **4,140**

Necklace, gold (18k yellow), centered by a ram's head w/emerald eyes suspended by two finely woven mesh chains w/ram's horn & repoussé spacers, signed "Lalaounis," 67.9 dwt., 16" l. (solder marks evident near clasp) **2,185**

Necklace, gold (18k yellow) & diamond, lariat style, foxtail chain w/diamond-set barrel terminals, diamond-set slide, hallmark, 36" l. **1,840**

Necklace, gold (18k yellow), & enamel, the trace links interrupted at intervals by multicolor enamel ladybugs, Italian hallmarks, 32" l. **1,725**

Necklace, gold, 18k yellow gold wide double-band braided choker-type w/tiny links, 15 1/2" l., 1" w. **2,645**

Necklace, gold (18k yellow) & moonstone, a mesh chain suspending 13 graduating moonstones, 7.40 - 12.00 mm., 15 1/2" l. (minor damage to chain) **805**

Gold Snake Necklace

Necklace, gold (18k. yellow), open mesh links set w/four textured spacers, completed by two brushed gold snake heads set w/cabochon rubies & faceted emeralds & rubies, 15" l. (ILLUS.) **1,380**

Necklace, gold (18k yellow), platinum & pearl, centered by a golden grey South Sea pearl, flanked by two collet-set circular yellow stones, joined by six fine trace link chains, completed by a barrel clasp, 16" l. **863**

Necklace, gold (20k) & jadeite, featuring round & oval-shaped jadeite cabochons alternated w/round gold disks enhanced by Chinese characters, pendant-clasp accented w/a carved, round-shaped jadeite disk, approx. 16 1/4" l. **1,380**

Necklace, gold (22k) & tourmaline, collet-set tumbled pink, green & blue tourmaline links, signed "Tracy Dara Kamenstein," 17 1/2" l. **2,530**

Necklace, gold, cultured pearl, ruby & diamond, a single strand of 40 pearls measuring 7 1/2 to 8 mm. centering a 14k yellow gold openwork looped floral pendant w/two large ruby half-beads & 28 round faceted rubies weighing about 9 carats, the border set w/96 round faceted melée diamonds weighing about 1.45 carats suspending a bellflower pendant set w/26 round melée diamonds weighing about .40 carats centering a large ruby half-bead weighing about 3 carats joined by a 14k yellow gold tongue-in-groove clasp set w/five round faceted rubies weighing about .50 carats, 15" l. **2,300**

Necklace, gold, openwork beads alternating w/hollow beads w/bead & wiretwist decoration, floral engraved spacers, 40.5 dwt, 34" l. (break to chain) **1,035**

Gold & Pearl Vine Design Necklace

Necklace, gold & pearl, a vine design set w/baroque pearls, detailed gold leaves & textured gold buds topped w/baroque pearls, 16" l. (ILLUS.).. **1,725**

Necklace, gold, ropetwist design, the textured 18k yellow gold rope links intertwined w/an 18k white gold double trace link chain, Italian hallmarks, 70.5 dwt., 19 1/2" l. . **1,495**

Necklace, gold, sapphire & diamond, a 14k yellow gold herringbone chain suspending a blue sapphire & diamond pendant set w/three dark blue sapphires weighing about 2 carats, alternating w/32 round brilliant-cut diamonds weighing about 1 carat, chain can be made longer, 20" l. **920**

Necklace, ivory & silver, six carved ivory balls w/Chinese motifs spaced by a fancy silver link chain, 30 1/2" l. (shrinkage cracks to ivory) **546**

Necklace, jade beads, a single strand of round jadeite jade beads, the 14k yellow gold clasp w/a single oval-shaped cabochon-cut jade, 40" l. **2,300**

Necklace, labradorite & silver, floral chain links spaced by fluted beads terminating in a labradorite & silver-capped pendant, signed "Peruzzi, Boston," 32" l. **345**

Necklace, natural pearl, double-strand, one strand w/63 pearls, the other w/65 pearls, each about 3 to 8.15 mm., w/a rectangular clasp decorated w/an emerald-cut diamond & accent w/four small emeralds mounted in platinum, about 14" l. **15,525**

Necklace, natural pearl, single strand, 79 graduated pearls from 3.5 to 8.25 mm., 18" l. **12,650**

Multi-strand Black Onyx Bead Necklace

Necklace, onyx beads, ten strands of black onyx beads accented w/14k yellow gold spacers, barrel-shaped gold & black onyx clasp randomly set w/small round, single-cut diamonds, 36" l. (ILLUS. of part)... **460**

Opal & Gold Necklace

Necklace, opal & 14k yellow gold, featuring round-shaped opal cabochons measuring from approx. 7.00 x 7.00 x 2.50 to 4.00 x 4.00 x 2.00 mm., fancy links, 16 3/4" l. (ILLUS. of part).. **1,840**

Necklace, opal & chrysoprase, centered by a cabochon oval opal measuring approx. 17.82 x 13.37 x 9.05 mm., surrounded by round rubies within a foliate frame suspending a chrysoprase drop, completed by oval cabochon chrysoprase links, 10k gold mount, hallmark (two chrysoprase & one ruby missing)........ **288**

Opal & Diamond Necklace

Necklace, opal, diamond & 14k gold, large oval opal flanked by four diamond melée, suspended from chain of graduating oval opals highlighted by six old European-cut diamonds in bellflower motif links, cracks to two opals, approx. total diamond weight 1.50 cts. (ILLUS. of part)............................ **3,680**

Necklace, opal & diamond, designed w/14 oval triplets prong-set within 18k gold abstract textured mounts, spaced by collet-set diamonds, No. 3086, signed "Gilbert Albert"........................... **4,025**

Fine Black Opal & Diamond Necklace

Necklace, opal & diamond, the textured chain suspending an oval cabochon-cut black opal that weighs approx. 8.63 cts. & exhibits a fine color pattern of predominantly red, blue, green, orange & yellow "fire," surrounded by 28 marquise-shaped brilliant-cut diamonds w/a total weight of approx. 2 cts., the central portion of the chain set w/round, brillant- and baguette-cut diamonds w/a total approx. weight of 1.60 cts., mounted in 18k white gold & platinum, 16" l. (ILLUS.).............................. **13,800**

Necklace, opal & gold, opal beads graduating from 4.8 to 9.0 mm., spaced by 14k gold beads w/wiretwist decoration, 25 1/2" l. **863**

Necklace, pearl, 36 South Sea black pearls ranging in size from 9.60 to 13.50 mm., the silver & gold round clasp set w/a ruby & diamond **9,200**

Necklace, pearl, 38 cultured pearls measuring approx. 9.0 to 9.3 mm., platinum & diamond pavé-set ball clasp 15 3/4" l. (together w/seven extra pearls)................................. **4,888**

Necklace, pearl, 52 cultured pearls measuring 7.5 to 8.0 mm. completed by a 14k gold clasp, hallmark for Mikimoto, 16 3/4" l. **3,220**

Necklace, pearl, a double strand of cultured pearls, ranging from approx. 8.70 to 9.40 mm., w/a 14k gold knot-style clasp w/pavé bead-set diamond accents, 16" l. **3,565**

Necklace, pearl, a strand of 33 coin-shaped freshwater pearls ranging in size from approx. 12.00 to 14.50 mm. w/bezel-set cabochon jade & 18k yellow gold clasp, 17 1/2" l. **1,035**

Necklace, pearl, a strand of graduated black Tahitian pearls measuring 10.00 to 14.00 mm., completed by an 18k yellow gold clasp set w/tapered baguette-cut diamonds, 19 1/2" l. **16,100**

Necklace, pearl, a strand of grey cultured pearls, measuring approx. 7.40 to 7.80 mm., 14k yellow gold clasp surmounted by an abstract ceramic face, signed "Sallyann Wekstein" **460**

Necklace, pearl, a torsade comprising 14 twisted strands of cultured pearls measuring approx. 2.75 mm. each, joined by a jeweled buckle clasp, pavé-set w/round diamonds, edged w/channel-set square-cut rubies, emeralds & sapphires, mounted in 18k yellow gold, 15" l. **4,600**

Cultured Pearl & Amethyst Necklace

Necklace, pearl & amethyst, a double strand of 113 cultured pearls terminating in an 18k yellow gold clasp centering an oval faceted amethyst within an interwoven white & green enamel frame accented w/eight round brilliant-cut diamonds, Italian maker's mark (ILLUS.)............................. **4,600**

Pearl & Diamond Necklace

Necklace, pearl, diamond & 18k white gold, dog collar design composed of a rectangular diamond plaque of openwork filigree design, further accented w/diamond foliate bars & flanked by a row of white gold diamond-set flowers & leaves, approx. 1.55 cts. diamonds, pearls measure approx. 4.0 mm. (ILLUS. of part)............ **3,450**

Necklace, pearl & diamond, abstract heart-shaped design comprising a caged baroque South Sea pearl accented w/prong-set round multicolored diamonds & a prong-set champagne color marquise diamond, approx. total wt. 1.20 cts., w/a handcrafted hinged link chain, 14k yellow gold mount & findings, signed "King," 19" l. **2,875**

Necklace, pearl, opera-length, the continuous single strand w/97 creamy white baroque pearls measuring 7 to 7.5 mm. alternating w/96 black baroque pearls measuring 7 to 7.5 mm, 32" l. **719**

Pearl Necklace w/Ornate Clasp

Necklace, pearl, single strand composed of graduated slightly baroque cultured pearls ranging from 6.4 mm. to 11 mm., fastening w/a 14k yellow gold clasp set w/multicolored stones (ILLUS. of part)............................. **920**

Necklace, pearl, single strand featuring 31 South Sea baroque cultured golden pearls alternating white cultured pearls & completed w/an 18k yellow gold, pearl & diamond foliate design clasp **8,050**

Necklace, pearl, single strand of 37 graduated cultured natural colored black South Sea pearls measuring 9.2 to 14.5 mm. joined by a 14k white gold barrel form tongue-in-groove clasp set w/four round brilliant-cut diamonds, 19" l.. **9,200**

Necklace, pearl, single strand of 85 cultured pearls approx. 9 to 9.5 mm. in diameter, 33 1/4" l. **4,600**

Necklace, pearl, single strand of graduated black South Sea cultured pearls ranging in size from 11.00 to 14.70 mm., 18k. white gold pavé-set diamond ball clasp, approx. 1.00 cts., 18" l. **14,950**

Necklace, pearl, strand of 35 multicolored South Sea cultured pearls, ranging in color from silver to greyish brown to greyish purple, 14k white gold & pavé-set diamond ball clasp, 19" l. **3,565**

Necklace, pearl, three strands of cultured pearls w/a large floral design clasp decorated w/marquise-shaped & round brilliant-cut diamonds having a total weight of approx. 5 cts., mounted in 18k yellow & 14k white gold, approx. 17 1/2" l. **7,245**

Necklace, peridot, 14 strand torsade of faceted beads completed by an 18k gold reverse-hook clasp, 18-19 1/4" l. **3,220**

Multi-strand Peridot & Sapphire Necklace

Necklace, peridot & sapphire, composed of 30 strands of small peridot & sapphire beads w/an 18k white & yellow gold leaf design clasp, 16" l. (ILLUS.) **1,955**

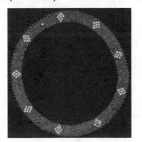

Ruby & Diamond Necklace

Necklace, ruby & diamond, composed of seven rows of round-cut rubies, approx. 72.00 cts., accented by diamond-shaped segments set w/a total of 81 round-cut brilliant-cut diamonds, approx. 4.45 cts., mounted in 18k yellow gold (ILLUS.) **14,950**

Cartier Ruby & Diamond Necklace

Necklace, ruby, diamond & platinum, comprising 80 graduated baguette-cut diamonds spaced by 83 circular-cut rubies, French hallmarks, signed "Cartier Paris No. 05037," 15 1/2" l. (ILLUS. of part) **27,600**

Ruby & Diamond Necklace

Necklace, ruby & diamond, the 9k yellow gold braided design w/ten oval diamond & ruby set links, a center floral design centered by a diamond surrounded by round faceted rubies & suspending a floral pendant set w/diamonds & rubies & surrounded by a diamond-set frame, oval & round faceted rubies approx. 6.80 cts., round brilliant-cut diamonds approx. 3.50 cts., 16" l. (ILLUS.) **1,265**

Sapphire & Diamond Necklace

Necklace, sapphire & diamond, composed of 48 oval-shaped sapphires having a total weight of approx. 48 cts., each separated by two round brilliant-cut diamonds having a total weight of approx. 4 cts., mounted in 18k white gold, 16" l. (ILLUS.) **9,775**

Necklace, sapphire, graduated oval beads ranging from approx. 4.30 to 2.80 mm., centered by three larger beads separated by two diamond rondelles, completed by a bezel-set marquise-cut diamond clasp, weighing approx. 0.50 cts., platinum mount, signed "Tiffany & Co.," 14" l. **4,255**

Necklace, sterling silver & 18k gold, sterling silver "chaine d'ancre" links, 18k yellow gold toggle clasp, signed "Hermes, Paris," 38" l. **3,795**

Necklace, sterling silver & topaz, collar-type, comprising four tapered & jointed sterling silver links centered by a large rectangular smoky topaz, ca. 1970s **633**

Necklace, turquoise & 18k gold, bezel-set oval turquoise joined by fine chain links, 45" l. **1,265**

Turquoise & Pearl Bib Necklace

Necklace, turquoise & pearl, bib-style open net design consisting of multiple gold quatrefoils each set w/a round turquoise, suspending a fringe of 22 freshwater pearls, mounted in 18k yellow gold, 15 1/2" (ILLUS.) **1,725**

Choker w/Tourmaline & Peridot Clasp

Necklace/clip brooch, pearl, tourmaline & peridot, choker-type torsade of 16 strands of cultured freshwater pearls centering a large domed clasp of tumbled tourmalines, peridots & freshwater pearls in 14k yellow gold, intricately pierced, heart-shaped wire back-plate, the pearl strands detach on both sides of the clasp & a retractable clip allows the piece to be worn as a brooch, choker approx. 19" l. (ILLUS.) **4,025**

Necklaces, diamond, choker-type, each w/two rows of elongated octagonal links accented w/368 pavé-set diamonds, total wt. approx. 17.32 cts., w/fittings to be worn as one necklace, 18k yellow gold mount, 104 dwt., pr. **17,250**

Pendant, carved tourmaline, oval form, depicting the profile of a classical female within a 14k gold frame, decorated w/wiretwist accents (missing pin stem) **518**

Pendant, Chinese amethyst, carved as a bird perched on a branch w/fruit, amethyst bead terminal, seed pearl accents, completed by a purple macramé cord **115**

Brown Diamond Pendant

Pendant, diamond & 14k white gold, a brown moon-shaped diamond, approx. 0.55 cts., suspended within a swirled foliate design set w/round diamonds, approx. 0.70 cts. (ILLUS.) **805**

Pendant, diamond & 18k gold, heart-shaped design w/21 pavé-set square-cut diamonds, diamond-set bail, approx. total weight 5.27 cts., suspended from a fine trace link chain, both signed "Tiffany & Co.," accompanied by a Tiffany appraisal... **4,600**

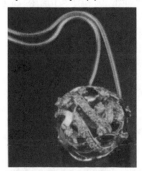

Gold & Diamond Ball Pendant

Pendant, diamond & 18k yellow gold, abstract openwork ball set at intervals w/bead-set & circular-cut diamonds, approx. total wt. 1.57 cts., suspended from a snake chain, signed "Jose Hess," 10.5 dwt., 18" l. (ILLUS.) **1,093**

Pendant, diamond, an oval-shaped brilliant-cut diamond weighing approx. 3.0 cts., decorated at the top w/three small round brilliant-cut diamonds set in the hinged bail, mounted in 14k white gold... **4,140**

Pendant, diamond, bezel-set w/a cushion-shaped brilliant-cut faint pink diamond weighing 2.57 cts., suspended from an 18k yellow gold delicate link chain, approx. 19 1/4" l., together w/GIA report stating the diamond is faint pink, natural color, VS2 clarity.................................... **10,925**

Pendant, diamond, double leaf design bead-set w/round diamonds suspending two round old European-cut diamonds w/total weight approx. 0.5 ct., further suspending an emerald-cut diamond weighing 2.89 cts., mounted in platinum, w/15" l. platinum chain........... **9,200**

Pendant, diamond, heart design bead-set w/round brilliant-cut diamonds, approx. 1.10 cts., together w/a 16" l. platinum link chain.................... **1,495**

Pendant, diamond, heart shape w/diagonal pattern of 38 invisibly set square diamonds, approx. 1.52 cts., framed in 14k bicolor gold........ **920**

Diamond, Enamel & Pearl Pendant

Pendant, diamond, pearl & enamel, a scalloped circular form decorated w/a six petal flower pattern centering a cultured pearl & further set w/old mine- & rose-cut diamonds in a geometric design on pastel green plique-a-jour enameling, diamond decorated bail, mounted in platinum (ILLUS.) **4,140**

Pendant, diamond & platinum, a heart-shaped pendant pavé-set w/23 assorted round diamonds, approx. 2.10 cts., completed by a white gold trace link chain **1,150**

Pendant, diamond solitaire, heart-shaped diamond approx. 1.00 ct. in a platinum bezel suspended from a fine platinum trace line chain, 17" l...**3,565**

Pendant, emerald & diamond, the heart-shaped emerald surrounded by 16 marquise-cut diamonds, diamond-set bail, approx. total wt. .64 cts., completed by a fine 14k white gold chain.......................... **1,093**

Pendant, gold (18k yellow), irregular-shaped plaque engraved w/a seated nude, hallmark, signed "Jean Mahie" **431**

Antique Coin & Gold Pendant

Pendant, gold (18k yellow), tourmaline & pearl, round form centered by an antique coin, the frame inscribed "Elizabeth - First - 1533 - 1603" & set w/four tourmalines & a small round diamond & suspending a teardrop-shaped cultured pearl, approx. 17.1 dwt. (ILLUS.) .. **1,150**

Pendant, jade, tapering rectangular naturalistic carved jade suspended from a geometric gold cap, completed by a woven green cord, 18k & 24k yellow gold mount, signed "Janiye," 23" l. **920**

Pendant, opal & diamond, an oval opal cabochon w/bail set w/a round diamond, approx. .80 ct. & two pear-shaped diamonds, total approx. .25 ct., completed by a 14k yellow gold chain **4,600**

Multi-stone Pendant

Pendant, platinum & diamond, designed as a floral spray w/rock crystal & blue stone flowers, carved peridot leaves & diamond-set branches, suspended from a fine platinum baton, trace link & lapis bead chain, 9 1/2" l. (ILLUS.) **2,530**

Pendant, portrait-type, centered by an oval watercolor of a woman within an engraved 18k yellow gold & pearl-set silver frame, pearl-set bow top, engraved back **575**

Pendant, sapphire & diamond, 18k yellow gold four-prong mount center set w/a large oval faceted dark blue sapphire weighing approx. 5.30 cts., surrounded by 22 round brilliant-cut diamonds, weighing approx. .50 cts., bail set w/a round brilliant-cut diamond weighing approx. .03 cts., 1/2" w., 1" l. **575**

Pendant, sapphire & diamond, heart-shaped linear pavé-set design of buff-top sapphires spaced by bead-set diamonds, diamond bail, millegrain accents, platinum mount **2,300**

Tiffany Fish Pendant

Pendant, sapphire & diamond, modeled as a long-tailed fish, the body decorated w/26 round faceted sapphires & five round faceted demantoid garnets, the mouth, head & tail decorated w/round single-cut diamonds & the eyes accented w/two cabochon-cut rubies, mounted in 18k yellow gold, signed "Tiffany, Schlumberger" (ILLUS.) **5,175**

Pendant, silver, amethyst & pearl, foliate design set w/faceted collet-set amethysts & freshwater pearls, suspending a pear-shaped amethyst pendant drop, silver-gilt mount, Austrian hallmark **201**

Pendant, stained ivory stone & 14k gold, circular form, depicting a flute player surrounded by birds & flowers within a gold frame, initialed "E.K." **575**

Topaz Pendant & Ring

Pendant, topaz & diamond, an elongated, rectangular-shaped topaz weighing approx. 11 cts., the top accented w/round brilliant-cut & marquise-shaped diamonds w/a total weight of approx. 0.40 cts., mounted in 18k white gold (ILLUS. right)....... **1,610**

Pendant & chain, diamond & gold, the 14k white gold wishbone & rectangular arched design pendant set w/three emerald-cut diamonds weighing about .75 carats surrounded by 29 single-cut diamonds weighing about .50 carats, together w/a 14k white gold chain joined by a sterling silver ring clasp, 16 1/2" l. **1,265**

Pendant & chain, gold & diamond, puffed heart-shape, 14k textured yellow gold barrel-form design set w/six round brilliant-cut diamonds weighing about .15 carats suspending a heart-shaped pendant set w/ten round brilliant-cut diamonds weighing about .30 carats, together w/a 14k yellow gold circular link chain, 17" l. **604**

Pendant & chain, gold, molded crystal & amethyst, the hand-crafted tested 14k yellow gold floral headdress set w/seven round faceted amethysts weighing about .50 carats, the headdress enclosing a molded crystal face of a young girl, w/a gold-filled curb-link chain, signed "Walter Bauscher," pendant 1 1/2 x 2 1/4" **575**

Diamond & Cultured Pearl Pendant/brooch

Pendant/brooch, diamond, pearl & 14k yellow gold, the modified triangular-shaped brooch designed w/ribbon & star motifs, center set w/a cultured pearl, surrounded by 160 round diamonds, approx. 5.50 cts., & suspending a cultured pearl drop (ILLUS.)................................ **5,750**

Pendant/brooch, diamond, ruby & sapphire, designed as an eagle in flight, 18k yellow & white gold mount, the body pavé-set w/round brilliant-cut diamonds, approx. 1.90 cts., wings bordered w/54 round faceted rubies, approx. 1 ct. & 37 round faceted blue sapphires, approx. .75 cts., 2 1/2" w. **1,380**

Pendant/brooch, diamond, sapphire & 14k white gold, floral design w/seven leaves topped by a flower w/five petals, center set w/an oval blue sapphire surrounded by a circle of diamonds, each petal set a/round faceted blue sapphire, further set w/approx. 75 round brilliant & single-cut diamonds, sapphires approx. 1.65 cts., diamonds approx. .40 cts., 1 x 2 1/4".................................. **920**

Gold & Black Jade Pendant/Pin

Pendant/pin, gold (18k & 22k) & jade, large Mayan black jade bead flanked by contemporary gold strip design, converts to pin, boxed, signed "Janiyé" (ILLUS.) **1,495**

Perfume bottle pendant, crystal, amethyst & 18k gold, the bottle of carved quartz crystal, the lid of 18k yellow gold set w/a faceted cushion-cut Siberian amethyst measuring   approx.

14.20 x 11.80 mm., suspended from an 18k gold chain & finger ring, collar signed "Tiffany & Co." (chips to bottle)............................. **805**

Gold & Diamond Perfume Pendant

Perfume pendant, gold & diamond, amphora design w/ram's head handles & a wide band of collet-set pink, yellow & white diamonds, cabochon ruby, emerald & sapphire accents (ILLUS.)....... **805**

Pill box pendant, gold & enamel, circular form w/chased & engine-turned design, inlaid w/black enamel monogram & foliate border, signed "Tiffany & Co.," 12.1 dwt. **374**

Pin, crystal & gold, sailboat design w/a carved crystal sail, accented by a red enamel stripe, 14k gold mount, hallmark..................... **1,035**

Pin, diamond & 14k white gold, Caduceus design, set w/an old European-cut diamond approx. 0.92 cts., further set w/26 bead-set diamonds, approx. total wt. 0.50 cts. & eight bead-set rubies **1,610**

Pin, diamond, circular design set w/29 round brilliant-cut diamonds weighing approx. 3.2 cts., mounted in platinum **2,300**

Diamond & Garnet Dragonfly Pin

Pin, diamond & garnet, dragonfly design w/demantoid garnet-set tail, scrolled openwork wings w/collet- & bead-set diamonds, ruby eye accents, platinum-topped 18k yellow gold mount (ILLUS.)............................. **4,313**

Pin, diamond & gold, designed as a whale, bead-set w/round brilliant-cut diamonds, cabochon ruby eye, ribbed gold accents, 18k yellow gold mount, Mauboussin, French hallmarks... **3,450**

Pin, diamond, gold riding crop surmounted by a 14k gold horseshoe set w/seven old mine-cut diamonds (gold solder at clasp)................................. **316**

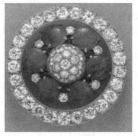

Diamond & Jade Circle Pin

Pin, diamond, jade & platinum, a circle design set w/25 round full-cut diamonds, total approx. 6.25 cts., hallmarked M & Co., together w/an insert pin designed w/six jade cabochons alternately set w/six small round diamonds surrounding a dome pavé-set w/41 small round diamonds, total approx. 2 cts. (ILLUS.) **8,625**

Pin, diamond & platinum, a swan depicted in a stylized floral setting, set throughout w/54 full-cut diamonds, total approx. 2.50 cts. together w/single-cut diamonds, total approx. 2.50 cts., approx. 14.3 dwt. **4,025**

Pin, diamond, ruby & demantoid, an openwork swirl design surmounted by a crown, silver-topped 14k yellow gold mount **2,760**

Pin, diamond, ruby & gold, model of a chick, the 18k yellow & white gold mount in the form of a chick pavé-set w/approxi. 47 round brilliant-cut diamonds weighing about 1 carat, the eye set w/ one round faceted ruby, signed "Kevn 'H'," 3/4 x 1"... **1,100**

Pin, diamond & ruby, model of a dragonfly centered by an old mine-cut diamond, weighing approx. .61 cts. w/diamond-set wings & ruby-set back, platinum-topped 18k yellow gold mount **4,370**

Pin, emerald & diamond, a circle set w/21 round emeralds & three sprays of pear- & marquise-shaped diamonds set in platinum, approx. total diamond wt. 1.83 cts., 18k yellow gold mount, signed "SB, No 39854 5" (large chip to one emerald) **2,070**

Pin, enamel & 18k gold, modeled as a frog, the body decorated w/light & dark green enamel, collet-set diamond eyes, stamped "Italy,"14.7 dwt. (chips & loss to enamel) .. **460**

Pin, enamel & 18k yellow gold, a flowerhead comprising five green enamel petals w/gold beads in center accented by seven prong-set sapphires, 18k yellow gold mount **1,035**

Enamel & Diamond Frog Pin

Pin, enamel & diamond, modeled as a frog, guilloché green enamel body w/30 collet-set diamonds, 18k yellow gold mount (ILLUS.) **2,185**

Pin, enamel & pearl, a purple enamel flower centered by a 6.00 mm. pearl, 18k yellow gold mount, signed "Tiffany & Co." **920**

Figural Bee Pin

Pin, gold (18k yellow), mother-of-pearl & ruby, a three-dimensional bee design w/four round, faceted rubies set in the body, round brilliant-cut diamond-set eyes & antennae, mother-of-pearl wings accented w/twisted gold wire, French hallmark, maker's mark & signed "Chaumet" (ILLUS.) **2,185**

Floral Pearl & Diamond Pin

Pin, gold (18k yellow), pearl & diamond, designed as a large daisy-type flower, center set w/a mabé pearl, the petals & leaf set w/58 round diamonds, total approx. 1.20 cts & outlined in a gold twisted border, approx. 15.4 dwt., hallmarked for Phillip Morris (ILLUS.).............................. **1,265**

Pin, gold (18k yellow) & ruby, modeled as a frog, the body set w/seven small round diamonds, approx. .40 cts. & 30 faceted rubies, signed "VCA," approx. 9.3 dwt.......... **2,990**

Pin, moonstone, flower design set w/round moonstone petals, red stone center accents, 14k yellow gold stem, leaf & mount, hallmark for Wordley, Allsopp & Bliss, Newark...................................... **489**

Pin, pearl & 14k yellow gold, circle design set w/ten 5.5 mm. cultured pearls, interspersed w/twisted gold rondelles, signed "Tiffany Germany".. **460**

Pin, pearl & 18k gold, designed as a bee, the body set w/a South Sea cultured pearl measuring approx. 10.80 x 9.80 mm., gold wings & legs, head accented w/cabochon red stone eyes & diamond melée........................ **546**

Pin, peridot, circle design set w/15 oval peridot, 14k yellow gold mount.............................. **575**

Pin, peridot & gold, circle form w/faceted oval peridots alternating w/14k yellow gold leaves, gold bead accents, signed "Tiffany & Co.".............. **1,093**

Pin, platinum & diamond, scroll design set w/round diamonds, approx. 3.71 cts., in a feather motif, signed "Mauboussin, Paris," French hallmarks (two diamonds missing)...................................... **2,530**

Pin, ruby, diamond & garnet, modeled as a ladybug, body

& articulated wings set w/rubies & diamonds, cabochon tsavorite garnet accent, ruby eyes, 18k gold mount............. **1,610**

Jeweled Bow Pin

Pin, ruby, diamond & gold, designed as a knotted bow & suspending an ovoid drop set w/numerous pink rubies, the knot accented w/diamond melée, minor lead solder evident, Alemany & Co. (ILLUS.)................................... **6,325**

Pin, sapphire & 14k gold, a flower design w/blue sapphire petals centered by a pearl, yellow & blue sapphire & diamond accents, 14k gold mount, signed "Tiffany & Co."... **1,840**

Pin, sapphire & diamond, circular design w/an alternating pattern of round sapphires & old European-cut diamonds, approx. total diamond wt. .60 cts., platinum-topped 14k yellow gold mount...................... **1,380**

Pin, silver & enamel, designed as a cat's head, enhanced w/black enamel & glass stones.. **172**

Pin, silver, jade & diamond, stylized bird-form, a silver mount, the body & head set w/18 round diamonds weighing about .35 carats, the wings set w/two carved mottled green jade panels, 2 x 2"...................................... **546**

Pin, topaz & diamond, clover design, the leaves set w/four heart-shaped smoky topaz stones, round diamond in center & diamond-set stem, 14k yellow gold mount............. **487**

Pin/pendant, diamond & platinum, wreath-shaped w/bow at top suspending a pear-shaped diamond, approx. .75 ct. & two marquise-cut diamond leaves approx. .30 ct., the bow & inner circle of pin set w/68 baguette-cut diamonds, approx. 5 cts., framed by two rows composed of 33 round diamonds, approx. 5 cts., approx. 15.1 dwt. **6,900**

Pin/pendant, diamond, sapphire & white gold, the circular openwork design center set w/a round diamond, approx. .35 ct., additionally set w/rose-cut diamonds & defined by 12 round sapphires, approx. 5.3 dwt. **1,840**

Ring, amethyst & emerald, centered by a sugarloaf-shaped cabochon amethyst , approx. 21.30 x 17.40 x 10.06 mm., the shoulders w/28 bezel-set round emeralds, 18k yellow gold mount, hallmark **1,495**

Ring, aquamarine & blue topaz, center set w/a large rectangular-cut aquamarine & a rectangular-cut blue topaz, the 18k yellow gold mounting set w/six small round diamonds **862**

Ring, aquamarine & diamond, a cushion-shape aquamarine weighing approx. 8.94 cts., framed by 25 circular-cut diamonds, approx. total 25. 1.0 cts., 18k white gold mount **1,725**

Aquamarine & Diamond Ring

Ring, aquamarine & diamond, an emerald-cut aquamarine, approx. 3.04 cts. in a border of round brilliant & tapered baguette-cut diamonds, approx. 0.97 ct., 18k white gold mount (ILLUS.) **1,150**

Ring, aquamarine & diamond, centered by a clip-cornered emerald-cut aquamarine, measuring approx. 18.65 x 15.42 x 10.55 mm., flanked by eight round brilliant-cut diamonds, platinum mount, stamped "Handmade" **2,070**

Ring, aquamarine & diamond, pear-shaped aquamarine measuring approx. 12.6 x 9.4 x 6.00 mm., framed by 16 circular-cut diamonds, approx. total weight 0.64 cts., platinum mount, signed "Tiffany & Co." **1,610**

Ring, aquamarine & diamond, set w/an emerald-cut aquamarine weighing approx. 44.00 cts., shoulders set w/36 circular-cut & 24 parallelogram diamonds in a chevron design, approx. total 5.14 cts., platinum mount **4,313**

Ring, aquamarine, gentleman's, bezel-set step-cut aquamarine, measuring approx. 15.90 x 14.10 x 11.50 mm., heavy 14k white gold mount **460**

Ring, aquamarine, sapphire & diamond, centered by an emerald-cut sapphire, measuring approx. 14.91 x 11.68 x 8.83 mm., flanked by two round brilliant-cut diamonds & four round sapphires, 14k gold mount **633**

ring, cat's-eye chrysoberyl & diamond, man's, the chrysoberyl weighing approx. 8.00 cts., gypsy-set in a platinum mount, flanked by two trapezoidal-shaped diamonds weighing approx. 0.75 cts. each **8,050**

Ring, chalcedony, tapering band style centered by an oval lavender chalcedony, flanked by two gold medallions within a wiretwist border, gold bead accents, 14k bicolor gold mount, hallmark for Elizabeth Gage **1,265**

Ring, chrysoberyl, diamond & 18k yellow gold, centering a round cabochon-cut cat's eye chrysoberyl, weighing approx. 15.5 cts., flanked by two tapered baguette-cut diamonds **16,100**

Ring, citrine, a mixed-cut citrine within a pierced, chased & engraved, 18k gold & sterling silver mount **316**

Ring, citrine & diamond, an oval faceted yellow citrine weighing approx. 12.55 cts. surrounded by 24 round brilliant-cut diamonds weighing approx. 1.20 cts., 18k white gold mount **920**

Ring, coral & diamond, a high-domed, fluted, oval-shaped coral surrounded by a row of 29 round brilliant-cut diamonds (five are single-cuts), mounted in 18k yellow gold **690**

Ring, coral & diamond, centered by an oval angel skin coral measuring approx. 11.40 x 8.80 mm., surrounded by round brilliant-cut prong-set diamonds, approx. total wt. 0.50 cts., platinum mount, signed "Trio" **748**

Ring, crystal, centered by a reverse-painted crystal lion's head, 14k beaded gold frame **546**

Ring, diamond & 14k white gold, a swirl design centering a round light brown diamond, approx. 1.21 cts., surrounded by channel-set round white diamonds, approx. 1.21 cts. **805**

Ring, diamond & 14k yellow gold, asymmetric foliate design mounted w/two round-cut brilliant-cut & ten marquise-cut diamonds, approx. 1.50 cts. **1,725**

Ring, diamond & 14k yellow & white gold, set w/five round full-cut diamonds, total approx. 1.50 cts. **2,070**

Ring, diamond & 18k white gold, wide eternity band composed of six rows of pavé-set diamonds, approx. 3.20 cts. **4,025**

Ring, diamond & 18k yellow gold, centering one round brilliant-cut diamond, approx. 1.90 cts., flanked by rows of six tapered baguette-cut diamonds, approx. 0.85 cts. **5,520**

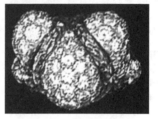

Triple Dome Diamond Ring

Ring, diamond & 18k yellow gold, pavé-set diamond triple dome style, approx. 6.00 cts., the three sections separated by textured gold bands (ILLUS.) **3,450**

Ring, diamond, a round brilliant-cut diamond, approx. 9.30 cts., held in a heavy box attached to an 18k yellow gold flexible curb link chain shank **15,525**

Ring, diamond, a round brilliant-cut diamond solitaire weighing approx. 3 cts., mounted in platinum **14,950**

Ring, diamond, a yellow diamond weighing approx. 2.0 cts., within a navette-shaped pierced mount set throughout w/84 old European-, rose- & old mine-cut diamonds, platinum-topped 14k yellow gold w/millegrain accents **3,450**

Ring, diamond, an emerald-cut diamond weighing 3.53 cts., mounted in 18k yellow gold, w/Italian hallmark & maker's mark, w/GIA report **23,000**

Ring, diamond, band style, continuously set w/240 pavé-set diamonds, approx. total wt. 2.50 cts., 14k yellow & white gold mount **1,495**

Diamond Bypass Ring

Ring, diamond, bypass design set w/a step-cut pear-shaped light yellow diamond, approx. 0.82 ct. & a colorless diamond, approx. 0.73 ct., framed by clusters of baguettes & marquise-shaped diamonds, platinum mount, stamped "S, C & L" for Shreve, Crump & Low (ILLUS.) **7,475**

Ring, diamond, centered by a marquise-cut diamond, approx. .67 cts., within an abstract butterfly mount, set w/baguette- & round-cut diamonds, approx. total wt. .58 cts., platinum mount **1,610**

Ring, diamond, centered by a prong-set yellowish green round brilliant-cut diamond, weighing approx. 1.22 cts., mounted in a star shape inside a pentagon, accented by round diamonds, 14k white gold mount, accompanied by London Precious Stone Laboratory Origin of Color report stating natural color **1,610**

Large Diamond Ring

Ring, diamond, centering a large round brilliant-cut diamond weighing approx. 9.40 cts., surrounded by six marquise-shaped brilliant-cut diamonds & 18 tapered baguette-cut diamonds, total weight of approx. 3.20 cts., w/a Dant Palais pendant conversion feature, mounted in platinum (ILLUS.) **35,650**

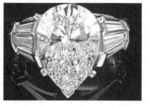

Pear-shaped Diamond Ring

Ring, diamond, centering a pear-shaped brilliant-cut diamond weighing 5.92 cts., flanked by six baguette-cut diamonds, mounted in platinum, accompanied by GIA report (ILLUS.) **36,800**

Ring, diamond, centering a round brilliant-cut diamond weighing approx. 0.90 ct. w/six round single-cut diamonds in the shoulders, mounted in 14k white gold, accompanied by a cradle ring decorated w/14 round brilliant-cut diamonds set in floral leaf designs, weight approx. 0.60 cts., mounted in 14k white gold **6,900**

Ring, diamond, centering an old European-cut diamond weighing approx. 5.50 cts. w/24 small round, single-cut diamond accents, mounted in platinum **13,800**

Ring, diamond, collet-set oval old European-cut yellow diamond, approx. 1.75 cts., framed by concentric rows of calibré-cut emeralds & sapphires, platinum mount......... **2,875**

Ring, diamond, eternity band channel-set w/tapered baguettes weighing approx. 2.32 cts., platinum mount..... **2,645**

Ring, diamond, eternity band set in an alternating pattern of 18 bezel-set circular-cut diamonds w/gold spacers, approx. total wt. 2.16 cts., 18k yellow gold mount......... **1,265**

Ring, diamond, eternity band set w/a row of 23 marquise-shaped brilliant-cut diamonds, prong-set at a diagonal to the finger, mounted in 18k white gold, approx. 2.30 tcw.............. **1,725**

Ring, diamond eternity band set w/baguette-cut diamonds, platinum mount......... **1,093**

Ring, diamond, eternity band set w/graduated marquise-cut diamonds, approx. 7.00 cts., 14k white gold mount... **5,175**

Ring, diamond, "Etoile" style, centered by a circular-cut intense yellow diamond weighing 1.02 cts., framed by ten pear-shaped colorless diamonds w/total weight of 1.44 cts., platinum mount, signed "Tiffany & Co.," boxed **13,800**

Ring, diamond, five collet-set old European-cut diamonds approx. total wt. 1.65 cts., 18k yellow gold mount w/pierced gallery.................. **1,495**

Ring, diamond, gentleman's, gypsy-set w/a round brilliant-cut diamond weighing approx. .40 cts., brushed 14k white gold mounting.............. **345**

Ring, diamond, gentleman's Masonic ring w/a bezel-set old European-cut diamond, 14k yellow gold & enamel mount............ **2,300**

Ring, diamond & gold, dinner-type, 22k yellow gold wide mount, the top portion set w/a pavé of 67 graduated round brilliant-cut diamonds weighing about 2.90 carats, Cartier, size 5 1/4.............. **3,680**

Ring, diamond & gold, domed pavé-set diamond top, approx. total wt. 2.00 cts., gold borders, woven 18k yellow gold shank (minor fraying).... **1,955**

Ring, diamond & gold, man's contemporary style, bezel-set emerald-cut yellow diamond bordered by 14 bead-set diamonds within a white gold geometric framework, textured 18k yellow gold mount........................ **575**

Ring, diamond & gold, solitaire, the 18k white gold four-prong A-Box mount set w/one round brilliant-cut diamond weighing about 1.03 carats flanked by two round brilliant-cut diamonds weighing about .28 carats, size 5 1/4.............. **4,140**

Ring, diamond & gold, the 14k yellow & white gold six-prong Tiffany mount set w/one round brilliant-cut diamond weighing exactly 2.39 carats, size 4 1/2................ **6,900**

Ring, diamond & gold, twin-style dinner-type, the 14k white gold bypass-designed mount set w/two round brilliant-cut diamonds weighing about .95 & 1 carat flanked by ten baguette diamonds weighing about .30 carats, size 6................ **4,600**

Ring, diamond, man's, centered by a circular-cut diamond weighing approx. 0.40 cts, 14k yellow gold mount...... **288**

Ring, diamond, man's twin-stone design w/two old European-cut diamonds weighing approx. 1.35 cts. & 1.23 cts., bead-set in squared white gold mountings, 14k yellow gold mount, marked "F.R. Co.".............. **6,038**

Pear-shaped Diamond Ring

Ring, diamond & platinum, a center pear-shaped diamond enhanced w/two tapered baguettes, approx. 7.20 cts. (ILLUS.) **13,800**

Ring, diamond & platinum, a center round brilliant-cut diamond flanked by baguette-cut diamonds, approx. 1.00 ct. **1,495**

Ring, diamond & platinum, bypass design, two transitional-cut diamonds, each measuring approx. 1.29 cts., flanked by straight baguettes **6,900**

Ring, diamond & platinum, centered by pentagonal light yellow diamond, approx. 3.00 cts., flanked by half-moon shape & 19 baguette-cut diamonds **6,900**

Ring, diamond & platinum, eternity band continuously set w/channel-set baguette-cut diamonds, approx. 2.10 cts. **1,725**

Ring, diamond & platinum, eternity band-style, the platinum channel mount set w/33 round brilliant-cut diamonds weighing about 1 carat, size 7 1/2 .... **1,150**

Ring, diamond & platinum, mounted w/a round brilliant-cut solitaire weighing approx. 4.75 cts., accompanied by G.I.A. certificate stating the diamond is of "G" color & "Internally Flawless" in clarity **46,000**

Ring, diamond & platinum, oblong-shaped design w/three emerald-cut diamonds surrounded by 16 round brilliant-cut diamonds **2,300**

Ring, diamond & platinum, reticulated mount set w/an old European-cut diamond weighing approx. 1 ct. flanked by four smaller round old European-cut diamonds weighing approx. 2 cts., surrounded by six round brilliant-cut, six marquise, two pear-shaped & 14 baguette diamonds weighing approx. 2.80 cts. **6,900**

Ring, diamond & platinum, the platinum fishtail-design mount set w/five round brilliant-cut diamonds weighing about 1.05 carats, size 8 1/2 .. **863**

Ring, diamond & platinum, the platinum four-prong Tiffany mount set w/one round brilliant-cut diamond weighing about 2.85 carats flanked by two tapered baguette diamonds weighing about .50 carats, size 9 .... **19,500**

Ring, diamond & platinum, twin-stone design, old European-cut diamonds, each weighing approx. 0.92 & 0.99 cts., within a floral mount (chips to girdle) **4,025**

Ring, diamond & platinum, wedding band continuously set w/23 round brilliant-cut channel-set diamonds, approx. 1.15 ct. **805**

Ring, diamond, rectangular openwork 18k white gold mount, set w/European-cut diamonds weighing a total of approx. 1.50 cts. **1,150**

Ring, diamond & ruby, an oval prong-set Burma ruby approx. 1.00 cts., flanked by six circular-cut diamonds, approx. total wt. 0.50 cts., 18k yellow gold ribbed mount **1,150**

Ruby & Diamond Ring

Ring, diamond & ruby, bombé cross-over design centering a round faceted ruby approx. 3.37 cts. on one side & an old mine-cut diamond approx. 2.44 cts. on the other side, w/pavé-set round brilliant-cut diamonds w/total weight of approx. 7.75 cts., mounted in platinum (ILLUS.)............................ **13,800**

Ring, diamond, sapphire,18k yellow gold & platinum, the oval tablet center set w/three oval sapphires surrounded by 16 round diamonds, total approx. .90 cts., signed "Tiffany & Co."............................ **2,530**

Ring, diamond & sapphire, bypass style w/a prong-set sapphire measuring approx. 8.25 x 5.21 mm., & an old mine-cut diamond weighing approx. 1.90 cts., gold mount............................ **5,405**

Ring, diamond, sapphire, emerald & 18k gold, cocktail ring centered by a cushion-shaped old mine-cut diamond weighing approx. 1.98 cts., surrounded by three step-cut emeralds, approx. 3.08 tcw. & a cushion-, oval- & square-cut sapphire, approx. 5.21 tcw., further enhanced by smaller bead-set sapphires, collet-set diamond accents & bead-set diamond shoulders mounted in platinum............................ **5,750**

Ring, diamond & sapphire, three-stone design centered by a prong-set emerald-cut diamond weighing approx. 3.50 cts., flanked by two prong-set emerald-cut sapphires measuring approx. 7.38 x 6.40 x 4.58 mm. & 7.50 x 6.52 x 4.55 mm., platinum mount, hallmark............ **13,800**

Ring, diamond, set w/a cluster of 15 round brilliant-cut diamonds weighing approx. 2.50 cts., 14k white gold mount............................ **1,610**

Ring, diamond, set w/cluster of round colorless & treated fancy colored diamonds, approx. 2.75 cts., 18k yellow gold mount............................ **920**

Ring, diamond solitaire, a prong-set emerald-cut diamond, measuring approx. 14.56 x 8.25 x 5.19 mm., weighing approx. 6.10 cts., flanked by tapered baguettes in a platinum mount............................ **14,950**

Ring, diamond solitaire, a prong-set oval-cut diamond weighing approx. 5.44 cts. & measuring approx. 16.932 x 8.97 x 5.53 mm., within a platinum mount, French hallmarks, w/G.I.A. certificate............................ **65,200**

Ring, diamond solitaire, an oval-shaped brilliant-cut diamond weighing approx. 2.0 cts., flanked by two tapered baguette-cut diamonds, mounted in platinum................ **3,910**

Ring, diamond solitaire, centered by a marquise-cut diamond, approx. 4.20 cts., baguette-set platinum mount, signed "Yard," accompanied by GIA certificate.................... **49,450**

Ring, diamond solitaire, centered by a pear-shaped diamond, weighing 2.71 cts., flanked by baguette-cut diamonds, platinum mount, accompanied by GIA certificate............................ **21,850**

Ring, diamond solitaire, centered by a round brilliant-cut diamond, approx. 5.5 cts., flanked by tapered baguettes, platinum mount..... **25,300**

Ring, diamond solitaire, centered by an emerald-cut diamond, approx. 11.00 cts., flanked by tapered baguettes, platinum mount..... **41,400**

Ring, diamond solitaire, centered by an old European-cut diamond, approx. 3.75 cts., further set w/ten bead-set diamonds in a scroll design, 14k white gold mount **10,350**

Ring, diamond solitaire, centering a round brilliant-cut diamond weighing approx. 0.95 ct., mounted in an 18k yellow gold sculpted tile design shank, w/maker's mark **2,415**

Ring, diamond solitaire, emerald-cut diamond weighing approx. 3.75 ct., flanked by straight baguettes, platinum mount............ **13,800**

Ring, diamond solitaire, gypsy-set w/a round, old European-cut diamond weighing approx. 2.25 cts., mounted in 18k white gold....... **8,625**

Ring, diamond solitaire, man's, box-set w/old European-cut diamond weighing approx. 2.25 cts., geometric engraved shoulders.......... **4,888**

Ring, diamond solitaire, man's, centered by a claw-set old European-cut diamond weighing approx. 0.95 cts., 14k yellow gold mount (minor chips)............ **1,150**

Ring, diamond solitaire, round brilliant-cut diamond weighing 1.07 cts., platinum & yellow gold filigree mount, accompanied by GIA report **4,140**

Ring, diamond solitaire, round brilliant-cut diamond weighing 1.43 cts., 18k white gold six-prong mount......... **8,050**

Ring, diamond solitaire, set w/a circular-cut diamond weighing 3.01 cts., flanked by bezel-set diamond trillions, total weight 0.92 cts., 18k gold mount, signed "Cartier"........ **28,750**

Ring, diamond solitaire, set w/a round brilliant-cut diamond weighing approx. 8.35 cts., mounted in 18k white gold........ **24,150**

Ring, diamond solitaire, set w/a transitional old European, round brilliant-cut diamond weighing approx. 3.55 ct., mounted in 18k white gold........ **7,360**

Ring, diamond solitaire, the center w/a round brilliant-cut diamond, approx. 3.00 cts., flanked by tapered baguettes, platinum mount..... **17,250**

Ring, diamond solitaire, the platinum four-prong A-box mount set w/a round brilliant-cut diamond weighting approx. 4 cts. flanked by two tapered baguette diamonds weighing approx. .40 cts.... **20,700**

Ring, diamond, three round bezel-set diamonds, approx. total wt. 1.70 cts., 14k yellow gold heavy mount, hallmarks **5,060**

Ring, diamond, three stone style, three collet-set round diamonds, weighing approx. .73 cts., .98 cts., & .75 cts., in a tiered diamond-set frame, heavy 14k white gold mount........ **5,175**

Ring, diamond, twin-stone, round, bezel-set fancy yellow & brownish-orange diamonds, each approx. 1.00 ct., in an 18k white gold abstract bypass motif mount w/diamond accents......... **4,313**

Unusual Diamond Ring

Ring, diamond, unusual split shank, scroll design decorated w/three bezel-set round brilliant-cut diamonds weighing approx. 1.40 cts., 1.10 cts. & 1 ct. each, mounted in 18k yellow gold, w/maker's mark (ILLUS.) **9,200**

Ring, emerald, centered by a cushion-cut cabochon emerald measuring 12.30 x 11.7 mm. surrounded by prong-set diamonds, approx. 1.20 cts., domed basketweave 14k yellow gold mount (one diamond missing) **345**

Ring, emerald, diamond & 18k yellow gold, center w/bezel-set oval emerald, approx. 3.35 cts., surrounded by 43 baguette-cut diamonds, approx. 1.50 cts. **5,175**

Ring, emerald & diamond, a square-cut emerald weighing approx. 2.10 cts. surrounded by eight round brilliant-cut & four square-cut diamonds, weighing approx. .85 cts., platinum mount, emerald possibly Columbian **3,450**

Emerald & Diamond Ring

Ring, emerald & diamond, an emerald-cut emerald measuring approx. 7.82 x 6.76 x 3.12 mm., prong-set in 18k yellow gold, surrounded by 12 pear-shaped diamonds, approx. total wt. 0.95 cts., platinum mount, No. 6252 (ILLUS.) **3,105**

Ring, emerald & diamond, band style centered by a cluster of emeralds flanked by a tiered alternating pattern of round diamonds & emeralds, 18k yellow gold mount **489**

Emerald & Diamond Dinner Ring

Ring, emerald & diamond, dinner-type, set w/a marquise emerald weighing approx. .75 cts., surrounded by 19 square & baguette diamonds weighing approx. .85 cts. & five round brilliant-cut diamonds weighing approx. .15 cts., 18k yellow gold mount (ILLUS.) **460**

Ring, emerald & diamond, five-stone design, set w/three emerald-cut emeralds weighing approx. 0.80 cts., 0.53 cts. & 0.50 cts., spaced by two old European-cut diamonds, each weighing approx. 0.88 cts. & 0.93 cts., pierced, scrolled gallery, 18k gold mount **5,750**

Emerald & Diamond Dinner Ring

Ring, emerald, diamond & platinum, center set w/a square-cut emerald weighing approx. 5.25 cts., surrounded by 16 round old European-cut diamonds weighing approx. 2.40 cts., the shoulders of the ring set w/six smaller round old European-cut diamonds weighing approx. .10 cts. (ILLUS.) **5,290**

Garnet & Diamond Ring

Ring, garnet & diamond, centered by a demantoid garnet approx. 8.00 x 6.20 x 3.80 mm. framed w/18 single-cut diamonds, 14k white gold chased mount w/millegrain accents (ILLUS.) **1,955**

Jeweled Snake Ring

Ring, garnet, ruby & diamond, designed as a coiled snake w/a demantoid garnet, ruby & diamond bead-set head & tail, 14k yellow gold mount (ILLUS.).. **1,495**

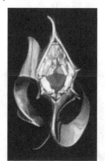

Free-form Diamond Ring

Ring, gold (14k yellow) & diamond, a free-form design mounted w/a kite-shaped diamond, approx. 1.25 cts. (ILLUS.)... **1,093**

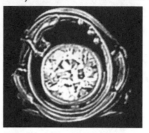

Diamond Ring in Vine Design

Ring, gold (14k yellow) & diamond, old European-cut diamonds set in center of free-form vine design mount, approx. 2.95 cts. (ILLUS.).......... **5,175**

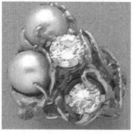

Diamond & Pearl Ring

Ring, gold (14k yellow), diamond & pearl, the grapevine style mounting centered by two round brilliant-cut diamonds, total approx. 2 cts. & two cultured pearls, approx. 10.7 dwt. (ILLUS.)...................... **5,462**

Ring, gold (14k yellow) & diamond, styled as a coiled serpent w/engraved scale detailing, the head mounted w/a rectangular diamond weighing approx. 0.40 cts., the eyes set w/small red stones, hallmarked for Larter & Sons, Newark.............................. **546**

Ring, gold (14k yellow) & sapphire, openwork mount of leaf & vine design centered by a star sapphire, flanked by round, faceted sapphires, all bezel-set....................................... **403**

Ring, gold (14k yellow), star sapphire & diamond, centered by a star sapphire cabochon, approx. 18 cts., flanked by three small round diamonds, approx. .20 cts... **1,265**

Ring, gold (18k), ruby & diamond, domed design, top w/invisibly-set rubies flanked by two rows of round-cut diamonds............ **1,380**

Ring, gold (18k white), diamond, sapphire & emerald, Florentine finish bypass style set w/30 round brilliant-cut diamonds, weighing approx. .30 cts., the tops of the ring set w/one oval cabochon blue sapphire weighing approx. .35 cts. & one oval cabochon emerald weighing approx. .30 cts............ **489**

Ring, gold (18k white), pearl & diamond, Florentine finish mount set w/a blue-grey cultured pearl measuring 10 mm. surrounded by five fancy shape diamonds weighing approx. .15 cts. **173**

Ring, gold (18k yellow) & citrine, centered by an emerald-cut citrine within a domed, textured gold mount, gold wire accents, signed "Schlumberger" for Tiffany & Co............ **1,725**

Ring, gold (18k yellow) & diamond, bombé design set w/alternating rows of round brilliant-cut diamonds, approx. 2.16 cts. & twisted gold wire........ **1,150**

Ring, gold (18k yellow) & diamond, bombé style, lattice design of three rows of twisted gold wire, centers set w/round diamonds, approx. 2.22 cts. **1,035**

Ring, gold (18k yellow) & diamond, comprising six rows of ropetwist bands, accented by three white gold bead-set diamond curved X's, signed "Tiffany, Schlumberger" **2,990**

Ring, gold (18k yellow) & diamond, florentine finished bombé style centered by a brilliant-cut diamond, approx. 5.10 cts. w/small round- & baguette-cut diamond accents **40,350**

Gold, Diamond & Pearl Ring

Ring, gold (18k yellow), diamond & pearl, the wide tapered band edged w/gold beads & pavé-set w/58 round full-cut diamonds, total approx. 1.25 cts., set across the top w/three cultured pearls contained in beaded collars, signed "Chanel" & numbered, approx. 12.5 dwt. (ILLUS.) **2,530**

Ring, gold (18k yellow) & gem, domed form decorated w/randomly-placed round faceted sapphires, emeralds & rubies & round brilliant-cut diamonds flush-mounted in star-cut designs, numbered & signed "Chaumet, Paris" **748**

Ring, gold (18k yellow), gentleman's, band style w/central chased foliate motifs, 13.70 dwt. **345**

Ring, gold (18k yellow) relief-molded chased lion's head, etched red stone eyes, stamped "France," hallmark, 7.1 dwt............ **489**

Ring, gold (18k yellow), sapphire & diamond, center w/an oval-shaped cabochon-cut sapphire weighing approx. 2.30 cts., flanked by square- & baguette-cut diamonds having a total weight of approx. 0.75 ct............ **3,220**

Ring, gold (18k yellow) & sapphire, eternity band w/collet-set faceted round sapphires spaced by twisted gold bars, French hallmarks **460**

Ring, gold (18k yellow) & sapphire, wide gold band centered by a row of calibré-cut sapphires, signed "Poiray, No. 9195," French hallmark **1,553**

Ring, gold (18k yellow) & silver, gentleman's, centered by a Greek Macedonian silver drachma depicting Alexander the Great w/a lion headdress, ca. 336 B. C., 10.6 dwt. **460**

Gentleman's Ring w/Roman Denarius

Ring, gold (18k yellow) & silver, gentleman's, centered by a Roman Republic silver denarius depicting the Roman god Janus, ca. 119 B.C., 14.5 dwt. (ILLUS.)............ **719**

Ring, gold, morganite & diamond, dinner-type, the 18k yellow gold floral-designed mount set w/an oval faceted morganite (pink beryl) weighing about .20 carats surrounded by 16 tapered baguette diamonds weighing about .50 carats, size 6..... **345**

Ring, green jade, sapphire, ruby, diamond & gold, dinner-type, the 18k yellow gold four-prong mount set w/one oval cabochon apple green jade stone measuring 18.2 x 13 x 6.45 mm. flanked by two pear-shaped blue sapphires weighing about 1 carat, four marquise rubies weighing about 1.20 carats & eight round brilliant-cut diamonds weighing about .30 carats, size 6 1/2 ..... **863**

Ring, jade & 18k yellow gold, a prong-set oval jade measuring approx. 16.20 x 11.00 mm. **1,955**

Ring, jade, an oval jade flanked by three diamond melée, 18k white gold................ **575**

Jade & Diamond Dinner Ring

Ring, jade & diamond, 18k white gold openwork mount center set w/a rectangular cabochon apple green jade stone measuring 12.4 x 5.5. mm., flanked by 42 round brilliant-cut diamonds, approx. .50 cts. (ILLUS.) **316**

Ring, jade & diamond, centered by an oval cabochon jadeite jade, measuring approx. 12.97 x 10.55 x 5.75 mm. in a round- & baguette-cut diamond-set 18k white gold mount, millegrain accents **12,650**

Ring, jade & sapphire, center set w/an oval cabochon green jadeite jade stone measuring 16.3 x 10.3 mm., flanked by two round faceted blue sapphires weighing approx. .60 cts., Chinese............. **345**

Ring, jadeite jade & diamond, a jade measuring 18.5 x 13.0 x 6.9 mm. framed by 18 circular-cut diamonds, approx. total wt. 2.70 cts., platinum mount (testing indicates the jadeite jade has not been enhanced)................................ **9,775**

Ring, jadite, diamond & amethyst, center oval-shaped lavender jadeite cacochon measuring approx. 18.50 x 14.30 x 7.00 mm., enhanced by round-cut amethysts & accented by full-cut diamonds............................. **518**

Ring, moonstone & cat's-eye, designed w/two oval prong-set moonstones outlined by 25 cat's-eye chrysoberyl, pierced gallery, 18k gold mount.. **1,093**

Ring, onyx & diamond, centered by an emerald-cut onyx measuring approx. 4.85 x 14 x 18.50 mm., flanked by ten old European-cut diamonds, approx. 1.40 cts., further set w/six colorless sapphires (scratch to onyx)..................................... **2,300**

Ring, opal, centered by a pear-shaped cabochon Mexican opal, measuring approx. 18.00 x 13.87 x 10.51 mm., platinum mount........................... **546**

Ring, opal & diamond, 14k white gold mounting centered by an oval opal surrounded by 24 small round diamonds, total approx. .50 ct., hallmarked by Fougera..... **747**

Ring, opal & diamond, centered by an oval black opal doublet surrounded by round tapered baguette-cut diamonds, 18k yellow gold mount... **1,380**

Ring, opal & diamond, centered by an oval black opal, measuring approx. 14.40 x 9.80 x 3.10 mm., surrounded by prong-set round brilliant-cut diamonds, approx. total wt. 1.00 cts., 18k yellow gold mount........... **2,300**

Ring, opal, diamond & gold, dinner-type, the tested 14k yellow & white gold mount set w/an oval cabochon white opal weighing about 4 carats surrounded by 40 round brilliant-cut diamonds weighing about 1.50 carats, size 6.. **748**

Ring, opal, flower design w/center carved opal, diamond accent, 14k yellow gold Florentine foliate-carved mount (cracks to opal)..................................... **259**

Ring, pearl, bypass design set w/two cultured pearls measuring approx. 8.69 mm. & 8.66 mm., highlighted w/six bead-set diamonds, 14k yellow gold mount, signed "Mikimoto"................................. **920**

Natural Pearl & Diamond Ring

Ring, pearl & diamond, a stylized, lozenge-shaped open crown framed w/round diamonds, centering three natural pearls measuring from approx. 7.8 mm. to 6.5 mm., flanked by two small natural pearls, approx. 3.7 mm., mounted in 18k white gold, accompanied by SSEF report stating all the pearls are natural (ILLUS.)................... **2,415**

Ring, pearl & diamond, centered by a golden pearl, measuring approx. 12.60 mm., surrounded by round & baguette-cut diamonds, approx. total diamond wt. .70 cts., 14k yellow gold mount, signed "Manning"...................... **1,265**

Ring, pearl, diamond & gold, dinner-type, 14k yellow gold floral-designed mount set w/a South Sea pearl measuring 14 mm. surrounded by 12 baguette diamonds weighing about 1 carat alternating w/42 round brilliant-cut diamonds weighing about .65 carats, size 7........... **1,610**

Ring, pearl, diamond & platinum, featuring a South Sea cultured pearl, approx. 10.0 mm., accented w/two oval-cut horizontally-set diamonds, approx. 0.70 cts. **2,645**

Ring, pearl & diamond, set w/a button-shaped South Sea pearl measuring 14.3 mm., surrounded by two tiers of 48 round brilliant-cut & baguette-cut diamonds, approx. 1.75 cts. **1,610**

Ring, pearl & diamond, set w/a Tahitian black cultured pearl measuring 11.6 mm. surrounded by 21 round brilliant-cut diamonds, weighing approx. .55 cts. **1,840**

Ring, pearl & diamond, shield shape, centered by a cultured pearl measuring approx. 6.20 mm., framed by eight old European-cut diamonds, approx. total wt. 0.80 cts., further surrounded by nine cultured pearls each measuring approx. 3.20 mm., 14k yellow gold mount **1,093**

Ring, peridot & diamond, centered by an oval peridot measuring approx. 12.61 x 10.61 x 7.25 mm., flanked by six round diamonds, 14k white gold mount **374**

Peridot & Diamond Ring

Ring, peridot & diamond, designed w/a marquise-cut peridot, measuring approx. 20.68 x 9.29 x 7.00 mm., set at an angle in a diamond foliate-style mount, approx. total diamond wt. .96 cts., ruby accents, 18k yellow gold mount, French hallmark (ILLUS.) **920**

Ring, platinum, diamond & emerald, centered by a triangular-cut diamond, approx. .44 cts., surrounded by a row of emeralds & a row of round brilliant-cut diamonds, approx. total wt. .84 cts., engraved platinum mount (one emerald missing) **1,380**

Ring, platinum & diamond wedding band channel-set w/23 round diamonds, total approx. 1.40 cts., signed "Tiffany & Co.," approx. 3.1 dwt. **2,070**

Ring, platinum, sapphire & diamond, centered by a cushion-cut sapphire, approx. 8.59 x 8.22 x 7.50 mm., surrounded by eight round brilliant-cut diamonds, approx. 2.65 cts., signed "Boucheron, Paris, No. 49147" (slight abrasions to sapphire) **14,950**

Ring, platinum, sapphire & diamond, centered by an oval sapphire, measuring approx. 8.65 x 6.68 x 5.12 mm., surrounded by round brilliant-cut diamonds, approx. total wt. .42 cts. **1,725**

Ring, ruby, diamond & 14k white gold, centered by an oval-shaped ruby measuring approx. 8.90 x 6.55 x 3.65 mm, encircled by full-cut diamonds **1,610**

Ring, ruby, diamond & 18k yellow gold, checkerboard design featuring three rows of horizontally-set rubies, approx. 4.50 cts., further accented w/small round brilliant-cut diamonds, approx. 0.25 cts. **1,610**

Ruby & Diamond Ring

Ring, ruby & diamond, alternating shaped bands of channel-set rubies & bead-set diamonds w/an integral plume decoration set w/rubies & diamonds, 14k gold mount (ILLUS.) **1,265**

Ruby and Diamond Ring

Ring, ruby & diamond, center oval faceted ruby, weighing approx. 5 cts., flanked by two round brilliant-cut diamonds w/total weight of approx. 1.35 cts., mounted in 18k yellow gold, Italian hallmark (ILLUS.) **17,250**

Ring, ruby & diamond, center w/bezel-set old European-cut diamond, approx. 2.35 cts., within a triple row of 40 bead-set round diamonds, approx. 1.12 cts., spaced by two rows of channel-set rectangular rubies, platinum-topped 14k yellow gold mount **5,980**

Ruby & Diamond Bowknot Ring

Ring, ruby & diamond, designed as a double bowknot, set w/a cushion-shaped ruby approx 8.70 x 7.00 x 5.20 mm. & a circular-cut diamond approx. 1.70 cts., within a ruby & diamond tapered baguette mount, fitted box for Black, Starr & Frost (ILLUS.) **12,650**

Ring, ruby & diamond, three stone design, set w/an oval double cabochon natural star ruby measuring approx. 8.29 x 7.47 x 6.26 mm., estimated by formula to weigh 3.72 cts., flanked by round brilliant-cut diamonds, approx. total weight 0.898 cts., 14k yellow gold mount **5,750**

Ring, ruby eternity band, platinum mount **978**

Sapphire & Gold Ring

Ring, sapphire & 14k gold, set w/two clip-cornered triangular-cut sapphires, measuring approximately. 15.48 x 14.25 x 8.13 mm. & 15.71 x 14.17 x 9.17 mm., white gold mount (ILLUS.) **863**

Ring, sapphire & 18k white gold, centered w/heart-shaped sapphire & pavé-set diamond lettering, "Happy Hearts," inscribed "LOVE," signed "Chopard" **1,610**

Sapphire & Diamond White Gold Ring

Ring, sapphire, diamond & 14k white gold, center oval-shaped sapphire measuring approx. 11.90 x 8.70 x 4.50 mm., surrounded by two rows of full-cut diamonds weighing a total of approx. 1.40 cts. (ILLUS.) **2,875**

Ring, sapphire & diamond, 14k yellow gold four-prong floral design mount center set w/a round faceted pink sapphire, approx. .65 cts., the petals set w/44 round brilliant-cut diamonds spaced by baguette diamonds, approx. 1 ct. **288**

Ring, sapphire, diamond & 18k yellow gold, centering a row of oval-cut sapphires, approx. 2.10 cts., bordered by round brilliant-cut diamonds, approx. 0.30 cts. **920**

Ring, sapphire & diamond, 24 square-cut channel-set blue sapphires weighing approx. 2.85 cts., flanked by 24 round brilliant-cut pavé-set diamonds, weighing approx. .55 cts., 18k yellow gold mount **863**

![Yellow Sapphire & Diamond Ring]

Yellow Sapphire & Diamond Ring

Ring, sapphire & diamond, a center oval-shaped, faceted yellow sapphire weighing approx. 5.70 cts., flanked by six round brilliant-cut diamonds w/an approx. total weight of 0.50 ct., mounted in 18k white gold (ILLUS.).... **3,450**

Ring, sapphire & diamond, a collet-set sapphire measuring approx.   8.35 x 7.95 x 3.45 mm., highlighted by four old European-cut diamonds, approx. total wt. 0.75 cts., a millegrain platinum & diamond mount w/pierced shank, European hallmark............................. **2,990**

Pear-shaped Sapphire Ring

Ring, sapphire & diamond, a prong-set pear-shaped sapphire measuring approx. 8.75 x 6.82 x 4.78 mm., surrounded by 13 bezel-set round diamonds, the shoulders having a row of channel-set tapered square-cut sapphires bordered by bead-set round diamonds mounted in platinum-topped 18k yellow gold, approx. total wt. 0.75 cts. (ILLUS.)........ **3,450**

Ring, sapphire & diamond, center set w/an old mine-cut diamond, approx. 2.10 cts., further enhanced by four corner prong-set sapphires measuring   approx. 3.30 x 4.50 mm., 14k yellow gold mount (chips to girdle of diamond, chips to sapphires) **8,050**

Ring, sapphire & diamond, centered by a cushion-cut sapphire   approx. 10.08 x 8.98 x 7.12 mm., surrounded by marquise- & circular-cut diamonds, approx. total 1.40 cts., stamped "S, C & L" for Shreve, Crump & Low, accompanied by AGTA colored stone certificate....... **41,400**

Ring, sapphire & diamond, centered by an oval sapphire, approx. 2.15 cts., flanked by three small round diamonds, total approx. .78 cts., 18k yellow gold mount, signed "Cartier 632431"......... **4,600**

Ring, sapphire & diamond, centered by an oval sapphire measuring   approx. 11.2 x 8.8 x 4.7   mm., flanked by trillion-shaped diamonds, each approx. 0.36 cts., 18k yellow gold mount, Cartier, accompanied by original Cartier bill of sale...... **5,463**

Unusual Yellow Sapphire & Diamond Ring

Ring, sapphire & diamond, centering a pear-shaped, faceted yellow sapphire weighing approx. 16.70 cts. w/four heavy prongs, each set w/square princess-cut diamonds, the ring having a heart-shaped outline when viewed from the side profile, decorated w/two rows of square princess-cut diamonds in the shoulder portions & round brilliant-cut diamonds on the sides, having a total weight of approx. 7 cts., mounted in platinum & 18k yellow gold, Italian hallmark, Spoleto Gioielli (ILLUS. of top & profile)............ **14,950**

Sapphire & Diamond Ring

Ring, sapphire & diamond, centering an oval-shaped cabochon-cut sapphire weighing approx. 30 cts. decorated w/two baguette-cut diamonds on each side, total weight of approx. 2.5 cts., mounted in platinum (ILLUS.).............................. **11,500**

Ring, sapphire & diamond, centrally set w/an oval-shaped cabochon-cut sapphire weighing approx. 11 cts., surrounded by round single-cut diamonds & accented on each side w/a

round brilliant- & baguette-cut diamond, mounted in platinum.............................. **4,830**

Ring, sapphire & diamond, collet-set oval yellow sapphire within a diamond-set openwork band w/engraved foliate decoration, 18k white & yellow gold mount, signed "M. Buccelatti".............................. **3,910**

Ring, sapphire & diamond, man's, centered by a gypsy-set oval sapphire cabochon, flanked by old mine-cut diamonds, weighing approx. 0.50 cts. each, 14k yellow gold mount, signed "H.O." ... **1,150**

Sapphire & Diamond Bypass Ring

Ring, sapphire, diamond & platinum, bypass style, diagonally set w/one trapezoid-shaped diamonds, approx. 1 ct. & a similarly shaped sapphire, approx. 1 ct. & enhanced w/26 baguette-cut diamonds, total approx. .75 cts. (ILLUS.).............................. **4,600**

Ring, sapphire, diamond & platinum, centered by a round sapphire, approx. 5.10 cts., the openwork mounting w/millegrain detailing & set w/34 round diamonds, total approx. 1 ct...... **2,530**

Ring, sapphire, diamond & platinum, rectangular mixed cut pink sapphire weighing approx. 3.40 cts. flanked by 12 square & tapered baguette diamonds weighing approx. .50 cts............................. **4,600**

Ring, sapphire & diamond, set w/an oval Ceylon sapphire measuring approx. 12.5 x 10.8 x 4.8 mm., framed by 14 old mine-cut diamonds, approx. total wt. 1.50 cts., 14k gold mount..... **2,760**

Ring, sapphire & diamond, set w/an oval orange-pink sapphire measuring approx. 8.7 x 6.5 x 5.2 mm. within a scrolled platinum mount decorated w/calibré-, baguette- & circular-cut diamonds (one diamond missing)..................... **5,175**

Ring, sapphire & diamond, "The Peacock Ring," designed w/a marquise-cut sapphire center surrounded by round diamonds, 14k yellow gold mount, signed "Erte"................. **403**

Ring, sapphire, joined bands, one centered by an emerald-cut yellow sapphire, the other w/an emerald-cut blue sapphire, each measuring approx. 6.10 x 9.70 x 4.80 mm. flanked by tapered baguettes, 18k yellow gold mount................. **4,600**

Ring, sapphire, man's, cabochon sapphire measuring approx. 11.8 x 9.5 x 6.5, flanked by two baguette-cut diamonds, textured 14k white gold mount.............. **3,450**

Ring, star sapphire & diamond, a bezel-set oval star sapphire, measuring approx. 8.85 x 9.98 x 3.15 mm., surrounded by collet-set round diamonds approx. total wt. 0.35 cts., millegrain accents, platinum mount (gold solder evident)............................... **1,610**

Ring, star sapphire & diamond, a center oval cabochon-cut star sapphire

weighing approx. 20 cts., flanked by two square-cut & two tapered baguette-cut diamonds w/a total approx. weight of 1.10 cts., mounted in platinum..................... **4,370**

Ring, star sapphire & diamond, centered by a star sapphire measuring approx. 12.05 x 10.88 x 7.89 mm.flanked by baguette-cut diamonds & surrounded by round diamonds, platinum mount (surface scratch)......... **1,150**

Ring, star sapphire, diamond & platinum, a central oval star sapphire measuring approx. 12.78 x 10.03 x 8.14 mm., flanked by two trapeze-cut diamonds, the shoulders further set w/six round-cut diamonds, hallmark for F. & F. Felger, Inc., Newark (chip to back of sapphire).................. **3,220**

Ring, tanzanite & 14k gold, centered by an oval faceted tanzanite, measuring approx. 17.62 x 12.76 x 11.72 mm. within a foliate gold mount, round brilliant-cut diamond accents............................. **3,220**

Ring, tanzanite & diamond, a circular-cut tanzanite measuring approx. 7.50 mm., flanked by brilliant-cut diamonds, approx. total wt. 1.15 cts., 14k gold mount................. **1,610**

Ring, tanzanite & diamond, three oval tanzanites framed by 16 round brilliant-cut diamonds, approx. total diamond weight 0.88 cts., all prong-set, 14k yellow & white gold mount............................. **978**

Ring, tanzanite, set w/an oval-shaped faceted tanzanite weighing approx. 3.63 cts. & flanked by two round brilliant-cut diamonds having a total weight of approx. 0.20 ct., mounted in a wide bombé mounting of 18k white gold **2,990**

Ring, topaz & diamond, centered w/a rectangular-shaped, faceted topaz weighing approx. 9.50 cts., the sides accented w/round & small emerald-cut diamonds w/an approx. total weight of 0.60 ct., mounted in 18k white gold (ILLUS. left w/topaz pendant, page 227) **1,725**

Ring, tourmaline & 18k yellow gold, contemporary style, triangular pink tourmaline flanked by diamond melée in a triangular cartouche **863**

Ring, tourmaline, centered by an oval cabochon green tourmaline, measuring approx. 14.35 x 12.50 x 6.20 mm., flanked by four round diamonds, 18k white gold mount **259**

Ring, turquoise & diamond, centered by a prong-set sugarloaf turquoise, approx. 19.5 x 15.68 mm., surrounded by 18 round brilliant-cut diamonds, approx. total wt. 2.16 cts., mounted in 18k yellow gold, signed "David Webb" **1,610**

Ring, turquoise & diamond, marquise cabochon turquoise framed by 16 old mine-cut diamonds, 14k yellow gold mount **863**

Ring, turquoise, ruby & diamond, centered by a pear-shaped turquoise highlighted by round brilliant-cut diamonds & round rubies, 18k yellow gold scroll mount, signed "David Webb" **1,725**

Ring, zircon & diamond, centered by a square-cut yellow/brown zircon, measuring approx. 9.95 x 9.93 x 6.51 mm., surrounded by tapered baguette & round diamonds, approx. total wt. .60 cts., 14k yellow gold mount **288**

Ring/pendant, platinum, emerald & diamond, the platinum ballerina-design mount set w/a square-cut emerald weighing about 1.35 carats surrounded by 16 round brilliant-cut & 24 tapered baguette diamonds weighing about 2.85 carats, the shank is removable & top portion can be used as a pendant, size 5 .... **2,070**

Rings, gold (18k yellow), stackable set, one w/channel-set square-cut diamonds, approx. 0.96 cts., one w/channel-set square-cut rubies, approx. 1.68 cts., one channel-set w/approx. 1.08 cts. emeralds & one w/channel-set w/approx. 1.20 cts. sapphires, set of four **2,530**

Slide, gold (14k), shield form slide surmounted by a scroll decoration w/blue stone & seed pearl accents, suspended by a wiretwist chain w/applied plaque stamped "Boston," 33.2 dwt., 31" l. **690**

Slide & chain, gold, fancy link chain suspending a lobed slide set w/seed pearls w/black enamel highlights, foxtail pendant, 14k yellow gold, 24.3 dwt, 18 1/4" l. **805**

Stickpin, cultured pearl & diamond, a small ring at the top w/a row of small rose-cut diamonds centering a 5.6 mm. pearl, mounted in a platinum-topped 18k yellow gold pin **311**

Stickpin, diamond, centered by an old European-cut diamond, diamond-set square platinum-topped gold mount **1,840**

Stickpin, diamond & enamel, designed as the head of an owl w/polychrome enamel feathers & old European-cut diamond eyes, silver-topped 14k yellow gold mount, signed "Tiffany & Co." (minor scratch to back, minor enamel loss) **1,725**

Stickpin, diamond, set w/a round diamond, weighing approx. 1.12 cts., platinum basket, 14k yellow gold stickpin **2,875**

Stickpin, moonstone, emerald & 14k yellow gold, designed w/an oval moonstone surrounded by channel-set emeralds in gold mount **345**

Stickpin, natural pearl, the top w/an ovoid pearl measuring 11.6 x 9.7 mm., mounted on a 14k yellow gold pin **3,450**

Unusual Peacock Stickpin

Stickpin, opal, model of a peacock carved from boulder opal w/the original matrix

forming the tree branch & decorated w/an oval, faceted ruby, mounted in 18k yellow gold, numbered, French hallmarks & maker's mark, Branché Avignon (ILLUS.) ... **4,830**

Stickpin, ruby, jade & diamond, centered by cabochon ruby bead flanked by rose-cut diamond rondel w/jade bead terminals **1,955**

Wedding band, diamond & platinum, channel-set w/29 square-cut diamonds, approx. 2.30 cts. **2,300**

Sets

Garnet & Citrine Bracelet & Earrings

Bracelet & earrings, gold (18k yellow), garnet & citrine, the hinged bangle bracelet w/a matte finish & set across the top w/rectangular-cut citrines & garnets, together w/matching pair of demi-hoop clip-on earrings, total approx. 69.3 dwt., the set (ILLUS.) **1,725**

Bracelet & necklace, gold (18k yellow), contemporary style pieces w/brushed fancy links, can be converted into one necklace w/hidden swivel clasp accented w/cabochon sapphire, 46.6 dwt, necklace 17 1/2" l., bracelet 7 1/2" l., the set **1,093**

Bracelet & necklace, gold, snake link in a double twist design, signed "Tiffany & Co.," bracelet 7 1/2" l., necklace 16 3/4" l., the set **2,185**

Coral & Diamond Suite

Bracelet, necklace & ring, coral & diamond, the double strand coral bead necklace w/a center circle set w/diamonds suspending a detachable coral heart pendant decorated w/diamonds, the bracelet w/three oval-shaped cabochon-cut coral surrounded by diamonds on an 18k white gold link chain, the oval coral ring accented w/diamonds, all designed in 18k white gold & set w/round brilliant-cut, single-cut & marquise-shaped diamonds w/approx. total weight of 4 cts., necklace 15" l., the set (ILLUS.).. **6,325**

Diamond & Enamel Bracelet

Bracelet & ring, gold (14k yellow), diamond & enamel, the rigid bracelet a circular domed spoke design, each spoke decorated w/dark blue enameling w/a round brilliant-cut diamond set between each spoke & in the top & center w/blue enameled sides, each decorated w/a centerline of five round brilliant-cut diamonds, ring w/matching design, bracelet 6", the set (ILLUS. of bracelet).................... **2,300**

Leopard Head Bangle Bracelet

Bracelet & ring, gold (18k yellow), gem & diamond, the bangle-type bracelet of hinged bypass design featuring two gem & diamond set detailed leopard heads, together w/matching bypass design ring, the set (ILLUS. of bracelet).................... **4,025**

Matching Diamond Bracelet & Ring

Bracelet & ring, platinum & diamond, comprised of a bracelet centered by a collet-set diamond surrounded by a row of synthetic sapphires & single-cut diamonds on a diamond-set box link bracelet, platinum mount, millegrain accents, together w/a matching ring, the set (ILLUS.).................... **2,185**

Floral Design Bracelet, Ring & Earrings

Bracelet, ring & earrings, gold (18k yellow), the bracelet a rigid, hinged bangle w/floral textured openwork design, together w/matching ring & semi-hoop earrings, bracelet 7", signed "Buccellati," maker's mark, the set (ILLUS.).................... **2,530**

Leaf-shaped Brooch

Brooch & dress clips, gold (18k), sapphire & diamond, the openwork brooch designed as a leaf set w/sapphire & diamond florets, diamond-set platinum-topped stem, together w/two matching dress clips, the set (ILLUS. of brooch).................... **5,175**

Brooch & earrings, amethyst & nephrite, a flower brooch designed as a bouquet of pansies w/amethyst quartz carved petals, diamond accents & nephrite jade carved leaves, 18k yellow gold, together w/matching clip earrings, the set.................... **748**

Brooch & earrings, gold (14k yellow), a domed floral design brooch of thick gold wire, together w/pair of matching earclips, signed "Tiffany & Co.," hallmark, total wt. 24.2 dwt..................... **1,035**

Gold "Pick-up-Sticks" Brooch & Earrings

Brooch & earrings, gold (18k yellow), sapphire & diamond, "Pick-up-Sticks" design, the brooch composed of criss-crossed gold rods w/beaded ends containing eight faceted sapphires & four round diamonds, approx. .32 cts., together w/matching pair of earrings, the set (ILLUS.).......................... **1,035**

Georgina Gold & Diamond Brooch & Earrings

Brooch & earrings, gold (18k yellow), the brooch in a contemporary "bird's nest" design pierced w/a crossed pair of 14k white gold "twigs," together w/pair of similar contemporary design earrings, each piece decorated w/a round brilliant-cut diamond, approx. diamond total weight of 0.75 ct., Georgina, the set (ILLUS.).............. **1,035**

Pearl & Emerald Brooch & Earrings

Brooch & earrings, pearl & emerald, the 14k yellow gold brooch designed as a stylized fern set w/five cultured pearls & emeralds, matching clip earrings, hallmark, the set (ILLUS.).. **345**

Contemporary Gold Brooch

Brooch & earrings, ruby & 18k yellow gold, designed as a flower centered by 19 bead-set rubies within a frame of six textured gold leaves, the stem designed as a curving snake, together w/matching earrings, Italian gold marks, the set (ILLUS.)
.... **1,150**

Leaf Brooch & Earrings

Brooch & earrings, ruby & 18k yellow gold, the brooch designed as a textured leaf entwined by a smooth gold vine enhanced w/ruby "berries," together w/similar clip earrings, hallmark, the set (ILLUS.) **518**

Sea Urchin Brooch & Earring

Brooch & earrings, ruby, diamond & 14k yellow gold, designed as sea urchins, the brooch accented w/one circular-cut diamond & each clip-style earring accented w/three circular-cut rubies & two diamonds, minor solder to finding, the set (ILLUS. of part) **1,150**

Brooch & earrings, ruby & diamond, a floral spray brooch set en tremblant w/108 rubies & 36 bead set & bezel-set diamonds, 18k white gold mount, matching pair of clip earrings, the set **4,888**

Brooch/pendant & earrings, enamel & 18k gold, oval brooch centered by an urn-shaped vessel suspending a similar vessel & two gold pendants decorated throughout w/opaque polychrome & pink translucent enamel, black enamel tracery highlights, w/matching earrings, the set **633**

Agate Cameo & Pearl Brooch & Earrings

Cameo brooch & earrings, agate, the brooch depicting a woman in profile, sur-

rounded by prong- & box-set pearls, suspending a fringe of pearls, together w/matching pair of earpendants, 18k yellow gold mount, European & export hallmarks, the set (ILLUS.) **1,610**

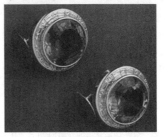

Citrine & Gold Cuff Links

Dress set, citrine & 14k yellow gold, pair of cuff links, each featuring one round-cut citrine measuring approx. 16.80 x 16.80 x 11.30 mm., together w/three matching shirt studs, each centering one round-cut citrine measuring approx. 7.50 x 7.50 x 5.50 mm., the set (ILLUS. of cuff links) **460**

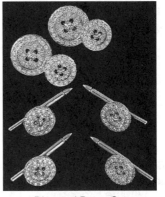

Diamond Dress Set

Dress set, diamond, a pair of gentleman's double-sided cuff links designed as buttons, each pavé-set w/round brilliant-cut diamonds, together w/four matching shirt studs, an approx. total weight of 5 cts., mounted in platinum, the set (ILLUS.) **8,050**

Dress set, gold (10k bicolor) & onyx, a pair of double-sided cuff links enhanced by round-shaped black onyx, together w/six matching shirt studs, the set (some damage) **230**

Dress set, gold (14k) & moonstone, a pair of oval cabochon moonstone cuff links, together w/similar round moonstone studs, hallmark for Larter & Sons, the set **1,265**

Dress set, gold (14k yellow) & hematite, the cuff links designed w/hematite beads set in gold claw mountings, together w/three matching studs, 18k yellow gold mounts, 14k gold findings, the set **1,495**

Dress set, gold (14k yellow), onyx, mother-of-pearl & diamond, a pair of double-sided cuff links, each centering one full-cut diamond framed by mother-of-pearl, completed by faceted black onyx, together w/three matching shirt studs, the set **1,265**

Dress set, gold (14k yellow) & sapphire, a pair of rectangular-shaped brushed gold plaques centered by a row of calibré-cut sapphires, cabochon sapphire terminals on T-bar, signed "Tiffany & Co., No. S449," together w/a set of three matching shirt studs, No. 941, the set **2,875**

Dress set, gold (18k white), onyx & diamond, pair of cuff links of circular design featuring square-cut onyx & round brilliant-cut diamonds in checkboard pattern, together w/four matching studs, approx. 0.70 cts. (ILLUS.) **2,300**

Dress set, gold (18k yellow), a pair of man's gold knot cuff links & three dress studs, 16.1 dwt., signed "Schulmberger, Tiffany & Co.," w/fitted box, the set **2,070**

Dress set, onyx & 18k yellow gold, gentleman's, pair of cuff links & three shirt studs each of circular shape, centrally inlaid w/a black onyx disk & engraved "Bulgari" along the wide gold bezel, numbered, w/original fitted leather box, the set **1,495**

Dress set, onyx, platinum & 18k yellow gold, pair of circular onyx cuff links, centering a small seed pearl, the platinum border further set w/tiny seed pearls, together w/four matching studs, the set **690**

Dress set, opal & 18k yellow gold, gentleman's, pair of cuff links centered by an oval opal, 18k yellow gold frame, together w/four matching studs, signed "Ming's," the set **2,300**

Dress set, ruby & 14k gold, a pair of elliptical form cuff links centered by bezel-set rubies, together w/two matching collar studs, hallmark, 9.8 dwt., the set **1,093**

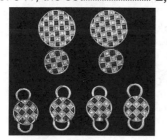

Onyx & Diamond Dress Set

Aquamarine Earrings & Ring

Earrings & ring, aquamarine, each piece centering an oval-shaped, cabochon-cut cat's eye aquarmarine in an 18k yellow gold ribbed frame w/satin finish, maker's mark & signed "Bach," aprox. total weight of the three stones .45 cts., the set (ILLUS.) **3,680**

Earrings & ring, gold (18k yellow), aquamarine & diamond, the ring center set w/an emerald-cut aquamarine weighing approx. 15 cts., accented w/round single-cut diamonds in a multiple flame design, the earrings of similar multiple flame design randomly set w/small emerald-cut aquamarines & round brilliant- & single-cut diamonds, the set **8,050**

Necklace & bracelet, gold, designed w/large oval reeded & polished trace links, Portuguese hallmarks, necklace 30" l., bracelet 7 1/4" l., the set.............. **1,265**

Necklace & bracelet, gold & diamond, yellow curb link chain centered by diamond melée links in white gold together w/matching bracelet, necklace 15" l., bracelet 7 1/2" l., the set **920**

Necklace & bracelet, pearl, the necklace composed of a triple strand w/approx. 163 natural colored light golden yellow freshwater cultured pearls measuring 8 to 8 1/2 mm., together w/a matching triple strand bracelet w/69 pearls, each joined by matching 14k yellow gold button form tongue-in-groove clasps, necklace 17" l., bracelet 7 1/2" l., the set... **1,035**

Necklace & bracelet, sterling silver, choker-type, rope twist sections w/14k yellow gold accents, hook & eye clasp w/red cabochon stones, matching bracelet, No. 371314, signed "D. Yurman," the set................. **1,610**

Necklace & bracelet, sterling silver, twisted silver torque design necklace w/similar bracelet, signed "Hermes, Paris," hallmark, the set **1,150**

Necklace & bracelet, tortoiseshell & 18k yellow gold, the necklace composed of alternating gold & tortoiseshell curb links, together w/matching bracelet, pieces combine to form one necklace, necklace 16 3/4" l., bracelet 7 5/8" l. (two worn links) **2,185**

Necklace, brooch & earrings, gold (yellow) & diamond, contemporary leaf fringe necklace, a leaf spray brooch w/round brilliant-cut diamond accents, approx. 1.30 cts., together w/matching pair of leaf earrings, each set w/three round brilliant-cut diamonds, approx. total wt. .30 cts., necklace 15 1/2" l., the set.................... **2,070**

Necklace & earrings, beryl, gold & diamond, the necklace of twisted 18k yellow gold wire domed links centered by graduated emerald-cut green beryl w/43 round diamond accents, approx. total wt. 3.97 cts., together w/similar clip earrings, 14k yellow gold mount, the set.... **2,990**

Necklace & earrings, diamond & 18k gold, the necklace styled w/192 graduating bezel-set diamonds grouped in clusters of three, together w/matching pair of earrings w/diamonds weighing approx. 0.36 cts., necklace w/approx. total 3.40 cts., 15 1/2" l., the set.................... **3,910**

Gold Necklace & Earrings

Necklace & earrings, gold (18k yellow), a leaf design w/very finely textured finish, separated by small gold nugget-like designs w/matching earrings, signed w/Italian hallmarks, M. Buccellati, necklace approx. 15 3/4" l., the set (ILLUS.)............ **4,600**

Necklace & earrings, pearl, a 24 1/2" l. strand of 70 pearls measuring approx. 7.90 mm., completed by a pearl, diamond & 14k white gold clasp, matching earrings, the set................. **863**

Necklace, earrings & brooch, gold, enamel & diamond, the necklace designed w/an alternating pattern of fancy links set w/numerous rose-cut diamonds outlined in cobalt blue enamel, 14" l., together w/matching earrings, the pendant brooch mounted w/two pear-shaped rose-cut diamonds in buttercup mountings surrounded by diamonds & decorated w/blue enamel scrolls, the set (chip to one rose-cut)............ **4,025**

Lapis Lazuli & Diamond Set

Necklace, pendant & bracelet, lapis lazuli & diamond, the necklace designed w/circular links of lapis lazuli alternating w/navette-shaped, twisted gold links that each contain a row of five round, brilliant-cut diamonds, the bracelet of similar design, the large oval-shaped pendant-drop decorated w/an oval-shaped, pierced lapis lazuli surrounded by two twisted gold wires, w/a circle of 12 round brilliant-cut diamonds at the top, all mounted in 18k yellow & white gold, approx. total weight of diamonds 2.50 cts., necklace 26" l., bracelet 7 1/2" l., the set (ILLUS. of part)........... **1,150**

Necklace, ring & earrings, jade & 14k gold, a single strand of 57 white jade beads completed by a Chinese motif clasp symbolizing good luck, 22" l., together w/an oval-shaped white jade ring & pair of matching clip earrings, retailed by Gump's, the set................. **403**

Pendant & earrings, diamond & aquamarine, the pendant centered by a pear-shaped aquamarine weighing approx. 14.25 cts., surrounded by 21 round brilliant-cut diamonds, together w/matching pair of earrings, approx. total diamond wt. 2.83 cts., 18k yellow gold mounts, the set. **1,840**

Pendant & earrings, diamond & pearl, 14k white gold neck wire suspending a 9.80 mm. South Sea pearl & diamond pendant, together w/similar ear posts, approx. total wt. 0.49 cts., marked for designer Karina Mattei, boxed, the set......................... **1,955**

Mabe Pearl & Diamond Pendant

Pendant & earrings, pearl & diamond, the pendant set w/a pear-shaped mabe pearl measuring approx. 21.52 x 13.98 mm., framed in bead-set round brilliant-cut diamonds, together w/a matching pair of clip earrings, each w/a chevron of round brilliant-cut diamonds at the top, approx. total diamond wt. of set 1.65, 14k yellow gold mounts, the set (ILLUS. of pendant) **1,495**

Watches

Bracelet Watch, No. 41597, Model 18KW or 1859, 11 jewels, key wind & set from back, P.S. Bartlett **600-1,100**

Concealed Face Bracelet Watch

Bracelet watch, gold (14k yellow), wide gold geometric design belt & tassel bracelet w/14k yellow gold case w/hinged lid, high-relief floral motif highlighted w/black enamel, silver matte finish rectangular dial w/black enamel Arabic & yellow goldtone circular hour chapters, ca. 1950, P. Buhre, Swiss, 6 1/2" l. (ILLUS.).. **345**

Bracelet Watch

Bracelet watch, gold (18k pink), ruby & diamond, rigid bracelet w/concealed dial, two overhanging triple grips holding watch, alternating w/diamond-set decoration, four-body, solid, polished guilloché bombé cover set w/diamonds & surrounded by rubies, matte silver dial w/applied gold indexes & Arabic numerals, "Bâton" gold hands, dial, case & movement signed, Vacheron & Constantin, Genève, ca. 1952 (ILLUS.) **2,070**

Cuff links/watch, gold (18k yellow), hinged design w/decorative rectangular plaque, one surmounted by a watch signed "Uti, Paris, No. 35997," French hallmarks **575**

Platinum & Diamond-set Dress Watch

Dress watch, platinum & diamond, keyless, three-piece w/satiné back & diamond-set band & bow, the bezel w/baguette diamond indexes, silver satiné dial w/minute ring on border of bezel, white gold "feuilles" hands, signed on dial, case & movement, Patek Philippe & Cie, Genève, ca. 1944 (ILLUS.) **7,245**

Gold & Diamond-set Fob Watch

Fob watch, gold (18k yellow) diamond-set keyless, four-body "Louis XVI," pavé-set overall w/old-cut diamonds, hinged gold cuvette, white enamel dial w/Roman numerals & blue outer Arabic minute ring, gold "Louis XV" hands, ca. 1880, Swiss (ILLUS.) **2,622**

Cartier Art Deco Fob Watch

Fob watch, Art Deco style, rectangular w/18k white gold geometrically decorated top set w/cabochon sapphires, yellow gold bezel set w/diamonds, plain 18k yellow gold back, hinged & set w/two cabochon sapphires, one mounted to a spring-loaded mechanism to open covers, matte white w/Arabic numerals, blued steel hands, 15 jewel, dial signed "Cartier," back cover engraved inside "European Watch and Clock Co., Inc. France," France, ca. 1920 (ILLUS.) **3,565**

Gold & Enamel Fob Watch

Fob watch, gold (18k yellow) & enamel, four-body, massive, "bassine," engine-turned in a vermicelli pattern, the back decorated w/a flower in high relief against a green, yellow & scarlet flinqué enameled ground, hinged gold cuvette w/engine-turned border, white enamel dial w/Roman numerals & outer Arabic minute ring, blued steel hands, ca. 1900, Swiss (ILLUS.) **759**

Gold & Garnet Fob Watch & Clip

Fob watch w/clip, gold (18k yellow), four body keyless "bassine," polished, the back set w/a large garnet cabochon within a stylized chased foliage frame, hinged gold cuvette, matching gold & garnet clip, white enamel w/Arabic numerals & sunk subsidiary seconds, gold hands, 15 jewel, dial & movement signed "Longines," made for L. Peslier à Avalon, Swiss, ca. 1890 (ILLUS.) ... **1,380**

Unique Lapel Watch

Lapel watch, designed as a violin, two-piece, polished, frosted silver dial w/applied gold indexes, gold "feuilles" hands, signed on dial, case & movement, Rolex, ca. 1950s (ILLUS.).............................. **4,140**

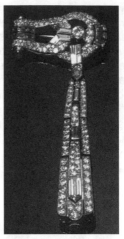

Art Deco Lapel Watch

Lapel watch, diamond & emerald, Art Deco style, the top designed as a stylized buckle set w/round cabochon-cut & calibré-cut emeralds on one end, the diamond side supporting a long tapering segmented ribbon set w/one hexagonal- & one bullet-shaped diamond, round, baguette- & trapezoid-cut diamonds, mounted in platinum, the watch on reverse side w/Vacheron Constantin movement, 18 jewel, rhodium-plated, designed by Verger, France, ca. 1928, French hallmarks, maker's mark & signed (ILLUS.) **19,550**

Art Deco Diamond & Onyx Lapel Watch

Lapel watch, diamond & onyx, Art Deco style, a hexagonal design set w/a row of round single-cut diamonds w/a small row of French-cut black onyx, the top w/a V-

shaped design set w/a triangular-shaped diamond within a frame of French-cut
black onyx (one onyx missing) w/round, single-cut diamonds decorating the V
which pivots to reveal a
small square watch w/white
dial w/black Arabic numerals
& gunmetal blue hands,
frame numbered & signed
"Golay Fils & Stahl," mount-
ed in platinum (ILLUS.) **8,050**

Antique Enamel & Diamond Watch

Lapel watch, enamel & diamond, enameled portrait
surrounded by rose-cut diamond scrollwork & green
guilloché enamel, verso depicting a lute & doves, 18k
yellow gold case, white porcelain dial w/black Arabic
numerals, dust cover in-
scribed "Grand Prix/Par-
is/1889," suspended from a
fleur-de-lis pin set w/old European-cut diamonds, seed
pearl accents, 18k yellow
gold mount, one small diamond missing, minor enamel
loss, boxed (ILLUS.) **2,875**

Art Nouveau Lapel Watch

Lapel watch, enamel & gold,
Art Nouveau style, engraved
18k yellow gold case decorated w/purple guilloché
enamel & highlighted by a
central gold star w/rose diamond accents, suspended
from a lapel pin designed as
a diamond bicycle wheel
flanked by guilloché enamel
wings & a spray of diamond
stars, white porcelain dial
w/black Arabic numerals &
subsidiary seconds dial
w/gold numerals, scroll
hands, tiny scratches to
case, in original fitted box labeled "Patek Philippe & Co.,
Geneve, Grand Prix a Paris
1889, Membre du Jury-Paris
1900" (ILLUS.) **4,485**

Lapel watch, pearl & diamond, the bicolor 18k gold
case w/pavé-set rose-cut diamonds & pearls, cream
porcelain dial w/blue Arabic
numerals, dust cover in-
scribed "Jane 1 er Janvier
1895," suspended from a
crown form & foliate
watch/pin set w/pearls,
round diamond accent, 14k
yellow gold mount, American
hallmark, Bailly ct. Gagnant,
Lyon (crack to crystal) **978**

Art Deco Enamel Pendant Watch

Pendant watch, Art Deco style geometric black enamel pendant centered by an oval whitetone dial, blacktone Arabic numerals, freshwater pearl crown, front centered by a diamond-set plaque suspended from a diamond & onyx bail, completed by a black silk cord (ILLUS.).. **2,530**

Pendant watch, Art Nouveau style, green enamel case w/applied 18k yellow gold foliate design, rose-cut diamond accents, hallmark, white porcelain dial, royal blue Arabic numerals, LeCoultre & Cie............................... **978**

Diamond Pendant Watch

Pendant watch, diamond, Art Deco style, pierced & engraved rectangular case set throughout w/round diamonds, triangular blue stone accents, suspended from a sterling silver curb link chain,

cream colored dial w/black Arabic numerals, L. & S.L. Nerny, 20" l. (ILLUS.)............... **1,265**

Diamond Heart Pendant Watch

Pendant watch, diamond & platinum heart-shaped scroll & foliate motif case bead-set w/rose-, single- & full-cut diamonds, suspended by a black silk cord w/diamond slide & swivel clasp, the C.H. Meylan, Brassus watch w/round white porcelain dial, black Arabic numerals, Louis XIV hands, high grade jeweled nickel movement, Edwardian (ILLUS.) **6,900**

Art Deco Pendant Watch

Pendant watch, diamond & sapphire, Art Deco style, diamond & sapphire encrusted case centered by a bezel-set marquise diamond, bail set w/a pear-shaped & round diamond, mounted in platinum w/millegrain accents, platinum bar link & seed pearl chain, No. 30735, Tiffany & Co., 19" l. (ILLUS.).................... **5,463**

Diamond & Sapphire Pendant Watch

Pendant watch, diamond & sapphire, round case encrusted w/bead-set round diamonds set in platinum & sapphires set in 18k yellow gold, diamond-set bow, movement No. 16622, porcelain dial w/black Roman numerals, scroll hands, ca. 1905, Tiffany & Co., Edwardian, accompanied by Tiffany & Co. appraisal (ILLUS.) **8,050**

Gold & Enamel Pendant Watch

Pendant watch, gold (18k yellow) & enamel, keyless, three-body, entirely decorated w/a powder blue flingué enamel, the back w/painted white enameled flowers on the border & applied w/a rose-cut diamond set basket of flowers, suspended from a ribbon & bowl design set w/rose-cut diamonds, hinged gold cuvette engraved w/name of owner, frosted engine-turned silver dial w/Arabic numerals, gold

Breguet hands, signed on dial, case & movement, Vacheron & Constantin, Genèe, ca. 1915 (ILLUS.) **2,070**

Smith Patterson Pendant Watch

Pendant watch, hunting case, Art Noveau style, Smith Patterson Co., goldtone dial w/black Roman numerals, initialed case, chased & engraved griffin brooch, hallmarked for Bippart, Griscom & Osborn, 14k yellow gold (ILLUS.) **443**

Rare Gold & Enamel Pendant Watch

Pendant watch/locket, gold (18k yellow) & enamel, five-body, designed as a book, the enameled spring-loaded lid on cover painted w/a muse over a black ground, outer pierced gold decoration, the back cover w/engraved decoration over an azure enameled ground, hinged lockets for four portraits inside the back, hinged gold cuvette, white enamel dial w/Roman numerals, blue steel "spade" hands, signed on cuvette, Patek Philippe & Cie, Genève, ca. 1875 (ILLUS.) **13,800**

Howard, Davis & Dennison Pocket Watch

Pocket watch, 20 size, 15 jewels, 8 day, two main-springs & gilt movement, ca. 1852, the first 17 were made for the officials of the company, Howard, Davis & Dennison (ILLUS.) **30,000-80,000**

American Watch Co. Pocket Watch

Pocket watch, Bridge Model, 16 size, 23 jewels, gold train, Adj.5P, American Watch Co. (ILLUS.) **1,100-2,500**

Art Deco Dress Watch

Pocket watch, enamel & 18k gold, Art Nouveau style, keyless, four body, solid "demi-bassine" back & bezel in multicolored cloisonné enamel flowers, leaves & fruits on black enamel background, gold hinged cuvette engraved w/medals awarded at different expositions, gold w/gold Roman numerals on black enamel round cartouches, center w/similar decoration to case, case & movement signed "Longines," ca. 1910 (ILLUS.) **4,255**

Pocket Watch with Horse Portraits

Pocket watch, enamel & 18k yellow gold, keyless "Reglage de Precision," four body, "demi-bassine" front cover w/finely painted portraits of two horses over translucent blue enamel w/"basket pattern" engine-turning, within a round white opaque & translucent dark blue frame, back cover w/painted horseshoe intertwined w/laurel leaves over the same background & frame as the front, gold hinged cuvette, bow & crown chased w/scrollings, matte-gilded Arabic numerals, "Cathedrale hands," dial & case signed "Borel Fils & Cie, Neuchâtel," Borel's trademark on movement, made for H. Shtulevich, Elisabethgrad, ca. 1910 (ILLUS.) **5,750**

Pocket watch, gold (14k tricolor) hunting case, Elgin, 3/4 plate nickel movement, white enameled dial w/Roman numerals, subsidiary seconds dial, gold cuvette, tricolor gold case centered by a monogrammed medallion on one side & a floral bouquet on the other, ca. 1885, dial & movement signed "Elgin," case marked "P.K. & Co." 374

Lady's Gold Pocket Watch

Pocket watch, gold (14k yellow) & enamel, hunting case, lady's, engraved case No. 15500 w/black enamel tracery, polychrome enamel decoration of a man & a woman dancing in the moonlight, the verso w/blue enamel decoration, white porcelain dial w/black Roman numerals (ILLUS.) 489

Gold Hunting Case Pocket Watch

Pocket watch, gold (14k yellow), hunting case, white porcelain dial w/black Ro-

man numerals, Hampden, movement No. 596090, loose crystal, engraved gold case w/scalloped edge, No. 65487 (ILLUS.) 460

Pocket watch, gold (18k), hunting case, American Watch Co., 3/4 plate nickel movement marked "Appleton Tracy & Co., Nr. 702529," white enameled dial w/Roman numerals, subsidiary seconds dial, gold cuvette, case engraved w/floral scrolls trimmed w/black enamel, ca. 1873, case, dial & movement signed 345

Pocket watch, gold (18k) hunting case, American Watch Co., full plate gilt movement marked "Appleton, Tracy & Co., Nr. 778941," white enameled dial w/Roman numerals, subsidiary seconds dial, gold cuvette, engine-turned case w/floral engraving, ca. 1875, movement & dial signed, case signed "B & T" 575

Antique Gold Hunter Case Pocket Watch

Pocket watch, gold (18k yellow) chased hunting case, polychrome goldtone foliate dial, fussee movement no. 1367 marked "Dublin," coppertone Roman numerals, key missing, mid-19th c. (ILLUS.) 1,265

Rare Presentation Watch

Pocket watch, gold (18k yellow), fine & rare hunting case, four-body, massive, "bassine et filets," engine-turned w/reeded band, the cover centered w/a black champlevé enameled scene depicting a life rescue at sea, the back w/the emblem of the United States of America, dedication engraved inside cover, "presented by Ulysses S. Grant (1869-1877), President of America, to Capt. J. Petterson for the rescue of the crew of the AM. BARK PLEIADES - 1870," white enamel dial w/Roman numerals & sunk subsidiary seconds, blued steel "spade" hands, signed on dial & back plate, American Watch Co., Waltham, Massachusetts, ca. 1870 (ILLUS.)............................ **11,040**

Rose Gold Open face Pocket Watch

Pocket watch, gold (9k rose) open face w/goldtone floral engraved dial, black enamel Roman numerals, subsidiary seconds dial, engraved dust cover, key wind, hallmarks, together w/a 9k rose gold fancy link chain, swivel hook, T-bar & shield fob, hallmarks, 15 1/2" l. (ILLUS.)......... **489**

Gold & Enamel Pocket Watch

Pocket watch, gold & enamel hunting case, 18k yellow gold case inlaid w/cobalt blue enamel on both sides & further enhanced by rose-cut diamonds & gold foliate detail, chips to enamel, Racine Perrot, No. 37207, key wind, white porcelain dial w/black Roman numerals (ILLUS.)............................... **690**

Pocket watch, hunting case, lady's, Empress JMG Co., pendent-type, gold-filled case w/floral-engraved outer case w/engraved scalloped edge, monogrammed inside & dated 1911, enameled dial w/seconds hand, case marked by the Ideal Watch Case Co., 15 jewels.................... **280**

Fine American Waltham Pocket Watch

Pocket watch, hunting case, man's, American Waltham, 14k gold case, 17 jewels adjustable, shield engraving on the case, works marked by P.S. Barlett, Waltham, Massachusetts, ca. 1906 (ILLUS.)................................... **952**

Pocket watch, hunting case, man's, American Waltham Co., P.S. Bartlett, white enameled dial & small second, blued steel hands, Roman numerals, movement #1331680, patent pinion, 14k yellow gold case w/engine-turned design & monogrammed crest.................... **743**

Pocket watch, hunting case, man's, American Waltham Watch Co., white enameled dial & small second, Roman numerals & red Arabic second numerals, blued steel Brequet-style hands, movement #5150465, safety pinion, coin silver case w/chased decoration, sterling watch chain.............. **154**

Pocket watch, hunting case, man's, American Watch Co., Waltham, Massachusetts, white enameled dial & small second, Roman numerals, movement #1,200941, patent pinion, 18k yellow gold case w/engine-turned background & chased scroll work & monogrammed crest.. **220**

Pocket watch, hunting case, man's, Bautte (Jq. Fd.), Geneve, white dial w/Roman numerals, chased case w/bicolor floral bouquet on one side & mixed metal & enamel decoration on reverse, scalloped edges, 18k yellow gold (damaged enamel) **260**

Pocket watch, hunting case, man's, Elgin National Watch Co., 14k mixed-color gold ornately engraved case w/floral yellow, green & rose gold

engraving surrounded a repoussé engraving of a deer in rose gold, the reverse engraved w/a center shield of rose gold surrounded by floral designs in yellow, white, green & rose gold bordered w/scalloped edge front & back, 17 jewels, ca. 1924...... **3,360**

Pocket watch, hunting case, man's, Elgin National Watch Co., G.M. Wheeler, white enameled dial & small second, blued steel hands, Roman numerals, movement #278696, patent pinion, gold-filled case w/chased scroll work & shield & engine-turned background, w/key & gold-filled T-bar chain... **248**

Gruen Pocket Watch & Chain

Pocket watch, hunting case, man's, Gruen, No. 96516, white dial w/black Arabic numerals, subsidiary seconds dial, chased & engraved case depicting a griffin, includes 48" l. trace link chain accented w/eight small cultured pearls & swivel hook, 14k yellow gold (ILLUS.)........... **575**

Pocket watch, hunting case, man's, Hampton Watch Co., Springfield, Massachusetts, white enameled dial w/small second & blued steel hands, Roman numerals, movement #475644, gold-filled case w/floral chased decoration & horse head on one cover, gold-filled socket chain w/rose gold-filled baby fob engraved on one side w/"BABY BORN June 13th 1900 CARRIE BORN May 23rd 1873" & the reverse w/"BABY DIED November 23rd 1900 CARRIE DIED March 31st 1901" **242**

Pocket watch, hunting case, man's, Illinois Watch Co., Springfield, Illinois, patent pinion, gilt dial w/small second hand & raised Roman numerals, movement #654721, center scene of buildings, gold-filled case w/interior engraved "Jan 27, 1900" & exterior floral & scroll chase decorated w/one bowl depicting buildings, w/key & gold-filled T-bar chain **275**

Pocket watch, hunting case, man's, Illinois Watch Co., Springfield, Illinois, white enameled dial & small second, blued steel hands, Roman numerals, movement #740317, ornate gold-filled case w/chased design of building & flowers **286**

Pocket watch, hunting case, man's, Illinois Watch Company Bunn model, Springfield, Illinois, 18k yellow gold engraved case, 21 ruby jewels, adjusted teperature, five positions, Isochronison, double rolled, working, ca. 1910 .... **532**

Jurgensen Pocket Watch

Pocket watch, hunting case, man's, Jurgensen (J. Alfred), No. 785, white procelain dial, subsidiary dial for seconds, fancy hands, highly jeweled movement, patent 1865, Copenhagen, 18k gold (ILLUS.) **3,000**

Pocket watch, hunting case, man's, U.S. Watch Co., Waltham, Massachusetts, white enameled dial & small second decorated w/mauve & gilt flowers, each Arabic numeral surrounded by a pink circle, movement #20811, smooth gold-filled case w/floral etched edge **330**

Pocket watch, hunting case, man's, Zenith, 14k gold engraved case, ca. 1900, mint condition **1,568**

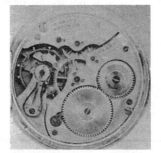

Abbott Watch Co. Pocket Watch

Pocket watch, hunting case, No. 993932, 16 size, 17 jewels, gold jeweled settings, Abbott Watch Co. (ILLUS.) **125-350**

Pocket watch, Model 1886, 16 size, 21 jewels, gold train, w/tadpole regulator, American Watch Co. **450-800**

Pocket watch, Model 1892, 17J, 24 hour dial used by astronomers, marked "Sidereal" on dial, Sidereal.... **1,200-2,400**

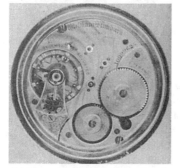

Waltham Standard Pocket Watch

Pocket watch, No. 10,099,625, Grade 1892, 18 size, 19 jewels, Adj5P, open face, note engine & coal car (locomotive) engraved on movement , Waltham Standard (ILLUS.)................. **1,000-2,000**

Vanguard Pocket Watch

Pocket watch, No. 10,533,465, Model 1892, 18S, 23J, diamond end stone, gold jewel settings, exposed winding gears, Vanguard (ILLUS.) **300-500**

Pocket watch, No. 1205, Model 1857, 18 size, 15 jewels, under sprung, key wind, Dennison, Howard, Davis **1,000-1,800**

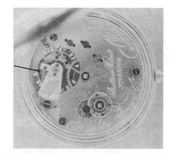

Appleton, Tracy 20 Size Pocket Watch

Pocket watch, No. 125004, Model 20KW, 20 size, 15 jewels, w/vibrating hairspring stud, Appleton, Tracy & Co. (ILLUS.).............. **1,400-2,800**

Pocket watch, No. 13446, Model 1857, 18 size, 15 jewels, engraved on back "4 PR. Jewels," P.S. Bartlett........ **150-300**

Appleton, Tracy 18 Size Pocket Watch

Pocket watch, No. 1,389,078, Model 1877, 18 size, 15 jewels, stem wind, quick train, hunting case, Appleton, Tracy & Co. (ILLUS.) **75-150**

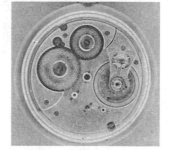

Pennsylvania Special Pocket Watch

Pocket watch, No. 14,000,015, Model 1892, 18 size, 21 jewels, Pennsylvania Special (ILLUS.).. **1,600-3,000**

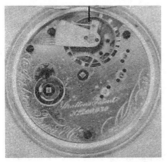

Appleton, Tracy 16 Size Pocket Watch

Pocket watch, No. 140030, 15J, 16 size, w/vibrating hairspring stud, key wind & set from back , Appleton, Tracy & Co. (ILLUS.) **1,000-2,000**

Pocket watch, No. 14,752, 1st Serial No. 13,701, Model 1857, 18 size, 15-16 jewels, "Chronodrometer" on dial, "Appleton Tracy & Co." or "P.S. Bartlett," key wind & set, 1/4 jump seconds, Appleton, Tracy & Co. **2,000-4,000**

Pocket watch, No. 15,097,475, Model 1892, 18 size, 21 jewels, railroad grade, Adj.5P, Grade 845 .... **300**

Adams & Perry Watch Co. Pocket Watch

Pocket watch, No. 1681, movement, 20 jewels, gold jeweled settings, key wind & pendant set, Adams & Perry Watch Co. (ILLUS.) ... **2,000-4,000**

Pocket watch, No. 19, movement 16 jewels, gold train & escape wheel w/pivoted detent, key wind & key set, Allison, J.H. **600-1,500**

Canadian Railway Time Service Pocket Watch

Pocket watch, No. 22,017,534, Model 1892, 18 size, 17 jewels, marked, Canadian Railway Time Service (ILLUS.) **600-1,000**

Appleton, Tracy 20 Size Pocket Watch

Pocket watch, No. 250107, 20 size, 15-17 jewels, Fogg's safety pinion, pat. Feb. 14, 1865, key wind & set from back, Appleton, Tracy & Co. (ILLUS.) **100-250**

J. Watson Pocket Watch

Pocket watch, No. 28,635, 18 size, 11 jewels, "Boston, Mass." engraved on movement, hunting case, key wind key set, ca. April 1863, J. Watson (ILLUS.) **1,000-2,500**

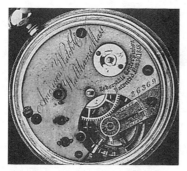

American Watch Co. Pocket Watch

Pocket watch, No. 36369, Model 18KW, 18 size, 15 jewels, reversible center pinion, patented Nov. 30th, 1858, American Watch Co. (ILLUS.)............... **2,400-5,000**

Pocket watch, No. 5,000,297, Model 1888, 16 size, 19 jewels, gold jewel settings, gold train, high grade movement, American Watch Co............ **85-250**

Pocket watch, No. 501,561, Model 16KW or Model 1868, 16 size, key wind & set from back, gold train, American Watch Co. **400-1,000**

Pocket watch, No. 552,526, Model 1870, 15J, 18 size, key wind & set from back, this grade was the first American watch to be advertised as a railroad watch, Crescent Street **150-400**

Pocket watch, No. 778763, Model 1857, 18S, 15J, w/factory stem wind, Fogg's Patent, Waltham Standard **200-325**

Pocket watch, No. 80111, Model 1862, 20 size, 17-19 jewels, gold balance & escape wheel, gold jeweled settings, key wind, key set from back, American Watch Co. **2,000-4,000**

Pocket watch, open face, 16 size, 17 jewels, gold jeweled settings, Abbott Watch Co. **325-750**

Pocket watch, open face, gold (18k yellow) case enameled w/butterflies & flowers edged in cobalt blue enamel, red guilloché & seed pearl accents open face, white porcelain dial, Roman numerals, blue steeled hands, unusual skeletonized polished steel movement signed "Bovet, London," bow set w/pearls, enamel watch key, English hallmarks on back cover (surface scratches to case, some enamel damage to edge, hairline to dust cover) **3,910**

Pocket watch, open face, gold (18k yellow), repeating, white porcelain dial w/black Arabic numbers, subsidiary seconds dial w/red Arabic numbers, dated "1898," triple signed "Tiffany & Co., New York," No. 90409............. **3,450**

Pocket watch, open-face, man's, American Waltham, Riverside model, 16 size, double roller, gold-filled, pendant set, 15 jewel **100-150**

Pocket watch, open-face, man's, American Watch Co., Keller & Bros., Allentown, Pennsylvania, white enameled dial & small second, Roman numerals, movement #2751998, safety pinion, gold-filled case w/engine-turned cover & chased floral work on rim **220**

Pocket watch, open-face, man's, Appleton, Tracy & Co., Waltham, Massachusetts, 17-jewel movement, white enameled dial w/small second hand, Arabic numerals, blued steel hands, gold-filled smooth case, gold-filled chain & small pocket knife, signed................ **193**

Pocket watch, open-face, man's, Patek Phillippe & Co., No. 161442, Geneve, white dial, Roman numerals, 18k yellow gold, (missing bail)................ **575**

Pocket watch, open-face, man's, Tiffany & Company, New York, 18k yellow gold case w/21 jewel Swiss movement, works marked "AG Agassiz W. Co.," w/a 14k yellow gold watch chain, ca. 1900, the set **1,512**

Silver Sector Watch

Pocket watch, silver, keyless "Sector Watch," four body, fan-form, back w/low relief decoration depicting an Arab on horseback, camels, palm tree & sunset in background, hinged silver cuvette, matte silver w/hour Arabic sector, blue steel hands, back signed "Holy Frèes" & movement signed "Record Watch Co.," ca. 1920 (ILLUS.) **2,185**

Pocket watch, open-face, man's, marked "H.H., Bevete S.G.D.G., Paris" on face, gold colored metal case w/white face in Roman numerals, lines indicate minutes between each numeral, one-piece thin gold hands, back depicts French cathedral, 1 5/8" d. **210**

Gold Ring Watch

Ring watch, gold (18k yellow), enamel & diamond, two-piece, oval band & shoulder chased w/foliage decoration, the scarlet flinqué enameled bezel inlaid w/rose-cut diamonds, gold slide over winding holes, white enamel dial w/Roman numerals, blued steel "spade" hands, ca. 1870, Swiss (ILLUS.) **6,900**

Unusual Ring/Wrist watch

Ring/wrist watch, gold (14k yellow), tonneau shape decorated in a twisted rope pattern w/sapphire set winding crown, one shoulder containing the clasp, the shank unfolding for the length of the bracelet, pink gold tonneau shape dial w/black Arabic numerals, blued steel "bâton" hands, signed on dial, case & movement, Uti, Paris, ca. 1960s (ILLUS.) **8,280**

Wrist watch, 15 jewels, 5 min. repeater, 14k, Driva... **3,000-4,000**

Wrist watch, 15 jewels, "Arlington also Hawthorne," gold-filled, ca. 1929, Illinois **175-250**

Wrist watch, 15 jewels, curved case, ca. 1930s, base metal, Abra........................ **30-55**

Wrist watch, 15 jewels, engraved case, ca. 1930s, gold-plated, Abra **30-55**

Wrist watch, 15 jewels, repeater, repeats on gong, repeater wound by bolt above hand, stainless steel, ca. 1930, Driva.................... **3,500-4,500**

Wrist watch, 17 jewels, "Ardsley also Hudson," gold-filled, ca. 1929, Illinois...... **150-225**

Wrist watch, 17 jewels, "Black Star," 14k gold, ca. 1940, E. Huguenin **300-425**

Wrist watch, 17 jewels, cal. 1361, 14k gold, ca. 1948, Doxa............. **100-175**

Wrist watch, 17 jewels, carved case, ca. 1930s, base metal, Abra........................ **30-55**

Wrist watch, 17 jewels, center sec., gold-filled, ca. 1949, Doxa... **40-70**

Doxa 17 Jewel Wristwatch

Wrist watch, 17 jewels, center sec., stainless steel, Doxa (ILLUS.).............................. **45-65**

Wrist watch, 17 jewels, center second-hand, auto-wind, gold filled, Hirco **30-70**

Wrist watch, 17 jewels, chronologgical, cal. 1220, stainless steel, ca. 1940, Doxa **175-275**

Wrist watch, 17 jewels, chronological, 2 reg., gold-filled, ca. 1942, Doxa........ **250-400**

Wrist watch, 17 jewels, chronological, by Valj., 3 reg., 14k gold, Abercrombie & Fitch.............................. **900-1,200**

Wrist watch, 17 jewels, chronological, by Valj., 3 reg., stainless steel, Abercrombie & Fitch................................... **350-500**

Wrist watch, 17 jewels, chronological, by Valj., 3 reg., stainless steel, ca. 1950, Abercrombie & Fitch.......... **350-500**

Doxa 17 Jewel Wristwatch

Wrist watch, 17 jewels, chronological, cal. 1220, gold-filled, ca. 1940, Doxa (ILLUS.)............................. **175-275**

Wrist watch, 17 jewels, curved, 14k C&B, ca. 1990s, Baume & Mercier............... **500 -800**

Wrist watch, 17 jewels, diam. mystery dial, 14k white gold, ca. 1950s, Baume & Mercier................................... **500-800**

Baylor Wristwatch

Wrist watch, 17 jewels, diamond on bezel & dial, 14k gold, ca. 1948, Baylor (ILLUS.)............................. **175-275**

Wrist watch, 17 jewels, direct read, aluminum case, ca. 1925, Illinois.................. **2,000-2,500**

Illinois Direct Read Wristwatch

Wrist watch, 17 jewels, direct read, chrome case & band, ca. 1925, Illinois (ILLUS.)................................. **225-325**

Wrist watch, 17 jewels, engraved case, base metal, Abra............................. **30-55**

Wrist watch, 17 jewels, fancy hidden lugs, 14k gold, Beltone.............................. **125-200**

Baume & Mercier Wristwatch

Wrist watch, 17 jewels, fancy lugs, auxillary second hand, 14k gold, ca. 1955, Baume & Mercier (ILLUS.).............. **250-400**

Wrist watch, 17 jewels, flip up top, 14k gold, Hydepark... **400-550**

Doxa "Grafic" Date Wristwatch

Wrist watch, 17 jewels, "Grafic" date, 14k gold, Doxa (ILLUS.)..................................... **100-175**

Wrist watch, 17 jewels, hidden lugs, 14k gold, Baylor **125-195**

Wrist watch, 17 jewels, hidden lugs, gold-filled, Baylor **40-75**

Wrist watch, 17 jewels, jump hour, stainless steel, Abra **250-395**

Wrist watch, 17 jewels, Model 207 on Movement, model 250 on case, 14k gold, Illinois **300-425**

Wrist watch, 17 jewels, RF#49300, 14k gold, ca. 1965, Baume & Mercier... **150-225**

Baume & Mercier Wristwatch

Wrist watch, 17 jewels, seconds window, auto-wind, base metal, ca. 1950s, Baume & Mercier (ILLUS.)..................................... **100-175**

Wrist watch, 17 jewels, step case, ca. 1930s, base metal, Abra............................... **30-55**

Wrist watch, 18 jewels, "Riviera", 18k gold & stainless steel, ca. 1980s, Baume & Mercier........................... **400-525**

Wrist watch, Babe Ruth, Babe on dial, leather strap, ca. 1948, U.S. Time (no box, fair condition)..... **225-300**

Wrist watch, datejust, quick set, oyster stainless steel band, 30 jewel, ca. 1970s, Rolex................... **900-1,100**

Wrist watch, Foster model, leather band, gold buckle, 14k gold, 10 jewel, Hamilton **300-550**

Wrist watch, lady's, "Atlas," Roman numerals on bezel, original Tiffany & Co. leather strap & blue felt pouch, 18k yellow gold, Tiffany & Co. (minor scratches to bezel)....... **978**

Wrist watch, lady's, enlongated oval gold tone dial, rectangular bezel w/stylized hinge lugs, satin band, 18k yellow gold, Bueche Girod...... **978**

Wrist watch, lady's, Oyster Perpetual, date, crenelated bezel, silvertone dial, abstract indicators, sweep seconds hand, magnifying glass on date aperture, jubilee bracelet, stainless steel, Rolex................... **1,035**

Wrist watch, lady's, Uti movement, round goldtone dial w/ruby indicators, one-half framed in graduating calibré-cut channel-set rubies, snake link bracelet, French hallmarks, 18k yellow gold, Lehman (dial slightly discolored)............................ **1,495**

Wrist watch, man's, Geneve, square black abstract indicators, heavy mesh bracelet, 18k yellow gold, Universal (minor scratches to crystal)..... **460**

Wrist watch, man's, No. 46600J, engraved dial w/black tracery enamel, black leather strap, yellow gold clasp, Italian hallmarks, 18k yellow gold, Gianmaria Buccellati **6,900**

Wrist watch, man's, No. A250565, tank-style w/reeded bezel & dial, invisible clasp, black leather Boucheron strap, French hallmarks, original leather pouch, 18k white gold, Boucheron **2,128**

Man's Cartier Wrist watch

Wrist watch, man's, rectangular convex white dial w/black Roman numerals, rounded gold bezel, black leather strap, 18k yellow gold, Cartier (ILLUS.)................ **1,380**

Wrist watch, Mickey Mouse, embossed "Mickey's" on metal band, ca. 1933, Ingersoll, mint in box, (originally priced $2.95) **600-800**

Wrist watch, No. 16233, stainless steel, two-tone 18k gold, Jubilee bracelet, 31 jewel, Rolex.................... **2,100-2,500**

Wrist watch, No. 16610, stainless steel w/subdate, flip lock, oyster band, 31 jewel, Rolex........................... **1,850-2,350**

Wrist watch, No. 1675, GMT Master, stainless steel, 30 jewel, ca. 1970s, Rolex **1,000-1,350**

Wrist watch, No. 2940, stainless steel, bubble-back, original dial, ca. 1940s, Rolex **1,200-1,800**

Wrist watch, No. 2940, stainless steel, Rolex............. **800-1,200**

Wrist watch, No. 5500, Air King, stainless steel, heavy oyster bracelet, 26 jewel, ca. 1970s, Rolex **600-775**

Wrist watch, quartz, enamel dial, tank, 14k gold, ca. 1990s, Baume & Mercier **200-350**

Wrist watch, Sea Master, embossed back, Man on Moon, stainless steel band, manual wind, ca. 1969, Omega.... **600-850**

Abercrombie & Fitch Seafarer Wrist watch

Wrist watch, Seafarer, chronological, waterproof, 18k gold, Abercrombie & Fitch (ILLUS.)............................. **1,100-1,600**

Wrist watch, Seafarer, chronological, waterproof, stainless steel, Abercrombie & Fitch.. **350-500**

Swiss Bangle-type Bracelet Watch

Wrist watch, bangle-type, gold (18k yellow) & diamond, keyless "Boule de Genève" type, diamond-set design decorated at the top w/diamond-set applied gold triangular segments, glazed back cover w/view of movement, dark blue enamel w/white Arabic numerals, gold hands, Swiss, ca. 1895 (ILLUS.)... **3,910**

Wrist watch, diamond, Art Deco style tonneau-shaped case decorated w/old European-, brilliant- & single-cut diamonds mounted on the sides & in a geometric design on each end, silver-colored dial, black Arabic numerals & gunmetal blue hands, mounted in platinum w/black strap................................. **5,175**

Art Deco Diamond & Onyx Wrist watch

Wrist watch, diamond & black onyx, Art Deco style, a rectangular case bordered w/black onyx & small diamond accents w/a row of round single-cut diamonds & two baguette-cut black onyx on each end, attached to the black band by an open shield-shaped decoration set w/round diamonds, platinum mounting (ILLUS.).......... **3,910**

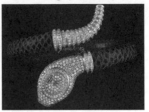

Unusual Diamond Wrist watch

Wrist watch, diamond & leather, the bracelet depicting a snake w/a wrap-around leather "snakeskin" textured band, pavé-set w/round diamonds in the head & tail w/ruby accents in the eyes & tip of tail, the oval-shaped dial pavé-set w/round single-cut diamonds mounted in 18k yellow gold, numbered & signed "Chopard," 6" l. (ILLUS.)... **5,750**

Wrist watch, diamond & platinum, Art Deco lady's model, a rectangular case framed w/round single-cut diamonds, the ends decorated w/round & square-cut diamonds & sapphire accents, mounted in platinum w/an adjustable platinum mesh bracelet, Glycine, 1930s, signed & numbered **2,070**

Wrist watch, diamond & platinum, Art Deco lady's model, an oval case decorated w/pavé-set round single-cut diamonds w/a total weight of .90 cts., engraved sides, attached to an adjustable platinum mesh band w/a 14k white gold clasp, Swiss movement, mounted in platinum w/a sapphire winding stem, name engraved on back of case, signed & numbered by Baume & Mercier, Geneva, Switzerland................. **1,840**

Wrist watch, diamond & platinum, Art Deco lady's model, rectangular case decorated w/round diamonds w/a total weight of 1.25 cts., mounted in platinum, attached to a black cord bracelet w/a gold-filled deployant clasp, 5 3/4" l. **1,725**

Wrist watch, diamond & platinum, Art Deco lady's model, rectangular case framed by round single-cut diamonds accented by triangular- and marquise-cut diamonds, the bracelet decorated w/round, single- and baguette-cut diamonds, total diamond weight of 4.30 cts., mounted in platinum, Pastor Watch Co., 7" l. **5,750**

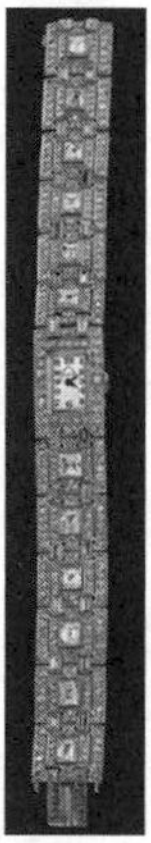

Art Deco Diamond Wristwatch

Wrist watch, diamond & platinum, Art Deco style w/a repeated, rectangular, geometric link design, each centering an emerald-cut diamond flanked by round, single-cut diamonds, the links bridged by a pair of baguette-cut diamonds, having a total weight of approx. 20 cts., the rectangular watch w/white face, black Arabic numerals, mounted in platinum, signed on dial, Vacheron & Constantin, approx. 7" l. (ILLUS.) **27,600**

Wrist watch, diamond & platinum, the silver circular dial surrounded by diamonds & flanked by two circular links set w/diamonds, completed by diamond-set line-type band, signed "Cartier" **3,680**

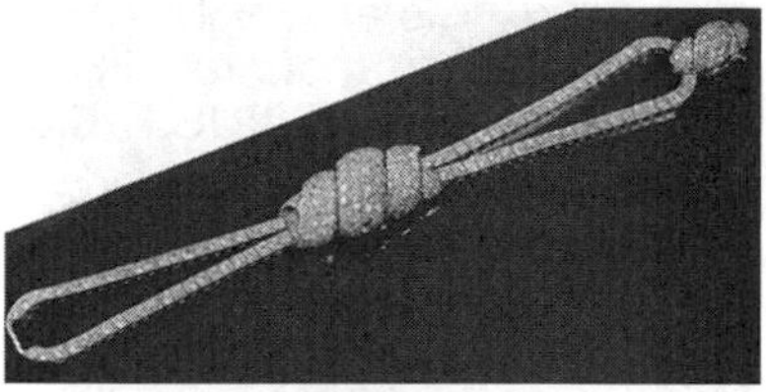

Diamond Wrist watch

Wrist watch, diamond, the cover having a bombé design w/three sections of pavé-set round, brilliant-cut diamonds w/a double row bracelet of round brilliant-cut diamonds & a smaller, bombé designed diamond-set catch w/approx. total weight of 13. cts. for all 222 diamonds, mounted in platinum, measuring approx. 17.3 cm., 6 3/4" l., watch w/Swiss 17 jewel, unadjusted, monometallic balance anti-shock movement, signed & numbered, 1960s, Van Cleef & Arpels, New York, New York (ILLUS.) **17,825**

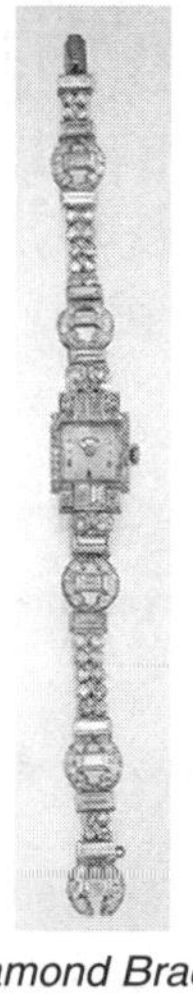

Hamilton Diamond Bracelet Watch

Wrist watch, diamond, the rectangular-shaped watch is decorated on the top w/round single- & baguette-cut diamonds w/round brilliant-, single- & baguette-cut diamonds lining the bracelet, all having a total weight of approx. 8 cts., mounted in platinum, 6 1/2" l. (ILLUS.) .. **6,325**

Rolex Wristwatch

Wrist watch, gentleman's 9k white & yellow gold, rectangular, two-body, massive, polished, yellow gold case, white gold fillet on stepped sides, white gold stripes in relief on bezel, flat top crystal, two-tone silver dial w/painted Arabic numerals, auxiliary seconds dial, dial, case & movement signed, Rolex, Prince Railway, 1930s (ILLUS.)............................ **6,555**

Rare Gentleman's Wrist watch

Wrist watch, gentleman's rare early tonneau-shaped, two-body, solid polished, hinged bezel, gold screw bars, champagne dial w/radium-coated radial Arabic numerals, "Skeleton" radium-coated hands, velvet strap w/18k yellow gold Patek Philippe buckle, dial, case & movement signed, Patek Phillippe & Cie, Genève, ca. 1915 (ILLUS.)... **31,740**

Jaeger Reverso Wrist watch

Wrist watch, gentleman's, rectangular, stainless steel "Staybrite" & 18k yellow gold, four-body, solid, polished, reeded bezel, dust-protecting cap, matte silver dial w/painted gold Arabic numerals, painted black Arabic numerals on a satiné silver ring dial for minutes, "Epée" yellow gold hands, ca. 1940s, dial, case & movement signed, Jaeger, Reverso (ILLUS.)........................ **6,210**

Wrist watch, gold (14k), 17 jewels, double teardrop lugs, ca. 1945, Driva.......... **125-200**

Lady's Gold & Diamond Wrist watch

Wrist watch, gold (14k white) & diamond, the straight lattice-work band set w/96 round diamonds, total approx. .96 cts., centering an oval case w/conforming white dial w/black Roman numerals & surrounded by 24 round diamonds, total approx. 1.20 cts., signed "Baume & Mercier Geneve" (ILLUS.)... **4,025**

Unusual Retro-style Wrist watch

Wrist watch, gold (14k yellow), Retro-style, Florentine finish triangular case, joined by a twin strand 14k yellow gold rope bracelet w/hinged locking clasp, rectangular white enamel dial w/raised clrcular & triangular goldtone hour chapters, Acme Watch Co., ca. 1940, 7" l. (ILLUS.) **345**

Wrist watch, gold (18k), 17 jewels, chronological by Venius W. Co., Hilton W. Co. **300-400**

Cartier Diamond & Gold Wrist watch

Wrist watch, gold (18k yellow) & diamond, the curved link gold bracelet centrally lined w/two rows of round brilliant-cut diamonds having a total weight of approx. 3.50 cts., the back winding watch contains a Swiss 17 jewel, unadjusted, 2 1/2 ligne size movement by Blancpain Rayville S.A., "Cartier" signed on dial, 7" l. (ILLUS.) **5,750**

Wrist watch, gold (18k yellow) & malachite, the deployment band centering a circular case, the conforming malachite dial w/date aperture, the dial signed "Rolex Oyster Perpetual Datejust" **2,990**

Wrist watch, gold & diamond, silvertone rectangular dial w/black abstract indicators, covered w/a buckle design set w/17 round-cut & four baguette-cut diamonds, integral textured 18k white gold band, approx. tdw. 1.58 cts., Piaget, 7" l. **2,530**

Wrist watch, reeded round cover centered by a star sapphire w/baguette-cut diamonds, surrounded by single-cut diamonds, reeded round bracelet links, each centered by a round star sapphire & two baguette-cut diamonds, 14k white gold mount, Lucien Piccard, ca. 1950 .... **575**

Wrist watch, silver case, Swiss movement, marked "Arthur Bond Yokohama," ca. 1915, Japan **500-700**

Bibliography

Books
Ball, Joanne Dubbs, *Costume Jewelers The Golden Age of Design:* Schiffer
Publishing LTD, 1990.

Bell, Jeanenne, *Answers to Questions About Old Jewelry 1840-1950:*
Books Americana Second Edition, 1985.

Dolan, Maryanne, *Collecting Rhinestone Jewelry, An Identification & Value
Guide:* Books Americana, 1984.

Gordon, Angie, *Twentieth Century Costume Jewelry:* ADASIA
International, 1990.

Miller, Harrice Simons, *The Official Identification and Price Guide to
Costume Jewelry:* House of Collectibles First Edition, 1990.

Catalogue
Sears Roebuck & Co. 1908 #117, DBI Books Inc., 1971.

Article
Cohen, Marion, *Inside the Costume Jewelry Box:* Antique Trader Weekly,
September 17, 1997.